Mastering Purchasing Management for Inbound Supply Chains

Thomas A. Cook

CRC Press
Taylor & Francis Group
Boca Raton   London   New York

CRC Press is an imprint of the
Taylor & Francis Group, an **informa** business

CRC Press
Taylor & Francis Group
6000 Broken Sound Parkway NW, Suite 300
Boca Raton, FL 33487-2742

© 2011 by Taylor and Francis Group, LLC
CRC Press is an imprint of Taylor & Francis Group, an Informa business

No claim to original U.S. Government works

Printed in the United States of America on acid-free paper
10 9 8 7 6 5 4 3 2 1

International Standard Book Number: 978-1-4200-8619-5 (Hardback)

Library of Congress Cataloging-in-Publication Data

Cook, Thomas A., 1953-
    Mastering purchasing management for inbound supply chains / Thomas A. Cook.
      p. cm.
    Includes bibliographical references and index.
    ISBN 978-1-4200-8619-5
    1. Purchasing--Management. 2. Business logistics. I. Title.

HF5437.C66 2011
658.7'2--dc22   2010013409

Visit the Taylor & Francis Web site at
http://www.taylorandfrancis.com

and the CRC Press Web site at
http://www.crcpress.com

To Ray O'Connell. Thanks for all your challenges, inspiration, dedication, and friendship. I do miss you.

Contents

Prologue

Every company is looking to overseas markets to purchase from, partner with, or manufacture in. Importing finished products, components, raw materials, and related items is the status quo and the future for all industries, trades, and businesses that will survive and do well in the new millennium.

Globalization is as integral as the assembly line, use of technology, and diversification in corporate cultures. But managing the globalization and, more specifically, the foreign purchasing thought process and the import logistics is a skill set that must be mastered. The entire competitive advantage of the process to source globally hinges on the decisions made by purchasing managers and their corporate counterparts. Not understanding all the parameters of "landed costs"—duties, taxes, harmonized classifications, transfer pricing—will immediately kill any benefits of the decision to source on foreign shores. The impact of decisions will be negative, costly, and potentially problematic for the survival of the lean and mean new corporate culture in purchasing management.

This book needed to be published so those whose numbers are growing quite significantly can favorably impact their decisions on how they manage their purchasing in foreign markets. The book will provide the reader with a comprehensive guide to identifying all the decision-making issues involved with purchasing in foreign markets, and then provide a how-to outline on how best to manage this import process to gain competitive advantage. The book will dissect all the issues and place them in a better order and sequence for purchasing managers to more easily execute, implement, and control for best practices in imports, logistics, and landed cost modeling.

Acronyms

ABI—Automated Broker Interface
ACE—Automated Customs Environment
ACS—Automated Commercial System
AES—Automated Export System
AESTIR—Automated Export System trade interface requirements
AGR—License exception code for agricultural commodities
BIS—Bureau of Industry and Security
BL—Bill of lading
BTA—Bioterrorism Act
CAFTA-DR—Central American Dominican Republic Free Trade Agreement
CBP—Customs and Border Protection
CCL—Commerce Control List
CFR—Code of Federal Regulations
CIP—Carriage and insurance paid to
CPT—Carriage paid to
CSI—Container Security Initiative
C-TPAT—Customs-Trade Partnership against Terrorism
DHS—Department of Homeland Security
DOT—Department of Transportation
DPL—Denied Parties List
EAR—Export Administration Regulations
ECCN—Export Control Classification Number
EEI—Electronic Export Information
EIN—Employee Identification Number
FCA—Free carrier at
FDA—Food and Drug Administration
FOB—Freight on board
FPPI—Foreign Principal Party in Interest
FTA—Free Trade Agreement
FTD—Foreign Trade Division
FTR—Foreign Trade Regulations

FTZ—Foreign trade zone
HAWB—House airway bill
HBL—House bill of lading
HTS—Harmonized Tariff System
HTSUS—Harmonized Tariff System of the United States
IATA—International Air Transportation Association
ICE—Immigration and Customs Enforcement
ID—Identification
INCOTERMS—International commerce terms
IRS—Internal Revenue Service
ISF—Importer Security Filing
ITN—Internal transaction number
MAWB—Master airway bill
MBL—Master bill of lading
N/A—Not applicable
NAFTA—North American Free Trade Agreement
NDC—Nondutiable charge
NLR—No license required
OFAC—Office of Foreign Assets Control
PEA—Postentry amendment
POA—Power of attorney
RVC—Regional value content
SCAC—Standard Carrier Alpha Code
SCH B—Schedule B
SLI—Shipper's letter of instructions
SNAP—Simplified Network Application Process
SOP—Standard operating procedure
STELA—System for Tracking Export License Applications
TSA—Transportation Security Administration
TSCA—Toxic Substance Control Act
USDA—U.S. Department of Agriculture
USPPI—U.S. principal party in interest
XTN—External transaction number

Chapter 1

Purchasing Management 101

In order to manage inbound supply chains with great effectiveness, from a purchasing management perspective, one needs to first understand the basics of purchasing management. Getting this right sets the foundation for successful global purchasing initiatives, which is the focus of this book.

What Is Purchasing Management?

Corporations, in running their daily operations, require the acquisition of goods and services. This needs to be accomplished with efficiency, cost-effectiveness, and meeting company objectives within set constraints. Purchasing management is either a part-time or full-time corporate initiative to accomplish this successfully. As companies mature, this initiative becomes its own profession and fiefdom within the corporation. In the thousands of corporations that landscape our economy, purchasing is an executive position, department, or cost or profit center, and is a critical function of corporate governance.

There are numerous organizations around the world that focus on this subject: the National Association of Purchasing Managers in New York (NAPM), the Institute of Supply Chain Managers (ISM), and the Council of Supply Chain Professionals (CCSMP), and to name a few. These organizations clearly attest to the great height and strength purchasing managers have achieved in corporate America and within all companies worldwide. They are dedicated to promoting the career, developing skill sets, raising the qualifications, and enhancing qualities and standards within all aspects of business.

Purchasing management can be summed up to a dedicated position created within a corporation to manage the acquisition of goods and services.

How Does Purchasing Management Work?

In order to understand how purchasing works, we begin with trying to identify what are common goals in this area of responsibility. Purchasing managers acquire goods and services. To do this well, they need to:

1. Know what the needs are of the corporation now and into the future
2. Know what the options are in fulfilling these needs
3. Know how to obtain the best deal to fulfill these needs
4. Know how to maintain these deals for the long term

Purchasing managers in many corporations will be involved in every area of the company where there is "spend," defined as allocated monies for the acquisition of goods and services. Real estate, leasing agreements, office supplies, equipment, raw materials, spare parts, inventory, supplemental products, cleaning services, contractor services, and construction are many of the goods and services that purchasing managers control or influence.

Purchasing Management and Corporate Governance

Purchasing managers follow the lead dictated by senior management. Depending upon the structure of the corporation, the purchasing manager may be in senior management, and if that is the case, he or she will follow the guidelines set by the CEO or the board of directors. The guidelines help prevent favoritism, graft, and corruption in the purchasing process and assist in making the function work effectively. The guidelines not only affect purchasing managers and their staff directly, but also affect other corporate managers who have purchasing responsibilities as part of their overall job description.

Many corporations have very specific laws, regulations, and guidelines set for their purchasing managers to follow. They deal with honesty, integrity, safety, ethical, moral, and related issues. For example:

■ Company X will not accept any gifts from potential vendors of any size or amount.
■ Company Y will always obtain three closed bids before making a purchase.
■ Company Z will always receive all proposals in a RFP or RFQ format (companies use RFP and RFQ for formalizing the bidding process from potential vendors) as dictated by the offer, in writing and delivered in a specific format and venue.
■ Company XY will only make purchases through a purchase order (PO) process established by the corporate controller.

What Makes Purchasing Managers Effective?

Many corporations measure the effectiveness of their purchasing managers by the amount of their spend compared against various benchmarks. Factored into this equation would be the success of the purchasing program; i.e. does the company obtain what it needs in a timely and effective manner?

We discussed earlier what the basic purchasing managers had to accomplish. Those purchasing managers who fulfill all these areas the best become the best. How they can do that is our next focus.

Know What the Needs Are of the Corporation Now and into the Future

1. Establish internal pipelines of communication and information flow, and know where everybody is and where they are going.
2. Structure regular meetings with the "movers and shakers" within the corporation that have control and influence of all the corporate functions.
3. Learn to ask questions and be inquisitive without being offensive.
4. Be a good listener and set an atmosphere for fellow employees to open up and talk to you.
5. If you are not directly part of the senior management team, then you need to establish an open communication link with them, as that is where all critical decisions are made that will affect the responsibilities of the purchasing manager. You want to be "in the loop" in advance proactively, not after the fact reactively.
6. Make sure that senior management weighs the importance of purchasing management and supports all your initiatives to handle your responsibilities in the most effective way. *This is critical.*
7. Establish your presence; that creates a sense that everyone will benefit from keeping you in their communication network.
8. Schedule meetings with critical areas in manufacturing, supply chain, logistics, and customer service that afford you and them timely access to information and situation status reports.

Know What the Options Are in Fulfilling These Needs

1. Be very proactive in seeing potential vendors and suppliers. *Make the time. Accept appointments.*
2. Visit with vendors and suppliers and spend money and time in establishing the very best of working relationships.
3. Attend industry-related trade shows.
4. Network in trade associations, related business groups, and events.
5. Keep up with industry periodicals.

6. Take a class at least once a year in a related subject.
7. Learn to navigate the Internet for potential options. We are not recommending Internet for the sake of making a final purchasing decision, but as one of your tools to learn potential options.

Know How to Obtain the Best Deal to Fulfill These Needs

1. Learn who the primary competition to your current vendors and suppliers are and what they have to offer.
2. Set the parameters of what you need as best, least, and willing to accept.
3. Know what those parameters are for your vendor and supplier.
4. *Develop negotiation skills. We cannot emphasize this matter enough.* Take a professional class on negotiation skills. The cost and time will come back to you in spades.
5. Leverage your strengths. Minimize your weaknesses.
6. Think long term, which will usually provide benefits for better deals.
7. *Pay quickly.* Many times you can receive a cash discount for paying in less than ten days.

Know How to Maintain These Deals for the Long Term

1. Vendors and suppliers will offer better pricing for longer-term agreements.
2. Establish relationships that become personal and offer "bridges" to get through more difficult times.
3. Look for partnership relationships that have more of a *we* approach than an *I* one, and look to establish reasonable compromises for the integrity of the overall long-term benefit.
4. Obtain information flow that outlines future needs that can be somehow worked into contemporary contracts. For example: "Our needs for next year will double with this purchase, so what you might lose on a unit cost basis will be made up in volume when we renew the contract for next year."
5. Respect the needs of your vendors and suppliers. Be somewhat flexible in their requests and issues.
6. Don't focus on the smaller issues. View the bigger picture and make your "marks" on these, where you can have a bigger impact, so you do not get lost on the smaller issues that will have less impact on the bottom line.
7. Look to vendors and suppliers to offer other services and goods, so you are buying more and have more to negotiate on. Consolidation may also provide other ancillary benefits.
8. When finalizing a decision, always analyze the value for the dollars spent. The cheapest may come with a hidden cost that could prove very consequential. You need to make sure that you are getting the best bang for your dollar.

Value added is a critical component in assessing vendor options and offers a more sustainable relationship. Anyone can be 10% cheaper, but can they be 10% better?

Additional Best Practices in Purchasing Management 101

1. *Keep good meeting notes and keep all understandings and agreements in writing.*
2. Be optimistic but also cautiously pessimistic. In other words, make them show you, when you are not absolutely certain.
3. *Always be honest, forthright, and deal with integrity.*
4. Be consistent, responsible, no-nonsense, and straightforward.
5. *Hold the line when you need to and be flexible when circumstances warrant.*
6. Pay attention to detail. At some point in the agreement process, someone needs to dot the *I*'s and cross the *T*'s. Many corporations will set an interface with legal at this point.
7. *Always include finance and accounting in the decision-making process.* For example: Don't agree to pay in ten days when accounting may be having a cash flow problem and needs more time at this particular moment.
8. Check out at least three referrals. Call and scrutinize. Try to talk to accounts they may have lost and find out what happened.
9. *When possible, sleep with the vendor before getting married.* If you can have a test run before agreeing to anything that will result in a final commitment, do so.
10. When disputes occur, and they will, utilize the concept of compromise; that will balance out what will ultimately be fair and responsible.

Master Negotiation Skills

When we consider the basic components of purchasing 101, we should recognize that an integral aspect of purchasing is negotiating good deals and contracts for you and your company. All purchasing managers know this. The skill set of negotiation is a critical component of purchasing management. But in foreign sourcing and global purchasing, the basics of negotiation are more complex and convoluted, and require an even more skilled approach.

Language, cultural, and localized trade practices can create significant differences in negotiating locally vs. overseas. It can take a learning curve of years, experience, and trials and tribulations to master this area of foreign negotiation skills management.

There are a number of classes and programs available to assist one in honing these skills sets. Karass, AMA, and the World Academy all present very viable options. Some negotiation skill sets for managers involved in purchasing, supply chain, and inbound logistics include:

1. Spend time in meeting with and learning your options from various service providers. Accept visits and hear what they have to say. This information flow will prove invaluable.

2. Study your options ahead of a purchasing meeting. Strategize proactively based upon an information flow of what you have as viable options, choices, and variables in what you are eventually looking to accomplish.

3. Exercise patience in the negotiation process. Many times, getting what you want can take time over several meetings and discussions. Usually when someone is trying to sell to you, you have an advantage when you demonstrate resilience, conviction, and a willingness to "wait" until the right time to say yes or no, or even maybe.

4. Make sure you are fully aware of your strengths and weaknesses. And know those of your adversary in the negotiation. This knowledge can be critical to knowing when to be aggressive and when to be sheepish or reticent.

5. Make sure you know what your goals are and identify the realm of what you are looking to obtain and what you will be willing to accept.

6. Be willing to compromise and never say never. Sometimes it will be worth trading off a short-term consideration for a long-term and tenured benefit.

7. Should you need to compromise, make sure you know the total downside. For inbound logistics, this could mean that you now have agreed to a situation where additional risk has been imposed from government agencies, such as Customs and Border Protection (CBP). Before agreeing to the compromises, do your homework and identify the risks, rewards, and trade-offs.

8. In freight negotiations, longer-term contracts often allow for better pricing, as well as bundling of services into fewer providers and carriers, which can also produce the potential of better pricing and lower costs.

9. Develop excellent working relationships with all key providers, suppliers, vendors, and channel partners. Take the time to "break bread" with these key partners and be proactive in initiatives to get to know them on both a business and a personal basis. This will go a long way in allowing future negotiations to go more simply and obtaining better results.

10. Make partners of those you negotiate with. Work with mutually vested interests. This is a time-tested and proven factor in long-term relationships that afford smoother, more productive problem resolution and the achieving of more favorable results. In purchasing this would include all suppliers, vendors, providers, channel partners, freight forwarders and customhouse brokers, third-party companies and the like.

11. International business requires a fine-tuned ability to negotiate with numerous cultures, people from all walks of life and in vast demographic, political, and economic differences. Take the time and initiative to learn the nuances of

the cultures, politics, economics, etc., in all the countries you source product from or operate locally in. This will go a long way in making sure you are more effective in the negotiation process, which may be very different from what happens in the United States.

Follow these tips and suggestions, and better agreements, more lucrative contracts, and more desired results will be in the cards for you.

Chapter 2

Foreign Purchasing Management 101

As companies source products overseas, the purchasing manager's job becomes more challenging—some would say more difficult. This chapter identifies the issues and risks, and then focuses on the foundation for what needs to be done to accomplish successful offshore operations and purchasing.

Why Is Foreign Purchasing Different from Domestic Purchasing?

There are many reasons that the job is harder for foreign purchasing managers than domestic ones as outlined in detail in the following pages:

- Distances involved
- Demographics
- Language
- Culture
- Politics
- In-country risks
- Receivable exposure
- Currency risk
- Insurance risks
- Political risks
- Legal differences

- Logistics and supply chain
- Dependence on providers
- Customs (domestic and international)
- Regulatory affairs
- Access to qualified personnel
- Travel costs
- Sarbanes–Oxley

The issues outlined above provide an array of risks and exposures that the purchasing manager faces in global business, not seen to the same extent in domestic business. Foreign purchasing managers must learn a new level of skill sets that increase their opportunity for successful offshore purchasing, inbound logistics, and the import supply chain.

Distances Involved

The maximum distance in the United States for business activity is under 4,000 miles and averages around 1,000 miles. In global business, the potential distance exceeds 10,000 miles and averages over 7,000 miles. Distance equates to risk. Opportunity for delays, loss, damage, and other fortuities increases significantly.

Demographics and Infrastructure

If you analyze the countries that you will be purchasing from and all the demographic issues, you could be dealing with the 500-pound gorilla pretty easily. When you combine the demographic issues with infrastructure concerns, the problems could be huge. As an example, if you look at the People's Republic of China (PRC), it is a huge location, with very difficult topography through which to navigate freight. Distances, time frames, and meeting scheduling goals become twice as difficult than in Western countries.

We anticipate in the United States that when we make a call, it will go through. This is not necessarily the case in all countries. Road systems, port options, energy demand access, and communication systems are but a few of the infrastructure needs that could easily present inadequacies in certain countries that make them less favorable options in developing as vendors and suppliers for your purchase contracts. These become challenges that we have to deal with when making a decision to purchase goods and services from overseas markets. Some countries have most of these issues under control; others have little or no control whatsoever.

Language

Our ability to communicate is a very critical component of the necessary collaboration that needs to exist in a foreign sourcing option. Most American businessmen depend upon the English speaking capability of their foreign vendors and suppliers. But those experienced in global business know that while they might speak English well, their comprehension may be significantly below acceptable. Comprehension and the understanding of what we mean can be a culture difference, a personal difference, or otherwise, but we have witnessed more problems as a result of two parties in agreement in concept, but the deal fails because the definitions are different—all emanating from a difference in comprehension.

Culture

Cultural differences remain both an interesting aspect of doing business globally and an obstacle. Our failure to deal with cultural, religious, and people-related differences can cause a lot of problems in foreign purchasing. Many corporations proactively provide cultural sensitivity training to their foreign nationals, and if they don't, they would be in a better position to have some sort of formal program.

In many cultures the people need to feel secure in the relationship and how you react within their culture before they will do business with you. Mistakes in cultural issues can become deal breakers or make negotiations much more complicated.

Politics

Politics plays a critical role in business matters and can often open up an opportunity or close it down. In international business, this becomes very convoluted as you are not just dealing with American politics and the politics of the country you are sourcing from, but all the countries that could potentially affect your business ties in a region, in a trading block, or in a certain demographic of the world. A good example of this is in the Middle East. The politics of the region greatly affects the business process in any specific country. Another example is in South America, where the politics are greatly interconnected regionally, particularly as they relate in dealing with American interests.

True to form, global executives budget time, develop information flows, and obtain country- or region-specific intelligence to utilize in their decision-making processes.

In-Country Risks

One needs to pay close attention to the internal political, economic, and infrastructure activities of a country one is sourcing from. There are local politics, regional politics, and centralized occurrences that will potentially wreak great havoc on your supply chain that are very different from the country's politics as a nation. A good example of this is in China, where regional and major city differences are huge in what happens from one part of the country to the next. China puts out one face to the world, but those who have experience in China know that the realities at the local level are very different. What is going on in Hong Kong can be very different from what is going on in Shanghai. Another country that has very different circumstances in politics and internal issues from various regions is Mexico. What is happening at the border in Laredo can be very different from what is happening in the port city of Veracruz.

Receivable Exposure

When a U.S. company does not pay its receivable obligation, we have legitimate remedies to obtain payment. Many of these remedies do not exist or work well in certain countries. This then increases the exposure of the U.S. company in collecting foreign receivables.

Currency Risk

The inability to convert a local currency to U.S. dollars or another acceptable currency can be a major risk. Almost every country of the world, and certainly all the major trading nations where American companies source from, has a state or national bank that controls the flow of the local currency in and out of the country. When those countries have to remit local funds to pay against foreign currencies, they must have the financial ability to be able to accomplish that task. That is, do they have the funds available to buy the foreign currency?

Typically, at any point in time, over one hundred countries have difficulty in accomplishing payment on a timely basis, mainly because of major imbalances of trade in the country. They import vastly more than they export. Brazil, Colombia, the Philippines, Russia, and Malaysia are but a few of the countries that pose this risk. Purchasing managers and all those executives involved in the global supply chain, typically as dictated by finance, will have much better results in the movement of monies worldwide when they pay attention to the subject of currency convertibility. Working with qualified and experienced bankers will go a long way in mitigating these types of currency issues.

Insurance Risks

Once corporations begin to source overseas, risks follow. Personnel travel globally, creating workers' compensation, health, and related exposures. Investments, assets, and intellectual property rights begin to collect. Protection of these assets becomes a necessary evil. Foreign liabilities, casualty exposures, products liability, automobiles—all begin to add up and could present significant financial risks. In the supply chain, inventories, transportation (cargo) risks, goods in transit, etc., all become insurable exposures. Larger corporations will typically have risk management divisions to assist in managing the purchasing and administrating of insurance programs that will deal with all types of risks and exposures.

Political Risks

Confiscation, nationalization, expropriation, and deprivation all pose serious exposures to companies that have assets and investments in foreign domiciles. What we are referring to are exposures caused by a political chain of events that can cause financial loss to your company. Past examples of occurrences include Peru, Brazil, Iran, Nicaragua, the Philippines, Nigeria, Liberia, Argentina, Iraq, and Lebanon—all countries that had various arrays of a political eventuality that caused a loss or damage to assets of companies from the United States or elsewhere. These types of exposures are very complicated and require a very specific type of expertise to assist you in evaluating, analyzing, and providing various risk management tools to bring favorable resolutions.

Legal Differences

The differences in the legal systems between countries are vast, just as are the differences between the foods they eat, the side of the road they drive on, and how they practice their religions. This is a huge matter that has to be managed with professional legal counsel in the United States, for those law firms that specialize in this area, along with local legal expertise in the countries you are doing business with. Numerous contracts will need to be created. The contracts become the foundations for relationships and can be a very critical element of your firm's success in foreign purchasing.

Logistics and Supply Chain

Every factor related to logistics and supply chain management becomes more complicated and challenging to navigate once the goods are sourced in overseas markets. Principal responsibilities are:

- Timely shipments
- Safe and secure movement of goods
- Cost-effective logistics

These all become more complicated to handle because of the issues raised in this chapter.

The purchasing manager who is buying goods from overseas markets must have these related issues factored in to the inbound equation, and must more openly address the necessary skill sets required to move freight inbound and manage the three criteria listed above.

Dependence on Providers

Purchasing managers and their team of colleagues will typically not have all the necessary skill sets to manage inbound supply chains successfully. They will depend upon a slew of service providers:

- Freight forwarders
- Customhouse brokers
- Third-party logistics providers
- Specialized warehouses and truck companies
- International carriers

These providers will make or break the cost-effectiveness and functionality of just how the inbound supply chain will work. Choosing and managing these providers is a skill set all by itself and is covered in Chapter 7 in much greater detail.

Customs (Domestic and International)

U.S. Customs (CBP) is a very important component of the inbound supply chain. The purchasing manager has to develop skill sets in both Customs regulation and accessing capabilities of third parties to assist in these endeavors. Knowledge of import controls will be a key to successful inbound logistics. Successful inbound logistics adds to the purchasing manager's decision to source overseas and handle the inbound correctly and cost-effectively.

Regulatory Affairs

There are hundreds of import regulations that a purchasing manager needs to know about in order to import successfully. Unless they have a full-time qualified person on site 24/7, they will typically hire the resources of attorneys, consultants, or providers that can provide this expertise. One such regulation new in 2009 is called ISF or 10+2. This Importer Security Filing requires a significant flow of information from the importer to CBP prior to departure from the overseas sourcing location and loading onto the inbound conveyance. This requires an entirely different approach to inbound logistics that will affect purchasing decisions and vendor requirements.

The Appendix outlines in great detail just how ISF works. This should be read by all purchasing managers, because major changes on import data requirements began in 2009 and are continuing into 2011.

Access to Qualified Personnel

Purchasing managers will need to access qualified personnel either from staff who have received training or from external third parties. The success of the overseas purchase will be determined by the quality of the expertise providing advice into the inbound business processes.

Travel Costs

Costs to travel overseas for purchasing managers, technicians, engineers, operations, and logistics personnel can be very expensive, sometimes as much as $10,000 for a week's visit. It must be planned out well and cost-effective strategies utilized to minimize these expenses. But more importantly, these costs must be factored in to the decision-making process of determining the overall cost-effectiveness of offshore sourcing.

In many studies that the author has accomplished on behalf of corporations who look to source overseas, these travel expenses can greatly nullify the lower cost purchasing at point of origin. The landed cost then becomes much higher.

Sarbanes–Oxley

Public companies who operate global supply chains must develop Sarbanes–Oxley (SOX) business processes in their inbound logistics so as to be Sarbanes–Oxley compliant. Too often the import process is left out of the SOX initiatives, leaving the public company vulnerable to SEC/IRS scrutiny, fines, and penalties.

Develop Resources

Purchasing managers need to develop an array of resources to get up-to-the-minute information on issues affecting their global supply chains.

Magazines

Managing Imports and Exports: www.pacman.com
American Shipper: www.americanshipper.com
Journal of Commerce: www.joc.com

Cargo Business News: www.cargobusinessnews.com
World Trade Magazine: www.worldtrademazazine.com

Key International and Supply Chain Web Sites

1travel.com: www.onetravel.com
ACW (Air Cargo Week): www.aircargoweek.com
Addresses and salutations: www.bspage.com
AES Direct (Automated Export System): www.aesdirect.gov
Africa Online: www.africaonline.com
AgExporter: www.fas.usda.gov
Air Cargo World: www.aircargoworld.com
AIRCARGO News: www.air-cargo-news.com
Airforwarders Association: www.airforwarders.org
Airline toll-free numbers and Web sites: www.princeton.edu/Main/air800.
 html
American Association of Port Authorities (AAPA): www.aapa-ports.org
American Computer Resources, Inc.: www.the-acr.com
American Countertrade Association (ACA): www.countertrade.org
American Institute for Shippers' Associations (AISA): www.shippers.org
American Journal of Transportation (AJOT): www.ajot.com
American River International: www.worldest.com
American Shipper: www.americanshipper.com
American Short Line and Regional Railroad Association (ASLRRA): www.
 aslrra.org
American Stock Exchange: www.amex.com
American Trucking Association (ATA): www.trucking.org
ASXTraders: www.ASX.com
ATA Carnet (Merchandise Password): www.uscib.org
ATMs around the world: www.fita.org/marketplace/travel.html#atm
Aviation Consumer Action Project: www.acap1971.org
Aviation Week: www.aviationnow.com
Bureau of Customs and Border Protection: www.cbp.gov
Bureau of Industry and Security (BIS): www.bis.doc.gov
Bureau of National Affairs, International Trade Reporter Export Reference
 Manual: www.bna.com
Business Advisor: www.business.gov
Business Traveler Info Network: www.business-trip.com
Career China: www.dragonsurf.com
Cargo Systems: www.cargosystems.net
Cargovision: www.editorial@cargovision.org
Census Bureau, Foreign Trade Division: www.census.gov/foreign trade
Central Europe Online: www.centraleurope.com

Chicago Stock Exchange: www.chicagostockex.com

Chinese news (in English): www.einnews.com/china

Classification schedules: www.census.gov/ftp/pub/foreign-trade/www/schedules.
html

Commerce Business Daily: www.cbdnet.gpo.gov

Commercial Carrier Journal (CCJ): www.etrucking.com

Commercial encryption export controls: www.bis.doc.gov/Encryption/Default.
htm

Compliance consulting of importers/exporters: www.compliancemaven.com

Compliance Maven: www.compliancemaven.com

Correct way to fill out the shipper's export declaration: www.census.gov/ftp/
pub/foreign-rade/www/correct.way.html

Country risk forecast: www.controlrisks.com/html/index.php

Create your own newspapers: www.crayon.com

Culture and Travel: www.ciber.bus.msu.edu/busres/static/culture-travel-
language.htm

Currency: www.oanda.com

Daily Intelligence Summary: www.dtic.mil/doctrine/jel/doddoct/data/d

Database at the UN World Bank: www.worldbank.org/data/onlinedatabases/
onlinedatabases

Department of Transportation: www.dot.gov

Diverse languages of the modern world: www.unicode.org

DOT's Office of Inspector General: www.oig.dot.gov

Dr. Leonard's Healthcare Catalog: www.drleornards.com

Dun & Bradstreet: www.dnb.com

Economic Times (India): www.economictimes.com

Economist: www.economist.com

Electronic Embassy: www.embassy.org

Embassies and consulates: www.embassyworld.com

Embassy Web site: www.embassy.com

European Union (EU): www.europa.eu.int

Excite travel: www.excite.com/travel

The Expeditor: www.theexpeditor.com

Export Administration Regulations (EAR): www.ntis.gov/products/type/database/
export-regulations.asp

Export Assistant: www.cob.ohio-state.edu

The Exporter: www.exporter.com

Export hotline: www.exporthotline.com

Export-Import Bank of the United States (EXIMBANK): www.exim.gov

Export Legal Assistance Network (ELAN): www.fita.org/elan

Export Practitioner (Export Regulations): www.exportprac.com

Far Eastern Economic Review: www.feer.com

Federal Register Notice on the Status of AES and AERP: www.access.gpo.gov

Federation of International Trade Associations (FITA): www.fita.org

Financial Times: www.ft.com

For female travelers: www.journeywoman.com

Global Business: www.gbn.org

The Global Business Forum: www.gbfvisa.com

Global Business Information Network: www.bus.indiana.edu

Global Information Network for Small and Medium Enterprises: www.gin.sme.
  ne.jp/intro.html

Global law and business: www.law.com

Glossary of internalization and localization terms: www.bowneglobal.com/
  bowne.asp?page=9&language=1

Glossary of ocean cargo insurance terms: www.tsbic.com/cargo/glossary.htm

Government resources: www.ciber.bus.msu.edu/busres/govrnmnt.htm

Hong Kong Trade Development Counsel (TDC): www.tdctrade.com

iAgora Work Abroad: www.iagora.com/pages/html/work/index.html

IMEX Exchange: www.imex.com

Import-Export Bulletin Board: www.iebb.com

Inbound Logistics: www.inboundlogistics.com

Incoterms 2000: www.iccwbo.org/home/menu_incoterms.asp

Independent Accountants International: www.accountants.org

Information on diseases abroad: www.cdc.gov

Inside China Today: www.einnews.com

Intellicast weather (4-day forecast): www.intellicast.com/LocalWeather/World

Intermodal Association of North America (IANA): www.intermodal.org

International Air Cargo Association (TIACA): www.tiaca.org

International Air Transport Association (IATA): www.iata.org

International Association for Medical Assistance to Travelers (IAMAT): www.
  iamat.org

International Business: Strategies for the Global Marketplace Magazine: www.
  internationalbusiness.com

International Chamber of Commerce (ICC): www.iccwbo.org

International commercial law monitor: www.lexmercatoria.org

International economics and business: dylee.keel.econ.ship.edu/econ/index.html

International Executive Service Corps (IESC): www.iesc.org

International Freight Association (IFA): www.ifa-online.com

International law check: www.law.comindex.shtml

International Maritime Organization (IMO): www.imo.org

International Monetary Fund (IMF): www.imf.org

International Society of Logistics (SOLE): www.sole.org

International Trade Administration (ITA): www.ita.doc.gov

International trade shows and business events: www.ciber.bus.msu.edu/busre

International trade/import-export jobs: www.internationaltrade.org/jobs.html

International trade/import-export portal: www.imakenews.com

Intershipper: www.intershipper.com

IWLA: www.warehouselogistics.org

Journal of Commerce Online: www.joc.com

Latin Trade: www.latintrade.com

Libraries: www.libraryspot.com/librariesonline.htm

Library of Congress: www.loc.gov

Local times around the world: www.times.clari.net.au

Logistics Management & Distribution Report: www.manufacturing.net/magazine/logistic

London Stock Exchange: www.londonstockexchange.com

Mailing lists: www.ciber.bus.msu.edu/busres/maillist.htm

Marine Digest: www.marinedigest.com

Market research: www.imakenews.com

Matchmaker site: www.ita.doc.gov/efm

Medical conditions around the world: www.cdc.gov/travel/blusheet.htm

More trade leads: www.ibrc.bschool.ukans.edu

NAFTA Customs: www.nafta-customs.org

National Association of Foreign Trade Zones: www.NAFTZ.org

National Association of Purchasing Management (NAPM): www.napm.org

National Association of Rail Shippers (NARS): www.railshippers.com

National Business Travel Associaton: www.biztraveler.org

National Customs Brokers & Forwarders Association of America (NCBFAA): www.ncbfaa.org

National Institute of Standards and Technology (NIST): www.nist.gov

National Law Center for Inter-American Free Trade: www.natlaw.com

National Motor Freight Traffic Association (NMFTA): www.nmfta.org

New records formats for commodity filing and transportation filing: www.customs.ustreas.gov

New York Times: www.nytimes.com

North American Industry Classification System (NAICS): www.census.gov/epcd/www/naics.html

Office of Anti-Boycott Compliance: www.bis.doc.gov/AntiboycottCompliance

Online Chambers of Commerce: www.online-chamber.com

Online newspapers: www.onlinenewspapers.com

Original Notice/Bureau of Census regarding a classification of the definition of the exporter of record for SED reporting purposes: www.access.gpo.gov

Overseas Private Investment Corp. (OPIC): www.opic.gov

Pacific Dictionary of International Trade and Business: www.pacific.commerce.ubc.ca/ditb/search.html

Passenger rights: www.passengerrights.com

PIERS (Port Import/Export Reporting Service): www.PIERS.com

Ports and Maritime Service Directory: www.seaportsinfo.com

Professional Association of Import/Export Compliance Managers: www. compliancemaven.com

Resources for international job opportunities: www.dbm.com/jobguide/ internat.html

Reuters: www.reuters.com

Russia Today: www.russiatoday.com

SBA: www.sbaonline.com

SBA Office of International Trade: www.sba.gov/oit

SBA offices and services: www.sba.gov/services

Schedule B export codes: www.census.gov/foreign-trade/schedules/b

Search engine: www.google.com

Service Corps of Retired Executives (SCORE): www.score.org

Shipping International: www.aajs.com/shipint

Shipping Times (Singapore): www.business-times.asia1.com.sg/shippingtimes

SIC codes: www.trading.wmw.com/codes/sic.html

Small Business Administration (SBA): www.sba.gov

Small Business Association: www.sbaonline.gov

Small Business Development Centers (SBDC): www.sba.gov/sbdc

Statistical data sources: www.ciber.bus.msu.edu/busres/statinfo.htm

STAT-USA and NTDB: www.stat-usa.gov

The Times: www.londontimes.com

Tokyo Stock Exchange: www.tse.or.jp

Trade and Development Agency (TDA): www.tda.gov

Trade Compass: www.tradecompass.com

Trade Information Center (TIC): www.ita.doc.gov/td/tic

Trade law Web site: www.hg.org/trade.html

Trade Net: www.tradenet.gov

Trade Point USA: www.tradepoint.org

Trade statistics: www.ita.doc.gov/media

Trading floor harmonized code search engine: www.trading.wmw.com

Traffic world: www.trafficworld.com

Transportation Intermediaries Association (TIA): www.tianet.org

Transportation jobs and personnel: www.quotations.com/trans.htm

Travlang: www.travlang.com

UK service for small businesses that provides preliminary information on trade: www.dti.uk/ots/explorer/trade.html

UN International Trade Center (ITC): www.intracen.org

Unibex: www.unibex.com

United Nations (UN): www.un.org

United States–Mexico Chamber of Commerce: www.usmcoc.org/nafta.html

Universal Travel Protection Insurance (UTPI): www.utravelpro.com

USA/Internet: www.stat-usa.gov

U.S. business advisor: www.business.gov

U.S. Census Bureau: www.census.gov

U.S. Census Bureau economic indicators: www.census.gov/econ/

U.S. Census Bureau Foreign Trade Division Harmonized Tariff Classification Schedule: www.census.gov/foreign-trade/www/schedules.html

U.S. Council for International Business (USCIB): www.uscib.org

U.S. Customs Services: www.cbp.gov

USDA Foreign Agricultural Service (FAS): www.fas.usda.gov

USDA Shipper and Export Assistance (SEA): www.ams.usda.gov/tmd/tsd

U.S. Department of Commerce (DOC): www.doc.gov

U.S. Department of Commerce Commercial Service: www.export.gov/com_svc/

U.S. Department of Commerce International Trade Administration: www.ita. doc.gov

USDOC Trade Information Center: www.trade.gov/td/tic

U.S. Export Assistance Centers (USEAC): www.export.gov/eac.html

U.S. export portal: www.export.gov

U.S. Federal Maritime Commission (FMC): www.fmc.gov

U.S. foreign trade zones: www.ia.ita.doc.gov/ftzpage

U.S. government glossary and acronym of international trade terms: www.joc. com/handbook/glossaryofterms.shtml

U.S. Patent and Trademark Office (USPTO): www.uspto.gov

U.S. State Department travel advisory: www.travel.state.gov

U.S. Trade Representative (USTR): www.ustr.gov

Various utilities and useful information: www.ciber.bus.msu.edu/busres/statics/ online-tools-utilities.htm

Wall Street Journal: www.wsj.com

Wells Fargo: www.wellsfargo.com

The World Academy: www.TheWorldAcademy.com

World Bank Group: www.worldbank.org

World Chambers of Commerce Network: www.worldchambers.com

World Customs Organization (WCO): www.wcoomd.org

World Factbook: www.odci.gov/cia/publications/factbook/index.html

World Intellectual Property Organization (WIPO): www.wipo.int

World newspapers on-line: www.virtourist.com/newspaper

World Trade Analyzer: www.tradecompass.com

World Trade Centers Association (WTCA): www.iserve.wtca.org

World Trade Magazine: www.worldtrademag.com

World Trade Organization (WTO): www.wto.org

Worldwide shipping: www.ship.com

WorldPages: www.worldpages.com

Risk Management in the Global Supply Chain and Foreign Purchasing

There are any risks that are unique to global sourcing and foreign purchasing management. Some of these are:

- Political
- Economic
- Weather
- Physical
- Currency
- Distances and demographics
- Regulatory
- Overseas manufacturing
- Traveling personnel and foreign nationals

In most organizations the corporate risk manager has the responsibility to manage the risks of the corporation. These generally fall into property, liability, benefits, and international.

Typically there is no specific risk management expertise for the unique and more specific exposures that a company faces with respect to the operation and maintenance of its global supply chain. One reason for this is that the global supply chain incorporates a lot of different managers from a lot of different areas, and it is likely no one person has ownership of that overall responsibility. Having said that, the best-run corporations do address global supply chain exposures in their risk management programs. Those firms will typically have highly skilled insurance executives who understand the specialized risks and have developed the necessary skill sets of global risk management.

Overall, risk management is becoming an increasingly critical growth area of corporate structure, as it is now widely recognized that a favorable impact to the company's bottom line can be achieved by also having risk management as a component of normal business operations and practices.

Purchasing managers are now inheriting the risk management responsibility in corporations, as they are usually the senior officer engaged in foreign sourcing and overseas business development. This makes them responsible for:

- Identifying risks in their area of purview
- Managing risk assessments
- Taking actions and steps to reduce, mitigate, or transfer exposures
- Coordinating internal risk issues with corporate risk management
- Interfacing with outside providers, such as loss control firms, insurance brokers, insurance companies, etc.

- Educating, informing, and training other purchasing and supply chain personnel in all areas of risk management and mitigation
- Creating contingency and disaster management strategies and plans

A factor in the new millennium that directly impacts the responsibilities of the purchasing manager is how to best manage risk and therefore maximize profit in his or her organization. It is another key skill set he or she has to develop and manage.

Summary

A key issue with the above outlined concerns is that when something goes wrong internationally, in comparison to when something goes wrong domestically, it is the consequences that will be much more severe. And the ability to mitigate the problem is much more hampered. Awareness of the issues, information flow, and strategies to mitigate are key responsibilities of a purchasing manager operating in a global supply chain. Those companies that proactively engage all these concerns into their global business strategies will have more successful and profitable inbound supply chains.

Chapter 3

Import Logistics and Landed Cost Modeling

The movement of goods from foreign locations to final destinations here in the United States, and making sure that the costing models are true and accurate are critical responsibilities directly affecting the overall job description of purchasing management. This chapter offers important insight into this skill set.

Logistics Management

There are five key steps to successful import logistics management:

1. Hire the very best inbound logistics provider.
2. Know your true landed costs.
3. Control lead times.
4. Control the most favorable INCOTERMS of purchase.
5. Exercise due diligence, reasonable care, and supervision and control over the inbound process.

Hire the Very Best Inbound Logistics Provider

Hiring a good customhouse broker is one of the most important purchases an importer can make. *A good customhouse broker/freight forwarder will help ensure that the supply chain will function in a timely, safe, and cost-effective manner.*

Know Your True Landed Costs

It is very important to make sure you have properly allocated all the landed costs, which make up all the costs of goods landed from the origin through to the final destination, point of use, or final sale.

Import Landed Cost Formula

- Purchase price
- Method and cost for payment
- Currency exchange costs
- Foreign vendor packing charges
- Foreign inland transportation charges
- Foreign loading charges
- Foreign inspection fees
- Foreign port charges for CBP examination, and foreign port storage charges for no-load containers
- International transportation charges (air, ocean, and ground transportation)
- *Ad valorem* duties and taxes based on import value, specific duties and taxes based on import quantity, and compound duties based on both value and quantity
- Merchandise processing fees based on 0.21% of import value
- Harbor maintenance fee for ocean shipments based on 0.125% of import value
- Antidumping fees based on CBP investigation into fair market price value methods, countervailing duty fees based on CBP investigation into foreign bounties grants, and subsidies paid to foreign vendor that may have effected the price paid or payable
- Security manifest fees
- Fuel surcharge fees
- Handling and freight transfer fees
- Storage fees incurred on freight not picked up from the pier within three days of the date of availability
- International freight
- U.S. inland transportation fees
- U.S. warehousing, deconsolidation, storage, distribution, and break bulk fees
- Messenger fees
- U.S. Customs examination fees
- Other Department of Homeland Security (DHS) government agency examination fees (Agriculture, Fish and Wildlife Service, EPA)

Control Lead Times

Purchase order management requires timely ordering. In international purchasing, where more things are likely to hamper on-time services, lead time is a very crucial tool to mitigate potential exposures and costs.

Ocean freight is an economical mode of transporting freight globally. Air freight or expedited services can be as much as eighteeen times more expensive. A consequence of poor lead times is the movement toward more air freight shipping, which will impact the bottom line and increase landed costs.

Control the Most Favorable INCOTERMS of Purchase

All INCOTERMS are reviewed below. We recommend that purchasing managers utilize INCOTERMS that allow them to control the inbound freight from origin to destination. The two best options, depending upon a host of circumstances, are Ex Works origin and FCA outbound gateway. This gives you the best opportunity to:

- Control freight costs
- Know the status of the inbound shipment at all times
- Handle the clearance process, which you might end up being held accountable for anyway, as the importer of record or the ultimate consignee
- Use any mode of transportation

INCOTERMS

Language is one of the most complex and important tools of international trade. As in any complex and sophisticated business, small changes in wording can have a major impact on all aspects of a business agreement. Word definitions often differ from industry to industry. This is especially true of global trade, where such fundamental terms as *delivery* can have a far different meaning in the business than in the rest of the world.

For business terminology to be effective, phrases must mean the same thing throughout the industry. That is why the International Chamber of Commerce created INCOTERMS in 1936. INCOTERMS are designed to create a bridge between different members of the industry by acting as a uniform language they can use.

Each INCOTERM refers to a type of agreement for the purchase and shipping of goods internationally. There are thirteen different terms, each of which helps users deal with different situations involving the movement of goods. For example, the term *FCA* is often used with shipments involving

Ro/Ro or container transport; *DDU* assists with situations found in intermodal or courier service–based shipments.

INCOTERMS also deal with the documentation required for global trade, specifying which parties are responsible for which documents. Determining the paperwork required to move a shipment is an important job, since requirements vary so much between countries. Two items, however, are standard: the commercial invoice and the packing list.

INCOTERMS were created primarily for people inside the world of global trade. Outsiders frequently find them difficult to understand. Seemingly common words such as *responsibility* and *delivery* have different meanings in global trade than they do in other situations. In global trade, *delivery* refers to the seller fulfilling the obligation of the terms of sale or completing a contractual obligation. *Delivery* can occur while the merchandise is on a vessel on the high seas and the parties involved are thousands of miles from the goods. In the end, however, the terms wind up boiling down to a few basic specifics:

> Costs: Who is responsible for the expenses involved in a shipment at a given point in the shipment's journey?
> Control: Who owns the goods at a given point in the journey?
> Liability: Who is responsible for paying damage to goods at a given point in a shipment's transit?

It is essential for shippers to know the exact status of their shipments in terms of ownership and responsibility. It is also vital for sellers and buyers to arrange insurance on their goods while the goods are in their legal possession. Lack of insurance can result in wasted time, lawsuits, and broken relationships.

INCOTERMS can thus have a direct financial impact on a company's business. What is important is not the acronyms, but the business results. Often companies like to be in control of their freight. That being the case, sellers of goods might choose to sell CIF, which gives them a good grasp of shipments moving out of their country, and buyers may prefer to purchase FOB, which gives them a tighter hold on goods moving into their country.

This glossary will explain terms such as *CIF* and *FOB* and their impact on the trade process. In addition, since most international buyers and sellers do not handle goods themselves, but work through Customs brokers and freight forwarders, the glossary will cover how both fit in to the terms under discussion.

INCOTERMS are most frequently listed by category. Terms beginning with *F* refer to shipments where the primary cost of shipping is not paid for by the seller. Terms beginning with *C* deal with shipments where the seller pays for shipping. *E* terms occur when a seller's responsibilities are fulfilled when goods are ready to depart from its facilities. *D* terms cover shipments where the shipper or seller's responsibility ends when the goods arrive at some specific point. Because shipments are moving into a country, *D* terms usually involve the services of a Customs broker and a freight forwarder. In addition, *D* terms also deal with the pier or docking charges found at virtually all ports, and determining who is responsible for each charge.

Recently the ICC changed basic aspects of the definitions of a number of INCOTERMS; buyers and sellers should be aware of this. Terms that have changed have a star alongside them.

EX-Works: One of the simplest and most basic shipment arrangements places the minimum responsibility on the seller, with greater responsibility on the buyer. In an EX-Works transaction, goods are basically made available for pickup at the shipper or seller's factory or warehouse and delivery is accomplished when the merchandise is released to the consignee's freight forwarder. The buyer is responsible for making arrangements with the forwarder for insurance, export clearance, and handling all other paperwork.

FOB (free on board): One of the most commonly used and misused terms, FOB means that the shipper/seller uses his freight forwarder to move the merchandise to the port or designated point of origin. Though frequently used to describe inland movement of cargo, FOB specifically refers to ocean or inland waterway transportation of goods. Delivery is accomplished when the shipper or seller releases the goods to the buyer's forwarder. The buyer's responsibility for insurance and transportation begins at the same moment.

FCA (free carrier): In this type of transaction, the seller is responsible for arranging transportation, but he is acting at the risk and the expense of the buyer. Whereas in FOB the freight forwarder or carrier is the choice of the buyer, in FCA the seller chooses and works with the freight forwarder or the carrier. Delivery is accomplished at a predetermined port or destination point and the buyer is responsible for insurance.

FAS (free alongside ship)*: In these transactions, the buyer bears all the transportation costs and the risk of loss of goods. FAS requires the shipper or seller to clear goods for export, which is a reversal from past practices. Companies selling on these terms will ordinarily use their freight forwarder to clear the goods for export. Delivery is accomplished when the goods are turned over to the buyer's forwarder for insurance and transportation.

CFR (cost and freight): This term, formerly known as CNF (C&F), defines two distinct and separate responsibilities: one deals with the actual cost of merchandise (C), and the other (F) refers to the freight charges to a predetermined destination point. It is the shipper or seller's responsibility to get goods from its door to the port of destination. Delivery is accomplished at this time. It is the buyer's responsibility to cover insurance from the port of origin or port of shipment to the buyer's door. Given that the shipper is responsible for transportation, the shipper also chooses the forwarder.

CIF (cost, insurance, and freight): This arrangement is similar to CFR, but instead of the buyer insuring the goods for the maritime phase of the voyage, the shipper or seller will insure the merchandise. In this arrangement, the seller usually chooses the forwarder. Delivery, as above, is accomplished at the port of destination.

CPT (carriage paid to): In CPT transactions the shipper or seller has the same obligations found with CIF, with the addition that the seller has to buy cargo insurance, naming the buyer as the insured while the goods are in transit.

CIP (carriage and insurance paid to): This term is primarily used for multimodal transport. Because it relies on the carrier's insurance, the shipper or seller is only required to purchase minimum coverage. When this particular agreement is in force, freight forwarders often act, in effect, as carriers. The buyer's insurance is effective when the goods are turned over to the forwarder.

DAF (delivered at frontier): Here the seller's responsibility is to hire a forwarder to take goods to a named frontier, which is usually a border crossing point, and clear them for export. Delivery occurs at this time. The buyer's responsibility is to arrange with his forwarder the pickup of the goods after they are cleared for export, carrying them across the border, clearing them for importation, and effecting delivery. In most cases, the buyer's forwarder handles the task of accepting the goods at the border across the foreign soil.

DES (delivered ex ship): In this type of transaction, it is the seller's responsibility to get the goods to the port of destination or to engage the forwarder to move cargo to the port of destination uncleared. Delivery occurs at this time. Any destination charges that occur after the ship is docked are the buyer's responsibility.

DEQ (delivered ex quay)*: In this arrangement, the buyer or consignee is responsible for duties and charges and the seller is responsible for delivering the goods to the quay, wharf, or port of destination. In a reversal of previous practice, the buyer must also arrange for Customs clearance.

DDP (delivered duty paid): DDP terms tend to be used in intermodal or courier type shipments. Whereby the shipper or seller is responsible for dealing with all the tasks involved in moving goods from the manufacturing plant to the buyer or consignee's door, it is the shipper or seller's responsibility to insure the goods and absorb all costs and risks, including the payment of duty and fees.

DDU (delivered duty unpaid): This arrangement is basically the same as with DDP, except for the fact that the buyer is responsible for the duty, fees, and taxes.

Exercise Due Diligence, Reasonable Care, and Supervision and Control over the Inbound Process

The U.S. government, through several agencies, primarily Customs and Border Protection (CBP), requires all supply chains and the managers who run them to apply three standards to their inbound business process:

- Due diligence
- Reasonable care
- Supervision and control

These three standards are further defined by Customs regulations, precedence, and best practice operations.

Areas such as training of supply chain personnel, creating SOPs, use of technology, senior management involvement, etc., are all examples of managing these three areas.

Case Study in the Landed Costs in the Import Supply Chain

One needs to analyze the total costs in importing goods into the United States, including any costs once in the country. A profile of these costs follows:

Stereo Speakers from Beijing to Chicago

Unit cost: Ex Works factory	$61.00 USD ($18,300)
Inland freight: 40-foot container (300 units)	$1,200.00

(Continued)

Stereo Speakers from Beijing to Chicago (Continued)

Ocean freight	$3,100.00
Export handling	$220.00
Export clearance charges	$94.50
Import clearance	$125.00
Duties and taxes	$955.50
Other clearance	$70.00
Inland to Chicago	$755.00
Warehousing (60 days)	$122.00
Inland to customers	$246.00
Total landed (300 units)	$25,188.00
Per unit	$83.96

If you now dissect the costs, change any one line and you can seriously reduce your inbound supply chain costs. For example, if you chose the West Coast to both enter your goods and warehouse, you could reduce the inland freight costs by $600.00 ($755.00 minus $155.00 for local haulage). That would reduce the total cost by 2%. Negotiate with your West Coast customhouse broker to store the goods for sixty days free and you will save another 1%. Reduce your ocean freight by 10% and you will save another 1.2%.

So one can see how by a little manipulating, one could save almost 5%, which is in the importer's pocket or passed off to the customer in a competitive pricing scenario. More serious negotiations could result in even more savings.

Another example, which has more of a sourcing aspect, follows. You find a supplier in Mexico who can manufacture a similar product, at the same Ex Works price as the supplier in China. Obviously, this is an oversimplification, but for a sample business model it works well. It now comes in duty-free under NAFTA and the freight costs are reduced by 35%. Your savings would come to almost 11 to 13%.

There are a multitude of options and variations that a supply chain manager can manipulate to affect the landed cost and obtain competitive advantage. It is the supply chain's main objective to know what the best options are, the variable risks, and how to provide the most cost-effective options to its company's benefit.

Options in Reducing Landed Costs

Over the past thirty years I have observed well over a thousand corporations develop offshore manufacturing and build successful supply chains. Many go through arduous learning curves. Here are some suggestions that have worked to minimize the learning curve issues:

- Be patient in the decision-making process. Take considerable time to make conclusive decisions. Do the proper research and get as informed as possible. Don't let competitive pressures push you to make hasty choices you will regret down the road.
- Utilize external support services. Consultants who specialize in developing foreign market and manufacturing options can prove invaluable. Their fees will be covered in the financial gains in their use.
- Align yourself with quality service providers whose expertise can make or break the success of your supply chain. Take the time and chose wisely. This includes:
  - Logistics service providers
  - Freight forwarders
  - Customhouse brokers
  - Third-party providers
  - Ocean and air carriers
  - Integrated carriers
  - Bankers
  - Attorneys
  - Consultants
  - Accounting firms
- Training and education facilities

All of these entities have personnel with years of experience and can provide lots of quality advice and counsel in any area that will affect your supply chain.

- Do beta testing when feasible, before making long-term decisions. Allow time for testing how a foreign manufacturer will perform, or any one of the supply chain partners, so you can "sleep with the party" before marrying.
- Design contracts that have easy "escape" clauses and have performance guidelines.
- Always, when feasible, have all the supply chain partners invest in the supply chain with capital expenditures, particularly the manufacturer. This will make for a more secure and longer-term commitment, as well as building a business model more likely to succeed.

Chapter 4

Import Compliance Management

Managing all the compliance and security initiatives of CBP and other government agencies is a major component of a successful import supply chain. This chapter dissects all the key issues and offers a comprehensive guide to follow to "get it right."

Import Management Overview

The United States imports twice as much as it exports. A major revenue source for the U.S. government is the revenue generated by taxes, duties, fees, and fines and penalties brought in by the tremendous import volume. Trade compliance management for imports is a very serious concern for corporations that purchase goods from foreign sources. The events of 9/11 made this an even more serious matter, and has now made it a number one priority for major importers to restructure their supply chain management functions to include trade compliance.

On that September day in 2001 supply chain managers of the world were focused on cost-effective purchasing, logistics, and operations. Disruption was not a pressing thought. No one in global trade really anticipated the 9/11 events. No contingency planning or disaster programs prethought that occurrence, thereby offering a "safe harbor" recourse or plan of action to mitigate the chain of occurrences that would follow and disrupt global supply chains, to this very day. It is amazing to my consulting practice that, as we enter 2010, a vast majority of firms involved in import, export, and domestic transportation have done very little regarding disaster planning or to pay attention to the new regulatory concerns that have and will affect their ability to manage supply chains.

When the world realized what was happening in New York City at the World Trade Center, over Pennsylvania, and at the Pentagon, it was just after 9:00 a.m. in the morning. Shock, disbelief, and rage, combined with a lot of fear, were everyone's original sentiment. The United States took action shortly after. It shut down areas of New York and Washington. Air traffic was brought to a halt. International business was now at a standstill. Within an hour there were no commercial planes in the air. Inbound air traffic was stopped, diverted, or halted. Truck transportation in certain areas was curtailed. Vessels coming in and out of U.S. ports were being restricted as to what they could do. People movement in and out of the United States was put on hold. Basically everything in motion or in transit was on hold.

As the hours, days, and weeks ensued and the situation was accessed, trade was reestablished and transportation corridors and lanes were reopened. Some supply chains took a few days, others a few weeks. Some never opened again or, when they did, were forever altered. Every import and export company was affected. Time frames, processes, documentation, or regulatory concerns impeded transportation infrastructures. There was no more doing business as usual. The bottom line has been as follows:

- It costs more to ship.
- More attention has to be paid to documentation and logistics detail.
- Regulations changed, making it more cumbersome to import and export.
- Corporations had to modify their supply lines.
- Purchasing management and selling decisions were altered.
- Carriers' futures were uncertain.
- Potential fines and penalties increased.
- An entire new corporate responsibility was created in security and compliance.

It is impossible for one person to represent all the governments' mind-set and attitude toward post-9/11 issues. There are just too many convolutions, strategies, and implemented programs that cause difficulty in deciphering and completely comprehending, due to:

1. The U.S. government recognized that it had to change its mind-set to manage the new threats of terrorism, compliance, and security management.
2. The complexities of all the government agencies that regulate and control inbound supply chains are so convoluted, and lines of accountability and responsibility are unclear, that any concerted, focused effort is almost impossible.

3. The happenings of 9/11 set a chain of events in motion that are still a work-in-process. There have now been two administration changes and numerous senior management changes to government personnel, all who have impacted regulatory policy.
4. As the political landscape changes, so do compliance and security issues.
5. Various government agencies, such as the Departments of Transportation and Commerce, State, and Treasury, are taking a different approach to terrorism. While the ultimate goals may be similar, their approaches can be very different.
6. Personnel at all levels are changing.
7. Different individuals in power positions are interpreting laws, regulations, and initiatives differently.
8. As time passes, many have forgotten the consequences of 9/11 and are becoming complacent against any new compliance/security/terrorist fighting initiatives that might affect the efficiencies of inbound supply chains.

What the author can do is offer an intelligent, informed opinion on what the government is thinking, as a result of significant analysis and an in-depth review of Web sites, media, presentations, and contacts with various personnel "in the know." The various agencies of the United States, with the Department of Homeland Security leading the charge, all had to ask questions to learn how our inbound supply chains operated:

■ How was our intelligence gathering mechanism working?
■ How were foreign nationals screened at the border?
■ How were "aliens" taught how to fly, with no questions asked?
■ How did terrorists move weapons through airline screening in Newark and Boston?
■ How did four planes fly and three crash into major targets, unimpeded?

The government was faced with some complex occurrences, had to come up with some short-term terrorist thwarting strategies, and keep open inbound supply chains, all at the same time. Some of the critical issues are as follows:

■ Prevent any futuristic terrorist actions
■ Access defensive strategies
■ Better our intelligence gathering and communicating ability
■ Have greater scrutiny over what and who can access America or our interests overseas
■ Better the U.S. government's interagency coordination and cooperation
■ Reorganize the government to better deal with terrorist issues
■ Enact long-term laws, regulations, and initiatives to keep low-cost inbound supply chains open and running

Inbound supply chain experts in tandem with various U.S. government agencies thought the following:

- Another 9/11 could not occur again.
- Inbound supply chains had to operate with the borders better secured from adverse persons and cargos.
- The government had to be reorganized to better utilize resources and combat terrorism.
- The exposures and enemy needed to be better identified.
- Better intelligence and resource development were necessary.
- The enemy needed to be targeted overseas and on foreign shores, and not here.
- Actions needed to be swift and decisive.
- Actions supported by other governments and country coalitions would not have to be absolutely necessary, but would improve opportunities for success.

The mind-set of the government followed these thoughts that ultimately led to actions, laws, regulations, reorganization, and military action. To name some that had an affect on global supply chains:

- ISF (10+2) Importer Security Filing
- Port Security Act
- Export Enforcement Act of 2007
- Customs becoming Customs and Border Protection (CBP)
- Liberating Afghanistan and Iraq ·
- Taking a harder line on countries that have terrorist strongholds or are known to interface with or harbor terrorist organizations
- USA Patriot Act
- Bioterrorism Act
- FDA Prior Notice
- Safe Explosives Act
- Aviation and Transportation Security Act
- Homeland Security Act
- Resolution 1373 (United Nations Counter Terrorism Committee)
- Custom-Trade Partnership against Terrorism (CTPAT)
- Container Security Initiative (CSI)
- Free and Secure Trade (FAST)/Prearrival Processing Systems (PAPS)
- Importer Self-Assessment (to pull in more CTPAT participants)
- Advanced Electronic Notice (twenty-four-hour rule and advanced notice for imports)
- Marine Transportation Security Act
- International Ship and Port Facility Security Code (ISPS)
- Advanced Passenger Information System (APIS)
- Interagency Border Inspection Systems (IBIS)

- Integrated Surveillance Intelligence System (ISIS)
- Radiation Isotope Identification Systems (RIIDS) issued to CBP field locations
- Remote Video Surveillance System (RVSS)
- Unmanned aerial vehicles (UAVs) to support the Arizona Border Initiative
- Geographic Information System (GIS) is another Southwest border program
- Tripling of the number of Border Patrol agents on the northern border
- Reassigning of two hundred agents to the Arizona-Mexico border
- Establishing additional checkpoints in strategically located border zones
- Deploying specially trained explosive and chemical detector dogs
- Interior Repatriation Program
- NEXUS (alternative inspection system to prescreen travelers)
- Secure Electronic Network for Travelers Rapid Inspection (SENTRI)
- National Targeting Center to centralize coordination of antiterrorism efforts
- Automated Targeting System (ATS) and Automated Export System (AES) used to assess cargo
- Student and Exchange Visitor System (SEVIS)
- Immigration Security Initiative (ISI)
- Border Safety Initiative (BSI)
- One Face at the Border Program
- Name change of BXA to BIS

These acts, changes, and new directional headings could be summarized as follows:

- The U.S. government was going to be proactive in fighting terrorism at the source and not waiting for it to hit our shores.
- Individuals and corporate America would be enlisted in providing various levels of cooperation in these new initiatives.
- Additionally, individuals and corporate America would trade off and compromise certain liberties, freedoms, and privileges in this effort.
- The government would enforce very strict guidelines on receiving prior information on inbound freight and people.

The U.S. government agencies that are peripherally involved in compliance and security and their user friendly Web sites are listed below.

Links to Government Sites

Bureau of Justice Assistance	http://www.ojp.usdoj.gov/BJA/
Bureau of Justice Statistics	http://www.ojp.usdoj.gov/bjs/
California Intelligence and Terrorism Alert Network	http://www.catitan.org/

Links to Government Sites (Continued)

Central Intelligence Agency	http://www.cia.gov/
Department of Homeland Security	http://www.dhs.gov/dhspublic/
Drug Enforcement Administration	http://www.usdoj.gov/dea/
Infragard: Guarding the Nation's Infrastructure	http://www.infragard.net/
International Association of Chiefs of Police	http://www.theiacp.org/
Internet Fraud Complaint Center	http://www.ifccfbi.gov/index.asp
INTERPOL	http://www.usdoj.gov/usncb/
MIPT Terrorism Knowledge Database	http://www.tkb.org/Home.jsp
National Center for Missing and Exploited Children	http://www.missingkids.com/
National Executive Institute Associates, Major Cities Chief's Association and Major County Sheriff's Association	http://www.neiassociates.org/
National Institute of Justice	http://www.ojp.usdoj.gov/nij/
National Sheriff's Association	http://www.sheriffs.org/
Regional Computer Forensic Laboratory, National Program Office	http://www.rcfl.gov/
Society of Former Special Agents	http://www.socxfbi.org/
Texas Coastal Region Advisory System	http://www.tcras.org/
U.S. Department of Justice	http://www.usdoj.gov/
U.S. Marshals Service	http://www.usdoj.gov/marshals/
U.S. State Department	http://www.state.gov/

Inbound Supply Chains Have Logistics Costs Escalate

Those parties servicing inbound logistics—forwarders, customhouse brokers, truckers, air and ocean carriers, etc.—were all required to beef up their compliance and security procedures. These actions increased their operating costs. Some of this expense was shared by various government agencies. Some was not. Most passed on the additional costs to the shippers. Fees as little as $25.00 per shipment to as much as 5% were added to freight bills, as surcharges for security.

After all the dust settled, it was discovered that most of the fees were legitimate. However, some were bogus or the amount was much too high and became a windfall for the carrier. In any event, inbound supply chains were run with additional cost. In 2006, these costs still add to the overall "landed costs" for importers and companies purchasing, manufacturing, and sourcing in foreign markets.

Detail to Documentation Was Much More Critical

For the individual traveling businessperson there were now layers of documentation required to come to and from the United States. Any executive who traveled internationally had to spend at least one to two additional hours going through security at certain airports. As we approach 2011, it is still difficult to travel internationally. Domestic is easier, but still problematic.

Freight coming to and from the United States underwent new documentation and procedures before being allowing to transit. One example of the government's response was the Twenty-Four-Hour Manifest Rule. This U.S. regulation required carriers to transfer detailed manifests to U.S. Customs and Border Protection, on inbound ocean freight, twenty-four hours prior to the vessel sailing from the foreign port. This new Twenty-Four-Hour Rule placed very tight communication and information transfer responsibilities on the overseas supplier, the inbound carrier, and the importer in the United States. Regulations changed, making it more costly, cumbersome, and frustrating to import and export. The new ISF regulations requiring a lot more detailed information to be provided to Customs prior to shipping from the country of origin is an example of the new, harsher import regulations.

The new focus on deemed export rules, as an example, covered in greater detail in Chapter 9, certainly made it more difficult for both importers and exporters to transfer information, knowledge, and wherewithal to foreign nationals. The deemed export regulations are cumbersome controls that redefine exports to include the transfer of information to foreign nationals to be handled as if they were physical exports. So if a corporation brought a foreign national from a subsidiary from an overseas plant to train here in the United States, the U.S. corporation would have to determine the "export readiness" of that learning process before it could be done. The nature of the knowledge transfer, the specific individual, and the county of utilization, along with the end use of the information, would all have to be taken into consideration before the training could even begin, if at all.

Corporations had to modify their supply lines. Many importers and exporters had to modify their supply lines. Infrastructure, choice of providers and carriers, third-party partners, modes of transit, packing, marking, and labeling became issues of change for logistics executives since 9/11. As mentioned before, the Twenty-Four-Hour Manifest Rule required importers who utilized ocean freight modes to make sure their suppliers provided detailed cargo manifests to carriers prior to export. Many overseas suppliers, to this day, struggle to meet that requirement and are forced to find other modes of transportation, such as air and truck, which might prove to be more expensive, adding cost to their landed cost calculations.

The increased threat of terrorism caused shippers of hazardous materials to raise the bar of due diligence in how their goods were packed, marked, and shipped. This added inconvenience, cost, and retraining of personnel and operational procedures.

Purchasing Managers Had to Learn New Skill Sets and Establish SOPs in Areas Not Previously Prioritized

When overseas suppliers refused to cooperate with certain CBP initiatives such as C-TPAT, CSI, and the Twenty-Four-Hour Manifest Ruling, purchasing managers often had no choice but to find more willing and cooperative contract manufacturers and suppliers. This changed the operating profile requirements of potential overseas suppliers, in that they now had to meet minimum capabilities in compliance, security, and information transfer. Many importers who also export chose not to exercise greater due diligence on reviewing Denied Parties Lists or paying attention to the Office of Foreign Assets Control (OFAC) sanctions list and found themselves in trouble with fines, penalties, and loss of import/export privileges.

The Air Carriers Suffered Greatly

When air travel became restricted immediately following 9/11, the airline industry took a big hit. Some airlines, such as United, Delta, and U.S. Air, have not been able to recover, and others, like Continental and American, have had major cutbacks. An entire new corporate responsibility was created in security and compliance. They have all reduced service parameters, cut the number of planes, and stopped flying certain routes, all of which has had an affect on shippers in reduced capacity and loss of certain trade lane competitive pricing options.

The economy took a hit from 9/11. Many transportation providers were affected. They merged, got bought, or went out of business. The landscape of trucking companies, third-party providers, and freight forwarders dramatically changed. The "big boys," such as UPS, Fed Ex, Danzas, Maersk Sea Land, and APL, while they had their share of post-9/11 issues, eventually benefited by acquiring or merging with many of the companies that could not successfully sustain their operations. At the end of the day there were fewer providers and carriers, and the ones that have survived are much larger.

Traffic managers now had to pay much closer attention to whom they were purchasing logistics services from. It became as much an art as a science. The due diligence of logistics purchasing was much more intense.

Financial Consequences to Importers and Global Supply Chain Participants

Every resource available to the author indicated a significant rise in government intervention and scrutiny, for example:

■ Dramatic increase in several government agencies' scrutiny of supply chains
■ Enforcement of both old and new regulations
■ More fines and penalties being issued

We were made aware that many carriers, including the integrated mega-carriers, were being fined regularly for violations, such as but not limited to hazardous material movements, Customs failures, and improper filing of Shipper's Export Declaration (SED) information. Shippers found themselves under increased scrutiny for an array of subjects that led to direct fines and penalties. Fines range from "administrative warnings" to $250 to more than $30 million. However, the greatest consequence is the loss of import or export privileges, which the government has a right to deny (and it does) on cases warranting that action. Additional consequences to this scrutiny are internal costs in time and personnel involvement, mandated infrastructure changes, and legal costs. Frustration, anguish, and disharmony can also be ill affects.

Supply Chain Security and Compliance Management Becomes a New Corporate Concern

When I graduated from the Maritime Academy, served in the military, and eventually came to the world of business and global trade in the late 1970s, Occupational Safety and Health Administration (OSHA) regulations were just beginning to dominate corporate cultures. Corporations were forced to comply with government regulations on workplace, personnel, and work environment scenarios or face serious fines, penalties, mandates, or be shut down. Eventually every corporation had to form a new management position: the OSHA compliance officer. Today, in the new millennium, it is a stalwart of corporate infrastructure.

That is where we are today in import and export compliance. Corporations are not sure what to do with the new regulatory environment in import and export supply chains. Do we ignore the current atmosphere and react to only mandatory issues? Do we become proactive and take significant initiatives in compliance and security? Do we take a moderated position and only do what is necessary now and do some contingency planning for future mandates? A perplexing problem with an easy answer. The best response is a methodic proactive strategy—one that grapples with the more immediate issues (CSI, Twenty-Four-Hour Manifest, Denied Parties List, USPPI, etc.) and plans a program over an eighteen- to twenty-four-month response to all the longer-term issues facing the supply chain in compliance and security, C-TPAT, creation of SOPs, training of operations personnel, etc. This would be a new position, and if not an independent job, then certainly another "hat" for someone to wear: the import/export compliance officer.

Supply chain executives, CFOs, purchasing managers, and logistics and import specialists all have had to raise the bar of their knowledge of how goods are imported into the United States. Their dependency on their customhouse broker could remain, but they had to exercise a new level of brokerage management:

■ Supervision and control
■ Due diligence
■ Reasonable care

When Customs put forth the Modernization Act in 1993, it increased the responsibility of importers all over the United States of every size, in every industry, from all levels of management and operations. When 9/11 occurred, it hastened and enhanced Customs initiatives to make sure that importers and all parties in the supply chain adhered to the regulations laid out in 1993, as well as all the new rules, regulations, and programs put forth since that event happened. Companies that managed their import operation as a secondary concern in their business model had to quickly prioritize import management 101 to the forefront of their corporate strategies and operational profile.

The following outline includes subject matters that all importers need to know as basic issues to successfully manage their relationship with Customs and Border Protection (CBP):

■ Importer of record
■ Reasonable care
■ Supervision and control
■ Ultimate consignee
■ Powers of attorney
■ Due diligence
■ Record keeping
■ Documentation (invoice) requirements
■ Assists
■ Drawback
■ HTS classification
■ Imported product/origin markings
■ Valuation
■ Duties and taxes
■ ISF

Reasonable Care

Reasonable care is the degree of care that an ordinary person would exercise in the normal course of business. It is the degree of care that an importer or his or her agent uses in the Customs business process of entering merchandise into the commerce of the United States. If an importer demonstrates reasonable care, it will serve as an immediate mitigating factor to any future fines, penalties, or Customs action. Many importers have faced fines and penalties for failure to "dot their *i*'s and cross their *t*'s." To ensure that reasonable care is taken, the importer of record should:

- Consult with qualified experts such as Customs brokers, consultants, and attorneys specializing in Customs law
- Seek guidance from Customs through the formal binding ruling program
- If using a broker, provide the broker with full and complete information, sufficient enough for the broker to make proper entry (import declaration) or provide advice as how to make entry
- Obtain analysis from accredited labs to determine the technical qualities of imported merchandise
- Use in-house employees who have experience and knowledge of Customs regulations and procedures
- Follow any binding rulings received from Customs
- Ensure that products are legally marked with the country of origin to indicate to the ultimate purchaser the origin of imported products
- Not classify his or her own identical merchandise or value identical merchandise in different ways
- Notify Customs when receiving different treatment by Customs for the same goods on different entries or different ports
- Examine entries (import declaration, CF 3461) prepared by the broker to determine the accuracy in classification and valuation

The broker should:

- Be considered an expert, hence must give competent advice
- Exercise due diligence to ascertain the correctness of information that he or she imparts to a client
- Not knowingly impart to a client false information relative to any Customs business
- Not withhold information from a client who is entitled to that information
- Establish internal procedures to limit advice being given by qualified licensed individuals
- Obtain and receive directly from the importer complete and accurate information sufficient to make the entry or provide proper advice regarding doing so

Supervision and Control

The responsibility to manage the entire import declaration process falls within the regulatory guidelines of the importer of record. Customs and Border Protection (CBP) mandated in the Modernization Act of 1993 a list of reasonable care standards that outline specific actions to be performed by the importer, demonstrating the ability to supervise and control entry declaration information tendered to Customs. In past practices deemed to be noncompliant, many importers relied solely on the actions of their designated Customs brokers without specific knowledge of their own responsibilities related to regulatory issues of Customs law. The concept of relying on the broker's actions was generally accepted as the means of proper importation by many trade participants. CBP has a different view of the Customs broker than that represented by this common practice.

Customs defines the Customs brokerage provider as a third party who is licensed by the Department of Homeland Security to conduct Customs business on behalf of an importer of record. Customs' position is that the importer of record is the responsible party who must ensure that proper information is provided to the brokerage provider, in all instances sufficient enough for the broker to make entry of the imported merchandise. CBP does not authorize the Customs broker to make any entry decisions on behalf of the importer.

Common noncompliant practices of a lack of supervision and control involve cases in which the broker would select a Harmonized Classification Number for imported products on behalf of the importer. These cases would involve the inability of the importer to properly utilize the Harmonized Tariff Schedule for proper reference abilities. An additional example involves the inability of the importer to schedule shipment arrivals, clearance, or delivery due to an exclusion from the logistics management process, with a total dependence on the import freight forwarder and Customs broker.

Ultimate Consignee

On most import transactions, the importer of record and the ultimate consignee are the same. The opinion of Customs is that the ultimate consignee caused the import to occur and is one of the responsible parties to the import transaction. Therefore, the ultimate consignee can be held accountable for regulatory requirements. This can have serious consequences for a company that purchases goods on a delivered duty paid (DDP) or free domicile basis. This term of sale dictates the seller is responsible for the payment of duties, freight, and Customs clearance.

Ultimate consignees mistakenly believe they can avoid the normal importing process and liabilities that go along with importing. Customs requires that if a buyer causes the import, the buyer must have the usual records required to import. This includes the bill of lading, entry documents, purchase order, and invoice. Records must also be retained for the usual five-year period. Ultimate consignees must be aware there may be an obligation to Customs even when they are not the importer of record.

Powers of Attorney

All importers should properly manage the number of Customs brokers who are conducting Customs business on their behalf. It is imperative that proper control be established and maintained to ensure that qualified persons are presenting all declarations. Many importers do not realize that the power of attorney (POA) is established for the protection of the importer of record to control the brokers who are conducting Customs business on their behalf. There is a rule that a Customs broker, who is authorized to conduct Customs business on behalf of an importer, must have a valid power of attorney to conduct such business or face a penalty of up to the value of the merchandise or loss of license.

Many importers have several brokers who, once issued a Customs power of attorney, become an extension of the traffic department of the importer. This authority is dangerous when not properly managed. Too many Customs brokers create an increased liability for error and mismanagement. Supervision and control over your brokerage providers becomes an unattainable goal when there are an unmanageable number of brokers with Customs powers of attorney for an importer.

Importers should perform extensive reviews of all brokerage services to critique the internal expertise being given to each and every entry. The average years of experience that are present in the operational levels of the brokerage service community that handles over 90% of the work volume, may not be licensed and may require some level of scrutiny.

It is the responsibility of the importer to properly manage the performance of the broker and regulate the brokers who meet satisfactory levels of compliance with the Customs power of attorney issuance management process. Only compliant and operationally effective brokers should be allowed to conduct Customs business on behalf of importers. Importers have power of attorney management as a tool to implement this requirement. Any broker who falls below the importer's standards of compliance will have his or her power of attorney revoked by letter of revocation sent to the port director of Customs at the port of entry.

All powers of attorney should be dated with a date of expiration, not to exceed an initial period of thirty days for renewal, pending proven performance. Once the importer is satisfied with the broker's performance, POAs should be issued for a period not to exceed one year.

Due Diligence

Due diligence is a term used in relation to the effort demonstrated by the broker or importer in the research, investigation, and determination of a decision related to a past, current, or future statement or act associated with the Customs declaration process. Customs and Border Protection acknowledges that common practice knowledge in many cases is the sole basis for the determination of a course of action taken by an importer or broker. CBP does not authorize either party to act solely on its interpretation of accepted or common practices. Customs has structured guidelines that consist of an expectation of definitive research of Customs laws and regulatory procedures to be investigated, referenced, and documented that will allow all importers and Customs brokers the ability to make educated and informed decisions in the import process.

Customs has dedicated a lot of effort toward the enhancement of its Web site, at www.cbp.gov, to serve as an automated tool of reference for most Customs business inquiries. CBP has the expectation that importers and Customs brokers will reference alternative resources, such as Customs rulings and prior case interpretations, as a precedence and platform for Customs business practice. If an importer or broker demonstrates the ability to use due diligence, this serves as an example of acceptable reasonable care and equates to an automatic mitigating factor toward any future Customs penalties, fines, or actions.

A company's due diligence business process should be well documented and incorporated into the inbound supply chain management SOPs.

Record Keeping

In Customs audits this is a significant area of scrutiny and can lead to serious fines and penalties when not administered correctly. Customs regulations state that all importers must establish proper record retention procedures to ensure that all records are maintained for five years from the date of entry. It is very important for importers to be aware of all records that they are required to maintain. The fact is that CBP requires that *all* documents associated with the import transaction be kept for the full period of five years.

Keep in mind that certain products governed by other agencies, such as food products by the Food and Drug administration, will have other record-keeping guidelines that also need to be followed.

Documentation (Invoice) Requirements

Copies of import transactional communications must include the following:

1. Purchase inquiry
2. Purchase verifications
3. Purchase negotiations between the buyer and seller of importer merchandise
4. Purchase order communications
5. Commercial invoice
6. Packing list information

7. Special Customs declarations/certifications
8. Customs import declaration (CF 3461)
9. Customs entry summary (CF 7501)
10. All communication records between the Customs broker and import compliance/traffic department in reference to each import transaction
11. Supervisory communication detailing supervision and control of import decisions between the importer and broker/freight forwarder/consultants/attorneys
12. All records of communication received from U.S. Customs
13. All records of communication relating to any statements/acts made to U.S. Customs
14. Notice of liquidations communication records
15. Communications records detailing receipt of merchandise into the importer's establishments or designated receiving stations
16. Communication records detailing the disposition of the merchandise after receipt or distribution
17. Records indicating actual proof of purchase of imported goods
18. Records indicating contract of carriage agreements, airway bills, and bills of ladings
19. Records indicating the exact amount of prepaid international freight or the insurance amount that was contained in the import sales transaction

Importers cannot delegate record-keeping duties to the Customs broker in lieu of maintaining records for themselves. Customs brokers must maintain the following documentation:

1. CF 3461 original (as prepared and released)
2. CF7501 original
3. Airway bill or bill of lading
4. Invoices (rated)
5. Packing lists
6. Special Customs invoices
7. Importer letter of instructions
8. Importer communications—inquiries and replies
9. Customs communications—inquiries and replies
10. Copies of all accounting transactions in which the broker is involved (monies received from the importer and or laid out on behalf of the importer)
11. Delivery orders and disposition of merchandise
12. FDA and all other government agency declarations and dispositions

Methods of Storage of Records

Customs regulations state that if a record has been created in hard-copy format those records must be maintained in hard-copy format. Records that were never created in a hard-copy format may be maintained in an alternate format if approved and deemed acceptable by Customs prior to the actual storage practice.

If the importer wishes to maintain records in an alternate method, he or she must obtain preapproval from:

U.S. Customs and Border Protection
Director of Regulatory Audit Division
909 S.E. First Avenue
Miami, Florida 33131

Alternative storage methods are those that are commonly used in standard business practices, such as machine-readable data, CD-ROM, and microfiche. Methods that are in compliance with generally accepted business practices will normally satisfy Customs requirements.

The importer must be able to substantiate and ensure that the imaging or media storage process preserves the integrity, readability, and security of the information contained in the original records. A standardized retrieval process must be implemented and exercised.

Assists

This is an often missed area by U.S. importers in their handling of imports where they provide technical assistance in product manufacturing by the overseas supplier. The import valuation declaration process has many components that require specific attention to purchasing and sourcing details that are included within the scope of proper value reporting practices. Many importers are not aware of these specific responsibilities of compliant reporting through the formal declaration process of imported articles. An example of a common practice error in the valuation declaration process is the omission of the proper reporting of assist values. Assists are defined as any materials, such as dies, molds, tools, and machinery, provided from the buyer of the imported merchandise to the seller of the imported merchandise at a reduced cost or free of charge.

Customs and Border Protection (CBP) defines the proper reporting value of imported merchandise to be all charges incurred in bringing the merchandise up to and on board a vessel or aircraft destined for the United States. This literal definition includes any charge or expense in obtaining materials that are used in the manufacturing or production of a finished article that is provided to the seller for use in such manufacturing or production. There is also an assist value inclusion for the transportation expense of shipping such materials to the seller from the U.S. buyer of the imported merchandise, which is often omitted from declarations of true assists. Assists are defined and clarified in the CFR Part 152.102 of "Customs Regulations," Title 19.

All import shipments that contain an assist must be accompanied by a proper commercial invoice that itemizes the value and existence of an assist as an invoice requirement.

There are also exemptions from the consideration of an assist declaration, which include design work, engineering work, and research and development fees undertaken in the United States that will not be treated as an assist. Once identified, each assist value will be added to the total Customs entry value.

Drawback

Customs manages a program that allows importers who eventually export the products that they imported to obtain access of up to 99% of the taxes and duties paid, upon evidentiary submission of proof of import, then export. Drawback is a privilege granted by Customs, which allows an importer to collect 99 percent of duties previously paid by exporting the merchandise from the United States or destroying the imported goods under Customs supervision. It is important to note that drawback is a privilege that can be taken away if Customs considers the drawback claimant in constant fraudulent violation concerning their drawback claims for refunds.

There are three main types of drawback:

Unused merchandise drawback: A 99 percent refund of duties paid on imported merchandise that is exported in the same condition as when imported and remains unused in the United States. The importer may claim a drawback for three years from the date of importation.

Rejected merchandise drawback: A 99 percent refund on imported merchandise that is received not conforming to the importer's standards of approval or the standards of any government agency (i.e., FDA, Department of Agriculture, FCC, Fish and Wildlife Service, Customs). The importer may claim a drawback for three years from the date of importation.

Manufacturing drawback: A 99 percent refund of duties paid on imported merchandise that is received and is to be further processed or manufactured in the United States. Customs will allow a 99 percent refund of duties paid on the imported merchandise for a period of up to five years from the date of importation.

It is key to note that unless given prior permission, all merchandise must be examined by Customs prior to export to qualify for the drawback privilege. A filer notifies Customs of its intent to file a drawback claim by filing a notice of intent (CF 7553). An importer must allow at least five working days prior to the export of the merchandise. Customs will notify the drawback claimant within two working days of its intent to examine or waive the examination. Drawback is a fantastic opportunity to recover previously paid duties on exportation or destruction. Careful attention must be paid to time limitations and correctness of information declared to Customs. Customs can pursue costly fines and penalties against a drawback claimant for incorrect claims submitted for refund. It is automatically reviewed as a fraudulent act, punishable by a penalty up to the domestic value of the merchandise. A frequent drawback claimant needs to consider a complete drawback program, containing adequate record-keeping procedures for proper filing.

Necessary Drawback Documentary Requirements

Following is a list of necessary drawback documents:

- Letter requesting a drawback claim to be filed on behalf of exporter
- CF 7501 entry summary
- Import commercial invoice
- CF 3461 entry/immediate delivery
- Import packing list
- Export invoice
- Export packing list

Careful consideration for drawback eligibility must be maintained by industry experts. This is a very trade specific area of expertise. Assistance from specialized brokers and consultants is a necessity.

HTS Classification

Merchandise that is entering the commerce of the United States requires specific identification to afford the governing agencies an opportunity to make the proper affirmation of release into the commerce of the United States utilizing commodity-specific controls of information. It is imperative that all merchandise entering the United States be properly identified through the delegation of a Harmonized Tariff Classification Number. CBP has a requirement for entry into the United States that all merchandise be identified by a correct commodity classification number referenced in the Harmonized Tariff Schedule of the United States.

It is the importer's responsibility to understand proper usage of HTSUS reference in order to provide such classification to Customs and Border Protection through the formal entry process. Many importers rely on their Customs brokerage service providers, who are licensed to conduct Customs business on their behalf, to derive the HTSUS classification codes. This practice is noncompliant and may result in costly fines and penalties to the importer for lack of reasonable care.

Education and training forums are an excellent means to increase the ability of the importer to become knowledgeable about proper classification principles.

Imported Product/Origin Markings

The country of origin marking on imported merchandise has always been a compliance responsibility of the importer of record. It is the importer's compliance responsibility to ensure that all merchandise that enters the commerce of the United States is properly marked with the proper country of origin of the merchandise to indicate to the ultimate purchaser of imported articles the specific country of origin of the product. Country of origin criteria play a role in applicable inclusion into possible tariff treaty duty preferential programs and rates of duty.

It is now an increasingly important process related to global security. Customs requires that the outermost carton be properly marked with the country of origin. This is crucial in the assessment criteria should an alert be distributed on increased scrutiny on products from a particular origin, so that CBP would be able to detect the origin of merchandise prior to opening the carton, drum, or box.

Proper country of origin marking procedures are outlined in the Customs Federal Regulations Part 134, which serves as an excellent guide for marking procedures.

Valuation

Merchandise entering the United States must be properly valued in the import clearance process. There exist many rules and standards that regulate the practice of compliant valuation declaration. It is the importer's responsibility to ensure that proper values are fully disclosed to Customs to afford CBP the opportunity to collect proper duties, fees, and taxes associated with each respective import transaction.

Many importers have traditionally relied on statements of value on commercial documents prepared by the foreign seller as the communication tool of valuation declaration, without any U.S. validation process of the correctness of information prior to the entry declaration submission to CBP. Customs has regulatory standards in place that require an importer to be informed about the proper principles of valuation, to include dutiable charges. Valuation determinations that are found to be incorrect and not conforming to the proper valuation principles in the regulatory structure may lead to fines and penalties against the importer of record. Education and training on specific valuation concepts are an essential component in proper import management.

Duties and Taxes

All duties and taxes must be remitted to Customs within ten days of clearance. These are determined by two key factors: the origin of the goods and the description as identified by the appropriate Harmonized Tariff Code (HTC). Secondary issues might be utilization of goods, such as in the case of samples or promotional items; the value; and who the ultimate consignee might be. Through various Web sites, publications, and resources available through Customs, one can obtain the tariffs to determine the applicable duties and taxes. This information also can be obtained from a customhouse broker or local Customs office.

Every importer's first bond condition is to pay duties, fees, and taxes on a timely basis. It is the importers responsibility to establish and verify that all duties, fees, and taxes are being submitted in accordance with CFR 19 113.62(a). The liability for payment must be met in most cases within ten days from the date of Customs clearance. The payment may be made directly from the importer to Customs via check or electronic payment methods of either ACH debit or ACH credit accounts. ACH is the Automated Clearing House method of payment.

Many importers use as a common practice the services of the brokerage provider to submit duty payment to Customs on their behalf. It is another luxury that the brokerage provider advances the duty payment on behalf of the importer as a service. Most companies like this added service that the brokerage community offers, as it minimizes the strain on the importers' accounting practices to validate correctness of information and issue payment to Customs within a ten-working-day time frame. Since the broker is advancing the duty payment the importer can take its time in the validation process, as most brokers afford thirty-day payment terms with their importers.

It is important to note that the use of this service does not relieve the importer of its responsibility to pay duties, taxes, and fees. The supervision process of how the duty payment process is being handled is the responsibility of the importer. Records of timely payment are maintained by the broker in cases where this advancement is being handled. Copies of the receipts of payments need be reviewed and retained by the importer.

There are various methods that can be used to achieve this goal, yet it must be met. In a Customs audit an importer will be asked how it managed the duty payment process. It is unacceptable to simply state, "My broker pays the duty for us." A system of accountability needs to be implemented to ensure that timely payment is being handled, and a level of understanding of just how it is being managed needs to be attained by the importer.

Copies of the final ACH statement will serve as proof of payment. Copies of checks with a receipted copy of the CF 7501 Customs entry summary will also represent timely payment. A stamped copy of the 7501 in itself is not proof of payment, only entry submission. Be careful that the brokerage provider provides a written explanation of the duty payment process.

ISF (10+2) Importer Security Filing

Effective January 26, 2009, U.S. Customs and Border Protection implemented the Importer Security Filing (ISF) program, more commonly known as the 10+2 program. Under the ISF program, U.S. Customs and Border Protection will require U.S. importers to file ten data elements, twenty-four hours prior to loading goods on an ocean vessel destined to the United States.

Contractually, we must clearly and effectively communicate this requirement to our suppliers and carriers to prevent delivery delays. As a best practice, companies should centralize the ISF in the United States. This will require us to work closely with our offshore suppliers and carriers to obtain necessary information for ISF. The ISF is similar to the Customs entry filing process. The ISF will be completed by the nominated Customs broker handling the import shipment on behalf of importers.

Importers will continue to forward best practices and supply additional recommendations on how to meet the new government requirement.

NOTE: As of this writing, this requirement is only applicable for ocean import shipments. It is anticipated that at some point in time all modes will be covered with ISF.

10 Mandatory Data Elements	Sample
1. Seller name and address: F. J. Tytherleigh Italia SRL Via Dell'Artigianato 75 57121 Livorno, Italy	2. Buyer name and address: NBTY Manufacturing 2100 Smithtown Avenue Ronkonkoma, New York 11779
3. Importer EIN: 11-3602075	4. Consignee EIN: 11-3602075
5. Manufacturer name and address: F. J. Tytherleigh Italia SRL Via Dell'Artigianato 75 57121 Livorno, Italy	6. Ship to party: NBTY Manufacturing 90 Orville Drive Bohemia, New York 11716
7. Country of origin: Italy	8. Commodity HTS number: 3924.10
9. Container stuffing location: Livorno, Italy	10. Consolidator (stuffing location): Italy ABC Freight Forwarder

Chapter 5

Customs Bonded Warehouses

An opportunity exists with a government initiative referred to as bonded warehouses that can offer companies a significant competitive advantage in how they import goods from overseas, which is reviewed in this chapter.

What Is a Customs Bonded Warehouse?

A Customs bonded warehouse is a building or other secured area in which dutiable goods may be stored, manipulated, or undergo manufacturing operations without payment or duty. Authority for establishing bonded storage warehouses is set forth in Title 19 of the United States Code (USC), Section 1555. Bonded manufacturing and smelting and refining warehouses are established under 19 USC 1311 and 1312.

Upon entry of goods into the warehouse, the importer and warehouse proprietor incur liability under a bond. This liability is generally canceled when the goods are:

- Exported or deemed exported
- Withdrawn for supplies to a vessel or aircraft international traffic
- Destroyed under Customs supervisions
- Withdrawn for consumption within the United States after payment of duty

Types of Customs Bonded Warehouses

Eleven different types or classes of Customs bonded warehouses are authorized under Section 19.1, "Customs Regulations" (19 CFR 19.1, amendments pending):

1. Premises owned or leased by the government and used for the storage of merchandise that is undergoing Customs examination, is under seizure, or is pending final release for Customs custody. Unclaimed merchandise stored in such premises shall be held under "general order." When such premises are not sufficient or available for the storage of seized or unclaimed goods, such goods may be stored in a warehouse of Class 3, 4, or 5.

2. Importers' private bonded warehouses used exclusively for the storage of merchandise belonging or consigned to the proprietor thereof. A Class 4 or 5 warehouse may be bonded exclusively for the storage of goods imported by the proprietor thereof, in which case it should be known as a private bonded warehouse.

3. Public bonded warehouse used exclusively for the storage of imported merchandise.

4. Bonded yards or sheds for the storage of heavy and bulky imported merchandise; stables, feeding pens, corrals, other similar buildings or limited enclosures for the storage of imported animals; and tanks for the storage of imported liquid merchandise in bulk.

5. Bonded bins or parts of buildings or elevators to be used for the storage of grain.

6. Warehouses for the manufacture in bond, solely for exportation, of articles made in whole or in part of imported materials or of materials subject to internal revenue tax, and for the manufacture for domestic consumption or exportation of cigars made in whole of tobacco imported from one country.

7. Warehouses bonded for smelting and refining imported metal-bearing materials for exportation or domestic consumption.

8. Bonded warehouses established for the cleaning, sorting, repacking, or otherwise changing the condition of, but not the manufacturing of, imported merchandise, under Customs supervision, and at the expense of the proprietor.

9. Bonded warehouses, known as duty-free stores, used for selling conditionally duty-free merchandise for use outside the Customs territory. Merchandise in this class must be owned or sold by the proprietor and delivered from the warehouse to an airport or other exit point for exportation by, or on behalf of, individuals departing from the Customs territory or foreign destinations. These stores may also sell other than duty-free merchandise.

10. Bonded warehouses for international travel merchandise, goods sold conditionally duty-free aboard aircraft, and not at a duty-free store. This is based on amendments to 19 USC 1555(c), approved 11/00. Regulations governing this type of warehouse are being written.

11. Bonded warehouses established for the storage of general order (GO) merchandise. GO is any merchandise not claimed or entered for 15 days after arrival in the United States (or final U.S. destination for in-bond shipments). The amended regulations establishing this class of warehouse are awaiting final approval and publication in the *Federal Register*.

Advantages of Using a Bonded Warehouse

No duty is collected until merchandise is withdrawn for consumption. An importer, therefore, has control over use of his money until the duty is paid upon withdrawal of merchandise for the bonded warehouse. If no domestic buyer is found for the imported articles, the importer can sell merchandise for exportation, thereby eliminating his obligation to pay duty.

Many items subject to quota or other restrictions may be stored in a bonded warehouse. Check with the nearest Customs office before assuming that such merchandise may be placed in a bonded warehouse. Duties owed on articles that have been manipulated are determined at the time of withdrawal from the Customs bonded warehouse.

Merchandise: Entry, Storage, Treatment

All merchandise subject to duty may be entered for warehousing except perishables, and explosive substances other than firecrackers and merchandise other than duty-free merchandise may be stored in the retail sales facility of a Class 9 warehouse and sold to persons departing the United States.

Full accountability for all merchandise entered into a Customs bonded warehouse must be maintained; that merchandise will be inventoried and the proprietor's records will be audited on a regular basis. Bonded merchandise may not be commingled with domestic merchandise and must be kept separate from unbonded merchandise. Merchandise in a Customs bonded warehouse may, with certain exceptions, be transferred from one bonded warehouse to another in accordance with the provisions of Customs regulations. Merchandise placed in a Customs bonded warehouse, other than Class 6 or 7, may be stored, cleaned, sorted, repacked, or otherwise changed in condition, but not manufactured (19 USC 1562).

Articles manufactured in a Class 6 warehouse other than cigars made from imported tobacco must be exported in accordance with Customs regulations. Waste or a by-product from a Class 6 warehouse may be withdrawn for consumption upon payment of applicable duties. Imported merchandise may be stored in a Customs bonded warehouse for a period of five years (19 USC 1557(a)).

How to Establish a Customs Bonded Warehouse

Application

An owner or lessee seeking to establish a bonded warehouse must make written application to his or her local Customs port director describing the premises, giving the location, and stating the class of warehouse to be established. Except in the case of a Class 2 or 7 warehouse, the application must state whether the warehouse is to be operated only for the storage or treatment of merchandise belonging to the applicant, or whether it is to be operated as a public bonded warehouse.

If the warehouse is to be operated as a private bonded warehouse, the application must also state the general character of the merchandise to be stored therein, with an estimate of the maximum duties and taxes that will be due on the merchandise at any one time.

Other Requirements

The application must be accompanied by the following:

- A certificate signed by the president or a secretary of a board of fire under-writers that the building is a suitable warehouse and acceptable for fire insurance purposes. At ports where there is no board of fire underwriters, certificates should be obtained and signed by officers of agents of two or more insurance companies.
- A blueprint showing measurements of the building or space to be bonded.

If the warehouse to be bonded is a tank, the blueprint should identify all outlets, inlets, and pipelines and be certified as correct by the proprietor of the tank. A gauge table showing the capacity of the tank in U.S. gallons per inch or fraction of an inch of height should be included and certified by the proprietor as correct.

When a part or parts of the building are to be used as a warehouse, a detailed description of the materials and construction of all partitions shall be included.

The Customs port director may ask for a list of names and addresses and a set of fingerprints for all company officers, principals, and employees of the applicant.

Duty-free shops (Class 9) have specific requirements governing their establishment. These requirements include location, exit points, record-keeping systems, and the approval of local governments.

Bonds Required

Bonds for each class of warehouse shall be executed on "Customs Bond," Form 301.

Where Are Customs Offices Located?

The U.S. Customs Service has more than three hundred ports of entry in the United States, Puerto Rico, and the U.S. Virgin Islands. Please consult your local telephone directory under federal government listings. You will find your local port director under "U.S. Treasury Department, Customs Service." The U.S. Customs (CBP) Web site is www.cbp.

Chapter 6

Foreign Trade Zones

Foreign trade zones like Customs bonded warehouses offer a tool for global supply chains that provide certain advantages. These advantages can make a company competitive in costing, operations, and client sales. This is reviewed in the chapter.

What Is a Foreign Trade Zone?

Foreign trade zones (FTZs) are restricted access sites authorized by the Foreign-Trade Zones Board, consisting of the Secretary of Commerce and the Secretary of the Treasury. FTZs, upon activation under regulations of the U.S. Customs Service, are secured areas under U.S. Customs supervision and are located in or near a U.S. Customs port of entry. Customs entry procedures do not apply, although FTZs are within the territory and jurisdiction of the United States.

Why Were Foreign Trade Zones Established?

- To encourage and expedite U.S. participation in international trade. Foreign goods may be admitted to an FTZ without being subject to Customs duties or certain excise taxes.
- To defer payment of duties until goods are entered into the commerce of the United States.

Under zone procedures, the usual Customs entry procedures and payment of duties are not required on foreign merchandise until it enters Customs territory for domestic consumption. Domestic goods admitted into a zone, in zone-restricted

63

status (for storage, destruction, or export), are considered exported when admitted to the zone for other government agency requirements, excise tax, and drawback purposes.

Zones are granted by the Foreign-Trade Zones Board to qualified public or private entities (port authorities, city/county economic developers). In a general purpose zone, the grantee usually has an operator to operate the zone. Operators can sublet to tenants, called users. In a subzone environment, the user and operator are usually the same.

Authority for establishing these facilities is granted by the Foreign-Trade Zones Board under the Foreign-Trade Zone Act of 1934, as amended (19 USC 81a–81u). The regulations of the Foreign-Trade Zones Board are published in 15 CFR Part 400. The regulations of the U.S. Customs Service governing the transfer of merchandise to and from zones are published in 19 CFR Part 146. The *Foreign-Trade Zones Manual* is available from the U.S. Customs Service by contacting the Office of Trade Programs, Office of Field Operations, Washington, DC 20229, or may be viewed on the Customs Web site at www.customs.gov.

Advantages of Using Foreign Trade Zones

The financial benefits are as follows:

Duty deferral: Customs duty and federal excise tax, if applicable, are paid only when merchandise is transferred from an FTZ to the Customs territory of the United States or transferred to a NAFTA country (Canada and Mexico).

Duty elimination: Goods may be imported into, and then exported from, a zone without the payment of duty and excise taxes except to certain countries, such as NAFTA countries, in which case any applicable duty and excise tax will be levied. Goods may also be imported into, and destroyed in, a zone without the payment of duty and excise taxes.

Inverted tariff relief: Inverted tariff relief occurs when imported parts are dutiable at higher rates than the finished product into which they are incorporated. For example, the duty rate on an imported muffler for an automobile is 4.5% if imported directly into U.S. commerce. However, if that muffler is brought into a foreign trade zone and incorporated into an assembled automobile, the duty rate on the finished automobile, including the muffler, is 2.5%.

Ad valorem tax exemption: Merchandise imported from outside the United States and held in a zone for the purpose of storage, sale, exhibition, repackaging, assembly, distribution, sorting, grading, cleaning, mixing, display, manufacturing, or processing, and merchandise produced in the United

States and held in a zone for exportation, either in its original form or altered by any of the above methods, are exempt from state and local *ad valorem* taxes.

Other benefits include the following:

No time constraints on storage: Merchandise may remain in a zone indefinitely, whether or not it's subject to a duty.

Satisfy exportation requirements: Merchandise entered into the United States on an entry for warehousing, temporary importation under bond, or transportation and exportation may be transferred to a foreign trade zone from the Customs territory to satisfy a legal requirement to export the merchandise. For instance, merchandise may be taken into a zone in order to satisfy an exportation requirement of the Tariff Act of 1930, or an exportation requirement of any other federal law insofar as the agency charged with its enforcement deems it advisable. Exportation may also fulfill requirements of certain state laws. Items admitted to a zone to satisfy exportation requirements must be admitted in zone-restricted status, meaning they are only for direct export, immediate export, and transportation and export.

Security and insurance costs: Customs security requirements and federal criminal sanctions are deterrents against theft. This may result in lower insurance costs and fewer incidents of loss for cargo imported into an FTZ.

Role of the Foreign Trade Zones Board Staff

- Review applications to establish or alter the boundaries of foreign trade zones
- Recommend approval of any zone or subzone application that is in the public interest
- Regulate the administration of foreign trade zones
- Inspect and examine the premises, operations, or accounts of the zone grantees and operators
- Revoke the grant of any zone for willful and repeated violations of the Foreign-Trade Zone Act after due notice and a hearing

The executive secretary is the chief operating official of the board.

Role of the U.S. Customs Service

- Maintain regulatory control over merchandise moving to or from a zone
- Ensure that all revenue is properly collected

- Ensure adherence to the laws and regulations governing the merchandise
- Ensure that merchandise has not been overtly or clandestinely removed from the zone without proper Customs permits

The Office of Regulations and Rulings, at Customs headquarters, provides legal interpretations of the applicable status, Customs regulations, and procedures.

Role of the Port Director

- Oversees the zone as the board representative
- Responsible for the supervision of the activities, including admission, operation, and transfer of merchandise
- Reviews port policy and comments on applications
- Approves the activation of the zone before any merchandise is admitted
- Approves discretionary requirements
- Requires an adequate FTZ operator's bond
- Assesses penalties and liquidated damages
- Initiates suspension of a zone, zone site, or zone activity, if necessary
- Recommends to the Foreign-Trade Zones Board that the privilege of establishing, operating, and maintaining a zone or subzone be revoked, if necessary

Frequently Asked Questions to CBP

The following are FAQs that are important to review and understand in implementing this competitive option into your global supply chain.

What Are the Types of Foreign Trade Zones?

There are two types of foreign trade zones: general purpose zones and subzones. General purpose zones are usually located in an industrial park, on raw land, or in port complexes whose facilities are available for use by the general public. Subzones are sites sponsored by a general purpose zone grantee on behalf of an individual firm or firms. Subzones are single-purpose sites for operations that cannot be feasibly moved to, or accommodated in, a general purpose zone, e.g., oil refineries, automobile manufacturers.

What May Be Placed in an FTZ?

Any foreign or domestic merchandise not prohibited by law, whether dutiable or not, may be admitted to a foreign trade zone. Conditionally admissible merchandise is subject to permits or licenses, or must be reconditioned to bring it into compliance with the laws administered by various federal agencies before entering the United States. Because zones are considered outside the Customs territory, requirements that would otherwise apply to imported merchandise are suspended as long as the merchandise remains in the FTZ. An example of conditionally admissible merchandise is a substance subject to the Toxic Substances Control Act (15 USC 2601 et seq.) that has not received approval by the Environmental Protection Agency for use in the United States. However, merchandise that is illegal, i.e., heroin, may not be imported under any circumstances.

Some federal agencies regulate storage and handling in the United States of certain types of merchandise, such as explosives. Depending on the nature of the requirements and the particular characteristics of the zone facility, such merchandise may be excluded. Most agencies that license importers or issue importation permits may block admission of merchandise that is not licensed or permitted into a zone.

The Foreign-Trade Zones Board may exclude from a zone any merchandise that in its judgment is detrimental to the public interest, health, or safety. The board ensures that foreign trade zones are not used to violate other trade laws of the United States.

Merchandise subject to quota restrictions may be admitted into a zone until a quota on entry is removed, or may be manufactured or manipulated in a zone into a product that is not subject to quota. The Foreign-Trade Zones Board can restrict or prohibit activity on public interest grounds.

What May Be Done in an FTZ?

Foreign and domestic merchandise permitted in a zone may be stored, sold, exhibited, broken up, repacked, assembled, distributed, sorted, graded, cleaned, mixed with foreign or domestic merchandise, otherwise manipulated, destroyed, or manufactured. On the other hand, machinery and equipment that is imported for use within a zone is not exempt from the payment of duty. Such equipment and supplies may include but are not limited to office furniture, machines, and equipment; construction machinery and materials; manufacturing machinery and equipment, tooling, and supplies; packaging machinery and equipment; food to be eaten in the zone; and water and fuel that do not become part of a zone product.

What May Not Be Done in an FTZ?

In specific cases, the Foreign-Trade Zones Board may prohibit or restrict any activity in a zone in order to protect the public interest, health, or safety. All manufacturing is reviewed in terms of government policy and its net economic effect.

Many products subject to an internal revenue tax may not be manufactured in a zone. These products include alcoholic beverages, products containing alcoholic beverages (except domestic denatured distilled spirits), perfumes containing alcohol, tobacco products, firearms, and sugar. In addition, the manufacture of clocks and watch movements is not permitted in a zone.

Retail trade is prohibited in zones, unless conducted under a permit issued by the zone grantee and approved by the Foreign-Trade Zones Board. Retail trade is then allowed only for the sale of domestic goods, or goods brought from the Customs territory following a regular Customs entry on which any applicable duties and taxes have been paid.

How Is Merchandise Admitted into a Zone?

Merchandise does not achieve zone status until a permit is given by the port director for its admission (except in the case of domestic status merchandise, for which no permit is required) and the zone operator signs for receipt of the merchandise into the zone.

Customs Form 214 Application

Merchandise may be admitted into a zone after application has been made on a Customs Form 214, "Application for Foreign Trade-Zone Admission and/or Status Designation," or its electronic equivalent, and a permit is issued by the port director. The application for admission is submitted to the port director, including a statistical copy on Customs Form 214A, to be transmitted to the Bureau of Census, unless the applicant has made arrangements for the direct transmittal of statistical information to that agency. The form will be signed by the zone operator, unless a separate individual or blanket approval has been given.

Application for admission may be made only by the person with the right to make entry. Right to make entry will be determined according to the provisions of Section 484(a) (19 USC 1484(a)), Tariff Act, Customs Directive 099 3530-002, and other pertinent servicewide instructions. However, a customhouse broker or foreign trade zone operator may prepare or file the application on behalf of the person with the right to make entry, if a proper power of attorney is on file.

The CF 214 will be presented to the location designated by the port director within a port of entry. Customs will review the application and supporting documentation for completeness and determine whether the application may be approved without a physical examination of the merchandise. Customs approves permits of admission for most low-risk shipments without examination.

Customs may examine merchandise to be admitted to a foreign trade zone to:

- Determine if the goods are admissible to the zone
- Determine the true liability of the zone operator for merchandise received in a zone under its bond

- Reduce the need for further examination of the merchandise if it is later transferred to Customs territory, in the same condition, for consumption or warehouse
- Ensure full compliance with all applicable laws and regulations

After document review and physical examination, as appropriate under the above provisions, the port director shall issue a permit for the admission of merchandise to a zone.

Direct Delivery

Direct delivery allows for the delivery of merchandise into a zone without prior application and approval on Customs Form 214. The operator, meeting all the requirements outlined below, shall file a written application with the appropriate port director at least thirty days before the special procedure is to become effective. The application will describe the merchandise to be handled or processed and the kind of operation that it will undergo in the zone (19 CFR 146.39).

Criteria to be met for direct delivery approval include the following:

- The merchandise is not restricted or of a type that requires Customs examination or documentation review before or upon its arrival at the zone (e.g., quota/visa merchandise).
- The merchandise to be admitted to the zone, and the operations to be conducted in the zone, are known well in advance, predictable and stable over the long term, and are relatively fixed in variety by the nature of the business conducted at the site.
- The operator is the owner or purchaser of the goods.

What Documents Are Needed for Admission?

The following documents must accompany the CF 214:

- Commercial invoice: The applicant shall submit two copies of an examination invoice meeting the requirements of Subpart F, Part 141 CR, for any merchandise, other than domestic status merchandise for which no permit is required, to be admitted into a zone. The notation on the invoice of tariff classification and value required by Section 141.90 CR need not be made, unless the merchandise is to be admitted in privileged foreign status.
- Evidence of right to make entry: The applicant for admission shall submit a document similar to that which would be required as evidence of the right to make entry for merchandise in Customs territory under Section 141.11 or 141.12 CR and CD 099 3530-002.

- Release order: Customs officers shall not authorize any merchandise for delivery to a zone until a release order has been executed by the carrier that brought the merchandise to the port, unless the merchandise is released back to that same carrier for delivery to the zone.
- Application to unlade: For merchandise unladen in the zone directly from the importing carrier, the application on Customs Form 214 shall be supported by an application to unlade on Customs Form 3171.
- Other documentation: The port director may require additional information or documentation as needed to examine the merchandise under Customs selective processing criteria, or to determine whether the merchandise is admissible to the zone. This includes documentation such as export certificates for certain steel products and machine tools under voluntary restraint and information needed for selectivity processing, such as importers' and manufacturers' numbers.

How Is Merchandise Removed from a Zone for U.S. Consumption?

Normal entry, classification, and appraisement procedures covering foreign merchandise entering the U.S. commerce are used.

What Are the Four Types of Zone Status?

Prior to any manipulation or manufacturing in the zone that would change the tariff classification, the port director will, if requested by the importer, give imported merchandise privileged foreign status (PF). The merchandise is classified and appraised and duties and taxes are determined, but not collected, as of the date the application is filed (First Proviso, Section 3(a) FTZA). Under this provision, the importer chooses to have the merchandise classified, for tariff purposes, as what it is at the time privilege is granted, rather than what it becomes at a later date.

Zone-restricted status is given to merchandise brought into a zone from the Customs territory for the purpose of exportation, destruction (except destruction of distilled spirits, wines, and fermented malt liquors), or storage. The merchandise is considered exported and cannot be returned to the Customs territory for consumption unless the Foreign-Trade Zones Board rules specifically that its return is in the public interest. Zone-restricted status merchandise may not be manipulated, manufactured, processed, or assembled in a zone.

Nonprivileged foreign status (NPF) is a residual category for foreign merchandise that does not have privileged or zone-restricted status. Articles in NPF status are classified and appraised in their condition at the time of transfer to the Customs territory and NAFTA countries.

Domestic status is available for merchandise that is:
- – Wholly grown, produced, or manufactured in the United States, on which all revenue taxes, if applicable, have been paid
- – Previously imported merchandise on which all duties and internal revenue taxes have been paid
- – Merchandise that was previously admitted into the United States free of duty

Articles of Mixed Status

Since manipulation and manufacturing may be permitted in a zone, a shipment of articles transferred to the Customs territory may be made up of merchandise that is privileged and nonprivileged, whether foreign or domestic status. The articles are appraised according to that status of the merchandise of which they are composed, or from which derived, as explained above. Privileged foreign status merchandise is classified in its condition at the time that privilege was granted. Privileged status merchandise has a fixed classification rate previously established at the time of request.

Where Is Additional Information Available?

The executive secretary of the Foreign-Trade Zones Board is located in the U.S. Department of Commerce, Washington, DC 20230, telephone (202) 482-2862. The Web site address is www.ita.doc.gov/import_admin/records/ftzpage/ftzhome.html.

For answers to specific questions, contact the U.S. Customs port director where the zone is located or the U.S. Customs Service Headquarters, Office of Trade Programs, Washington, DC 20229, telephone (202) 927-0510. Additional information can be found on the U.S. Customs Web site at www.customs.gov.

FTZs: Big-Time Competitive Advantage: An Overview

One of the best business methods for a company to gain competitive advantage in its global supply chain and foreign purchasing management decisions is to consider the use of foreign trade zones. These programs afforded under federal and state law offer significant tax advantages to companies that bring in raw materials and components and use American labor to assemble a finished product within the borders of the United States.

The basic model designates specific geographic areas within our borders as foreign trade zones. These can be industrial parks, housing numerous companies, or isolated plant locations. These locations operate under independent commercial management but follow guidelines dictated by federal, state, and U.S. Customs (CBP) practice. These free trade areas are designated locations that are not in the

U.S. economy or have not yet entered U.S. commerce. Therefore, goods and materials that come from overseas that enter these FTZs have not yet entered U.S. commerce. This then defers the final entry for Customs and duties and taxes until such a time that the goods or materials do enter our commerce. However, the goods and merchandise that come out from these FTZs are now in a different form—typically a finished product—for which the overall duties and taxes will be less than if they had been imported as a finished product from a foreign source.

The National Association of Foreign Trade Zones, located in Washington, D.C., which is the leading facilitator of foreign trade utilization, has identified this program as the leading source for U.S. companies to gain unparalleled competitive advantage against foreign competition. Companies such as BASF/Engelhard, BMW, Michelin, and Seiko are but a few of over five hundred corporations that have taken advantage of these federal and state-run programs to lower their costs and be more competitive.

The basic FTZ model works as follows:

No FTZ
> Company imports finished product from China
> Value of imports: $2 million
> Duty and taxes: 10%
> Landed cost (simplified): $2.2 million

With FTZ
> Company imports components from China into FTZ
> Value of imports: $1 million
> No duty and taxes until goods come out from the FTZ; advantage in cash
>> flow: $50,000
> Landed cost after finished product is imported: $2,050,000
Cost advantage: $150,000 per annum

Multiple these by millions when the supply chain is larger and the benefits could be very significant.

There are other advantages to keeping the assembly in the United States:

- Utilization of current employee base
- Stability in manufacturing process
- Better quality control
- Lower freight costs
- More options in risk mitigation

FTZs are becoming a very popular and lucrative method for purchasing managers to provide savings, economies, and more controlled supply chains.

The Web site www.naftz.org provides useful information.

Chapter 7

Choosing Providers Best Practices

Choosing the correct service provider, freight forwarder, and customhouse broker can make or break your inbound global supply chain. It is a very critical decision to be made requiring a specialized skill set, discussed in this chapter in order to make the very best selection.

Choosing Correctly

A very integral component of managing an inbound global supply chain is determining which service providers will partner with you in this endeavor. Make the wrong choice, and your supply chain will not run effectively. Make the right choice, and your supply chain will flourish.

The primary provider for import activity is the customhouse broker, sometimes referred to as the freight forwarder. This entity is supposed to provide expertise for moving your freight from an overseas point into the United States, handling all the logistics from the point of origin through to the destination. They will also handle the clearance, payment of duties and taxes, warehousing, and the forwarding to the final location.

This chapter views all the best practices a purchasing manager should follow to develop the best inbound transportation service provider option:

1. Determine your needs
2. Know your options
3. Develop an RFQ/RFP (RFPs and RFQs are formalized processes for vendor bidding)

4. Obtain referrals
5. Agree to service parameters first, then price
6. Set a review period, before long-term agreements
7. Agree to stewardship reporting
8. Periodically test your options
9. Focus on technology capabilities
10. View added-value benefits
11. Partnership mentality

Determine Your Needs

The purchasing manager must first determine what his or her company's needs are. A checklist of all the parameters of the inbound supply chain is a good start:

- Freight options: Air, truck, rail, ocean, courier, etc.
- Time frame or pickup and delivery requirements
- Nuances of your supply chain
- Value-added needs (dry ice packing, hazmat, etc.)
- Costs
- Packing, marking, or labeling
- Landed cost modeling
- Consolidation services
- Warehousing
- Carrier rate negotiations
- Carrier booking
- Documentation
- Tracking and tracing
- Record keeping
- Outlays of duties, taxes, value-added taxes, etc.
- Processing of payments or collection of funds, letters of credit, drafts, etc.
- Compliance issues
- Training needs
- Geographic profile
- Demographics of your supply chain

Once you have developed the list, you need to determine the salience of each area and its importance to you. This will assist you in determining which provider can help you in any or all of your needs, and just how to prioritize the importance of that help.

Know Your Options

A good purchasing manager will accept appointments from competing custom-house brokers from time to time. He or she will also participate in industry events that profile providers. In addition, it is important for the purchasing manager and his or her logistics personnel to read trade magazines, e.g., *Journal of Commerce*, *Cargo Digest*, *American Shipper*, *World Trade Magazine*, and *PACMAN: Managing Imports and Exports*.

All these habits will outline provider options and provide a good overview of services, capabilities, and current events about the industry that would be important in making a service provider decision. Firms in trouble, mergers and acquisitions, personnel changes, new services, etc., are but a few of the necessary issues that are important in assisting us in making the very best decision in choosing providers.

Develop an RFQ/RFP

Formalize the process of choosing the broker and forwarder. This will outline your needs and centralize all the data for the provider to submit a proposal. It will set service parameters and time frames. Any specific requirements, needs, nuances, or restrictions would be outlined here. All necessary deliverables are summarized in the proposal request. It establishes the best opportunity for an even playing field between competitors.

Obtain Referrals

It is highly recommended to request referrals from bidders. All of these should be followed up diligently. Ask for a referral on an account they recently lost and find out what happened. Referrals are one of the best methods to ensure you are making a good decision and provide support in regard to the decision you finally arrive at.

Agree to Service Parameters First, Then Price

Price will always be a serious part of the selection price, but do not prioritize it. First, establish which parties best meet your required service parameters. Weed out those who do not, and rank those who do. Once you come to the short list, then you can focus on price. This affords you a greater opportunity to get the best value for your spend.

Set a Review Period, before Long-Term Agreements

Bringing on a new service provider has certain risks. You have expectations based upon the proposal and screening process, but at the end of the day, reality sets in after the agreement is reached and it may be better or close to expectation—or it may fall short.

Allow an indoctrination period or probationary time frame. This could run for three to six months, before a longer-term agreement is solidified. This will make getting out of the deal a little easier if the provider does not reach anticipated deliverables. It will also provide leverage to make any necessary modifications to the intended longer-term agreement, as a result of realistic parameters, shortcomings, or changes being identified in the new interactions between you and the provider.

Agree to Stewardship Reporting

We provide a full outline later in this section on stewardship. This requires the provider, every year or so, to outline the status of the relationship with a focus on how it is doing and working for betterments and service enhancements.

Periodically Test Your Options

Providers tend to become complacent. Consistently challenge them and always know and test various options from competitors. This does not necessarily mean change, but it is a good tool for provider management.

Focus on Technology Capabilities

Technology can assist you in a number of areas:

- Expeditious transaction handling
- Compliance management
- Accuracy
- Transfer of data
- Tracking and tracing
- Management reports

Technology options need to be sought after and implemented when feasible.

View Added-Value Benefits

Always obtain the best value for your dollar spent. Insist on value-added options to all the services and programs that are available to you. This will help the supply chain run better and make for a healthier partnership.

Partnership Mentality

The best relationship is where both parties mutually benefit. This can best be achieved by having a partnership mentality right from the beginning. Problems and challenges will always be present. But when the mind-set is "partner," they will always be worked out favorably.

Stewardship Reports from Freight Forwarders: An Excellent Management Tool

An excellent option in managing service providers is to mandate, at least every one to two years, they provide you with an updated *stewardship report*. This report would be a recapitulation on the overall relationship. It can be utilized as a tool in measuring, benchmarking, and managing vendor performance. It would outline all the areas they are engaged in and just what is going on in the relationship and what needs to be done. For example:

- Pricing
- Service parameters
- New service offered
- Technology enhancements
- Improvements in business processing
- Reduction in documentation and time in handling orders and shipments
- Capabilities and skill set improvements of supply chain operations personnel
- Status of the "to do" list
- Percent change in service failures
- Problem mitigation
- Forecasting needs and growth strategies

These would be key parameters in a stewardship report, but it can be tailored to all the specific nuances of your supply chain operation. The real benefits of mandating a stewardship report are as follows:

- It helps to avoid *complacency* on the part of both parties—the vendor and the principal.
- It usually will affect prices favorably.
- Every time a company forces a vendor to do a self-analysis of the relationship, benefits and enhancements are uncovered.
- A perspective is developed on competitive options that may not necessarily produce a short-term gain, but most certainly will offer longer-term options for future benefit.
- It helps to keep the incumbent more honest.
- It brings a higher level of due diligence, professionalism, and internal scrutiny to "test the waters" on a less frequent basis.
- Competitive pressures on the incumbent will bring out features and benefits not previously provided.

Organizing the Stewardship Report

These items should be considered for most stewardship reports:

- General status of the relationship
- Accomplishments
- Open items list or agenda of things to do and their status (an Excel spreadsheet will work good here)
- Changes in operating service parameters (if applicable)
- Future issues, needs, and requests
- Government and regulatory considerations
- Technology issues
- Personnel changes
- Billing and payment status
- External influence issues, such as but not limited to economic conditions, industry issues, political influences, and geographic, demographic, or physical potentials
- Internal influence issues, such as but not limited to management changes, ownership or merger/acquisition circumstances, and financial changes
- Business process, SOPs, or operating profile changes
- Revised action plan for the coming year

These are all general requirements applicable to most organizations and global supply chains. It is important for readers to note that all of these profiles need to be tweaked for the specific needs and nuances of their operating profile.

The Process of Selecting Freight Forwarders, Customhouse Brokers, and Other Service Providers

The recommended process for selecting service providers can be outlined in nine steps:

1. Identify your expectations, parameters, needs, and service requirements.
2. Interview potential candidates.
3. Issue the RFP/RFQ.
4. Set deadlines for responsiveness.
5. Eliminate the peripheral candidates and bring the selection group from eight to ten persons to two or three.
6. Meet again with the two or three finalists to review the status of the process and discuss key selection criteria.
7. Ask for pricing and final revised proposals.

8. Make the selection. Set a time for testing the relationship, before making a longer-term agreement.
9. Structure a review process.

Identify Your Expectations, Parameters, Needs, and Service Requirements

As discussed earlier in this chapter, you need to create a very detailed outline of all your expectations and the key criteria for selecting the provider. This will also be the tool utilized for comparing quotes, proposals, and service options. You could benefit from working with all personnel engaged in the global supply chain in making sure you are covering all the necessary points.

Interview Potential Candidates

If you have done your job and met with various service providers in the past year or so, and you have information flow inbound to you on the industry, you should be in a position to select anywhere from six to ten potential candidates. You do not want to approach more than that amount, as the process will become too unwieldy. Six to ten is a reasonable purchasing management best practices amount.

Issue the Proposal Outline (RFP/RFQ)

Provide each candidate with a similar overview of expectations. Review it with them and make sure they understand all the parameters. Keep it simple. Avoid convolutions, complications, and too much detail, where it becomes inordinate.

Set Deadlines for Responsiveness

Set reasonable time frames for responses from the candidates. Thirty to forty-five days would be considered reasonable to obtain proposals. First, get it in writing, and then set meeting dates for oral presentations, where you deem it warrants that additional interface.

Eliminate the Peripheral Candidates and Bring the Selection Group from Eight to Ten Persons to Two or Three

Sometimes utilizing a committee to assist in the review and selection process is a helpful procedure. In this instance, it will help in rating all the candidates, leading to working with two or three finalists.

Meet Again

When the finalists are chosen, meet again with them to review the status of the process and discuss key selection criteria.

Ask for Pricing and Final Revised Proposals

Wait until the very end to obtain pricing and have a preliminary idea where this pricing will come in, so as to make sure your pricing structure is competitive. Make sure that you are accomplishing an "apples to apples" comparison to keep the overall process on an even playing ground. The quality of the original RFP/RFQ will help ensure an even playing ground.

Make the Selection: Set a Time for Testing the Relationship, before Making a Longer-Term Agreement

You do not need to structure long-term agreements from the outset. Set a trial period for review: 60, 90, or 120 days could work. Then when all the "bugs" are worked out, move ahead to a longer-term agreement. If it does not work out—meaning what was promised and what was delivered are two different things—then you can move on somewhat more easily.

Structure a Review Process

Anytime a change is made disruptions are likely to occur and time may need to be allotted for tweaking. To manage this process, a best practice approach is to proactively set a date for a meeting with all impacted parties attending to discuss and review what was promised, what was delivered, and how best to move forward.

Every major initiative in business requires modification, back-stepping, realignments, etc., to make it eventually work better and with the most effectiveness. This step will accomplish that. And it offers the best opportunity for both short-term and long-term success.

Summary

Choosing and then managing transportation service providers, freight forwarders, and customhouse brokers is an important area to engage in to make for the most effective global supply chain. It is a very critical skill set that purchasing managers need to master to obtain quality services, competitive pricing, timely deliveries, and value-added benefits.

Organizing the selection process is a significant step in ensuring that you are on your way to making not just a good selection, but an excellent one with long-term benefits to the supply chain's bottom line.

Chapter 8

China and India

Both China and India offer excellent options for U.S. companies to source from. With those opportunities come certain challenges that we need to manage as much as we manage any aspect of our global supply chain. This chapter offers us some insight into this issue.

China has grown into America's largest import partner, alongside Canada and Mexico. China's rise is a signature development of the early twenty-first century for U.S. economic and national security policy. For U.S. policy on exports, it offers the starkest example of the end of the cold war, when "trusted countries" had good customers for sophisticated U.S. exports and "adversary countries" were home to companies that must be denied U.S. technology and other items.

Now, almost all countries offer attractive opportunities for legitimate trade and security risks. U.S. export control policy toward China should evolve to keep up with these new realities in a manner consistent with our broader foreign policy. The Commerce Department today is publishing updated regulations that support U.S. companies in competing successfully in China while restricting the export of technologies that would contribute to China's military modernization.

China is one of America's most important overseas markets for high-technology items, and U.S. exporters are capturing the opportunity. Last year, U.S. high-tech exports to China grew by 44% to $17.7 billion—more than the entire value of U.S. exports to India, Russia, and Thailand. The share of these exports subject to Commerce Department export controls is tiny, but important. About $230 million worth of high-tech exports to China (1.3%) required a license in 2006. These were items like sophisticated electronic components that required an extra degree of scrutiny to ensure they would not be used in ways contrary to U.S. national security or foreign policy.

The United States welcomes a prosperous and peaceful China, integrated into the global economy. But China's rapid and opaque military modernization, punctuated by events such as its January 2007 test of an antisatellite weapon, demonstrates the continued need to apply additional prudent oversight to a small number of the most sensitive dual-use technologies and other items that by definition have both civilian and military applications. The new Commerce Department regulations strike the right balance in our complex relationship with China. First, they facilitate legitimate commercial trade by making it easier for U.S. companies to export items to Chinese companies that have a record of using them responsibly. At the same time, the new regulations place certain restrictions on high-technology items that could contribute to China's military buildup.

Specifically, the new Validated End-User (VEU) program will permit trusted customers in China to receive selected technologies and other items without the need for individual export licenses. Under the VEU program, exporters will be able to sell more easily to companies in China that have a responsible record of using sensitive U.S. items for their intended civilian purpose. This innovative new program promises to reduce time, expense, and uncertainty in the licensing process and make U.S. exporters more competitive in China. It will also act as a powerful market-based incentive, rewarding responsible practices by the many civilian firms in China that handle sensitive technology with care.

The updated regulations also will enhance U.S. security by imposing new and heightened scrutiny on a focused set of approximately twenty types of products and technologies, such as lasers and radar antennas, when they are intended for use in Chinese weapons systems. As military procurement relies ever more extensively on commercial, off-the-shelf products, this new targeted list of controls, which was carefully developed by the Departments of Commerce, Defense, and State, will help to ensure that dual-use products are not a back door to breaking the U.S. arms embargo on China.

The publication of the updated China policy regulations marks an end and a beginning. It is the end of a long debate about how to fine-tune export controls to strike the right balance in our complex relationship with China. This policy is also the beginning of new, enhanced opportunities for U.S. businesses to boost legitimate trade with one of the most important new economies in the world.

Undersecretary Mario Mancuso co-chaired the sixth annual HTCG in New Delhi, India, with Foreign Secretary Shivshankar Menon. Representatives from the Departments of Commerce, State, and Defense traveled with the undersecretary to this year's HTCG, which focused on defense and strategic trade, biotechnology, information technology, and nanotechnology issues.

What Is the HTCG?

The U.S.-India High Technology Cooperation Group (HTCG) was formed in 2002 to provide a forum for discussing U.S.-India high-technology trade issues and building the confidence necessary to facilitate trade in sensitive items. The HTCG Statement of Principles provides the framework under which the group operates. Work conducted within the HTCG has led to many positive developments in the U.S.-India trade relationship and has helped to promote bilateral high-tech trade, including:

■ Less than 0.5% of U.S. exports to India require a dual-use export license, and approximately 95% of license applications were approved in 2007.
■ From 2003 to 2007, processing times for dual-use applications dropped 37% to thirty-three days on average.
■ More than 87% of the value of controlled dual-use trade to India no longer requires a license as a result of the implementation, Next Steps in Strategic Partnership, a U.S.-India business development initiative, and trade in advanced technology products increased by over 145% from 2006 to 2007.
■ Increased private sector interaction has occurred with the two governments, including industry events under HTCG auspices and outreach activities targeting business communities in both the United States and India.

The HTCG is a two-day event every year that includes both industry and government dialogues. On the first day, U.S. and Indian industry representatives discuss ways in which the U.S. and Indian governments can facilitate trade and present the governments with their specific recommendations for each of the covered sectors. These industry recommendations provide a substantive basis for the government-to-government meetings on the second day of the event.

Successful Best Practices for Purchasing from China, India, and Other Emerging Countries

■ Learn the cultural issues, particularly those that affect trade.
■ Develop strong relationships with both senior and operations management.
■ Make fixed asset investments, as partners.
■ Protect your proprietary rights. Use consultants and counsel who specialize in these areas.
■ Stay ahead of the innovation curve of copycats, black marketers, and fraudulent competition.
■ Chose the very best in logistics providers where service, not cost, is an overriding factor.
■ Review and scrutinize all the pricing models, landed cost formulas, and reasons for purchasing overseas to make sure they represent good business models.
■ Make sure all your supply chain personnel understand all the variables that will apply differently to these sources, compared to more seasoned ones, such as Europe. Skill set development should be prioritized.

- Practice risk management and mitigation to a great extent in all the decisions made.
- Make sure there is cargo insurance in place to cover the risks of transportation and intermediate warehousing. Use qualified insurance expertise and make sure the insuring polices are "all risk" and "warehouse to warehouse" with the broadest insuring conditions.

Chapter 9

What Purchasing Managers Need to Know about Exporting

Companies that purchase goods from overseas will typically have some element of export trade as well. There are numerous government agencies and regulatory controls in place that are associated with stiff fines and penalties for nonadherence. This chapter takes a peek at all one needs to know about exporting purchases from overseas.

Purchasing managers will often become involved in export compliance management (even if by default), which makes this another area of information gathering and diligent business process application. There are many government agencies that are involved in regulating exports. Corporate supply chain management personnel who may have primary responsibilities for importing will typically have the basic need to understand export management as well. They may send over equipment, tools, dies, raw materials, components, etc. Or, as logistics personnel, they may have skill sets to negotiate. This section deals with some very basic issues that importers need to know about exporting.

The government agencies involved directly with export management include the following:

- Department of Transportation
- Census Bureau
- Department of Commerce (DOC)
- Bureau of Industry and Security

- Department of State
- Department of the Treasury
- Office of Asset Controls (OFAC)

One of the most important export documents is the Shipper's Export Declaration (SED), managed by the Census Bureau in concert with the DOC for monitoring export trade statistics. The SED also functions as a compliance document for other government agencies (Figure 9.1).

Trade statistics are vital to the negotiation of U.S. trade agreements. The Foreign Trade Statistic Regulations spell out for exporters what information must be reported and how to correctly report this information.

As a general rule, Shipper's Export Declarations are required for exports of products valued at over $2,500 per Schedule B number. In addition, Shipper's Export Declarations are required for shipments to and from Puerto Rico, shipments requiring export licenses, and shipments for goods falling under the Commerce Control List or U.S. Munitions List. A Shipper's Export Declaration

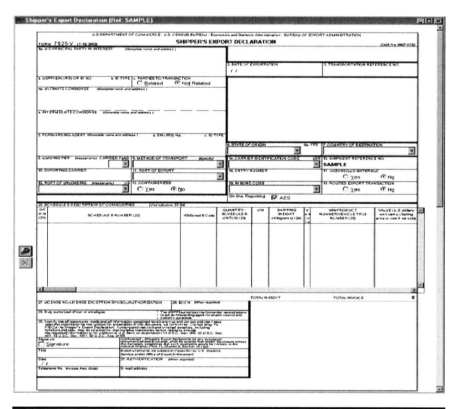

Figure 9.1 Sample of shipper's export declaration.

is not required for goods going to Canada, unless they require a license from the Department of State.

For many years the Shipper's Export Declaration was completed as a three-part document printed on goldenrod-colored paper. The shipper or his freight forwarder would present a copy of the Shipper's Export Declaration to the carrier. The carrier would then submit the forms to the government. Order entry clerks would eventually enter and code this information to formulate statistics and document the freight paper trail.

In order to expedite the processing of this information from both a statistical and a compliance standpoint, the Commerce Department implemented an electronic system to process the data contained on the Shipper's Export Declaration. This information can now be processed under the Automated Export System (AES). AES allows for the transfer of the SED information between Commerce, Customs, the Bureau of Industry and Security (BIS), and the shipper. The information is submitted prior to export (for the majority of shipments) and is much more timely.

AES became mandatory in October 2003 for items falling under the Commerce Control List or U.S. Munitions List. AES became mandatory for all export shipments requiring a Shipper's Export Declaration.

Incorrect data on the Shipper's Export Declaration/AES transmission can lead to potential delays if the information does not appear valid or Customs holds the shipment based on an incorrect Schedule B number indicated. A study by Customs and Border Protection indicated that too many errors are made in entering the data through AES. Exporters and forwarders are witnessing an increase in scrutiny by Census, BIS, and Customs crack down on these errors in the near future in their attempt to raise the accuracy level of the information transmitted.

AES is available for exporters and their forwarders. If a forwarder is using the AES on behalf of the exporter, the exporter must still meet its compliance responsibility. This is best accomplished by supplying the forwarder with the correct information to complete the Shipper's Export Declaration/AES transmission. The Foreign Trade Statistic Regulations contain a list of the specific responsibilities of the U.S. principal party in interest (USPPI) and the forwarder. A copy of the Foreign Trade Statistic Regulations can be found at http://www.census.gov/foreign-trade/regulations/regs062004.pdf.

From a compliance standpoint, exporters should receive a copy of the Shipper's Export Declaration that was filed electronically by the forwarder. Functionally, this document can be sent with the forwarder's invoice and should include a copy of the transportation document (air bill, ocean bill of lading, over-the-road bill of lading). In the case of a routed export, the copy may be sent with proof of export by the consignee's forwarder.

Department of Commerce (DOC)/Bureau of Industry and Security (BIS)

The BIS administers the Export Administration Regulations. Prior to 9/11, BIS was called the Bureau of Export Administration (BXA). Post 9/11, the name was changed to better reflect the agency's focus.

The mission of BIS is to advance U.S. national security, foreign policy, and economic interests. BIS activities include regulating the export of sensitive goods and technology, enforcing export controls and antiboycott regulations, and assisting U.S. industry in complying with international agreements.

The BIS regulates the export and reexport of most commercial items. These items are referred to as dual-use items that have both commercial and military or proliferation applications. The BIS also regulates commercial items without an obvious military use.

U.S. Principal Party in Interest (USPPI)

The party responsible for compliance in the export transaction is called the USPPI. The USPPI is the person in the United States who receives the primary benefit, monetary or otherwise, of the export transaction. Generally that person is the U.S. seller, manufacturer, order party, or foreign entity. The USPPI is responsible for:

- Providing the forwarder (or Census/BIS directly) with the correct information to properly file the Shipper's Export Declaration (SED)
- Maintaining documents and records verifying the shipment and transaction details
- Retaining documents for five years from the date of export and producing those documents at any time within the five-year period for inspection by Census, BIS, or Customs

Export Licensing

BIS maintains a list of controlled items that are based on commodities. This list is called the Commerce Control List (CCL). The Commerce Control List contains a list of products that have specific Export Control Classification Numbers (ECCNs). The ECCN is broken down into ten categories:

1. Nuclear materials, facilities, and equipment
2. Materials, chemicals, microorganisms, and toxins
3. Materials processing
4. Electronics

5. Computers
6. Telecommunications and information security
7. Sensors and lasers
8. Navigation and avionics
9. Marine
10. Propulsion systems, space vehicles, and related equipment

Each category is then broken down into five product groups:

A—Systems, equipment, and components
B—Test, inspection, and production equipment
C—Material
D—Software
E—Technology

Proper classification of the item to be exported is essential to determining any licensing requirements under the Export Administration Regulations (EAR). In many cases, the assistance of company product designers and engineers is a must, as the information used to ascertain the correct classification is very specific and technical. If an exporter is having difficulty classifying a product, it can turn to outside sources, such as consultants or the BIS.

In the classification process, a product will be found to either be on the list or not. In the case of an item found on the list, the exporter must review the destination country to determine if a license is required to ship to the country. The Commerce Country Chart is a matrix of reasons for control tied to the destination country and is contained within the Export Administration Regulations.

Figure 9.2   Undersecretary of Commerce Kenneth I. Juster (BIS director) (right) and Indian Foreign Secretary Shyam Saran (center) sign documents to conclude the first phase of the U.S.-India Next Steps in Strategic Partnership initiative. Undersecretary of State Marc Grossman (left) also participated in the signing ceremony.

If, after review of the Commerce Country Chart, a license is found to be necessary, the exporter will review his transaction to determine if a license exception is available. A license exception may be used in lieu of a license, provided the exporter performs the balance of his due diligence in the export transaction. This information is reported to Census and BIS upon export via the AES transmission.

If, after review of the Commerce Country Chart and review of the transaction, a license is found to be required prior to export, the exporter can apply for a license. This can be done electronically through the BIS Web site via the Simplified Network Application Process (SNAP).

If after review of the Commerce Control List a product is not found to be on list, the product may be shipped no license required (NLR), providing the exporter has performed his other responsibilities prior to export.

Denied Parties Screening

The additional compliance responsibilities include screening customers and avoiding business dealings with unauthorized parties. This includes knowing the end use of a product and determining if there are any red flags in the export transaction. In the event an exporter is uncomfortable with an export transaction or cannot ascertain answers to the end user as to end use, the exporter is not allowed to move ahead with the export. The red flag indicators are as follows:

1. Decide whether there are red flags.
2. If there are red flags, check out the suspicious circumstances and do not move ahead until any suspicious circumstances are eliminated.
3. Do not self-blind. Companies should not prevent staff from obtaining as much detail as possible regarding end use and end users of the product.
4. Reevaluate all information.
5. If there are still red flags and suspicions, refrain from the transaction and notify BIS.

In the event a transaction is still suspicious, the BIS should be notified so it can prevent the "shopper" from locating another vendor who may not be as aware of compliance and security issues.

Export personnel must be trained in how to deal with these red flags in jointly protecting the interests of the United States and their company.

Screening for denied parties is another responsibility exporters must comply with. Freight forwarders, ultimate consignees, intermediate consignees, and banking entities must be screened through the Denied Parties Lists. These lists are separately maintained within the Department of Commerce, Department of the Treasury, and Department of State.

- Denied Parties List (Department of Commerce): www.bis.doc.gov
- Entities List (Department of Commerce): www.bis.doc.gov
- Unverified List (Department of Commerce): www.bis.doc.gov
- Office of Foreign Asset Control Specially Designated Nationals List (Department of the Treasury): www.treas.gov
- Debarred Nationals List (Department of State): www.pmdtc.org

This screening process is managed best initially in a sales function. The sales department should screen the list prior to engaging in negotiations and even visiting a potential customer. If the company cannot ship to the customer, why waste time in trying to get the customer?

This process does not stop with sales. In some instances the Denied Parties Lists are updated daily. Conceivably an exporter could have screened the list prior to making the sales call, engaged in the sale, and now three months down the line is getting ready to ship the product. The list should be screened again. It is not enough for a company that utilizes a freight forwarder to rely on the forwarder to perform this function. While forwarders are responsible for their own compliance programs, the exporter is ultimately responsible for his or her own company's compliance.

Denied party screening should be included in a company's standard operating procedure and, depending on the lag time between time of sale and actual shipping, be conducted multiple times if necessary. Technology can assist in managing the denied party screening. Automated screening programs scan databases on existing customers as well as when entering new customers. Many such programs also contain other compliance features within the software program.

Deemed Exports

As mentioned in the beginning of this chapter, an export can be more than the movement of a good. An export of technology is deemed to take place when it is released to a foreign national within or outside the United States. This can be done through visual inspection, such as reading blueprints; when technology is exchanged orally; or when technology is made available by application under the guidance of persons with knowledge of the technology.

Technology is defined in the Export Administration Regulations as specific information for the development, production, or use of a product. Under the Export Administration Regulations, an export license is required for a deemed export because the technology does not qualify as no license required (NLR) and does not fall under an available license exception. U.S. companies must apply for an export license if they intend to transfer controlled technologies to foreign nationals in the United States, or transfer the same technology to the foreign national's country.

Antiboycott Compliance

Antiboycott regulations were adopted to encourage U.S. firms to refuse to participate in foreign boycotts that the United States does not sanction. The effect of these regulations is to prevent U.S. companies from being used to implement foreign policies of other countries that run counter to U.S. policy.

The antiboycott regulations of the Export Administration Regulations apply to all U.S. persons, defined to include individuals and companies located in the United States and their foreign affiliates. These regulations pertain to exports, imports, financing, forwarding, shipping, and other transactions that may occur offshore. Specifically, the laws prohibit:

- Agreements to refuse or actual refusal to do business with Israel or blacklisted companies
- Agreements to discriminate against other persons based on race, religion, sex, national origin, or nationality
- Agreements to furnish information about business relations with Israel or blacklisted companies
- Agreements to furnish information about the race, religion, sex, or national origin of another person
- Implementation of letters of credit containing prohibited boycott terms or conditions

The Export Administration Regulations require U.S. companies to report quarterly requests they have received to take actions to comply with unsanctioned boycotts. Standard operating procedures should contain a summary of possible boycott statements, including how to treat any statements received as well as how to report such statements to the BIS.

Department of Treasury/Office of Foreign Asset Controls (OFAC)

The Office of Foreign Assets Control (OFAC) of the U.S. Department of the Treasury administers and enforces economic and trade sanctions based on U.S. foreign policy and national security goals. These sanctions are targeted against foreign countries, terrorists, international narcotics traffickers, and those engaged in activities related to the proliferation of weapons of mass destruction. Many of these sanctions are based on United Nations and other international mandates, are multilateral in scope, and involve close cooperation with allied governments.

Under these sanctions, companies are prohibited from trading or engaging in financial transactions from individuals, companies, and countries on the sanctions list unless the company has received specific authorization to engage in said transaction. Countries included on the sanction list are the Balkans, Burma, Cuba, Iran, Iraq, Liberia, Libya, North Korea, Sudan, Syria, and Zimbabwe. In addition to the targeted countries, OFAC publishes a list of Specially Designated Nationals. This list contains over 3,500 names of companies and individuals who are associated with a targeted sanction.

OFAC has authority to permit a person or entity to engage in specific transactions that might ordinarily be prohibited. This is done through submission of a written request and acts as a license issued by the agency. If a company engages in a transaction with a sanctioned party, OFAC has the ability to block funds as a means of controlling property.

All U.S. persons must comply with OFAC regulations, including all U.S. citizens and permanent resident aliens regardless of where they are located, all persons and entities within the United States, all U.S. incorporated entities and their foreign branches, and in the cases of certain programs, such as those regarding Cuba and North Korea, all foreign subsidiaries owned or controlled by the United States

The fines for violations can be substantial. Depending on the program, criminal penalties can include fines ranging from $50,000 to $10 million and imprisonment ranging from ten to thirty years for willful violations. Depending on the program, civil penalties range from $11,000 to $1 million for each violation.

A recent listing of violations included such names as Daimler Chrysler, Exel Global Logistics, Fleet National Bank, and American Express. The penalty amount in these cases ranged from $2,700 to $58,994.

Department of State (DOS)

The Arms Export Control Act authorizes the president to control the export and import of defense articles and defense services. License or approval may only be granted to U.S. companies who are registered with Defense Trade Controls for export of such items.

The Department of State administers the International Traffic in Arms Regulations (ITAR). These regulations cover defense articles, defense services, and some commercial products. These articles are contained within the U.S. Munitions List (USML). The USML controls items designed, configured, or adapted for military use that do not have a predominantly civil application and do not have a performance equivalent (form, fit, and function) to those of an article used for civil applications. The USML also controls items specifically designed, developed, or modified for a military application, and the Department of State administers the ITAR. The following activities are controlled under the ITAR:

- Exports and reexports of defense articles or technical data
- Furnishing a defense service
- Temporary imports of defense articles

- Reexports of defense articles that are the product of U.S. technical data or incorporate any percentage of U.S. defense articles
- Proposals to sell significant military equipment
- Dealings with prohibited parties

Defense services under the ITAR consist of the following:

- Furnishing assistance to foreign persons, whether in the United States or abroad, in the design, development, engineering, manufacture, production, assembly, testing, repair, maintenance, modification, operation, demilitarization, destruction, processing, or use of defense articles
- Furnishing to foreign persons any technical data such as classified information, software, and information for the design, development, or production of defense articles, including blueprints, drawings, photographs, and plans

Under the ITAR an export includes the following:

1. Sending or taking a defense article out of the United States in any manner
2. Transferring registration, control, or ownership to a foreign person of any aircraft, vessel, or satellite covered by the USML, whether in the United States or abroad
3. Disclosing (whether visually or orally) or transferring in the United States any defense article to an embassy or agency of a foreign government
4. Disclosing technical data to a foreign person whether in the United States or abroad
5. Performing a defense service on behalf of a foreign person

Exporters who are involved in transaction that falls under the ITAR must have procedures in place to adhere to the regulations. Penalties for violations under the ITAR are severe:

- Policy of denial: The Department of State will not approve *any* exports (unless there is overriding proof the shipment is in the best interest of protecting national security)
- Three-year debarment
- Civil penalties not to exceed $500,000 per violation
    - Criminal penalties
    - Fine, not to exceed $1 million per violation
    - Imprisonment, not to exceed ten years per violation
- Both fine and imprisonment

It is very important for companies that source on foreign shores to also understand U.S export laws and regulations. No matter how well you manage inbound supply chains, a little mistake on the outbound leg may cause ramifications and consequences to the inbound supply chain that has penalties, fines, more scrutiny, and loss of privileges.

Managing TSA Regulations within a Logistics Organization

Why Pay Attention?

In February 2009 there were major changes to the Transportation Security Administration (TSA) cargo security program. Due to the nature of the information and the Sensitive Security Information (SSI), we are not permitted to share all the details. However, there are many changes, and if you are under the TSA umbrella and are governed by these regulations, you must be sure you put into effect all of the changes to the program. Noncompliance with the TSA regulations could be very costly: civil penalties of up to $10,000 per violation, and possible criminal fines or imprisonment. But there are other ramifications to noncompliance, such as a tarnished reputation in the business, inability to tender air cargo, loss of business, and being red flagged by the carriers.

The best way to avoid these pitfalls is to stay informed and current. This can be accomplished by attending the outreach seminars given by the TSA, reading industry-related materials, and frequent and recurrent training for staff. When a new security directive is issued, or when a change in the program occurs, don't wait for the annual recurrent training. Gather the troops for a mini-training session to be sure everyone is aware of any changes that will affect your company.

The next key to success in TSA compliance is to be sure that those who sit in the "ivory tower" are informed and involved. Any effective program, TSA or otherwise, requires key senior management buy-in. Officers of the company can flex the "big muscles" in order to accomplish goals toward compliance. An organization should also establish point people. The point person/people should be committed to compliance, genuinely care about security, be "user-friendly" to staff, and should be organized and keep good records. You should meet at least quarterly. This committee should develop an internal audit plan, discuss audit results, discuss and implement corrective actions, keep audit records to track progress toward compliance goals, and discuss any concerns or ideas for betterment. Promise pizza lunch meetings and see how quickly you will gather a committee.

Technology can play a key role in compliance and will certainly reduce the margin of errors as well as the time it takes to manage these regulations. The regulations are becoming too complex to continue on a manual platform. Automated systems can be set up to maintain compliance. Automated alerts can "pop up" to identify if an agent is an authorized representative, or to advise the known status of a shipper, or to alert the company compliance point person that recurrent training is due.

Audits

Audits of your TSA compliance should be conducted regularly, not less than quarterly. The committee should first identify each area of the program where compliance on its part is required. Then, prepare written audit guidelines. Follow guidelines during the audit to allow for continuity and consistency. Issue a written warning to the staff member(s) involved in noncompliant findings. Keep this in the employee file. The committee must invoke timely corrective actions. A report of findings after each audit should be discussed with the committee members and senior management. The audit report may be used as a tool in the next training conducted.

These TSA security measures and programs are continually developing and changing. The mind-set must be of the following:

■ Patience
■ Diligence
■ Understanding

Concluding Remarks

Purchasing managers are facing a whole new world of challenges in managing their responsibilities. These challenges become more intense when we move the purchasing into overseas markets. This book has outlined in great detail just what their challenges are and, more importantly, the necessary skill set the purchasing manager needs to develop to manage all these challenges successfully. The challenges are vast: political, economic, post-9/11, regulatory, logistics, costs, compliance, security, expedited shipping, etc. Those more experienced purchasing managers that have already gone through the learning curve of global supply chain operation know that they have to be more diligent, more knowing, and more capable to achieve the desired results dictated by the highest echelons of senior management. Key elements of this new arena are:

- Building streams of quality information flow
- Aligning with qualified service providers
- Mitigating risks and maximizing profits
- Developing numerous options
- Integrating all areas of the global supply chain
- Developing the necessary skill sets
- Exercising supervision and control over all aspects of the inbound logistics

Strategy, structure, and alignment are key summary points that this book utilizes for purchasing managers to consider in how they conduct themselves. We all have options on how we conduct our business life and affairs. To raise our level of performance, to act world class, to incorporate raising the bar, purchasing managers should heed all the advice and counsel outlined in this book. They need to incorporate the business practices, behaviors, and operating guidelines outlined in this book into their and their personnel's responsibilities.

The information flow is vast. The process to make use of the information is complex. The actions necessary to make the process successful require consistent diligence. This book provides the foundation and the blueprint for the purchasing manager to utilize for developing the strategies and actions to increase the opportunity for a smooth-running and successful inbound global supply chain. The challenges are vast, but they are not so vast as to be uncontrollable or unconquerable.

The author has a lot of experience in working with corporate America in utilizing the material in this book as a successful strategy and structure for best practice, risk management, and world-class operations that become reachable goals, expectations, and relevant achievements for all areas of global purchasing, offshoring, and inbound logistics. The readers learn that the challenges they face in global sourcing can be overcome by developing a process. The process is detailed in the structure of this book. It is time tested and proven in hundreds of corporations and purchasing programs throughout corporate America, from the very large to medium-sized and smaller organizations.

Read it. Think it through. Use it. Act on it. Incorporate it. Personalize and make it work. Is is a great resource for obtaining great results.

T.A.C.

Glossary

Abandonment: Refusing delivery of a shipment so badly damaged in transit, that it has little or no value.

Acceptance: An international banking instrument known as a time draft or bill of exchange that the drawee has accepted and is unconditionally obligated to pay at maturity.

Ad valorem: A tariff that is calculated based on a percentage of the value of the product.

Advising bank: A bank operating in the exporter's country that handles letters of credit for a foreign bank by notifying the exporter that the credit has been opened in its favor.

Agency for International Development (AID) shipments: The Agency for International Development is a U.S. government agency created to provide relief to developing countries that must purchase products and services through U.S. companies. Specialized export documentation is necessary to complete the transactions.

All-inclusive: Term of sale used to notate "all charges are included."

Allowance: Typically afforded a consignee as a credit or deduction on a specific export transaction.

All-risk cargo insurance: A clause included in marine insurance policies to cover loss and damage from external causes during the course of transit within all the terms and conditions agreed to by the underwriters.

Arbitration: Wording included in export contracts introducing an independent third-party negotiator into the dispute resolution in lieu of litigation.

Arrival notice: Advice to a consignee on inbound freight. Sometimes referred to as a prealert. Contains details of the shipment's arrival schedule and bill of lading data.

As is: An international term denoting that the buyer accepts the goods as is; it is a connotation there may be something wrong with the merchandise, and the seller limits its future potential liability.

Automated Broker Interface (ABI): The electronic transmission and exchange of data between a customhouse broker and CBP.

Automated Export Systems (AES): The electronic transmission of the Shipper's Export Declaration to Census, BIS, and CBP.

Automated Manifest System (AMS): The electronic transmission of a carrier/vessel's manifest between the carrier/steamship line and CBP.

Balance of trade: The difference between a country's total imports and exports. If exports exceed imports, a favorable balance of trade, or trade surplus, exists; if not, a trade deficit exists.

Barter: The direct exchange of goods or services without the use of money as a medium of exchange and without third-party involvement.

Bill of lading: A document that establishes the terms of a contract between a shipper and a transportation company under which freight is to be moved between specified points for a specified charge. Usually prepared by the shipper on forms issued by the carrier, it serves as a document of title, a contract of carriage, and a receipt of goods.

Bond: A form of insurance between two parties obligating a surety to pay against a performance or obligation.

Bonded warehouse: A warehouse authorized by Customs authorities for storage of goods on which payment of duties is deferred until the goods are cleared and removed.

Break bulk cargo: Loose cargo that is loaded directly into a conveyance's hold.

Bretton Woods Conference: A meeting under the auspices of the United Nations at Bretton Woods, New Hampshire, in 1944, that was held to develop some degree of cooperation in matters of international trade and payments and to devise a satisfactory international monetary system to be in operation after World War II. The particular objectives intended were stable exchange rates and convertibility of currencies for the development of multilateral trade. The Bretton Woods Conference established the International Monetary Fund and the World Bank.

Bunker adjustment fee (BAF): Fuel surcharge issued by a steamship line.

Bureau of Industry and Security (BIS): Department of Commerce agency responsible for Export Administration Regulations, formerly known as Bureau of Export Administration.

Carnet: A Customs document permitting the holder to carry or send merchandise temporarily into certain foreign countries without paying duties or posting bonds.

Certificate of origin: Document used to certify the country of origin for a product.

Clingage: When shipping bulk liquids, the residue remaining inside the conveyance after discharge.

Combi: An aircraft with pallet or container capacity on its main deck and belly holds.

Commission agent: An individual, company, or government agent that serves as the buyer of overseas goods on behalf of another buyer.

Commodity specialist: An official authorized by the U.S. Treasury to determine proper tariff and value of imported goods.

Consignment: Delivery of merchandise from an exporter (the consignor) to an agent (the consignee) under the agreement that the agent sell the merchandise for the account of the exporter. The consignor retains the title to the goods until the consignee has sold them. The consignee sells the goods for commission and remits the net proceeds to the consignor.

Consolidator: An agent who brings together a number of shipments for one destination to qualify for preferential rates.

Cost, insurance, freight (CIF): A system of valuing imports that includes all costs, insurance, and freight involved in shipping the goods from the port of embarkation to the destination.

Countertrade: The sale of goods or services that are paid for in whole or part by the transfer of goods or services from a foreign country.

Credit risk insurance: Insurance designed to cover risks of nonpayment for delivered goods.

Currency: National form for payment medium: dollars, pesos, rubles, naira, pounds, etc.

Distributor: A foreign agent who sells for a supplier directly and maintains an inventory of the supplier's products.

Dock receipt: Documented receipt the shipment has been received by the steamship line.

Draft: Negotiable instrument presented to the buyer's bank for payment.

Drawback: Duties to be refunded by government when previously imported goods are exported or used in the manufacture of exported products.

Domestic International Sales Corporation (DISC): Established in 1971 by U.S. legislation, DISCs were designed to help exporters by offering income tax deferrals on export earnings. DISCs were phased out in 1984.

Dumping: Exporting or importing merchandise into a country below the costs incurred in production and shipment.

Duty: A tax imposed on imports by the Customs authority of a country. Duties are generally based on the value of the goods (*ad valorem* duties), some other factor such as weight or quantity (specified duties), or a combination of value and other factors (compounded duties).

Embargo: A prohibition on imports or exports as a result of a political eventuality.

European Union (EU): The 27 nations, primarily in Europe, that have combined to form the world's largest single market of 495 million consumers. The EU includes Austria, Belgium, Bulgaria, Cyprus, Czech Republic, Denmark, Estonia, Finland, France, Germany, Greece, Hungary, Ireland, Italy, Latvia, Lithuania, Luxembourg, Malta, the Netherlands, Poland, Portugal, Romania, Slovakia, Slovenia, Spain, Sweden, United Kingdom.

Export: To send or transport goods out of a country for sale in another country. In international sales, the exporter is usually the seller or the seller's agent.

Export-Import Bank of the United States (Ex-Im Bank): Ex-Im Bank facilitates and aids the financing of exports of U.S. goods and services through a variety of programs created to meet the needs of the U.S. exporting community. Programs, which are tailored to the size of a transaction, can take the form of direct lending or loan guarantees.

Export management company: A private company that serves as the export department for several manufacturers, soliciting and transacting export business on behalf of its clients in return for a commission, salary, or retainer plus commission.

Export trading company: An organization designed to facilitate the export of goods and services. It can be a trade intermediary that provides export-related services to producers or can be established by the producers themselves, though typically export trading companies do not take title to goods.

Ex Works (EXW) from factory: The buyer accepts goods at the point of origin and assumes all responsibility for transportation of the goods sold. Also Ex Warehouse, Ex Mine, and Ex Factory as defined in INCOTERMS (Chapter 6).

Fair trade: A concept of international trade in which some barriers are tolerable as long as they are equitable. When barriers are eliminated, there should be reciprocal action by all parties.

Force majeure: Expressed as "acts of God." Conditions found in some marine contracts exempting certain parties from liability for occurrences out of their control, such as earthquakes and floods.

Foreign Corrupt Practices Act of 1977: U.S. legislation with stringent antibribery provisions and guidelines for record keeping and internal accounting control requirements for all publicly held corporations. The act makes it illegal to offer, pay, or agree to pay money or any item of value to a foreign official for the purpose of getting or retaining business.

Foreign Credit Insurance Association (FCIA): An insurance program, previously government managed and underwritten, now privately held, that insures commercial and political risks for U.S. exporters.

Foreign sales agent: An individual or company that serves as the foreign representative of a domestic supplier and seeks sales abroad for the supplier.

Forfaiting: The selling, at a discount, of a longer-term receivable or promissory note of a buyer.

Franchising: A form of licensing by the service sector for companies that want to export their trademark, methods, or personal services.

Free alongside (FAS): A system of valuing imports that includes inland transportation costs involved in delivery of goods to a port in the exporting country, but excludes the cost of ocean shipping, insurance, and the cost of loading the merchandise on the vessel.

Free domicile: Terminology used for door-to-door deliveries.

Free on board or Freight on board (FOB): A system of valuing imports that includes inland transportation costs involved in delivery of goods to a port in the exporting country and the cost of loading the merchandise on the vessel, but excludes the cost of ocean shipping and insurance.

Free port: An area such as a port city into which merchandise may legally be moved without payment of duties.

Free trade: A theoretical concept to describe international trade unhampered by governmental barriers such as tariffs or nontariff measures. Free trade typically favors the reduction or elimination of all tariff and nontariff barriers to trade.

Free trade zone or Foreign trade zone (FTZ): A port designated by the government of a country for duty-free entry of any nonprohibited goods. Merchandise may be stored, displayed, or used for manufacturing within the zone, and reexported without the payment of duties.

Freight all kinds (FAK): A mix of cargos traveling as one.

General Agreement on Tariffs and Trade (GATT): A multilateral treaty to which eighty-five nations (or more than 80% of world trade) subscribe; it is designed to reduce trade barriers and promote trade through tariff concessions, thereby contributing to global economic growth and development.

Generalized System of Preferences (GSP): Notes duty-free/reduced tariffs on imports from the countries listed on the GSP list.

Harmonized Tariff System of the United States (HTSUS): System of classifying products imported into the United States by number.

In bond: Transportation of merchandise under custody of a bonded carrier.

International Air Transportation Association (IATA): Regulates air cargo.

Harter Act: Legislation protecting a shipowner from certain types of claims that are due to actions of the crew.

Hazmat: Hazardous materials regulated by various government agencies, DOT/49 CFR, IATA, IMCO, Coast Guard, etc. Personnel who interface with hazmat cargos need to be certified to do so.

Hedging: A mechanism that allows an exporter to take a position in a foreign currency to protect against losses due to wide fluctuations in currency exchange rates.

Hold: The space below deck inside an ocean-going vessel.

Irrevocable letter of credit: A letter of credit in which the specified payment is guaranteed by the bank if all terms and conditions are met by the drawee (buyer). *See also* revocable letter of credit.

ISO 9000: Issued in 1987 by the International Organization for Standardization, ISO 9000 is a series of five international standards that establish requirements for the quality control systems of companies selling goods in the

European Union. It now includes many additional countries and companies throughout the world.

Joint venture: A business undertaking in which more than one company shares ownership and control.

Letter of credit: A document is issued by a bank per instructions from a buyer of goods that authorizes the seller to draw a specified sum of money under specified terms, usually the receipt by the bank of certain documents within a given period of time.

Licensing: A business arrangement in which the manufacturer of a product (or a company with proprietary rights over certain technology, trademarks, etc.) grants permission to some other group or individual to manufacture that product (or make use of that proprietary material) in return for specified royalties or other payment.

Logistics: The science of transportation covering the planning and implementation of specific strategies to move materials at a desired cost.

Mala fide: Misrepresentation or in bad faith.

Maquiladora: A tax-free program allowing the import of materials into Mexico for manufacturing of goods for export back to the United States. Now declining in importance as a result of NAFTA.

Marine insurance: Insurance covering loss or damage of goods during transit. It covers all modes of transport.

Market research: Specific intelligence about the market in which a seller proposes to sell goods or services. This information is gathered through interviews, commissioned surveys, and direct contact with potential customers or their representatives.

Marks and numbers: The references made in writing to identify a shipment on the exterior packing, typically referenced in the documentation.

North American Free Trade Agreement (NAFTA): An agreement that creates a single unified market of the United States, Canada, and Mexico.

Office of Foreign Asset Controls (OFAC): Department of the Treasury office issuing regulations on transfers/funding of money.

Paperless release: Electronic release of a shipment by CBP prior to hard copies being presented.

Open account: A trade arrangement in which goods are shipped to a foreign buyer without guarantee of payment. The obvious risk this method poses to the supplier makes it essential that the buyer's integrity be unquestionable.

Overseas Private Investment Corporation (OPIC): A government-sponsored organization that promotes investment in plants and equipment in less developed countries by offering guarantees comparable to those of the Ex-Im Bank.

Political risk: In exporting, the risk of loss due to such causes as currency inconvertibility, government action preventing entry of goods, expropriation, confiscation, or war.

Power of attorney: A document that authorizes a Customs broker or freight forwarder to act on the exporter or importer's behalf on issues relative to Customs clearance, transportation, documentation, etc.

Premium: Insurance dollars paid to an underwriter to accept a transfer of risk.

Prima facie: At face value.

Proforma invoice: (1) Invoice prepared by the supplier to the buyer, usually as a means to secure financing. (2) Invoice prepared by an importer when the supplier's invoice does not meet the invoice requirements set forth by CBP.

Protectionism: The setting of trade barriers high enough to discourage foreign imports or to raise the prices sufficiently to enable relatively inefficient domestic producers to compete successfully with foreign producers.

Purchasing agent: An individual or company that purchases goods in its own country on behalf of foreign importers, such as government agencies or large private concerns.

Remarketers: Export agents, merchants, or foreign trading companies that purchase products from an exporter to resell them under their own name.

Revocable letter of credit: A letter of credit that can be canceled or altered by the drawee (buyer) after it has been issued by the drawee's bank. Compared to an irrevocable letter of credit, which is totally binding without both parties' written agreement.

SOP: Standard operating procedure. Written guidelines on how corporate affairs are managed following consistent ideology, wording, and focus.

Tariff: A tax on imports or the rate at which imported goods are taxed.

Time draft: A draft that matures in a certain number of days, either from acceptance or date of draft.

Tracking: A forwarder or carrier's system of recording movement intervals of shipments from origin through to final destination.

Trade acceptance; *See* **acceptance.**

Transfer risk: The risk associated with converting a local foreign currency into U.S. dollars.

Transmittal letter: Cover communication outlining details of an export transaction and accompanying documentation.

Terminal handling charge: Fee assessed by a terminal for handling a shipment.

Twenty-foot equivalent (TEU): Twenty-foot equivalent or standard measure for a twenty-foot ocean freight container. Two TEUs represent one forty-foot standard container.

Ullage: Measuring the amount of liquid or dry bulk freight in the hold of a vessel by measuring the height of the stow from the opening on deck.

Uniform Customs and Practice: International rules governing documentary collections.

U.S. Agency for International Development (USAID): A U.S. governmental agency that carries out assistance programs designed to help the people of certain lesser developed countries develop their human and economic resources, increase production capacities, and improve the quality of human life as well as promote the economic or potential stability in friendly countries.

Value-added tax (VAT): An indirect tax assessed on the increase in value of goods from the raw material stage through the production process to final consumption. The tax to processors or merchants is levied on the amount by which they have increased the value of items that were purchased by them for use or resale. This system is used in the European Union.

Warehouse receipt: Receipt given to signify that goods have been received into a warehouse.

Weight breaks: Discounts to freight charges are given as the total weight increases at various weight breaks: 50 pounds, 100 pounds, 500 pounds, etc.

Wharfage: Charges assessed for handling freight near a dock or pier.

With average: A marine insurance term meaning that shipment is protected for partial damage whenever the damage exceeds an agreed percentage.

Zone: Freight tariffs are often determined by certain geographic areas called zones.

Appendix A

Importer Security Filing "10+2" Program

Frequently Asked Questions

On November 25, 2008, U.S. Customs and Border Protection (CBP) published an interim final rule entitled "Importer Security Filing and Additional Carrier Requirements" in the Federal Register (73 FR 71730). The interim final rule requires both importers and carriers to submit additional information pertaining to cargo to CBP before the cargo is brought into the United States by vessel. CBP has received numerous questions concerning the interim final rule. To assist the trade community in understanding the expectations of CBP concerning the Importer Security Filing and Additional Carrier Requirements rule, CBP in this document has provided responses to the most frequently asked questions. CBP will continually be updating and clarifying this document as necessary. Should you have additional questions that are not included in this document, please feel free to write to Security_Filing_General@cbp.dhs.gov. Please note that the responses to the FAQs are for informational purposes only and are non-binding. Questions relating to specific facts and circumstances of a prospective transaction can be the subject of a ruling request under Part 177 of the CBP regulations.

Contents

Most of the subject matter has been broken down into major topic areas and has been listed alphabetically. On the CBP Web site you can use the hyperlinks to navigate to help you with utilization of the Web site, where this information can also be obtained.

ABI
ACE
Agents
Amendments
    A. General
    B. Withdrawals

AMS
Bills of Lading
Bonds
    A. General
    B. Continuous Bonds
    C. Exemptions

Bulk and Break Bulk
Carnets
Client Representatives (CBP)
Coded Transactions
    A. Regular Shipments
    B. Informal Shipments (Personal Effects & Household Goods)
    C. To Order Shipments

Confidentiality
Contact Information (CBP)
Container Status Messages (CSMs)
Cruise Vessels and ISF
Data Elements (General and Specific Questions)
ISF-10 Elements
    A. Importer of Record Number
    B. Consignee Number
    C. Ship to Party
    D. Manufacturer (Supplier) Name/Address
    E. Country of Origin
    F. Commodity HTS-6
        • Parts

G. Container Stuffing Location
- Timing Flexibility
H. Consolidator (Stuffer) Name/Address
- Timing Flexibility

ISF-5 Elements
I. Foreign Port of Unlading

Enforcement Measures
A. Do Not Load (DNL) Messages
B. Liquidated Damages

Exemptions
A. 24-Hour Manifest Rule Exemptions ("Exempt" Break Bulk)
B. General ISF Requirements

Flexible Enforcement Period
FTZ Shipments
Identification Numbers
A. General
B. DUNS

Implementation Issues
A. Effective Date

Informal Shipments
A. General
B. Military Shipments
C. U.S. Goods Returned

Instruments of International Trade
ISF Filings
A. General
B. Self Filer
C. Timing Requirements
D. ISF-5 Filings
E. ISF Territories of Coverage (Geographic)
F. ISF Areas of Coverage (Mode of Transport)

ISF Importer
A. General
B. Transit Cargo (FROB, IE, TE)

Messaging
- A. General
- B. Accepted
- C. Unique Identification Number
- D. Accepted with Warning
- E. Rejected
- F. Status Advisory
- G. Duplicate ISF Filings
- H. ISF-5 Messaging

Mid Numbers
Outreach Efforts
Postal Codes
Powers of Attorney
Record Keeping Requirements
Rejected ISF Filings
Returned or Refused Shipments (including U.S. goods returned)
Self-Filing
Structured Review Period
Transmission Methods
Unified ISF-10 and Entry Filings
Unique Identification Number
Vessel Stow Plans
- A. Responsibility to File
- B. Exemptions
- C. E-mail address
- D. Formats
- E. Amendments

ABI

1. I would like to know if customs brokers are going to be able to use the Automated Broker Interface (ABI) system to do the Importer Security Filing (ISF).
   Yes.

2. How do we get signed up for the ABI system?
   Entities that want to become Importer Security Filing filers using either AMS or ABI should call 703-650-3500 to be assigned a Client Representative.

ACE

1. Will CBP create a Web portal in ACE so Importers can file their own Importer Security Filings?
   CBP will continue to explore additional ISF functionality as ACE is developed.

2. Will Custom House Brokers (CHBs) have the ability to query ISF performance reports from I track/Ace Portal? Will the account managers have access to this information? (see also Structured Review Period)

At this time CBP will not make available report cards through ACE; however, CBP is developing a reporting mechanism that will be provided to the ISF filers. Yes, account managers will have access to these report cards.

Agents

1. If we hire a customs broker to be our agent, does the broker have to be our agent for all of our ISF's during a single year?

No. Each ISF is done on an individual basis. An ISF Importer may file the ISF themselves, or hire an agent for each individual filing. There is no limit as to how many different agents an ISF Importer may use during the course of a year.

2. Can we use different agents for different filings? Can our agents use both AMS and ABI to do our filings? Will this affect our filings in any way?

The ISF Importer can elect to use different ISF Agents for each separate filing. Also, those ISF Agents may use either vessel AMS or ABI to do these separate filings. However, if a unified entry filing is being done, ABI must be used and the ISF Importer must self-file or use a licensed U.S. customs broker to do the filing on their behalf.

3. If an importer uses multiple CHBs, can the importer select one broker to do an ISF and another to make entry (on the same shipment)?

Yes, unless the filing is a "unified filing" in which case the filing must be done by a single entity.

4. Does the ISF Filer need to be located in the U.S.?

No.

5. Does the "filing agent" for the importer have to be a Licensed Customs Broker? Can it be the foreign freight forwarder?

A filing agent does not have to be a customs broker except for the case of a "unified filing." A foreign freight forwarder can also be a filing agent.

6. Service center notification—for 24-Hour Rule, there were specific details that went to CBP notifying that a service center had been appointed. Namely, Company Name, SCAC code, CBP assigned number, Bond number and effective date, and U.S. discharge ports that will be filed.

a. What is the process for nominating a service center for ISF 10+2 filing?

There is no process for nominating a party to submit the ISF. However, ABI filers may deal with their Client Representatives in establishing an account with reference to their service center.

b. There are instances where no SCAC code exists. Will there be a CBP assigned number and, if not, which identifier will be used in the service center nomination letter?

The filer needs a filer identification code. Either a SCAC if transmitting through AMS or an ABI filer code if filing through ABI. If a SCAC is not available for AMS participants, CBP will assign a 4 character identifier in order to be an AMS participant. For example, a broker who does not have a SCAC code will still need an identifier if they are using an AMS service center to file ISF transactions.

c. If the service center nomination comes from an assigned ISF agent, does a separate notification need to be sent for each customer they have been nominated by?

There is no process for nominating a party to submit the ISF.

Amendments

A. General:

1. When do we have to stop amending the ISF?

The Importer Security Filing must be amended if there is a change or more accurate information becomes available before the goods enter the limits of a port of first arrival in the United States. However, if the flexible filing option ("FR", "FT" or "FX") is used, the ISF must be updated with the correct or more accurate information as soon as it is known, but in any event no later than 24 hours prior to arrival of the vessel in the first U.S. port. If better information does not become available and/ or the original information is the best information, the ISF must still be completed using the "CT" amendment code.

2. Are changes to the ISF after arrival at the port of discharge allowed or required?

Generally, the requirement to update an Importer Security Filing terminates when the vessel calls at the U.S. port of discharge. However, CBP will not restrict updates outside of this window.

3. What happens if I fire my ISF Agent, but still need to update my ISF?

If an ISF Importer needs to update their own ISF that was initially submitted by their agent, the ISF Importer must contact a CBP Client Representative to have the original filing cancelled. After the original ISF has been cancelled by the CBP Client Representative, a new ISF may be submitted.

4. How will importers be able to amend the security filing if they don't have access to the Importer Security Filing elements in CBP systems?

If the ISF Importer used an agent to perform the filing, the ISF Importer should contact its agent for assistance in amending the ISF.

5. How do I handle shipments sold on the water?

The ISF will need to be updated if the shipment is sold in transit. At a minimum, the ISF Importer must notify CBP that the goods have been sold, and the party must update the Buyer (Owner) field and any other field that the party knows has changed as a result of the sale. The ISF Importer remains liable for the timing and accuracy of the ISF filing.

6. Can I amend the bill of lading number on the ISF?

Yes. From a transactional standpoint, the system will allow an ISF Filer to update an existing ISF with a new bill of lading number. However, the ISF Importer is ultimately responsible for the timely, accurate, and complete submission of the Importer Security Filing.

7. Can I replace (amend) an ISF-10 type shipment with an ISF-5 type shipment? Do I need to obtain Port Director approval first?

Yes. An ISF-10 filing can be replaced by an ISF-5 filing. As a matter of policy there is no requirement to obtain Port Director approval for these types of changes.

B. Withdrawals:
1. What happens if I enter an ISF and then the shipments do not ship?

Withdraw the ISF by deleting it.

2. Will you allow the entry to update the ISF?

No. Stand-alone ISF transactions can only be updated by replace transactions. Furthermore, unified entry transactions will only update the ISF if the entry is replaced along with an ISF replace transaction.

C. Codes:
1. CBP should create detailed amendment codes so changes to the ISF can be tracked more easily.

CBP agrees and will post a list of amendment codes in the next set of implementation guides.

2. If I decide to use the "flexible filing option" and submit my ISF under action reason code FR, FT or FX, will I be required to update my ISF filing?

Yes. If the ISF Importer elects to use the flexibilities provided for under the interim final rule by selecting the "FR", "FT" or "FX" code when submitting the initial ISF, the ISF must be updated with the action reason code of "CT" to denote the correct or more accurate information as soon as it is known, but in any event no later than 24 hours prior to arrival of the vessel in the first U.S. port.

One of the following action reason codes must be provided as part of an ISF-10 filing:

CT = Compliant Transaction—All data is present and is based upon the best information available at the time of the filing; no special flexibility rules apply. If "CT" is used, the ISF can be updated if necessary, but CBP does not necessarily expect to see updates for these filings. "CT" is also used to finalize a "FR", "FT" or "FX" filing.

FR = Flexible Range—A range of data for the Manufacturer, and/or Ship To Party, and/or Country of Origin, and/or Commodity HTSUS number has been provided. In these cases, the ISF must be updated as soon as better information becomes available, but in any event no later than 24 hours prior to arrival. If "FR" is used, CBP will be expecting to receive a timely update.

FT = Flexible Timing—The CS (Consolidator name/address) and/or the LG (Stuffing location) has not been provided. The ISF must be updated as soon as better information becomes available, but in any event no later than 24 hours prior to arrival. If "FT" is used, CBP will be expecting to receive a timely update.

FX = Flexible Range and Flexible Timing—A range of data as described in "FR" has been provided and the CS (Consolidator name/address) and/or LG (Stuffing location) has not been provided. The ISF must be updated as soon as better information becomes available, but in any event no later than 24 hours prior to arrival. If "FX" is used, CBP will be expecting to receive a timely update.

AMS

1. How do we get signed up for the AMS system?

Entities that want to become Importer Security Filing filers using either AMS or ABI should call 571-468-5500 to be assigned a Client Representative. You may also need to complete an Interconnection Security Agreement (ISA).

Antique Shipments

1. We import vintage furniture and accents that we buy ourselves overseas at small flea markets and street fairs. We gather our merchandise and stuff the shipping container ourselves, and then send that container to our location in the United States where we operate as domestic sellers. Are we the "buyer" as well as the "seller" at the time the ISF is required?

   Since you are purchasing and taking possession of the goods while overseas, it would be acceptable to list yourselves as both the Buyer (Owner) and Seller (Owner).

2. We have an invoice for each purchase but the people we buy from are not the actual manufacturer. Most of the people we buy from are antiques dealers and we have about 20 or 30 dealers per shipment. Do we consider the dealers as the "suppliers"? And if so, do we have to list every single one of them?

   You will need to provide the names and addresses of all the "suppliers" of the finished goods (i.e., the invoicing parties).

Bills of Lading

1. Is a bill of lading number required at the time of an ISF filing?

   Yes. The ISF Importer, or its agent, must obtain this information and provide it to CBP as part of the ISF filing. The ISF needs to be submitted at the lowest bill of lading level (i.e., house bill or regular bill) that is transmitted into the Automated Manifest System (AMS). The bill of lading number is the only common "link" between the ISF and the customs manifest data.

2. Please advise what to do if you do not have a bill of lading number at the time you submit the ISF. Most times the bill of lading numbers are not issued until after sailing.

   The ISF Importer must obtain the bill of lading number. The bill of lading number is an integral part of the security filing. Without the bill of lading number, the ISF cannot be matched to a customs manifest. The bill of lading number is part of the customs manifest information that is already required to be presented to CBP by the carrier or automated NVOCC 24 hours prior to vessel lading of cargo destined to enter the United States.

3. If the NVOCC is a non-AMS participant, should we file the master bill of lading instead of the house bill of lading with the ISF?

   The ISF needs to be submitted at the lowest bill of lading level (i.e., house bill or regular bill) that is transmitted into the Automated Manifest System (AMS). If the carrier creates and transmits a regular bill of lading number on behalf of a non-automated NVOCC or freight forwarder, the ISF filer must submit the regular bill of lading number that was transmitted into AMS as part of the ISF.

From the Importer Security Filing (ISF-10, ISF-5) CATAIR Version: June 1, 2009 Implementation Guide:

http://www.cbp.gov/linkhandler/cgov/trade/automated/automated_systems/sf_transaction_sets/isf_25_catair.ctt/isf_catair_102008.doc

Valid qualifier codes are:

OB (Ocean Bill of Lading – used for Regular Bills),

BM (House Bill of Lading)

For purposes of the Importer Security Filing, the following bill of lading definitions apply:

> Regular Bill—is defined as a non-Master bill of lading with no underlying house bills. For ISF, this is the bill reported to CBP in AMS, which is also referred to as "Straight Bill" or "Simple Bill". If multiple Regular Bills exist, the SF15 record is repeated accordingly.
>
> House Bill—is defined as a bill of lading issued under a Master Bill. For ISF, this is the House Bill reported to CBP in AMS. If multiple House Bills exist, the SF15 record is repeated accordingly.
>
> Master Bill—is defined as a bill of lading covering at least one or more underlying house bills of lading. If the filer chooses to provide the optional Master Bill for House Bills provided in the SF15 record, the Master Bill is reported in the SF20 record with an "MB" qualifier. As with the SF15 record, multiple SF20 records are used to report multiple Master Bills.
>
> CBP is requiring only the number for the bill of lading at the lowest level (i.e., the regular straight/simple bill of lading or house bill of lading) and not the master bill of lading number to be reported in an ISF.

4. Can I amend the bill of lading number on the ISF?

Yes. From a transactional standpoint, the system will allow an ISF Filer to update an existing ISF with a new bill of lading number. However, the ISF Importer is ultimately responsible for the timely, accurate, and complete submission of the Importer Security Filing.

5. What should I do when I file my ISF and I receive an "Accepted" message with a subsequent "Bill Not on File" message?

Every Importer Security Filing must reference at least one bill of lading number (BOL) at the lowest level transmitted to CBP in AMS (i.e., house bill or regular/simple bill). The BOL number is part of the customs manifest information that is already required to be transmitted to CBP by the carrier or automated NVOCC in AMS 24 hours prior to vessel lading of cargo destined to the U.S.

The return message "Accepted, no Bill on File" means that the ISF was accepted but the BOL number listed as part of the ISF did not match to a house BOL or regular/simple BOL on file within AMS. There are a few common reasons why there may be a no bill on file message:

The ISF filing preceded the transmission of the customs manifest information. In these cases, CBP will send out a match message as soon as the manifest data is received in AMS and the BOL number and BOL type match to the BOL number and BOL type referenced on the ISF.

The BOL number referenced on the ISF may contain a typographical error. In these cases, please check again with the parties that provided the BOL information. In addition, there is a query in ABI that can confirm whether or not a BOL number currently exists in AMS. CBP is working on improving this query. In the near future, CBP will also provide the BOL type (i.e., house, regular/simple or master) and whether or not an ISF is currently on file against a particular bill.

The BOL type referenced on the ISF does not match the BOL type in AMS.

Please do not send in a replace (amended) ISF to in order to try and force a match message as these types of actions could potentially impact your compliance profile. If you have gone through all these steps and you are confident that the BOL number transmitted as part of your ISF is the lowest level BOL in AMS, the correct bill type code was referenced, and your VOC or NVOCC transmitted the manifest information in AMS, you can contact your CBP Client Representative for assistance.

Bonds

A. General:
1. Will CBP phase in bond enforcement and will CBP's systems have bond edits in place January 26, 2010?

    Bonds are now required for most ISF filings (i.e., ISF Types 1, 2, 7, 8, 10). CBP's systems will soon have specific bond edits in place to enforce these new requirements.

2. How will a bond for an ISF be filed in cases where an importer, or its agent, does not have a continuous bond? How will this actually work? Will there be paperless single transaction bonds for ISF purposes?

    The ISF Importer, or its agent, will need to obtain a bond. The ISF Importer, or its agent, may obtain a continuous bond (type 1, 2, 3 or 4) or an Appendix D stand-alone ISF bond (single-transaction or continuous).

3. If an agent allows his bond to be obligated, is he considered the ISF Importer with all of the liabilities associated with the ISF filing?

   If an agent is submitting an ISF on behalf of another party and the agent posts its own bond, the agent agrees to have its own bond charged if there are breaches of obligations regarding the filing. However, the ISF Importer remains ultimately liable for the complete, accurate, and timely ISF filing.

4. Does an importer have to have the ISF stand-alone bond to be an ISF Importer?

   An importer does not have to have the ISF stand-alone bond to be an ISF Importer.

5. Will CBP accept one bond for the ISF filing and a second bond for entry? Is this true for a continuous bond as well as Single Transaction Bonds?

   Yes. CBP will accept one bond for the ISF filing and a separate bond for entry. However, if the ISF Importer and the Importer of Record are the same party and the ISF and entry are submitted to CBP via the same electronic transmission ("unified filing option"), that party must submit one bond that secures both the ISF and the entry.

6. If a unified entry filing (i.e., combined entry & ISF filing) is sent, does the bond obligated on the entry cover both the entry and the ISF? Is this true for both continuous bonds and single transaction bonds? If so does the limit of liability remain the same as it is now?

   Yes, the bond covers both. This is true for both continuous and single transaction bonds. The limits of liability are not changed by this rulemaking.

7. How will ISF bonding requirements be determined when the value of the cargo is unknown?

   The amount of the ISF bond is not based on the value of the cargo.

8. The interim final rule states that "CBP will enforce the importer security filing, vessel stow plan, and container status message requirement, through the assessment of liquidated damages, in addition to penalties applicable under other provisions of law." Can you give us an example of the types of penalties you had in mind in this regard. (Reference: 71760 - 3rd column, 3rd paragraph)

   Penalty statutes available to CBP include 19 U.S.C. 1595a(b) and 1436, depending upon the facts and circumstances of the violation. Penalty assessment and mitigation guidelines have been published in the CBP Bulletin. A copy of the "10+2" Mitigation Guidelines can be found in the legal bulletins section on the CBP.gov web site at the following location:

http://www.cbp.gov/linkhandler/cgov/trade/legal/bulletins_decisions/
bulletins_2009/vol43_07172009_no28/43genno28.ctt/43genno28.pdf
The guidelines begin on page 29 and end on page 41.

9. How does the agent agree in writing to allow its bond to be used for an importer who doesn't have a bond and why is this necessary? Is there draft language for such "agreement"? Will the agreement be acceptable on a per-ISF basis, a blanket basis, or either (at the filer's option)? (Reference: Page 71745 – 3rd column top of the IFR)

   The written agreement can be a power of attorney or other similar document. The agreement must make it clear that the agent is granting the ISF importer the authority to use its bond for ISF purposes. CBP will not intervene in how this agreement is to be drawn up.

10. The interim final rule provides that every ISF Filer/Importer must have a Basic Importation Bond under which the principal agrees to comply with the new provisions of part 149. To the extent that many ISF Filers/Importers have existing bonds, how does CBP intend to enforce this provision when the existing bonds do not contain this language? Is CBP suggesting that ISF Filers/Importers will need to obtain bond riders to reflect this change? How will CBP monitor compliance with this new bond requirement?

    All existing activity 1, 2, 3, and 4 bonds now contain this language. Riders are unnecessary.

11. Additions to bond regulations for type 1, 2, 3, and 4 (19 CFR §§ 113.62, 113.63, 113.64, & 113.73) provide for liquidated damages in the amount of $5,000 per violation in the event of a default in connection with ISF filing requirements. However, the ISF stand alone Continuous Bond (Appendix D bond) provides for payment of "any amount prescribed by law or regulation upon demand by CBP." Why is this provision different from the others? When asserting a claim against an ISF Continuous Bond, what law(s)/regulation(s) will CBP cite?

    The language in the Appendix D bond is different because the laws or regulations governing assessed amounts might change and the bond language will not need to be amended. The liquidated damages provisions covering ISF violations in 19 CFR §§ 113.62, 113.63, 113.64, & 113.73 govern. See p. 71781 of the Interim Final Rule.

12. Will you consider how to apply liquidated damages if two filings have been done and where one is correct and the other one is incorrect?

    There is a breach as to the incorrect filing. It will be a matter of enforcement discretion as to whether liquidated damages will be assessed.

13. Given the potential for rapid and substantial accumulation of liability, will CBP consider a prohibition or limit on customs brokers posting their bond(s) to secure the ISF?

    There is no current plan to impose such a prohibition or limit.

14. If the importer does not have a bond, can the filer obligate its own bond? Yes, the filer can obligate its own bond. See 19 CFR 149.5(b)

15. Will an import bond rider be required to fulfill the regulatory changes required in the ISF rule?

    No. The Rule amends the terms and conditions of the activity code 1 (basic importation), 2 (custodial), 3 (international carrier) and 4 (foreign trade zone operator) bonds to include the obligation to meet ISF filing requirements. No rider is necessary for any of these bonds.

16. What is the statute of limitations for liquidated damages for ISF violations? Will CBP consider making this consistent with the bond obligation for entry (i.e., one year)?

    Pursuant to 28 U.S.C. § 2415, the statute of limitations for ISF liquidated damages is six years from the date of the breach of the bond. CBP will not limit its authority to enforce the ISF requirements.

B. Continuous Bonds

   Type 1, 2, 3, and 4 (19 CFR §§ 113.62, 113.63, 113.64, & 113.73) (CBP Form 301))

   1. Is my current continuous bond sufficient to file an ISF?

      Yes, if you have a valid activity 1, 2, 3, or 4 continuous bond.

   2. Can the custodial bond (Type 2) be used for all of the ISF requirements?

      Yes.

   3. Can I use an FTZ bond to file an ISF for a shipment that is not being entered into an FTZ?

      Yes.

C. Single Transaction Bonds

   Type 1, 2, 3, and 4 (19 CFR §§ 113.62, 113.63, 113.64, & 113.73) (CBP Form 301))

   1. Can a single transaction bond (CBP Form 301) be used as a stand-alone ISF bond?

      No. A single transaction bond that is submitted on the CBP Form 301 secures the entry, payment of duties, etc. Only the Appendix D stand-alone ISF bond can be used as a stand-alone single transaction ISF bond.

2. Can a single transaction bond (CBP Form 301) be utilized when making a unified entry filing?

Yes. But the single transaction bond (CBP Form 301) may only be used in conjunction with a unified entry filing. In these cases, the single transaction bond will be used to cover both the ISF and customs entry requirements. Additionally, the single transaction bond (CBP Form 301) may only be used when the ISF Importer is the same as the Importer of Record.

3. As single transaction bonds for entry require a paper submission to CBP, how will a single transaction bond for a unified entry and submitted on the CBP Form 301 be matched to an electronic ISF filing? What is the process of notifying CBP that a single transaction bond is actually on file?

For ISF purposes, use of single transaction bonds using the CBP Form 301 is only allowed with the unified entry filing. If a single transaction bond is used, the ISF Importer must denote the usage of the single transaction bond on the ISF by identifying activity type 01 (basic importation), bond type 9 (single transaction), the surety code and the bond reference number. The bond reference number is a unique serial number that appears on CBP Form 301 and is used for surety company tracking purposes. It should be noted that this is not the same as the "Bond Number assigned by CBP", which is found in the "CBP use only" block.

In addition, the unique ISF transaction number should be noted in block 29 of the CBP Form 3461, customs entry, upon paper document submission to CBP for unified entry filings. This will alert CBP that the single transaction bond covers both the ISF and the entry.

4. How will the limit of liability be determined for a single transaction bond that secures a unified entry filing?

CBP will issue guidance after discussion with interested trade groups.

D. Appendix D Stand-Alone ISF Bonds:
  1. When is the final draft of the new Appendix D bond expected?

The amended 'Appendix D' bond was published in the 12/24/09 Federal Register notice.

2. Is the Appendix D bond expected to be used primarily for single entry bond importers (this is what we suspect)? Will the Appendix D bond also be used by bond holders who have a basic importation bond that is deemed insufficient to cover Importer Security Filing bond needs, or will continuous bond holders be required to increase their continuous activity code 1/2/3/4 bond?)

   The Appendix D bond may be used as a single or a continuous bond. The bond limits of liability were not changed by the rulemaking.

3. Will CBP create a new bond activity code for the Appendix D stand-alone bond?

   Yes. The Appendix D ISF bond will be designated as activity code "16".

4. How will the limit of liability be determined for an Appendix D stand-alone single transaction ISF bond?

   The bond amount for the Appendix D stand-alone ISF bonds will be $10,000.

5. How will the limit of liability be determined for an Appendix D stand-alone continuous ISF bond?

   The minimum bond amount for the continuous Appendix D bonds has been set at $50,000.

6. Under what circumstances will CBP require or allow the new Appendix D ISF stand- alone continuous bond in lieu of an Activity Code 1, 2, 3, or 4 continuous bond, or single transaction bond?

   If a party has a continuous Activity Code 1, 2, 3 or 4 (19 CFR §§ 113.62, 113.63, 113.64, & 113.73) bond, it needs to do nothing further with regard to bonding requirements. It has appropriate bonding so as to be eligible to submit ISF information. The decision to take out a bond on the CBP Form-301 with one of the noted Activity Codes or an Appendix D stand-alone ISF bond is one to be made between the bond principal and surety. CBP will accept either.

7. How should the ISF Importer or its agent provide a copy of the Appendix D stand-alone single transaction ISF bond to CBP?

   CBP requires that an electronic copy of the Appendix D stand-alone single transaction ISF bond be created and sent to CBP within 12 hours of receipt of an accepted ISF filing.

   Step 1: The ISF Importer, or its agent, must denote the usage of the Appendix D stand-alone single transaction ISF bond on the ISF by identifying bond activity code 16, bond type 9 (single transaction), the valid surety code and the bond reference number.

The bond reference number is the unique serial number issued by the surety that appears on the bond for surety company tracking purposes. This number ensures that CBP will not receive the same bond twice for multiple transactions.

Step 2: After CBP has received and accepted the ISF, the ISF filer will receive a unique ISF transaction number from CBP. The ISF Importer, or its agent, must affix a legible copy of the ISF transaction number (e.g., typed and of a font size 12) onto the Appendix D stand-alone ISF bond.

Step 3: An electronic copy of the bond containing the unique ISF transaction number must be created in a .pdf or .tif format and e-mailed to the ISF_Bond@cbp.dhs.gov mailbox within 12 hours of receipt of the unique ISF transaction number.

Note: The subject line of the e-mail must begin with "ISF" followed by the unique ISF transaction number (and only the unique ISF transaction number). Only 1 bond should be sent per transmission.

8. How should the ISF Importer or its agent provide a copy of the Appendix D stand-alone continuous ISF bond to CBP?

Appendix D stand-alone continuous ISF bonds must be submitted to, and approved by CBP's Office of Finance in advance of the filing of an ISF. Once approved, CBP will record the bond information within the Automated Commercial System (ACS) and issue a unique bond identification number.

Upon the filing of an ISF, the ISF Importer, or its agent, must denote the usage of the Appendix D stand-alone continuous ISF bond on the ISF by identifying the bond activity code 16, bond type 8 (continuous) and the importer ID number that the bond was recorded against.

E. Exemptions:
1. I do not have to secure my informal entry with a bond today. Will CBP provide for any exemptions to the bond requirements for the ISF?

The Interim Final Rule does not provide any exemptions to the bond requirements.

However, as a matter of policy, certain types of ISF coded transactions will not require a bond to cover the ISF filing requirements. The bond requirements have been waived for the following ISF coded transactions:

Type 3 Household Goods/Personal Effects
Type 4 Government and Military
Type 5 Diplomatic
Type 6 Carnets
Type 9 International Mail
(See also Coded Transactions)

Bulk and Break Bulk

(See also EXEMPTIONS)

1. Existing rules exempt bulk and some break-bulk cargoes (e.g., most forest, steel products) from the 24-Hour Rule reporting requirements. Please advise if these commodities are exempt from the new "10+2" rules as well.

   Bulk cargo is exempt from the ISF filing, vessel stow plan and container status messages requirements.

   Break-bulk shipments, while exempt from the vessel stow plan and CSM requirements, require the filing of an ISF.*

   For the purposes of the Importer Security Filing rule, the following definition will be used for bulk cargo:

   "Homogenous cargo that is stowed loose in the hold and is not enclosed in any container such as a box, bale, bag, cask, or the like. Such cargo is also described as bulk freight. Specifically, bulk cargo is composed of either: (A) free flowing articles such as oil, grain, coal, ore, and the like which can be pumped or run through a chute or handled by dumping; or (B) uniform cargo that stows as solidly as bulk cargo and requires mechanical handling for lading and discharging."

   *Customs and Border Protection (CBP), Cargo & Conveyance Security (CCS), has determined that the following list of commodities and commodity types can be classified as bulk cargo. To be classified as bulk, this cargo may not be containerized and must be easily identifiable as laden on the vessel. Any bundling of the following commodities must only be for the purposes of securing the cargo. This list may be changed and updated as deemed appropriate by CBP.

   - Coils of steel and other metals
   - Rails of steel and other metals
   - Wire rods of steel and other metals (may be coiled or flat)
   - Ingots of metal (precious or otherwise)
   - Round bars of steel or other metal
   - Deformed Bars/Rebars (of metal)
   - Plates (of metal)
   - Billets (of metal)
   - Slabs (of metal)
   - Pipes (of metal)
   - Beams (of metal)
   - Tubes/Tubing (of metal)
   - Angles, shapes and sections (of metal)
   - Sheets (of metal)

- Expanded metal
- Flat bars (of metal)
- Strand wire (of metal)
- Sawn Timber/Lumber as a commodity (not as packaging material)
- Paperboard/Fiberboard/Plywood as a commodity (not as packaging material)
- Paper products as commodity (wood pulp, newsprint and paper rolls and not as packaging material)
- Certain perishable goods, not in boxes, bags or containerized, and not frozen, but laden and stowed in a way similar to other types of bulk cargo (includes seafood and produce)
- Blooms (similar to "billets and of metal)
- Anodes/Cathodes, in sheets only (may be corrugated)

2. Existing rules exempt bulk and certain break-bulk cargoes (e.g. most forest and steel products) from the 24-hour timing requirements of the 24-Hour Manifest Rule. Please advise if these shipments are exempt from the new rules as well.

Break-bulk cargo that is exempt from the timing requirements of the 24-Hour Rule are automatically exempt from the timing requirements of the ISF filing. ISFs for break-bulk cargo that are exempt from the timing requirements of the 24-Hour Rule must be filed no later than 24 hours prior to arrival.

Only carriers may apply for and receive an exemption to the 24-Hour Manifest Rule for break-bulk cargo. Please review the latest information on the 24-Hour Manifest Rule, including definitions of bulk and break-bulk cargo at the following link:

http://www.cbp.gov/linkhandler/cgov/trade/trade_outreach/advance_info/vessel_faq.ctt/vessel_faq.doc

The preferred method of requesting an exemption is through email. Requests may be submitted to:

24hour.exemptions@dhs.gov

Exemption requests may be mailed to U.S. Customs and Border Protection, Cargo and Conveyance Security, Room 2.2-A, Attention: NTCC, 1300 Pennsylvania Avenue, NW, Washington, D.C. 20229.

Generally, exemption processing takes approximately two to three weeks for a complete review.

The following information should be supplied in order to be considered for an exemption (per 19 CFR 4.7(b)(4)(ii)(A)): The carrier's IRS number; the source, identity and means of the packaging or bundling of the commodities being shipped; the ports of call both foreign and domestic; the number of vessels the carrier uses to transport break bulk cargo, along with the names of the vessels and their International Maritime Organization numbers;

and the list of the carrier's importers and shippers, identifying any who are members of C-TPAT (Customs-Trade Partnership Against Terrorism). CBP reserves the right to request any additional information it deems necessary and appropriate to ensure adequate compliance with 19 CFR 4.7(b)(4) and to perform necessary national security risk analysis. NOTE: Any cargo stowed in containers, including containers referred to as "ship's convenience," will be considered general cargo. No such containerized cargo will be exempt from the manifesting reporting requirements. For example, palletized boxes of bananas (not loose or loaded directly into a hold) stowed in shipping containers will be treated the same as all containerized cargo requiring information to be submitted 24 hours prior to loading.

3. Is an ISF required for roll-on roll-off (RORO) cargo?

Yes. RoRo cargo is considered break-bulk and thus requires an ISF.

4. My question is regarding break-bulk cargo, specifically Chilean produce. We handle fruit that is imported on break-bulk vessels. Many times the holds of the vessel are filled to capacity. So the excess produce is loaded into *"ship's convenience"* (meaning that although the importer did not book containers, the steamship line loaded the fruit in containers), which are lashed on the deck. Is the fruit in the containers (on the break-bulk vessel) still considered break-bulk, exempt to the 24 hours prior to loading; or is it now considered containerized, subject to the 24 hours prior to loading?

Cargo placed in a container, even for "ship's convenience," is containerized cargo and requires an ISF. This is consistent with CBP's advance cargo declaration requirements as per the Trade Act of 2002 for cargo stored for "ship's convenience." See, http://www.cbp.gov/linkhandler/cgov/trade/trade_outreach/

advance_info/vessel_faq.ctt/vessel_faq.doc.

5. Does this new rule engage the shipment and imports of liquid cargoes (mainly crude oil) to ports or unloading offshore designated areas of the U.S., or does it only affect the import of containerized cargoes?

Bulk shipments (dry or liquid) are outside the scope of the rulemaking.

Carnets

1. I am curious as to how containerized import shipments traveling under a carnet are to be handled in regards to Commodity HTS numbers. Goods shipped under a carnet are required to be described on the General List, which is part of the carnet, but does not require the application of HTS numbers. When the final rule is ultimately in effect, will carnet goods now require classification pre-shipment?

Carnets are not exempted from the ISF requirements, including the six-digit HTS number.

2. What will the coded transaction for carnets look like? Will carnets need to be bonded?

Bonds will not be required for these types of transactions.

Carnets can be handled using a "Type 06" ISF filing. In most cases, CBP expects that a U.S. based agent will act as the ISF Importer on behalf of the actual ISF Importer.

For example:

ISF Type "06" Carnet Filing Guidelines

ISF Filer	ABI or AMS filer code
ISF Type:	06 "Carnet"
Carnet Issuing Country:	ISO Country Code (e.g., US)
Carnet Number:	Required for US (Optional for non-US)
ISF Importer: Agent or Importer	IRS#, CAN#, SSN
ISF Bond Holder: Not required	Exempt per policy
Bill of Lading Numbers(s)	SCAC/bill number(s) of the lowest AMS bill of lading number(s)
1. Importer of Record #: Agent or Importer	IRS#, CAN#, SSN if previously registered with CBP (CBP Form 5106) or passport number, country of issuance and date of birth 26
2. Importer of Record #: Agent or Importer	IRS#, CAN#, SSN (CBP will not permit the use of a passport number in lieu of an IRS#, CAN# or SSN#.)
3. Consignee #: "US Rock Band"	IRS#, CAN#, SSN or passport number, country of issuance and date of birth

4. Buyer (Owner): "US Rock Band" Name and address or IRS# or SSN if already on file with CBP (via CBP Form 5106)

5. Seller (Owner): "US Rock Band" Name and address or IRS# or SSN if already on file with CBP (via CBP Form 5106)

6. Ship to Parties: Name and Addresses of locations to be visited in the U.S. example: "Las Vegas Casino"

7. Manufacturer (Supplier): "US Rock Band" Name of company owning the goods and last foreign address.

8. Country of Origin:	ISO codes of all countries previously visited with under this carnet.

9. HTS Codes:	Generic 6-digit HTS codes that describe the general nature of the goods:
	For traveling theaters and trade shows,
	HTSUS codes of: 95089000 "Merry-go-rounds, boat-swings, shooting galleries and other fairground amusements; traveling theaters; parts and accessories thereof" and 90230000 "Instruments, apparatus and models, designed for demonstrational purposes, unsuitable for other uses, and parts and accessories thereof" are accepted.
	For rock bands, use 9208900040 for "Musical instruments NSPF"
10. Consolidator (Stuffer):	Follow normal requirements.
11. Container Stuffing Location:	Follow normal requirements.

Client Representatives (CBP)

1. Who do we contact at CBP if we are having system problems?

Parties should contact their assigned CBP Client Representative if they have any questions or are experiencing problems. If one has not yet been assigned, please call the general CBP Client Representative number at 571-468-5500.

Coded Transactions

CBP has programmed its system to accept 9 different ISF-10 Transaction types. More types will be added as needed (e.g., Type 10 for OCS shipments).

01 Standard	This transaction type covers the vast majority of commercial shipments.
02 Ship To	Should be used for shipments that have not yet been sold to a buyer in the U.S. Typically used for commodities shipments (e.g., coffee beans, cocoa, etc.).
03 HHG/PE	Should be used for all household goods & personal effects shipments. This includes shipments for returning military members, other U.S. governmental personnel and their families. No bond is required.
04 Gov't. & Military	Only to be used for actual government or military shipments and not the personal effects or household goods of individual government personnel. No bond is required.

05 Diplomatic	Only to be used by foreign entities entitled to diplomatic immunity. Returning U.S. diplomatic personnel are not entitled to use this transaction type. No bond is required.
06 Carnet	Covers shipments arriving under a carnet. No bond is required.
07 U.S. Goods	Reserved for shipments containing solely U.S. Goods Returned.
08 FTZ	Shipments Reserved for shipments going into a Foreign Trade Zone.
09 International Mail	Reserved for USPS mail shipments. No bond is required.
10 OCS Shipments	Reserved for shipments arriving from a U.S. outer continental shelf point or from vessels operating over a U.S. OCS point (e.g. rigs, derrick barges, seismic vessels).

A. Regular Shipments (ISF Type 01):

    1. I noticed there are several "types" of security filings. Which one should I use?

        The answer depends on the type of entry at issue. The most common ISF transaction type is the "Type 01" which is for most consumption entries. However, shipments that are expected to be sold prior to U.S. arrival should be filed under the ISF "Type 02" also known as the "To Order" ISF filing.

B. To Order Shipments (ISF Type 02):

    1. How do I handle shipments sold on the water?

        The ISF will need to be updated if the shipment is sold in transit. At a minimum, the ISF Importer must notify CBP that the goods have been sold, and the party must update the Buyer (Owner) field and any other field of which they are aware. The ISF Importer remains liable for the timing and accuracy of the ISF filing.

  C. Household Goods and Personal Effects (Informal Shipments) (ISF Type 03):

    1. Can CBP please explain in more detail how household goods and personal effects shipments can be handled? I act as an agent for several hundreds of these shipments per month. Typically, these shipments are on one bill of lading and are co-loaded in the same container. Can I provide my own IRS# as the "Importer of Record#" as long as I provide my clients information in the "Consignee#" field?

        Household goods (HHG) and personal effects (PE) can be handled by using a coded transaction type "03" filing. In this question the agent becomes the ISF Importer and would provide its own Importer of Record # as long as all of the actual consignees are properly identified within the ISF filing.

        Please note that this type of filing should also be used for household goods and personal effects shipments for returning members of the U.S. military, other U.S. government agencies, and their families. U.S. citizens working in a diplomatic capacity abroad must also meet these requirements. (see also Diplomatic Shipments)

2. Can the "Type 03 HHG/PE" coded transaction be used for personal use automobiles?

Yes. For automobiles or motorcycles, use an HTS from Chapter 87 such as 8703.21 (autos) and 8711.30 (motorcycles).

3. I purchased some large souvenirs on a recent vacation overseas and was not able to take them on the airplane with me. The bronze statues I purchased are for my own personal use and not for resale. Can I file a "Type 3 ISF" for these types of non-commercial shipments?

Yes. The "Type 3" ISF can be used to cover non-commercial shipments of this nature.

ISF Type "03" HHG/PE Filing Guidelines

ISF Filer:	ABI or AMS Filer Code
ISF Type:	03 "HHG/PE"
ISF Importer:	Agent or Importer IRS# 95-XXXXXXXXX
ISF Bond Holder:	EXEMPT per policy
Bill of Lading Numbers(s):	SCAC/bill number(s) of the lowest AMS bill of lading number(s)
1. Importer of Record #: Agent or Importer	IRS#, CAN#, SSN if previously registered with CBP (CBP Form 5106) or passport number, country of issuance and date of birth
2. Consignee # for John Smith	SSN XXX-XX-XXXX or passport number, country of issuance, and date of birth
Consignee # for Jane Smith	SSN YYY-YY-YYYY or passport number, country of issuance, and date of birth
Consignee # for Jan Doe	SSN ZZ-ZZ-ZZZZ or passport number, country of issuance, and date of birth
3. Buyer (Owner):	Owner's name and new address in the United States. Or IRS# or SSN if already on file with CBP (via CBP Form 5106)
4. Seller (Owner):	Owner's name and last foreign address
5. Ship to Parties:	Generally, the importer's new address in the United States.
6. Manufacturer (Supplier):	Owner's last foreign address.
7. Country of Origin:	Country code from Owner's last foreign address

8. HTS Codes:	Generic 6-digit HTS codes that describe the general nature of the goods:
	9804.00 for household goods and personal effects
	9805.00 for personal effects of U.S. Gov't extended duty employees & family or evacuees
9. Consolidator (Stuffer):	Follow normal requirements.
10. Container Stuffing Location:	Follow normal requirements.

D. Government and Military

E. Diplomatic: see Diplomatic Shipments

F. Carnets: see Carnets

G. U.S. Goods Returned: see U.S. Goods Returned

H. FTZ Shipments

I. International Mail Shipments

J. Outer Continental Shelf (OCS) Shipments: see Outer Continental Shelf (OCS)

Confidentiality

1. Will any of the new data that is being submitted be considered to be part of the carrier "manifest" and thereby become public record? Does CBP have a form that can be filled out to request confidentiality of ISF information?

   ISF information is not considered part of the carrier manifest. Pursuant to 19 CFR 103.31a, Importer Security Filing information that is electronically presented to CBP for inbound vessel cargo is per se exempt from disclosure under § 103.12(d), unless CBP receives a specific request for such records pursuant to § 103.5, and the owner of the information expressly agrees in writing to its release.

   (Also see the powers of attorney section)

2. Will the importer have access to carrier's data (CSMs and stow plans)?
   No.

Contact Information (CBP)

1. What type of assistance will CBP provide the trade to help us through this new process? Will there be a phone number available for general help?

   CBP will provide assistance to the trade via extensive outreach and postings on the CBP.gov Web site. In addition, National Account Managers and

Client Representatives are available to assist the trade. Parties may submit questions about the general application of the new requirements to CBP via the Security_Filing_General@cbp.dhs.gov mailbox. Questions relating to specific facts and circumstances of a prospective transaction can be the subject of a ruling request under Part 177 of the CBP regulations.

Container Status Messages (CSM)

1. How do you know that the repaired container will eventually be scheduled for the U.S.? How would this reporting requirement be complied with? Is the repair only required to show a CSM when the container is issued against a booking?

   The decision of whether a container is destined to arrive within the limits of a port in the United States is made by the carrier.

Cruise Vessels and ISF

1. Are ISFs required for non bulk cargo carried on a passenger vessel?

   Passenger vessels that are required to file cargo declarations (CBP Form 1302) must file ISFs as to the same cargo. However, ISFs are not required for ship's equipment.

2. Are vessel stow plans required for passenger vessels?

   A vessel stow plan is required if there are containers onboard the vessel.

3. How will vessel supplies for immediate exportation (VSIE) goods be handled? For example, liquor being stored in an FTZ on U.S. soil being laden on an outgoing vessel.

   Domestic cargo (whether of U.S. origin, or of foreign origin and having been formally entered), including cargo intended for repair or emergency work, that is transported between CBP ports, or other places within the customs territory of the United States, including an OCS facility, is not subject to Importer Security Filing requirements.

Data Elements (General)

1. Repeat Data: In many of our transactions, a single entity may be the same for several of the different required ISF elements. For instance, the "Seller (Owner) Name and Address" might be the same as the "Manufacturer (Supplier) Name and Address." Likewise, the "Buyer (Owner) Name & Address" might be the same entity as the "Importer of Record Number." Is it ok to repeat the same information if the entities are the same?

   Yes. If the information is exactly the same, it may be provided multiple times to cover the required ISF elements.

Data Elements (Specific)

A. Importer of Record Number:
   1. Can the importer of record number be a CBP assigned number?

      Yes. The Internal Revenue Service (IRS) number, Employer Identification Number (EIN), Social Security Number (SSN), or CBP assigned number of the entity liable for payment of all duties and responsible for meeting all statutory and regulatory requirements incurred as a result of importation must be provided. However, the consignee number is the IRS number, EIN, SSN, or CBP assigned number of the individual(s) or firm(s) in the United States on whose account the merchandise is shipped.

   2. What identification number is required for parties without U.S. social security numbers shipping household goods?

      In this instance, the passport number, passport country of issuance and date of birth will be accepted.

   3. Can a foreign entity be identified as the *Importer of Record Number*?

      Yes. However, a U.S. entity must be provided for the consignee number element.

B. Consignee Number:
   1. What identification number is required for parties without U.S. social security numbers shipping household goods?

      In this instance, the passport number, passport country of issuance, and date of birth will be accepted.

   2. The ISF-10 record asks for a Consignee. According to the ISF Implementation Guide, for unified entry, the EI-10 record is used to report the Ultimate Consignee, not Consignee. Are we to presume that the Ultimate Consignee and Consignee are the same?

      Yes, in this instance the Ultimate Consignee and Consignee must be the same.

C. Ship to Party:
   1. If the container has to be devanned in more than one location (i.e. container does multiple stops after arriving in the U.S. and drops cargo off at each location), does 10+2 require listing of all locations for the ship to addresses? You may see this scenario where it is one company but has multiple divisions underneath it. Thus, there would be only one BL reflecting the IOR but several separate divisions under the one IOR. What would CBP want to see as the ship to location—the first ship to location or all?

      Pursuant to new 19 CFR 149.3(a)(6), the name and address of the first deliver-to party scheduled to physically receive the goods after the goods have been released from customs custody must be provided. ISF

Importers are not required to provide subsequent ship to parties, however, they may do so if they choose.

2. Who should be listed as the "Ship to Party" when a shipment is shipped to a distribution facility that is owned by one company and operated by another related company?

    Pursuant to new 19 CFR 149.3(a)(6), the name and address of the first deliver-to party scheduled to physically receive the goods after the goods have been released from customs custody must be provided. The party physically receiving the goods must be provided and not an entity that merely owns the facility.

3. Please provide clarification regarding the data element "ship-to name and address." It would be helpful to have explanatory examples. The requirement is for the name and address of the first deliver-to party scheduled to physically receive the goods *after the goods have been released from Customs custody.*

    Please address the following scenarios:

    a. Full container load (FCL) cargo clears prior to arrival at the port of discharge. Is the terminal/pier the ship-to, since the cleared freight is no longer in customs custody? How would the ISF filer know this 24 hours prior to lading?

        In this scenario, the terminal was not the first deliver-to party scheduled to physically receive the goods after the goods have been released from Customs custody. Rather, the party who, at the time of ISF filing, was scheduled to physically receive the goods must be provided.

    b. FCL cargo moves inbond to an inland point by rail. After clearance at the inland port, the container is delivered to the ultimate consignee. Is the ship-to party the railroad, since they receive the cargo 1st after the freight leaves the pier, or is it the ultimate consignee since they receive the cargo first after Customs clearance?

        The bonded carrier should not be provided as the ship-to party. In this example, the identity of the ultimate consignee should be provided as the ship-to party.

    c. FCL or LCL cargo moves on a PTT to a CFS warehouse for transloading to trucks for delivery. The cargo clears Customs while at the CFS. Is the ship-to the CFS, or is it the ultimate consignee?

        The identity of the first deliver-to party scheduled to physically receive the goods after the goods have been released from Customs custody must be provided. In this instance, CBP wants the ultimate consignee's physical address where the goods are scheduled to be received.

D. Manufacturer (Supplier) Name/Address:
1. We import containers with thousands of parts, potentially having literally hundreds of different manufacturers, from a related party who, in turn, purchases the parts from those manufacturers. These parts may be commingled prior to importation. On the ISF filing, can we provide the identity of our related party to fulfill the Manufacturer (Supplier) ISF requirement, as this is the party from whom we actually buy the parts, or do we need to list all the manufacturer's individually?

 The party who supplied the goods can be provided as long as that party is a separate legal entity from the ISF Importer. If both of these parties are the same entity, the identity of the party who last manufactured, assembled, produced, or grew the commodity or the party who supplied the finished goods to the ISF Importer must be provided. Generally, the manufacturers provided on the CBP Form 3461 will satisfy the ISF requirement.

2. Please advise if we need to submit both the manufacturer and the supplier info on the 10+2 ISF filing. Or, will the supplier data be sufficient?

 The identity of the entity that last manufactures, assembles, produces, or grows the commodity *or* the name and address of the party supplying the finished goods in the country from which the goods are leaving must be provided. However, CBP would prefer that the identity of the actual manufacturer be provided where that entity is known.

3. Can the manufacturer (supplier) be a U.S. company?

 The manufacturer (supplier) can be U.S. a company if the party who last manufactured, assembled, produced, or grew (or supplied) the commodity is a U.S. company.

E. Country of Origin:
1. If the merchandise is assembled in one country but parts are from many other countries, which country of origin do I list?

 Generally, the country of origin for the imported product that is provided on the CBP Form 3461 will satisfy the ISF requirements.

2. Can you advise if the country of origin needs to be linked to each Harmonized Tariff Schedule of the United States (HTSUS) number or is it enough that the data is given electronically against each part number?

 The manufacturer (or supplier), country of origin, and commodity HTSUS number must be linked to one another at the line-item level. This linking is similar to the CBP Form 3461 requirements. Line-item linking is required at the ISF shipment level and not at the invoice, container, parts, or bill of lading level.

F. Commodity HTS-6:

1. When you talk about line-item linking requirement, are you talking at the HTS-6 digit level or at a SKU level on the commercial invoice from the manufacturer/supplier? I am asking as we have shipments from one manufacturer/supplier that might contain 100 different SKUs, but would only result in five HTS numbers.

   If the 100 different SKUs result in just five HTS numbers at the 6 digit level, the ISF Importer or their agent may provide the five HTS numbers. However, the manufacturer (or supplier), country of origin, and commodity Harmonized Tariff Schedule of the United States (HTSUS) number must be linked to one another at the line-item level. This linking is similar to the CBP Form 3461 requirements. Line-item linking is required at the ISF shipment level and not at the invoice, container, parts, or bill of lading level.

2. Parts: If an importer of parts brings in container loads of thousands of parts with multi manufacturers, country of origin, and Harmonized Tariff Schedule of the United States (HTSUS) numbers, do they upon filing the ISF have to show every part HTSUS number or can they show a general number such as 8714.190060, which is parts and accessories of motorcycles? The exact parts in the shipment may not be known upon filing the ISF and since 8714.190060 is specifically parts and accessories of motorcycles is it acceptable?

   The duty/statistical reporting number under which the article is classified in the HTSUS must be provided. The HTSUS number must be provided to the six digit level. The ISF Importer can submit an initial response or responses based on the best available data available at the time. However, the ISF must be updated as soon as more precise or more accurate information is available in no event less than 24 hours prior to arrival at a U.S. port (or upon lading at a foreign port that is less than a 24-hour voyage to the closest U.S. port).

3. FROB: How many HTS digits are required for foreign cargo remaining on board (FROB)?

   The commodity HTSUS number for FROB cargo must be provided to the six-digit level. The HTSUS number may be provided to the 10-digit level.

4. Garments on hangers: At the time of shipping, our electronic purchase orders that we provide to our overseas third party logistics provider (3PL) do not specify when garments will ship with hangers. Upon entry, however, our U.S. customs brokers have this information and classify the hangers separate from the garments because they qualify for the lower

duty treatment. For ISF purposes, do we need to provide the 6-digit HTS number for the hangers in addition to the HTS number for the garments that are hanging on them?

The ISF needs to include the 6-digit HTS number for the hangers if the ISF importer is aware of the existence of the hangers. If the ISF Importer is initially unaware that the hangers are shipped with the garments, then the ISF Importer should update the ISF as soon as they become aware of this information.

G. Container Stuffing Location:
   1. Regarding the Container Stuffing Location and Consolidator (Stuffer) (the 2 data elements that are to be filed as soon as possible, but no later than 24 hours prior to arrival)—is the timing flexibility just for the one-year flexible enforcement period?

   The flexibility as to timing for the Container Stuffing Location and Consolidator (Stuffer) elements will remain in place unless and until CBP determines that a change should be made. Interested persons are invited to submit written comments on the flexibility as to timing provided pursuant to the Interim Final Rule. CBP will consider these comments and, if CBP determines that a change to the flexibility as to timing is necessary, CBP will amend the regulations accordingly.

   2. If a single container is stuffed in multiple locations, can I enter all locations into the ISF?

   Yes. When a container is stuffed at more than one location and/or more than one container is on a single bill of lading, all of the stuffing locations for the goods listed on the bill of lading must be provided.

   3. The interim final rule states that for break bulk cargo, the Container Stuffing Location should be the party that made the goods "Ship ready." This term is somewhat vague when it comes to the shipping of motor vehicles on ro-ro vessels. Does "Ship ready" refer to the preparation for transport of the vehicle such as the application of protective tape and suspension blocks or does it refer to the actual movement onboard the vessel and lashing of the vehicle?

   "Ship ready" refers to the location(s) where the cargo is made ready (taped, banded, packaged, etc.) to be laden on the vessel. This could be the factory, terminal, intermediate warehouse, or other location.

   4. I need a simple way to explain what Container Stuffing Location & Consolidator (Stuffer) mean to my foreign shippers. Do you have anything that explains exactly what these 2 data elements are, and how my shippers can obtain the information, in simple terms?

Also, do you have a sample or mock-up of an ISF so that we can better understand what we'll be utilizing?

The container stuffing location(s) are the physical location(s) where the goods were stuffed into the container. This does not mean the location of the goods *within* the container. For break bulk shipments, this is the physical location(s) where the goods were made "ship ready."

The consolidator (stuffer) is the party who stuffed the container or arranged for the stuffing of the container. For break bulk shipments, this is the party who made the goods "ship ready" or arranged for the goods to be made "ship ready."

5. An export shipment is loaded into a container at a facility in Germany in which the brick and mortar, as well as the goods in the facility, are owned by Company AG. However, the facility is operated by a related firm, Company AG Logistics Services. Who would be listed as the "Container Stuffing Location" for the ISF? Company AG or Company AG Logistics Services?

    Provide the name of the operator of the facility and the address of the facility where the goods were stuffed into the container or made "ship ready."

H. Consolidator (Stuffer) Name/Address:
  1. Regarding the Container Stuffing Location and Consolidator (Stuffer) (the 2 data elements that are to be filed as soon as possible, but no later than 24 hours prior to arrival)—is the timing flexibility just for the one-year flexible enforcement period?

      The flexibility as to timing for the Container Stuffing Location and Consolidator (Stuffer) elements will remain in place unless and until CBP determines that a change should be made. If CBP determines that such a change is necessary, CBP will amend the regulations accordingly.

  2. If there are multiple stuffing locations and there are multiple consolidators, do all consolidators need to be listed? An example would be an NVOCC doing a milk run where it stops at multiple locations and the container is stuffed at each location by a different party. Would all stuffers need to be listed or just the party who arranged for the stuffing?

      In this scenario, the name of the party who arranged for the stuffing of the container should be provided.

  3. For a "Shipper Loaded" Container who is shipped by a manufacturer directly with the steamship line, who would be shown as the Consolidator or Stuffer?

If the manufacturer is the party who stuffed the container or arranged for the container to be stuffed, then the manufacturer is the consolidator (stuffer).

4. If I have one shipment going to one importer that has multiple containers which are stuffed by various consolidators, do I have to list them all as part of my ISF?

Yes. It is important to note that there can be more than one "Consolidator" involved in a transaction. CBP requires that if multiple "Consolidators" are involved (e.g., some co-load situations), multiple "Consolidators" need to be provided as part of the Importer Security Filing.

Unique ISF-5 Data Elements

I. Foreign Port of Unlading:

1. "Foreign port of unlading" is defined as the port code for the foreign port of unlading at the intended final destination. How should a location be reported when the location is not a port or when there is no port code associated with the destination?

If the intended final destination is not a port, or if there is no port code associated with the final destination, provide the nearest Schedule K code or UNLocode.

2. A vessel carrying transit cargo destined for Mexico departs from Hong Kong and discharges said cargo in Los Angeles, CA, USA. The cargo is then put on a truck bound for Laredo, TX, USA. The cargo exits the U.S. and enters Mexico at Nuevo Laredo, Mexico. The final destination of the cargo is Mexico City, Mexico. What do we use for the Foreign Port of Unlading?

For shipments that are being exported to Canada or Mexico via truck or rail, the UNLocode of the first foreign port of entry (or nearest city) after export from the United States may be used; in this case, MX LRD (the code for Nuevo Laredo) would be acceptable.

J. Place of Delivery:

1. A vessel carrying transit cargo destined for Mexico departs from Hong Kong and discharges said cargo in Los Angeles, CA, USA. The cargo is then put on a truck bound for Laredo, TX, USA. The cargo exits the U.S. and enters Mexico at Nuevo Laredo, Mexico. The final destination of the cargo is Mexico City, Mexico. What do we use for the "Place of Delivery?

In this case, the known "Place of Delivery" is Mexico City, Mexico (MX MEX)

Diplomatic Shipments (see coded transactions)

1. Can a returning U.S. diplomat, U.S. embassy personnel or other U.S. citizens working on behalf of the U.S. government use the Diplomatic Type 5 coded transaction?

    No. This shipment type is reserved for representatives of foreign governments and members of their families and their baggage and effects as provided for in 19 CFR 148.82.

    Returning U.S. personnel and their goods are not considered diplomatic shipments and are not eligible to use the Type 5 coded transaction.

2. Do bona fide diplomatic shipments require a bond to cover the ISF requirements?

    No.

3. What does the diplomatic type coded transaction look like? Must we provide all "10" ISF elements?

    Example of an ISF for a diplomatic shipment:

ISF Type "05" Diplomatic Shipment Guidelines

ISF Filer:	ABI or AMS Filer Code
ISF Type:	05 "Diplomatic"
ISF Importer: Agent or Imposter	IRS# of Agent or Customs Assigned Number (CAN#) of the foreign embassy or consulate in the United States
ISF Bond Holder:	EXEMPT per policy
Bill of Lading Numbers(s):	SCAC/bill number(s) of the lowest AMS bill of lading number(s)
1. Importer of Record #:	Agent or Importer IRS# of Agent or Customs Assigned Number (CAN#) of the foreign embassy or consulate in the United States
2. Consignee #	IRS# of Agent or Customs Assigned Number (CAN#) of the foreign embassy or consulate in the United States or passport number, country of issuance and date of birth of accepting party
3. Buyer (Owner):	The name and address of the foreign embassy or consulate in the United States. or the IRS#, CAN# of the foreign embassy or consulate in the United States
4. Seller (Owner):	The name and address of the foreign embassy or consulate in the United States. or the IRS#, CAN# of the foreign embassy or consulate in the United States

5. Ship to Parties:	Name and address of the party receiving the goods in the United States or the name and address of the foreign embassy or consulate in the United States. or the IRS#, CAN# of the foreign embassy or consulate in the United States
6. Manufacturer (Supplier):	Name and address of the foreign government
7. Country of Origin:	ISO country code of the foreign country
8. HTS Codes:	9806.00 Diplomatic effects/articles
9. Consolidator (Stuffer):	Follow normal requirements.
10. Container Stuffing Location:	Follow normal requirements.

Enforcement Measures

The full compliance (enforcement) date for the "10+2" requirements commenced on January 26, 2010, thus ending a 12-month flexible enforcement period during which CBP provided extensive outreach to educate the trade community on the new requirements.

As the flexible enforcement period has ended, the guiding principle is to exercise the least punitive measures available to obtain full compliance. In order to achieve maximum compliance with the least amount of disruption to the trade and to domestic port operations, CBP will apply a measured, common sense approach to enforcement. This deliberative approach towards enforcement should not be viewed by the trade community as a further extension of the structured review and flexible enforcement period.

At the outset, CBP will concentrate its enforcement efforts on importers who are not filing ISFs for U.S.-bound shipments. At the very least, non-compliant ISF Importers should expect to receive a warning and/or will experience delays in the release of their cargo while CBP analyzes and mitigates the potential risk of the cargo. At a minimum, non-compliant importers should expect their shipments to undergo non intrusive inspection (NII) exam upon arrival in the U.S.

As CBP's enforcement regime matures, non-compliant importers will continue to see increases in the amount of manifest holds and examinations, and will be subject to the greater use of stricter enforcement measures such as liquidated damages and do not load (DNL) holds. For C-TPAT companies that remain non-compliant, CBP will consider suspending, reducing and even revoking their C-TPAT status.

CBP will evaluate instances of non-compliance on a case-by-case basis and will consider factors surrounding potential violations before applying enforcement actions.

A. Do Not Load Messages:
1. If CBP issues a DNL for the ISF, how will the carrier know if it was because the ISF or manifest?

CBP will provide a message to the carrier via vessel AMS that the DNL was specifically due to the ISF.

B. Liquidated Damages:
1. Will CBP assess liquidated damages for multiple violations on one ISF?

    CBP will assess liquidated damages in accordance with the relevant mitigation guidelines which were published in the CBP Bulletin on July 17, 2009. While there may be multiple errors on an ISF transmission, in accordance with the guidelines, CBP may assess a claim for liquidated damages as follows: $5,000 per late ISF, $5,000 per inaccurate ISF, and $5,000 for the first inaccurate ISF update.

C. Mitigation Guidelines
1. Where can I find a copy of the ISF Mitigation Guidelines?

    The guidelines for the assessment and cancellation of claims for liquidated damages for failure to comply with the vessel stow plan, container status message, and importer security filing requirements were published in the Customs Bulletin on July 17, 2009 and are available through the link below.

    http://www.cbp.gov/linkhandler/cgov/trade/legal/bulletins_decisions/bulletins_2009/vol43_07172009_no28/43genno28.ctt/43genno28.pdf

Exemptions to ISF Requirements

A. 24-Hour Manifest Rule Exemptions (for "exempt" Break Bulk):
1. Existing rules exempt bulk and certain break-bulk cargoes (e.g. most forest and steel products) from the 24-hour timing requirements of the 24-Hour Rule. Please advise if these commodities are exempt from the new rules as well.

B. General ISF Requirements (Exemptions):
1. Are ISO tanks exempt from the ISF Requirements?

    ISO tanks are treated like any other containers. If the ISO tanks contain cargo, then they require the filing of an ISF. If the ISO tanks are empty (no residue), they do not require the filing of an ISF.
2. Are "containerized bulk" shipments exempt?

    No. Once cargo is placed in a container it can no longer be considered bulk cargo. See 19 CFR 4.7(b)(4)(i).
3. Are there any bond exemptions?

    Yes. (See Bonds)
4. What about outer continental shelf (OCS) shipments? Are they exempt from the ISF requirements?

    (See OCS shipments)

Flexible Enforcement Period (See also Enforcement Measures)

1. Is the flexibility (i.e., "acceptable range of responses" and "flexible timing") only for the flexible enforcement period or is it CBP's intent to keep the flexibility in the filing after the flexible enforcement period expires?

    The flexibility as to interpretation for the *Manufacturer (Supplier)*, *Ship to Party*, *Country of Origin*, and *HTSUS number*, and flexible timing provisions for the Consolidator (*Stuffer*) and/or *Container Stuffing Location* will remain in place unless and until CBP determines that a change should be made. If CBP determines that such a change is necessary, CBP will amend the regulations accordingly.

Identification Numbers

A. General:

1. Can you provide a list of all the widely recognized commercially accepted identification numbers for the ISF entities such as the buyer, seller, etc.?

    It was mentioned in the interim final rule that CBP will accept widely recognized commercially accepted identification numbers such as Dun and Bradstreet Data Universal Numbering System (DUNS) numbers. Are there any other numbers that will be accepted?

    CBP will allow the trade to provide widely recognized commercially accepted identification numbers such as DUNS numbers as an alternative to the name and address for the following elements: Seller, Buyer, Manufacturer (or supplier), Ship-to party, Container stuffing location, Consolidator (stuffer), and Booking party. In addition, CBP will accept Facilities Information and Resources Management System (FIRMS) codes for the ship-to party, when applicable. CBP will continue to consider, in coordination with the trade, accepting other widely recognized commercially accepted identification numbers.

B. DUNS:

1. Will CBP provide query functionality for DUNS numbers?
    No.

Implementation guides

CBP's most current implementation guides (data transaction sets) can be found at the following link:

   http://www.cbp.gov/xp/cgov/trade/automated/automated_systems/ sf_transaction_sets/

Informal Shipments (See also Coded Transactions)

A. General:
   1. Are ISFs required for informal shipments?
      Yes. ISFs are required for informal shipments.

B. Military Shipments:
   1. Are ISFs required for returning U.S. military household goods shipments?
      Yes. Please utilize the ISF "Type 03" Filing (See also Coded Transactions).

   2. Are bonds required for ISFs for U.S. military household goods shipments?
      No. The bond requirements for these types of shipments have been waived as a matter of policy.

   3. For U.S. military household goods, can the moving company contractor be the ISF Importer?
      Household goods and personal effects, including U.S. military household goods, can be handled by using a coded transaction type "03" filing. The agent can be the ISF Importer and provide its own importer of record number as long as all of the actual consignees are properly identified on the ISF filing.

C. Instruments Of International Trade (IIT):
   1. Are ship's equipment and carrier's intercompany moves exempt from the Importer Security Filing requirements?
      An Importer Security Filing is not required for ship's equipment. However, unless otherwise exempted, the ISF Importer must submit an Importer Security Filing for intercompany moves.

   2. Are ship's spares exempt from the ISF filing requirements?
      Yes.

   3. Is ship's equipment exempt from the ISF filing requirements?
      Yes.

   4. Are empty shipper (or importer) owned containers subject to the Importer Security filing requirements?
      No. But they must still be reported via vessel stow plans and container status messages where appropriate by the carrier.

ISF Filings

A. General:
   1. Can an ISF cover more than one vessel and voyage?
      No.

2. Is there going to be a paper ISF form?

   No. It is all electronic.

3. Since manifested quantity is not a part of the ISF filing, how will CBP handle multiple ISFs for one bill of lading?

   CBP will return a unique identification number for each unique ISF filing even if against the same bill of lading. (See also Unique Identification Number)

4. Can bills of lading on the same vessel and voyage for the same importer be combined in the same ISF if the ports of loading or discharge are different?

   An ISF filing covers a single "shipment" going to a single ISF Importer arriving on a single vessel voyage. While ISF filings may naturally match up with CBP Form 3461 entries, there is no actual requirement that they do so.

   ISFs are to be done at the "lowest" bill of lading level that has been (or will be) recorded in the vessel AMS system. CBP will accept an ISF at either the house bill of lading level or regular (i.e. simple, straight) bill of lading level. CBP will not accept ISFs that are filed against a Master bill of lading.

   Additionally, a single ISF may cover multiple bills of lading as long as they are all going to the same importer as part of the same shipment on the same vessel voyage.

5. It is possible to transmit one ISF for multiple bills of lading on the same vessel for one importer if they are one shipment. We see several possible scenarios here:

   • Multiple bills of lading for the same importer that will all be cleared under one entry

   • Multiple bills of lading for the same importer that will result in multiple entries for that importer

   The question now is does the word "shipment" mean entry as in example one? Or can the word shipment be applied to multiple entries as in example two? If the definition of "shipment" can be construed to mean example two, we are confused as to how we could file a combined ISF/entry. Would we simply pick any one of the entries and attach the ISF filing for all the bills of lading to that one?

   There are several possible filing options, as long as there is one shipment, one importer of record number, on the same vessel and same voyage number, including the following:

   ■ One ISF per bill of lading

   ■ One ISF to cover multiple bills of lading.

   ■ In a "unified entry" one ISF per entry regardless of the number of bills of lading (as long as these bills of lading are for the same shipment and are represented on the entry).

6. My company regularly imports to the U.S., Canada and Mexico; sometimes at the same time. At the time the ISF is required, we don't always know the specific destination for a particular shipment. For instance, sometimes the decision is made to divert a portion of a U.S. bound shipment to an FTZ or to Canada/Mexico after vessel sailing. In these cases, should I file an ISF-10 instead of an ISF-5 filing?

In these cases, an ISF-10 should be submitted. The ISF-10 must be updated at a later time with an ISF-5 if the decision is made to divert the shipment to Mexico or Canada via an IE or T&E or once better information becomes available prior to vessel arrival at the first U.S. port. However, if better information does not become available until after vessel arrival in the first U.S. port, the ISF importer is no longer bound to update the ISF-10 but may still do so at their discretion. As a matter of policy, updating an ISF-10 to an ISF-5 does not require Port Director approval. (See also Splits, Diversions and Rolling of Cargo)

B. Self Filer:
1. We currently use a broker to file our entry documents via the ABI interface. As an importer, is there a way to connect via the ACE system to only file the ISF-10? Will CBP create a Web portal in ACE so importers can file their own Importer Security Filings?

The ISF cannot be submitted through ACE at this time. However, CBP will continue to explore additional ISF functionality as ACE is developed.

C. Timing Requirements:
(See also Container Stuffing Location, Consolidator Name/Address)
1. Pursuant to the new regulations, some ISF elements must be submitted no later than 24 hours before the cargo is laden aboard the vessel at the foreign port. When cargo is first laden aboard a feeder vessel, are these elements required no later than 24 hours before the cargo is laden aboard the feeder vessel or the vessel destined to the United States? When are ISFs for FROB required?

For ISF elements that must be submitted no later than 24 hours before the cargo is laden aboard the vessel at the foreign port, the elements must be submitted no later than 24 hours before the cargo is laden aboard *a vessel destined to the United States*. Similarly, for FROB, the required elements must be submitted prior to lading aboard *a vessel destined to the United States*.

D. ISF-5 Filings:
1. On the I.E.'s and T&E's, are we required to transmit the inbond number prior to or at the same time the 5 additional elements are transmitted or can we transmit that later?

No. An inbond number is not required as part of the ISF.

2. Who is the responsible party for filing an ISF-5 for FROB? Who is responsible for filing the ISF-5 for IE and T&E shipments?

   Under the interim final rule, the party required to submit the Importer Security Filing is the party causing the goods to enter the limits of a port in the United States. This party is the carrier for FROB and the party filing for the immediate exportation (IE), transportation and exportation (T&E) for those types of shipments.

3. I am an automated NVOCC filing manifest data via AMS. Am I also responsible for submitting the ISF5 to CBP for FROB shipments? The IFR states that the carrier is the responsible party. However, NVOCCs are also specifically included as carriers under 19 CFR 4.7.

   As the Rule is currently written, the carrier, defined as the vessel operator, is responsible for filing the ISF-5 for FROB shipments. However, CBP is aware that NVOCCs are included as carriers in 19 CFR 4.7 but are not included as carriers in 19 CFR 149. CBP plans to address this issue through the regulatory process.

   Until such time as CBP addresses this issue, filers of ISF-5 FROB data will be treated with wide discretion by CBP relative to ISF enforcement issues, provided CBP receives the required ISF5 FROB data. In the interim, vessel operating carriers must submit the ISF-5 for FROB shipments if they have direct access to the data as the entity that received the booking directly from the shipper.

   In those instances where an NVOCC is filing manifest data via AMS, the NVOCC may file the ISF-5 for the appropriate transactions; and this action may be done without obtaining a power of attorney from the carrier. CBP will receive these transactions and process them using standard data edits and messaging.

   Carriers and NVOCCs will be operating under the same considerations as will importers and brokers during the graduated enforcement period for ISF.

E. ISF Territories of Coverage (Geographic):
   1. Are imports into Puerto Rico (ocean shipments from non-U.S. locations) subject to ISF/10+2 filing requirements?

      The rule covers cargo destined to arrive within the customs territory of the United States. Puerto Rico is part of the customs territory of the United States. Therefore, imports into Puerto Rico are subject to the filing requirements.

   2. Are shipments originating from a U.S. insular possession (such as U.S. Virgin Islands, American Samoa, or Guam) and being exported into the United States subject to the ISF/10+2 filing requirements?

Yes. U.S. insular possessions (such as U.S. Virgin Islands, American Samoa, or Guam) are not part of the customs territory of the United States.

3. Are ocean shipments from non-US locations into a U.S. insular possession (such as U.S. Virgin Islands, American Samoa, or Guam) subject to ISF/10+2 filing requirements?

No. U.S. insular possessions (such as U.S. Virgin Islands, American Samoa, or Guam) are not part of the customs territory of the United States.

F. ISF Areas of Coverage (Mode of Transport):
1. Are ISFs required for goods arriving in the U.S. via rail or truck? Will I need to do the ISF filing if my cargo will not be on a vessel until the point it is leaving the United States?

ISFs are only required for goods scheduled to arrive in the United States by vessel.

2. My goods are scheduled to arrive in Canada by vessel and will then be imported into the U.S. via truck or rail. While it's understood that an ISF is not required for shipments arriving into the U.S. via modes other than vessel, may I still file an ISF-10 for these shipments?

Yes, as long as there is an associated bill of lading at the lowest level in AMS.

G. Less than Container Load (LCL) Shipments
1. I am a small importer that rarely brings in a whole container; most shipments are a few pallets or boxes. If we are just bringing in small shipments and not containers do the same reporting requirements apply?

An ISF is required for non-bulk cargo, regardless of the size of the shipment.

ISF Importer

A. General:
1. What if I am the ISF Importer at the time the ISF was filed and I no longer want to take responsibility for the shipment?

The ISF Importer is ultimately responsible for the complete, accurate, and timely filing of the ISF. This responsibility cannot be transferred to another party.

2. How can an importer be responsible for an ISF if they are not aware of a shipment?

The party causing the goods to enter the limits of a port in the United States is the party responsible for filing the ISF. This party could be the owner, purchaser, consignee, or agent.

3. Can a foreign entity be the ISF Importer?

Yes. However, a U.S. entity must be provided for the consignee element.

B. Transit Cargo (FROB, IE, TE):

1. Can the NVOCC file an ISF even though there is no legal requirement to do so?

Yes, an NVOCC can file an ISF on its own behalf (as an ISF Importer) or file an ISF as an agent for another party.

2. If the VOC is the ISF Importer for FROB, does this mean the VOC is required to be the ISF filer for T&E and I.E. cargo?

No. The ISF Importer for both I.E. and T&E shipments is the party filing the I.E. and T&E documentation with CBP. If the VOC is the party filing the I.E. and T&E documentation with CBP, the VOC is also the ISF Importer.

3. We currently handle some shipments that move to an inland port on the ocean liner's I.T. Once the shipment arrives to the I.T. destination port, we cancel the I.T. with either an I.E. or T&E inbond to be exported. Since they will not be consumption entries, can we submit only the ISF-5?

An immediate transportation (IT) entry requires an ISF-10 filing. For T&E and I.E. shipments, the ISF importer must provide an ISF-5 or an ISF-10 in lieu of an ISF-5.

Messaging

A. General:

1. When an ISF is transmitted to CBP by a Customs broker through ABI and a response received back to the Filer, how will the carrier know it is okay to load the shipment? Will the carrier get a message?

CBP does not issue "affirmative load" messages. Additionally, there is no requirement that a carrier verify that an ISF has been filed against a particular bill of lading. However, at the request of the trade, CBP does provide a status notification message to both the ISF Filer as well as the appropriate carrier that an ISF has successfully matched to a bill of lading that is on file with CBP.

B. Accepted ISF Filings:

1. Can the ISF Importer provide the ISF unique identification number to the AMS notify party for shipments where the ISF has been matched to the manifest?

Yes. As a business decision, the ISF Importer may share their unique identification number with other parties. However, this must be done outside of the AMS system.

C. Unique Identification Number:
1. Will CBP provide feedback when the ISF is filed?

Yes. The possible return messages including, but not limited to: accept, conditional acceptance, and reject with reason codes. For those filings that CBP accepts, CBP will return a unique ID number.

If there are any errors, or if the submission is rejected, CBP provides a reason code.

2. Does the unique ID become part of the entry package?

No.

3. Will CBP return a unique identification number for a unified manifest ISF-5 filing?

Not at this time.

D. Accepted with Warning:
1. Is CBP expecting an update to the ISF for filings where a warning message is received?

CBP expects ISFs to be updated when a warning message is received.

E. Rejected ISF Filings:
1. If my initial ISF is rejected, can I simply amend it or must I create a new one?

If an "add" transaction is rejected, the ISF must be corrected and resubmitted as a new "add" since there is no active ISF record present in CBP's system to "replace" (i.e., amend).

2. Can I receive a unique transaction number for my rejected filings in order to "prove" that I attempted to submit an ISF?

No. Unique ID numbers will not be issued for rejected "add" ISFs. However, rejected "replace" transactions will return the provided ISF Transaction Number.

F. Status Advisory Messages:
1. The status advisory message confirming a match (or no match) with the bill of lading is to be sent to the ISF filer. If there are two filings against the same bill of lading, do both filers receive the status advisory message?

Each filer will receive a separate and unique match (or no match) message.

G. Duplicate Filings:
1. How will CBP prevent/handle duplicate filings? Will the confirmation provide an indication of duplicate submissions if the ISF is already on file?

Importer of record number per ISF filer. The only exception is a "Unified Entry Filing", which also includes the entry number as part of the unique combination.

If a second ISF filing is received with the same combination of these elements the second filing will be rejected if the ISF is submitted by the same filer. A reason for the rejection will be returned to the ISF filer in addition to the unique transaction number.

However, if a duplicate ISF is filed by a different filer, CBP will accept the duplicate ISF and send a warning message to the initial ISF filer that a duplicate was filed. In addition, CBP will send an "accepted with warning" message to the subsequent ISF filer to let them know that a different party previously filed an ISF against the same shipment. CBP expects the parties involved to contact the ISF importer in order to ascertain which ISF is the accurate one. Failure to do so may incur enforcement and/or compliance actions.

H. ISF-5 Messaging:
1. If a carrier submits a unified filing for the 24-hour manifest data and ISF-5 data, will an ISF acknowledgment or unique identification number (receipt#) for the ISF-5 be returned to the carrier?

No. Unified manifest/ISF-5 filings will not receive a unique identification number.

MID Numbers

1. Can the MID number be used in lieu of the name and address for the Manufacturer (or Supplier) element?

No, CBP will not accept a MID Number in lieu of a full name and address to fulfill the Manufacturer (Supplier) requirement on the ISF. However, entities such as manufacturers, importers, supplies, etc. may register their information with Dun & Bradstreet to obtain a DUNS number which can be used in lieu of a full name and address.

Outer Continental Shelf (OCS) Shipments

1. Do the Importer Security Filing requirements pertain to outer continental shelf (OCS) shipments?

Yes. See pg. 71757 of the IFR for more details.

2. Are there any special provisions for OCS shipments due to the close proximity to the U.S.?

Yes. As a matter of policy, CBP will allow the filing of ISFs for OCS shipments anytime prior to vessel lading. CBP will be adding a special coded transaction type for OCS shipments in the near future.

Outreach Efforts

1. How do I find information about any public outreach efforts in regard to the new Security Filing?

    Please check the CBP Web site for any upcoming public outreach events in your area at www.cbp.gov.

Postal Codes

1. During the flexible enforcement period the lack of a postal code will result in an "accepted with warnings" message. Is CBP expecting an update to the ISF for all filings where a warning message is received?

    Yes.

2. Some of our ISF entities are in countries that don't have a formalized postal code system. How will CBP handle ISF entities that are transmitted without a postal code?

    A postal code is not required as part of an address on an ISF for countries that do not currently utilize a postal code system. CBP is working on formalizing a list of countries that use postal codes. When this has been completed, CBP will provide this list to the trade.

Powers of Attorney

1. Will CBP require a "special" and separate power of attorney (POA) for ISF purposes? Currently, brokers use a generic POA that includes broad agency language for all importing activities, including customs brokerage and forwarding if applicable. CBP should accept the current POA used by brokers.

    CBP will not require a new or "special" POA. The sufficiency of a power of attorney will be decided on a case by case basis. However, 19 CFR 141.32 contains an example of an acceptable general power of attorney with unlimited authority.

Progress Reports

1. Will CBP provide feedback from the system to the importers / agents for ISF filing timeliness and/or accuracy?

Yes. Upon receipt of an ISF submission, CBP processes the data and provides immediate feedback to the ISF Filer. The return messages include an acceptance or rejection message. For those filings that CBP accepts, CBP will return a unique ISF transaction number. If there are any errors, or if the submission is rejected, CBP will provide a reason code.

In addition to the instant feedback provided on a submission by submission basis, CBP has developed a system generated "ISF Progress Report" that is sent back to each ISF Filer on a monthly cycle. To obtain an ISF Progress Report, ISF Filers must register via the following e-mail address: progress_report@cbp.dhs.gov

The email must provide the following information:

- Filer's corporate name
- Filer code used for filing Security Filings
- Point of Contact
- Point of Contact's telephone number
- Corporate email address to which to send the Performance Report.

CBP may contact the Point of Contact to verify the provided information.

2. Will ISF Importers be able to register and obtain a copy of their ISF Progress Report?

CBP currently allows Tier 3 C-TPAT and Tier 2 C-TPAT members the opportunity to register with CBP to receive their ISF Progress Reports directly from CBP. All other ISF importers must obtain a copy of their ISF Progress Report from their authorized ISF Filer.

3. How is CBP MEASURING TIMELINESS on the ISF Progress Reports?

The timeliness section of the ISF Progress Report is based upon the *vessel departure date minus 24 hours.*

If a carrier has received an exemption to the 24-Hour Manifest Rule for the timing provision of the manifest data for certain cargo shipments, i.e., "exempt" break bulk, the ISF is not required until 24 hours prior to vessel arrival into the United States. At this time, CBP is not specifically measuring the timeliness of these "exempt" break bulk shipments.

Record Keeping Requirements

1. What are the importer's recordkeeping requirements for an ISF filing?

The new regulations do not contain specific record keeping requirements other than retention of powers of attorney (see 19 CFR 149.5(c)). However, ISF parties should retain records necessary to demonstrate compliance with ISF filing requirements. In addition, the general 19 U.S.C. § 1508 recordkeeping requirements may be applicable to the ISF filer.

Returned or Refused Shipments

A. General
  1. If a container is loaded on a vessel in the U.S. and goes foreign but is not unladen until it returns to the U.S., what are the ISF filing requirements?

     An ISF is not required for cargo laden in the U.S. that goes foreign but is not unladen until it returns to the U.S.

  2. If cargo is refused admission by a foreign country after having been exported from the U.S. and the cargo has not left the custody of the carrier or the foreign customs service, will such cargo require an ISF?

     If the cargo was loaded at a foreign port on board a vessel destined for the U.S., an ISF must be submitted.

B. U.S. Goods Returned:
  1. Are there or will there be exceptions to the ISF filing requirements for U.S. goods returned?

     ISFs are required for U.S. goods returned.

  2. For U.S. goods returned, should the HTSUS Chapter 98 number or the HTSUS commodity number be provided?

     For U.S. goods returned, both the HTSUS Chapter 98 number and the HTSUS commodity number are required.

  3. For U.S. goods returned, can the manufacturer (supplier) be a U.S. company?

     The manufacturer (supplier) can be U.S. a company if the party who last manufactured, assembled, produced, or grew (or supplied) the commodity is a U.S. company.

  4. If my shipment contains a mix of U.S. Goods Returned and foreign manufactured goods, which ISF coded transaction type should I use? Type 01 or Type 07?

     If U.S. goods are commingled or mixed with non-U.S. goods, the "Type 01" Standard coded transaction type should be used. The "Type 07" U.S. Goods Returned coded transaction type is reserved for those shipments that consist entirely of U.S. goods.

Splits, Diversions and Rolling of Cargo

  1. On some occasions, after a vessel departs, our shipments get "split" and sent to new destinations. Do we need to provide new ISFs for these split shipments?

No. If new bills of lading are introduced into AMS for these shipments, the original ISF will need to be updated (i.e., amended) with these new bills of lading. In addition, the ISF Importer or their agent must also update any other data elements that may have changed such as the Ship-To Party name/address.

2. On some occasions, we have to "split" a shipment onto two different vessels. On others, the carrier rolls my cargo for their convenience. Do I need to provide two separate ISFs for these shipments?

    Yes. In these instances, the shipments must each be assigned a unique bill of lading number so two separate ISFs can be filed.

Structured Review Period

1. How will an importer demonstrate to CBP that they are making "satisfactory progress towards compliance?"

    CBP will consider the totality of the circumstances, on a case-by-case basis, when making this determination. ISF Importers should retain documentation demonstrating the steps that were taken during the structured review and flexible enforcement period.

    (See ISF Progress Reports)

Transmission Methods

(See also: ABI, ACE, and Vessel Stow Plans)

1. How must ISF information be submitted to CBP?

    The ISF may only be submitted through AMS or ABI.

Unified ISF-10 and Entry Filings

1. I have a question on how the unified filing is going to work under the ISF. Many of our shipments are sent inbond from the unlading port to the port of entry. This information will most likely not be available if we attempt to file a unified filing. Please explain how the unified filing will work—does all the entry data need to be submitted?

    Unified entry is not available for inbond entries. Under this scenario, the ISF Importer or their agent must use the stand alone ISF filing process.

2. For a unified entry filing, if the entry is rejected will the ISF filing be automatically rejected as well?

    The ISF filing will not be rejected merely because an entry filing is rejected.

3. For a unified entry, when do duties have to be paid?

All entries will be processed in accordance with all current laws and regulations. This includes unified entries.

Vessel Stow Plans

A. Responsibility to File:
1. Does an ISF Importer need to submit vessel stow plans or container status messages?

No. Carriers must submit vessel stow plans and container status messages.

B. Exemptions:
1. Are vessels exclusively carrying bulk and break-bulk cargo exempt from the requirement to provide a vessel stow plan?

Yes. Vessels *exclusively* carrying bulk and break-bulk cargo are exempt from the requirement to provide a vessel stow plan.

2. Are RoRo vessels exempt from the requirement to provide a vessel stow plan?

Yes, as long as there is no containerized cargo aboard.

C. E-mail Address:
1. Please advise the e-mail address that the carrier can submit the stow plan to.

To submit a stow plan file by e-mail, a carrier or their agent need only e-mail it as a .txt attachment to stowplan@cbp.dhs.gov. Be advised that the CBP system will only accept one stow plan file per e-mail.

D. Formats:
1. Are we able to submit stow plans by email in Microsoft Excel format?

CBP will accept the SMDG (smdg.org) versions of the UNEDIFACT BAPLIE stow plan. CBP is developing a MS Excel formatted vessel stow plan than may be used by carriers who do not currently use UNEDIFACT BAPLIEs at this time. Requests to use this alternative format will be reviewed and approved on a limited and case by case basis.

E. Amendments:
1. Clarification is needed regarding which changes or errors, if any, other than a previously unreported container, would warrant a stow plan amendment, and when or how frequently they would need to be filed.

It is understood that if a carrier found a stow plan error reflecting on the presence of a previously unreported container onboard, an immediate amendment would be needed.

Stow plans must be complete, accurate, and timely. However, CBP will consider the specific violation(s) when determining mitigation.

Appendix B

Importing Into the United States
Guide for Commercial Importers

On March 1, 2003, U.S. Customs and Border Protection, or CBP, was born as an agency of the Department of Homeland Security, merging functions of the former Customs Service, Immigration and Naturalization Service, Border Patrol, and Animal and Plant Health Inspection Service. Many changes took place in preparation for this merger and many have occurred since in order to safeguard U.S. borders against high-risk cargo, contraband, and unsafe imports. Visit the Web site (www.cbp.gov) for the latest information on specific laws, regulations or procedures that may affect your import transactions.

* * * * * *

This edition of *Importing Into the United States* contains material pursuant to the Trade Act of 2002 and the Customs Modernization Act (Title VI of the North American Free Trade Agreement Implementation Act), commonly referred to as the Mod Act.

The Customs Modernization Act (Title VI of the North American Free Trade Agreement Implementation Act [P.L. 103-182, 107 Stat. 2057]) became effective December 8, 1993. Its provisions have fundamentally altered the relationship between importers and CBP by shifting to the importer, the legal responsibility for declaring the value, classification, and rate of duty applicable to entered merchandise.

A prominent feature of the Mod Act is a relationship between CBP and importers that is characterized by *informed compliance*. A key component of informed compliance is the shared responsibility between CBP and the import community, wherein CBP communicates its requirements to the importer, and the importer, in turn, uses reasonable care to assure that CBP is provided with accurate and timely data pertaining to his or her importations.

Importing Into the United States provides wide-ranging information about the importing process and import requirements. CPB made every effort to include essential requirements, but it is not possible to cover all import laws and regulations. Also, legislative and administrative changes are always under consideration and can occur at any time. Quota limitations on commodities are also subject to change. Therefore, reliance solely on the information in *Importing Into the United States* may not meet the "reasonable care" standard required of importers.

Interested parties should contact their nearest CBP office for information on specific issues or questions. CBP ports of entry, with their addresses and phone numbers, can be found on CBP's Web site under "Ports."

The information in this book is provided to promote understanding of, and compliance with, importing laws and regulations, the information provided here is for general purposes only. Importers may also wish to obtain guidance from private-sector experts who specialize in importing, for example, licensed customs brokers, attorneys, or consultants.

Federal agencies whose laws CBP helps to enforce are listed throughout this book, as well as in the Appendix and on CBP's Web site.

Contents

U.S. Customs and Border Protection: Mission, Organization and Suggestions to Exporter
  1. Mission
  2. Organization
  3. Suggestions to the Exporter

Entry of Goods
  4. Entry Process
  5. Right To Make Entry
  6. Examination of Goods and Entry Documents
  7. Packing of Goods—Commingling

Informed Compliance
  8. Definition
  9. Reasonable Care Checklists
  10. Compliance Assessment/Compliance Measurement
  11. Notice to Small-Business Importers

Invoices
  12. Commercial Invoices
  13. Other Invoices
  14. Frequent Errors in Invoicing

Assessment of Duty
15. Dutiable Status of Goods
16. Containers or Holders
17. Temporary Free Importations
18. North American Free Trade Agreement (NAFTA)
19. Generalized System of Preferences (GSP)
20. Caribbean Basin Initiative (CBI) and the Caribbean Basin Economic Recovery Act (CBERA)
21. Andean Trade Preference Act (ATPA)/Andean Trade Promotion and Drug Eradication Act (ATPDEA)
22. U.S.–Israel Free Trade Area Agreement
23. U.S.–Jordan Free Trade Area Agreement
24. Compact of Free Association (FAS)
25. African Growth and Opportunity Act (AGOA)
26. U.S.–Caribbean Basin Trade Partnership Act (CBPTA)
27. U.S.–Chile Free Trade Agreement (US-CFTA)
28. U.S.–Singapore Free Trade Agreement
29. Antidumping and Countervailing Duties
30. Drawback—Refunds of Duties

Classification and Value
31. Classification—Liquidation
32. Conversion of Currency
33. Transaction Value
34. Transaction Value—Identical or Similar Merchandise
35. Other Bases: Deductive and Computed Value
36. Rules of Origin

Marking
37. Country of Origin Marking
38. Special Marking Requirements
39. Marking—False Impression
40. User Fees

Special Requirements
41. Prohibitions, Restrictions, and Other Agency Requirements
42. Alcoholic Beverages
43. Motor Vehicles and Boats
44. Import Quotas
45. Fraud

46. Foreign-Trade Zones
Foreign-Trade Zones

U.S. Customs and Border Protection: Mission and Organization

1. Mission

Before September 11, 2001, the major responsibility of the former U.S. Customs Service was to administer the Tariff Act of 1930, as amended. When Customs subsequently merged with other border enforcement agencies to become U.S. Customs and Border Protection, CBP's priority mission became homeland security: detecting, deterring, and preventing terrorists and their weapons from entering the United States.

This mission fits ideally with CBP's long-established responsibilities for protecting and facilitating international trade. CBP retains its traditional enterprise of protecting the nation's revenue by assessing and collecting duties, taxes, and fees incident to international traffic and trade. Further, by providing procedural guidance to the import community, CBP enhances and increases compliance with domestic and international customs laws and regulations. CBP thus helps importers assure that their shipments are free from terrorist or other malicious interference, tampering, or corruption of containers or commodities.

Today, CBP is the nation's premiere border enforcement agency, and it accomplishes this new mandate in part by executing the responsibilities for which it has always been known: controlling, regulating, and facilitating the movement of carriers, people, and commodities between the United States and other nations; protecting the American consumer and the environment against the introduction of hazardous, toxic, or noxious products into the United States; protecting domestic industry and labor against unfair foreign competition; and detecting, interdicting, and investigating smuggling and other illegal practices aimed at illegally entering narcotics, drugs, contraband, or other prohibited articles into the United States.

CBP is also responsible for detecting, interdicting, and investigating fraudulent activities intended to avoid the payment of duties, taxes and fees, or activities meant to evade the legal requirements of international traffic and trade; and for detecting, interdicting, and investigating illegal international trafficking in arms, munitions, currency, and acts of terrorism at U.S. ports of entry.

2. Organization

Field Operations Offices — CBP operates through a field-office structure that consists of 20 Field Operations offices around the United States. These field offices provide managerial oversight and operational assistance to 324 ports of entry around the nation and 14 preclearance offices in Canada and the Caribbean.

Established according to geographic region, Field Operations offices are the means by which CBP Headquarters distributes key policies and procedures to CBP officers and importing staff around the country. Each field office supervises a certain number of service or area ports, which are larger, full-service ports with staff subdivisions designated to handle commercial transactions, as well as smaller ports of entry that handle less traffic.

Field Operations offices provide guidance to the ports under their geographic jurisdiction to ensure the dissemination and implementation of CBP guidelines, policies, and procedures. Import transactions are conducted at service ports, area ports, and ports of entry, so these locations will be of primary interest to the trade community. CBP is also responsible for administering the customs laws of the United States Virgin Islands.

Ports of Entry

Ports of entry conduct the daily, port-specific operations like clearing cargo, collecting duties and other monies associated with imports, and processing passengers arriving from abroad. Port personnel are the face at the border for nearly all cargo carriers and people entering the United States. Ports of entry are the level at which CBP enforces import and export laws and regulations and implements immigration policies and programs. Port officers also perform agricultural inspections to protect the U.S. from potential carriers of animal and plant pests or diseases that could cause serious damage to America's crops, livestock, pets, and the environment.

For a detailed listing of ports of entry, please refer to: http://www.cbp.gov/xp/cgov/toolbox/ports/.

U.S. CBP Officers in Foreign Countries

Brussels, Belgium
CBP Attaché
U.S. Mission to the European Union
27 Blvd. Du Regent
1000 Brussels
011-32-2-508-2770

Ottawa, Canada
CBP Attaché
Embassy of the United States
P.O. Box 866 Station B
Ottawa, Ontario K1P 5T1
Tel: 613-688-5496

Hong Kong
CBP Representative
11/F., St. John's Building
33 Garden Road, Central
Hong Kong
Tel: 011-852-2230-5100

Rome, Italy
CBP Representative
American Embassy
Via Veneto 119/A
00187 Rome
Tel: 011-39-06-4674-2475

Tokyo, Japan
CBP Representative
American Embassy
10-5, Akasaka 1-Chome
Minato-ku
Tokyo 107-8420 Japan
Tel: 011-813-3224-5433

Mexico City, Mexico
CBP Attaché
American Embassy
Paseo de la Reforma 305
Colonia Cuauhtemoc
Mexico City, D.F., Mexico
C.P. 06500
Tel: 011-52-55-5080-2000

New Delhi, India
CBP Representative
24 Kasturba Gandhi Marg.
New Delhi
110021 India
Tel: 011-91-11-2331-0080

Panama City, Panama
CBP Representative
American Embassy
Calle 38 & Avenida Balboa
Panama City, Panama
Tel: 011-507-225-7562

Singapore
CBP Representative
American Embassy
27 Napier Road
Singapore 258508
Tel: 011-65-476-9020

Pretoria, South Africa
ICE Attaché
American Embassy
877 Pertorius
Arcadia, Pretoria 001
Tel: 011-27-12-342-8062

Bangkok, Thailand
CBP Representative
Sindhorn Building
130-1332 Wireless Road
Tower 2, 12th Floor
Bangkok 10330
Tel: 011-66-2-205-5015

London, United Kingdom
CBP Representative
American Embassy
24/31 Grosvenor Square
London, W1A 1AE
Tel: 011-44-207-894-0070

3. Suggestions to the Exporter for Faster Clearance of Your Merchandise:

1. Include all information required on your customs invoices.
2. Prepare your invoices carefully. Type them clearly. Allow sufficient space between lines. Keep the data within each column.
3. Make sure that your invoices contain the information that would be shown on a well-prepared packing list.
4. Mark and number each package so it can be identified with the corresponding marks and numbers appearing on your invoice.
5. Show a detailed description on your invoice of each item of merchandise contained in each individual package.
6. Mark your goods legibly and conspicuously with the country of origin unless they are specifically exempted from country-of-origin marking requirements, and with such other marking as is required by the marking laws of the United States.
7. Comply with the provisions of any special laws of the United States that may apply to your goods, such as laws relating to food, drugs, cosmetics, alcoholic beverages, radioactive materials, and others.
8. Observe the instructions closely with respect to invoicing, packaging, marking, labeling, etc., sent to you by your customer in the United States. He or she has probably made a careful check of the requirements that will have to be met when your merchandise arrives.

9. Work with CBP to develop packing standards for your commodities.
10. Establish sound security procedures at your facility and while transporting your goods for shipment. Do not give narcotics smugglers the opportunity to introduce narcotics into your shipment.
11. Consider shipping on a carrier participating in the Automated Manifest System (AMS).
12. If you use a licensed customs broker for your transaction, consider using a firm that participates in the Automated Broker Interface (ABI).

Entry of Goods

4. Entry Process

When a shipment reaches the United States, the importer of record (i.e., the owner, purchaser, or licensed customs broker designated by the owner, purchaser, or consignee) will file entry documents for the goods with the port director at the goods' port of entry. Imported goods are not legally entered until after the shipment has arrived within the port of entry, delivery of the merchandise has been authorized by CBP, and estimated duties have been paid. It is the importer of record's responsibility to arrange for examination and release of the goods.

Pursuant to 19 U.S.C. 1484, the importer of record must use reasonable care in making entry.

NOTE: In addition to contacting CBP, importers should contact other agencies when questions arise about particular commodities. For example, questions about products regulated by the Food and Drug Administration should be forwarded to the nearest FDA district office (check local phone book under U.S. government listings) or to the Import Division, FDA Headquarters, 301-443-6553. The same is true for alcohol, tobacco, firearms, wildlife products (furs, skins, shells), motor vehicles, and other products and merchandise regulated by the other federal agencies for which CBP enforces entry laws.

Addresses and phone numbers for these agencies are listed in the Addendum.

Goods may be entered for consumption, entered for warehouse at the port of arrival, or they may be transported inbond to another port of entry and entered there under the same conditions as at the port of arrival. Arrangements for transporting the merchandise inbond to an inland port may be made by the consignee or by a customs broker or by any other person with an interest in the goods for that purpose. Unless your merchandise arrives directly at the port where you wish to enter it, you may be charged additional fees by the carrier for transportation to that port unless other arrangements have been made. Under some circumstances, your goods may be released through your local port of entry, even if they arrive at a different U.S. port from a foreign country. Prior to the goods' arrival, arrangements for entry must be made at the CBP port of entry where you intend to file your duties and documentation.

Goods to be placed in a foreign trade zone are not entered at the customhouse.

Evidence of Right To Make Entry

Goods may only be entered by their owner, purchaser, or a licensed customs broker. When the goods are consigned "to order," the bill of lading, properly endorsed by the consignor, may serve as evidence of the right to make entry. An air waybill may be used for merchandise arriving by air.

In most instances, entry is made by a person or firm certified by the carrier bringing the goods to the port of entry. This entity (i.e., the person or firm certified) is considered the "owner" of the goods for customs purposes.

The document issued by the carrier for this purpose is known as a "Carrier's Certificate." An example of this certificate is shown in the Addendum. In certain circumstances, entry may be made by means of a duplicate bill of lading or a shipping receipt. When the goods are not imported by a common carrier, possession of the goods by the importer at the time of arrival shall be deemed sufficient evidence of the right to make entry.

Entry for Consumption

Entering merchandise is a two-part process consisting of: (1) filing the documents necessary to determine whether merchandise may be released from CBP custody, and (2) filing the documents that contain information for duty assessment and statistical purposes. Both of these processes can be accomplished electronically via the Automated Broker Interface (ABI) program of the Automated Commercial System (ACS).

Entry Documents

Within 15 calendar days of the date that a shipment arrives at a U.S. port of entry, entry documents must be filed at a location specified by the port director. These documents are:

- Entry Manifest (CBP Form 7533) or Application and Special Permit for Immediate Delivery (CBP Form 3461) or other form of merchandise release required by the port director,
- Evidence of right to make entry,
- Commercial invoice or a pro forma invoice when the commercial invoice cannot be produced,
- Packing lists, if appropriate,
- Other documents necessary to determine merchandise admissibility.

If the goods are to be released from CBP custody at the time of entry, an entry summary for consumption must be filed and estimated duties deposited at the port of entry within 10 working days of the goods' entry.

Surety

The entry must be accompanied by evidence that a bond has been posted with CBP to cover any potential duties, taxes, and charges that may accrue. Bonds may be secured through a resident U.S. surety company, but may be posted in the form of United States currency or certain United States government obligations. In the event that a customs broker is employed for the purpose of making entry, the broker may permit the use of his bond to provide the required coverage.

Entry Summary Documentation

Following presentation of the entry, the shipment may be examined, or examination may be waived. The shipment is then released if no legal or regulatory violations have occurred. Entry summary documentation is filed and estimated duties are deposited within 10 working days of the entry of the merchandise at a designated customhouse. Entry summary documentation consists of:

- Return of the entry package to the importer, broker, or his authorized agent after merchandise is permitted release,
- Entry summary (CBP Form 7501),
- Other invoices and documents necessary to assess duties, collect statistics, or determine that all import requirements have been satisfied. This paper documentation can be reduced or eliminated by using features of the ABI.

Immediate Delivery

An alternate procedure that provides for immediate release of a shipment may be used in some cases by applying for a special permit for immediate delivery on CBP Form 3461 prior to arrival of the merchandise. Carriers participating in the Automated Manifest System can receive conditional release authorizations after leaving the foreign country and up to five days before landing in the United States. If the application is approved, the shipment will be released expeditiously after it arrives. An entry summary must then be filed in proper form, either on paper or electronically, and estimated duties deposited within 10 working days of release. Immediate-delivery release using Form 3461 is limited to the following types of merchandise:

- Merchandise arriving from Canada or Mexico, if the port director approves it and an appropriate bond is on file,
- Fresh fruits and vegetables for human consumption arriving from Canada or Mexico and removed from the area immediately contiguous to the

border and placed within the importer's premises within the port of importation,

- Shipments consigned to or for the account of any agency or officer of the U.S. government,
- Articles for a trade fair,
- Tariff-rate quota merchandise and, under certain circumstances, merchandise subject to an absolute quota. Absolute-quota items require a formal entry at all times,
- In very limited circumstances, merchandise released from warehouse followed within 10 working days by a warehouse withdrawal for consumption,
- Merchandise specifically authorized by CBP Headquarters to be entitled to release for immediate delivery.

Entry for Warehouse

If one wishes to postpone release of the goods, they may be placed in a CBP bonded warehouse under a warehouse entry. The goods may remain in the bonded warehouse up to five years from the date of importation. At any time during that period, warehoused goods may be re-exported without paying duty, or they may be withdrawn for consumption upon paying duty at the duty rate in effect on the date of withdrawal. If the goods are destroyed under CBP supervision, no duty is payable.

While the goods are in the bonded warehouse, they may, under CBP supervision, be manipulated by cleaning, sorting, repacking, or otherwise changing their condition by processes that do not amount to manufacturing. After manipulation, and within the warehousing period, the goods may be exported without the payment of duty, or they may be withdrawn for consumption upon payment of duty at the rate applicable to the goods in their manipulated condition at the time of withdrawal. Perishable goods, explosive substances, or prohibited importations may not be placed in a bonded warehouse. Certain restricted articles, though not allowed release from custody, may be warehoused.

Information regarding bonded manufacturing warehouses is contained in section 311 of the Tariff Act (19 U.S.C. 1311).

Unentered Goods

If no entry has been filed for the goods at the port of entry, or at the port of destination for inbond shipments, within 15 calendar days after their arrival, the goods may be placed in a general-order warehouse at the importer's risk and expense. If the goods are not entered within six months from the date of importation, they can be sold at public auction or destroyed. Perishable goods, however, and goods subject to depreciation and explosive substances may be sold sooner.

Storage charges, expenses of sales, internal revenue or other taxes, duties, fees, and amounts for the satisfaction of liens must be taken out of the money obtained from the sale of the unentered goods. Claims for the surplus proceeds of sale may be filed with the port director at whose instruction the merchandise was sent to sale. Any claim for such proceeds must be filed within 10 days of sale and supported with an original bill of lading. A photostatic copy or certified copy of the bill of lading may be used if only part of a shipment is involved in the sale. Carriers, not port directors, are required to notify a bonded warehouse of unentered merchandise. Once notified, the bonded warehouse operator/manager shall arrange for the unentered merchandise to be transported to his or her premises for storage at the consignee's risk and expense. If the goods are subject to internal revenue taxes, but will not bring enough to pay the taxes if sold at public auction, they are subject to destruction.

Mail Entries

Importers have found that in some cases it is to their advantage to use the national postal service—that is, a country's mail system, rather than courier services—to import merchandise into the United States. Some benefits to be gained are:

- Ease in clearing shipments through CBP. The duties on parcels valued at $2,000 or less are collected by the letter carrier who delivers the parcel to the addressee,
- Savings on shipping charges: smaller, low-valued packages can often be sent less expensively through the mails,
- No formal entry required on duty-free merchandise not exceeding $2,000 in value,
- No need to clear shipments personally if under $2,000 in value.

Joint CBP and postal regulations provide that all parcel post packages must have a CBP declaration securely attached to the outer wrapping giving an accurate description of the contents and their value. This declaration can be obtained at post offices worldwide. Commercial shipments must also be accompanied by a commercial invoice enclosed in the parcel bearing the declaration.

Each mail parcel containing an invoice or statement of value should be marked on the outer wrapper, on the address side, "Invoice enclosed." If the invoice or statement cannot be conveniently enclosed within the sealed parcel, it may be securely attached to the parcel. Failure to comply with any of these requirements will delay clearance of the shipment through CBP.

Packages other than parcel post—for example, letter-class mail, commercial papers, printed matter, or samples of merchandise—must bear on the address side a label, Form C1, provided by the Universal Post Union, or the endorsement "May be opened for customs purposes before delivery," or similar words definitely waiving the privacy of the seal and indicating that CBP officers may open the parcel without recourse to the addressee. Parcels not labeled or endorsed in this manner and found to contain prohibited merchandise, or containing merchandise that is subject to duty or tax, are subject to forfeiture.

A CBP officer prepares the CBP entry (a form) for mail importations not exceeding $2,000 in value, and the letter carrier at the destination delivers the parcel to the addressee upon payment of duty. If the value of a mail importation exceeds $2,000, the addressee is notified to prepare and file a formal CBP entry (also called a consumption entry) for it at the CBP port nearest him. A commercial invoice is required with the entry.

A CBP processing fee of $5.00 will be assessed on each item of dutiable mail for which a CBP officer prepares documentation. The postal carrier will collect this nominal fee on all dutiable or taxable mail along with the duty owed. There is also a postal fee (in addition to prepaid postage) authorized by international postal conventions and agreements as partial reimbursement to the Postal Service for its extra work in clearing packages through CBP and delivering them.

NOTE: The following general exceptions apply to the $2,000 limit:

- Articles classified in Subchapters III and IV, Chapter 99, Harmonized Tariff Schedule,
- Billfolds and other flat goods,
- Feathers and feather products,
- Flowers and foliage, artificial or preserved,
- Footwear,
- Fur, articles of,
- Gloves,
- Handbags,
- Headwear and hat braids,
- Leather, articles of,
- Luggage,
- Millinery ornaments,
- Pillows and cushions,
- Plastics, miscellaneous articles of,
- Rawhides and skins,
- Rubber, miscellaneous articles of,
- Textile fibers and products,
- Toys, games, and sports equipment, and
- Trimmings.

The limit for these articles is $250, except for textiles (fibers and products). Virtually all commercial shipments of textiles require formal entry, regardless of value. Unaccompanied shipments of made-to-measure suits from Hong Kong, a category that includes single suits for personal consumption, also require a formal entry regardless of the suit's value.

Transportation of Merchandise Inbond

Not all merchandise imported into the United States and intended for domestic commerce is entered at the port where it arrives. The importer may prefer to enter the goods at a different location in the United States, in which case the merchandise will have to be further transported to that location. In order to protect United States revenue in these cases, the merchandise must travel in a bonded status from the port of arrival to the intended port of entry. This process is referred to as *traveling under Immediate Transportation procedures* and is accomplished by the execution of CBP Form 7512 (Transportation Entry and Manifest of Goods Subject to CBP Inspection and Permit). The merchandise is then placed with a carrier who accepts it under its bond for transportation to the intended destination, where the normal merchandise entry process will occur.

5. Right To Make Entry

Entry by Importer

Merchandise arriving in the United States by commercial carrier must be entered by the owner, purchaser, his or her authorized regular employee, or by the licensed customs broker designated by the owner, purchaser, or consignee. U.S. CBP officers and employees are not authorized to act as agents for importers or forwarders of imported merchandise, although they may give all reasonable advice and assistance to inexperienced importers.

Customs brokers are the only persons who are authorized by the tariff laws of the United States to act as agents for importers in the transaction of their customs business. Customs brokers are private individuals or firms licensed by CBP to prepare and file the necessary customs entries, arrange for the payment of duties found due, take steps to effect the release of the goods in CBP custody, and otherwise represent their principals in customs matters. The fees charged for these services may vary according to the customs broker and the extent of services performed.

Every entry must be supported by one of the forms of evidence of the right to make entry outlined in this chapter. When a customs broker makes entry, a CBP power of attorney is made in the name of the customs broker. This power of attorney is given by the person or firm for whom the customs broker is acting as agent. Ordinarily, the authority of an employee to make entry for his or her employer is established most satisfactorily by a CBP power of attorney.

Entries Made by Others

Entry of goods may be made by a nonresident individual or partnership, or by a foreign corporation through a U.S. agent or representative of the exporter, a member of the partnership, or an officer of the corporation.

The surety on any CBP bond required from a nonresident individual or organization must be incorporated in the United States. In addition, a foreign corporation in whose name merchandise is entered must have a resident agent in the state where the port of entry is located who is authorized to accept service of process on the foreign corporation's behalf.

A licensed customs broker named in a CBP power of attorney may make entry on behalf of the exporter or his representative. The owner's declaration made by a nonresident individual or organization which the customs broker may request must be supported by a surety bond providing for the payment of increased or additional duties found due. An owner's declaration executed in a foreign country is acceptable, but it must be executed before a notary public and bear the notary's seal. Notaries public will be found in all American embassies around the world and in most of the larger consulates.

Power of Attorney

A nonresident individual, partnership, or foreign corporation may issue a power of attorney to a regular employee, customs broker, partner, or corporation officer to act in the United States for the nonresident employer. Any person named in a power of attorney must be a resident of the United States who has been authorized to accept service of process on behalf of the person or organization issuing the power of attorney. The power of attorney to accept service of process becomes irrevocable with respect to customs transactions duly undertaken. Either the applicable CBP form (see Addendum) or a document using the same language as the form is acceptable. References to acts that the issuer has not authorized the agent to perform may be deleted from the form or omitted from the document. A power of attorney from a foreign corporation must be supported by the following documents or their equivalent when foreign law or practice differs from that in the United States:

- A certificate from the proper public officer of the country showing the legal existence of the corporation, unless the fact of incorporation is so generally known as to be a matter of common knowledge.
- A copy of that part of the charter or articles of incorporation which shows the scope of the corporation's business and its governing body.
- A copy of the document or part thereof by which the person signing the power of attorney derives his authority, such as a provision of the charter or articles of incorporation, a copy of the resolution, minutes of the board of

directors' meeting, or other document by which the governing body conferred this authority. In this case, a copy is required of the bylaws or other document giving the governing board the authority to designate others to appoint agents or attorney.

A nonresident individual or partnership or a foreign corporation may issue a power of attorney to authorize the persons or firms named in the power of attorney to issue like powers of attorney to other qualified residents of the United States and to empower the residents to whom such powers of attorney are issued to accept service of process on behalf of the nonresident individual or organizations.

A power of attorney issued by a partnership must be limited to a period not to exceed two years from the date of execution and shall state the names of all members of the partnership. One member of a partnership may execute a power of attorney for the transaction of customs business of the partnership. When a new firm is formed by a change of membership, the prior firm's power of attorney is no longer effective for any customs purpose. The new firm will be required to issue a new power of attorney for the transaction of its customs business. All other powers of attorney may be granted for an unlimited period.

CBP Form 5291, or a document using the same language as the form, is also used to empower an agent other than an attorney-at-law or customs broker to file protests on behalf of an importer under section 514 of the Tariff Act of 1930 as amended. (See 19 CFR 141.32.)

Foreign corporations may comply with CBP regulations by executing a power of attorney on the corporation's letterhead. A form of power of attorney used for this purpose is given below. A nonresident individual or partner may use this same form. The X Corporation, _____

(Address, city, and country)

organized under the laws of _____ hereby authorizes

_____

(Name or names of employee or officer in United States)

_____

(and address or addresses)

to perform on behalf of the said corporation any and all acts specified in CBP Form 5291, Power of Attorney; to accept service of process in the United States on behalf of the X Corporation; to issue powers of attorney on CBP Form 5291 authorizing a qualified resident or residents of the United States to perform on behalf of the X Corporation all acts specified in CBP Form 5291; and to empower such resident or residents to accept service of process in the United States on behalf of the said X Corporation.

Because the laws regarding incorporation, notation, and authentication of documents vary from country to country, the agent to be named in the power of attorney should consult the port director of CBP at the port of entry where proof of the document's existence may be required as to the proper form to be used and the formalities to be met.

6. Examination of Goods and Entry Documents

Examination of goods and documents is necessary to determine, among other things:

- The value of the goods for customs purposes and their dutiable status,
- Whether the goods must be marked with their country of origin or require special marking or labeling. If so, whether they are marked in the manner required,
- Whether the shipment contains prohibited articles,
- Whether the goods are correctly invoiced,
- Whether the goods are in excess of the invoiced quantities or a shortage exists,
- Whether the shipment contains illegal narcotics.

Prior to the goods' release, the port director will designate representative quantities for examination by CBP officers under conditions that will safeguard the goods. Some kinds of goods must be examined to determine whether they meet special requirements of the law. For example, food and beverages unfit for human consumption would not meet the requirements of the Food and Drug Administration.

One of the primary methods of smuggling narcotics into the United States is in cargo shipments. Drug smugglers will place narcotics inside a legitimate cargo shipment or container to be retrieved upon arrival in the United States. Because smugglers use any means possible to hide narcotics, all aspects of the shipment are examined, including container, pallets, boxes, and product. Only through intensive inspection can narcotics be discovered.

Textiles and textile products are considered trade-sensitive and as such may be subject to a higher percentage of examinations than other commodities.

CBP officers will ascertain the quantity of goods imported, making allowances for shortages under specified conditions and assessing duty on any excess. The invoice may state the quantities in the weights and measures of the country from which the goods are shipped or in the weights and measures of the United States, but the entry must state the quantities in metric terms.

Excess Goods and Shortages

In order to facilitate duty allowances for goods that do not arrive and to determine whether excess goods are contained in the shipment, the importer (or foreign exporter) is advised to pack the goods in an orderly fashion; properly mark and number the packages in which the goods are contained; list each package's contents on the invoice; and place marks and numbers on the invoices that correspond to those packages.

If the CBP officer finds any package that contains an article not specified on the invoice, and there is reason to believe the article was omitted from the invoice by fraud, gross negligence, negligence on the part of the seller, shipper, owner, or agent, a monetary penalty may be imposed, or in some cases, the merchandise may be seized or forfeited. (See e.g., 19 U.S.C. 1592.)

If, during the examination of any package that has been designated for examination, the CBP officer finds a deficiency in quantity, weight, or measure, he or she will make a duty allowance for the deficiency. An allowance in duty may be made for those packages not designated as long as the importer notifies the port director of the shortage before liquidation of the entry becomes final and establishes to the port director's satisfaction that the missing goods were not delivered.

Damage or Deterioration

Goods that the CBP officer finds to be entirely without commercial value at the time of arrival in the United States because of damage or deterioration are treated as a "nonimportation." No duties are assessed on these goods. When damage or deterioration is present with respect to part of the shipment only, allowance in duties is not made unless the importer segregates, under CBP supervision, the damaged or deteriorated part from the remainder of the shipment. When the shipment consists of fruits, vegetables, or other perishable merchandise, allowance in duties cannot be made unless the importer, within 96 hours of unloading the merchandise and before it has been removed from the pier, files an application for an allowance with the port director. Allowance or reduction of duty for partial damage or loss as a result of rust or discoloration is precluded by law on shipments consisting of any article partially or wholly manufactured of iron or steel, or any manufacture of iron or steel.

Tare

In determining the quantity of goods dutiable on net weight, a deduction is made from the gross weight for just and reasonable tare. Tare is the allowance for a deficiency in the weight or quantity of the merchandise caused by the weight of the box, cask, bag, or other receptacle that contains the merchandise and that is weighed with it. The following schedule tares are provided for in the CBP Regulations:

> **Apple boxes.** 3.6 kilograms (8 lb.) per box. This schedule tare includes the paper wrappers, if any, on the apples.
> **China clay in so-called half-ton casks.** 32.6 kilograms (72 lb.) per cask.
> **Figs in skeleton cases.** Actual tare for outer containers plus 13 percent of the gross weight of the inside wooden boxes and figs.
> **Fresh tomatoes.** 113 grams (4 oz.) per 100 paper wrappings.
> **Lemons and oranges.** 283 grams (10 oz.) per box and 142 grams (5 oz.) per half-box for paper wrappings, and actual tare for outer containers.
> **Ocher, dry, in casks.** Eight percent of the gross weight; in oil in casks, 12 percent of the gross weight.
> **Pimentos in tins,** imported from Spain.

Size can	Drained weights
3 kilos	13.6 kilograms (30 lb.) — case of 6 tins
794 grams (28 oz.)	16.7 kilograms (36.7 lb.) — case of 24 tins
425 grams (15 oz.)	8.0 kilograms (17.72 lb.) — case of 24 tins
198 grams (7 oz.)	3.9 kilograms (8.62 lb.) — case of 24 tins
113 grams (4 oz.)	2.4 kilograms (5.33 lb.) — case of 24 tins

Tobacco, leaf not stemmed. 59 kilograms (13 lb.) per bale; Sumatra: actual tare for outside coverings, plus 1.9 kilograms (4 lb.) for the inside matting and, if a certificate is attached to the invoice certifying that the bales contain paper wrappings and specifying whether light or heavy paper has been used, either 113 grams (4 oz.) or 227 grams (8 oz.) for the paper wrapping according to the thickness of paper used.

For other goods dutiable on the net weight, an actual tare will be determined. An accurate tare stated on the invoice is acceptable for CBP purposes in certain circumstances.

If the importer of record files a timely application with the port director of CBP, an allowance may be made in any case for excessive moisture and impurities not usually found in or upon the particular kind of goods.

7. Packing of Goods—Commingling

Packing

Information on how to pack goods for the purpose of transporting them may be obtained from shipping manuals, carriers, forwarding agents, and other sources. This section, therefore, deals with packing goods being exported in a way that will permit CBP officers to examine, weigh, measure, and release them promptly.

Orderly packing and proper invoicing go hand in hand. You will speed up the clearance of your goods through CBP if you:

■ Invoice your goods in a systematic manner,
■ Show the exact quantity of each item of goods in each box, bale, case, or other package,
■ Put marks and numbers on each package,
■ Show those marks or numbers on your invoice opposite the itemization of goods contained in the package that bears those marks and numbers.

When packages contain goods of one kind only, or when the goods are imported in packages the contents and values of which are uniform, the designation of packages for examination and the examination for CBP purposes are greatly facilitated. If the contents and values differ from package to package, the possibility of delay and confusion is increased. Sometimes, because of the kinds of goods or because of the unsystematic manner in which they are packed, the entire shipment must be examined.

Pack and invoice your goods in a manner which makes a speedy examination possible. Always bear in mind that it may not be possible to ascertain the contents of your packages without full examination unless your invoice clearly shows the marks and numbers on each package (whether box, case, or bale) and specifies the exact quantity of each item of adequately described goods in each marked and numbered package.

Also, be aware that CBP examines cargo for narcotics that may, unbeknownst to the shipper or the importer, be hidden inside. This can be time-consuming and expensive for both the importer and for CBP. Narcotics inspections may require completely stripping a container in order to physically examine a large portion of the cargo. This labor-intensive handling of cargo, whether by CBP, labor organizations, or private individuals, results in added costs, increased delays, and possible damage to the product. Importers can expedite this inspection process by working with CBP to develop packing standards that will permit effective CBP examinations with a minimum of delay, damage, and cost.

A critical aspect in facilitating inspections is how the cargo is loaded. "Palletizing" cargo—loading it onto pallets or other consolidated units—is an effective way to expedite such examinations. Palletization allows for quick cargo removal in minutes using a forklift compared to the hours it would take manually. Another example is leaving enough space at the top of a container and an aisle down the center to allow access by a narcotic-detector dog.

Your cooperation in this respect will help CBP officers decide which packages must be opened and examined; how much weighing, counting, or measuring must be done, and whether the goods are properly marked. It will simplify the ascertainment of tare and reduce the number of samples to be taken for laboratory analysis or for other customs purposes. It will facilitate verification of the packages and contents, as well as the reporting by CBP officers of missing or excess goods. And it will minimize the possibility that the importer may be asked to resubmit for examination packages that were already released under the belief that the ones originally designated for examination were sufficient for that purpose.

Packing a combination of different types of goods makes it impracticable for CBP officers to determine the quantity of each type of product in an importation. Such packing can also lead to a variety of other complications in the entry process. No problem will arise, however, from the orderly packing of several different kinds of properly invoiced goods in a single package. It is indiscriminate packing that causes difficulty.

Commingling

Except as mentioned hereafter, whenever articles subject to different rates of duty are so packed together or combined such that CBP officers cannot readily determine the quantity or value of each class of articles without physically separating the shipment or the contents of any package, the combined articles will be subject to the highest rate of duty applicable to any part of the commingled lot, unless the consignee or his agent separates the merchandise under CBP supervision.

The three methods of ready ascertainment specified by General Note 3(f) of the Harmonized Tariff Schedule are:

1. Sampling,
2. Verification of packing lists or other documents filed at the time of entry, or
3. Evidence showing performance of commercial settlements tests generally accepted in the trade and filed in the time and manner as prescribed in the CBP Regulations.

Segregation of merchandise is at the risk and expense of the consignee. It must be done within 30 days (unless a longer time is granted) after the date of personal delivery or the date of mailing a notice to the consignee by the port director that the goods are commingled. The compensation and expenses of the CBP officers supervising the segregation must be borne by the consignee.

Assessing duty on the commingled lot at the highest applicable rate does not apply to any part of a shipment if the consignee or his agent furnishes satisfactory proof that:

1. Such part is commercially negligible, is not capable of segregation without excessive cost, and will not be segregated prior to its use in a manufacturing process or otherwise; and
2. The commingling was not intended to avoid the payment of lawful duties.

Any article for which such proof is furnished shall be considered for all CBP purposes as a part of the article, subject to the next lower rate of duty, with which it is commingled.

In addition, the highest-rate rule does not apply to any part of a shipment if satisfactory proof is furnished that:

1. The value of the commingled articles is less than the aggregate value would be if the shipment were segregated;
2. The shipment is not capable of segregation without excessive cost and will not be segregated prior to its use in a manufacturing process or otherwise; and
3. The commingling was not intended to avoid the payment of lawful duties.

Any merchandise for which such proof is furnished shall be considered for all CBP purposes to be dutiable at the rate applicable to the material present in greater quantity than any other material.

The above rules do not apply if the tariff schedules provide a particular tariff treatment for commingled articles.

Informed Compliance

8. Definition

Informed compliance is a shared responsibility between CBP and the import community wherein CBP effectively communicates its requirements to the trade, and the people and businesses subject to those requirements conduct their regulated activities in accordance with U.S. laws and regulations. A key component of informed compliance is that the importer is expected to exercise reasonable care in his or her importing operations.

Informed compliance benefits both parties: When voluntary compliance is achieved, CBP resources need not be expended on redundant examinations or entry reviews for the importer's cargo found to be dependably compliant. From the trade perspective, when voluntary compliance is attained, compliant importers are less likely to have their shipments examined or their entries reviewed.

CBP publishes a wealth of information to assist the import community in complying with CBP requirements. We issue rulings and informed compliance publications on a variety of technical subjects and processes. Most of these materials can be found online at www.cbp.gov.

We urge importers to make sure they are using the latest versions of any printed materials.

9. Reasonable Care Checklists

Reasonable care is an explicit responsibility on the part of the importer. Despite its seemingly simple connotation, the term reasonable care defies easy explanation because the facts and circumstances surrounding every import transaction differ, from the experience of the importer to the nature of the imported articles. Consequently, neither CBP nor the importing community can develop a reasonable care checklist capable of covering every import transaction.

CBP recommends that the import community examine the list of questions below. These questions suggest methods that importers may find useful in avoiding compliance problems and in meeting the responsibilities of reasonable care.

These questions are intended to promote compliance with CBP laws and regulations, but be aware that the list is advisory, not exhaustive. The checklist is intended as a guide and *has no legal, binding, or precedential effect on CBP or the importing community.*

The questions apply whether the importer of record conducts the transactions(s) him- or herself, or whether the importer hires others to do it.

General Questions for All Transactions:

1. If you have not retained an expert (e.g., lawyer, customs broker, accountant, or customs consultant) to assist you in complying with CBP requirements, do you have access to the *CBP Regulations* (Title 19 of the Code of Federal Regulations), the *Harmonized Tariff Schedule of the United States* (generally referred to as the Harmonized Tariff Schedule), and *CBP Bulletin and Decisions*? (All three are available from the Superintendent of Documents, Tel. 202-512-1800.) Do you have access to the CBP Web site at www.cbp.gov, or other research service that provides the information to help you establish reliable procedures and facilitate compliance with CBP law and regulations?

2. Has a responsible, knowledgeable individual within your organization reviewed your CBP documentation to assure that it is full, complete and accurate? If the documentation was prepared outside your organization, do you have a reliable method to assure that you receive copies of the information submitted to CBP, that it is reviewed for accuracy, and that CBP is apprised of needed corrections in a timely fashion?

3. If you use an expert to help you comply with CBP requirements, have you discussed your importations in advance with that person, and have you provided him or her with complete, accurate information about the import transaction(s)?

4. Are identical transactions or merchandise handled differently at different ports or CBP offices within the same port? If so, have you brought this fact to CBP officials' attention?

Questions by Topic: Merchandise Description & Tariff Classification

Basic Question: Do you know what you ordered, where it was made, and what it is made of?

1. Have you provided a complete, accurate description of your merchandise to CBP in accordance with 19 U.S.C. 1481? (Also, see 19 CFR 141.87 and 19 CFR 141.89 for special merchandise description requirements.)

2. Have you provided CBP with the correct tariff classification of your merchandise in accordance with 19 U.S.C. 1484?

3. Have you obtained a CBP ruling regarding the description of your merchandise or its tariff classification (see 19 CFR Part 177)? If so, have you followed the ruling and apprised appropriate CBP officials of those facts (i.e., of the ruling and your compliance with it)?

4. Where merchandise description or tariff classification information is not immediately available, have you established a reliable procedure for obtaining it and providing it to CBP?
5. Have you participated in a CBP classification of your merchandise in order to get it properly described and classified?
6. Have you consulted the tariff schedules, CBP informed compliance publications, court cases, or CBP rulings to help you properly describe and classify the merchandise?
7. Have you consulted with an expert (e.g., lawyer, customs broker, accountant, customs consultant) to assist in the description and/or classification of the merchandise?
8. If you are claiming a conditionally free or special tariff classification or provision for your merchandise (e.g., GSP, HTS Item 9802, NAFTA), how have you verified that the merchandise qualifies for such status? Do you have the documentation necessary to support the claim? If making a NAFTA preference claim, do you have a NAFTA certificate of origin in your possession?
9. Is the nature of your merchandise such that a laboratory analysis or other specialized procedure is advised for proper description and classification?
10. Have you developed reliable procedures to maintain and produce the required entry documentation and supporting information?

Valuation

Basic Questions: Do you know the "price actually paid or payable" for your merchandise? Do you know the terms of sale? Whether there will be rebates, tie-ins, indirect costs, additional payments? Whether "assists" were provided or commissions or royalties paid ? Are amounts actual or estimated? Are you and the supplier "related parties"?

1. Have you provided CBP with a proper declared value for your merchandise in accordance with 19 U.S.C. 1484 and 19 U.S.C. 1401a?
2. Have you obtained a CBP ruling regarding valuation of the merchandise (see 19 CFR Part 177)? Can you establish that you followed the ruling reliably? Have you brought those facts to the attention of CBP?
3. Have you consulted the CBP valuation laws and regulations, *CBP Valuation Encyclopedia*, CBP informed compliance publications, court cases, and CBP rulings to assist you in valuing merchandise?
4. If you purchased the merchandise from a "related" seller, have you reported that fact upon entry? Have you assured that the value reported to CBP meets one of the "related party" tests?

5. Have you assured that all legally required costs or payments associated with the imported merchandise (assists, commissions, indirect payments or rebates, royalties, etc.) have been reported to CBP?

6. If you are declaring a value based upon a transaction in which you were/are not the buyer, have you substantiated that the transaction is a bona fide "sale at arm's length" and that the merchandise was clearly destined to the United States at the time of sale?

7. If you are claiming a conditionally free or special tariff classification or provision for your merchandise (GSP, HTS Item 9802, NAFTA), have you reported the required value information and obtained the documentation necessary to support the claim?

8. Have you produced the required entry documentation and supporting information?

Country of Origin/Marking/Quota

Basic Question: Have you ascertained the correct country of origin for the imported merchandise?

1. Have you reported the correct country of origin on CBP entry documents?

2. Have you assured that the merchandise is properly marked upon entry with the correct country of origin (if required) in accordance with 19 U.S.C. 1304 and any other applicable special marking requirements (watches, gold, textile labeling, etc)?

3. Have you obtained a CBP ruling regarding the proper marking and country of origin of the merchandise (see 19 CFR Part 177)? If so, have you followed the ruling and brought that fact to the attention of CBP?

4. Have you consulted with a customs expert regarding the correct country-of-origin/proper marking of your merchandise?

5. Have you apprised your foreign supplier of CBP country-of-origin marking requirements prior to importation of your merchandise?

6. If you are claiming a change in the origin of the merchandise or claiming that the goods are of U.S. origin, have you taken required measures to substantiate your claim (e.g., do you have U.S. milling certificates or manufacturers' affidavits attesting to production in the United States)?

7. If importing textiles or apparel, have you ascertained the correct country of origin in accordance with 19 U.S.C. 3592 (Section 334, P.L. 103-465) and assured yourself that no illegal transshipment or false or fraudulent practices were involved?

8. Do you know how your goods are made, from raw materials to finished goods, by whom and where?

9. Have you ensured that the quota category is correct?

10. Have you checked the *Status Report on Current Import Quotas* (Restraint Levels), issued by CBP, to determine if your goods are subject to a quota category with "part" categories?
11. Have you obtained correct visas for those goods subject to visa categories?
12. For textile articles, have you prepared a proper country declaration for each entry, i.e., a single country declaration (if wholly obtained/produced) or a multi-country declaration (if raw materials from one country were transformed into goods in a second)?
13. Can you produce all entry documentation and supporting information, including certificates of origin, if CBP requires you to do so?

Intellectual Property Rights

Basic Question: Have you determined whether your merchandise or its packaging use any trademarks or copyrighted material or are patented? If so, can you establish that you have a legal right to import those items into and/or use them in the United States?

1. If you are importing goods or packaging bearing a trademark registered in the United States, have you established that it is genuine and not restricted from importation under the "gray-market" or parallel-import requirements of United States law (see 198 CFR 133.21), or that you have permission from the trademark holder to import the merchandise?
2. If you are importing goods or packaging that contain registered copyrighted material, have you established that this material is authorized and genuine? If you are importing sound recordings of live performances, were the recordings authorized?
3. Is your merchandise subject to an International Trade Commission or court-ordered exclusion order?
4. Can you produce the required entry documentation and supporting information?

Miscellaneous

1. Have you assured that your merchandise complies with other agencies' requirements (e.g., FDA, EPA, DOT, CPSC, FTC, Agriculture, etc.) and obtained licenses or permits, if required, from them?
2. Are your goods subject to a Commerce Department dumping or countervailing-duty investigation or determination? If so, have you complied with CBP reporting requirements of this fact (e.g., 19 CFR 141.61)?
3. Is your merchandise subject to quota/visa requirements? If so, have you provided a correct visa for the goods upon entry?

4. Have you assured that you have the right to make entry under the CBP Regulations?
5. Have you filed the correct type of CBP entry (e.g., TIB, T&E, consumption entry, mail entry)?

Additional Questions for Textile and Apparel Importers

Section 333 of the Uruguay Round Implementation Act (19 U.S.C. 1592a) authorizes the Secretary of the Treasury to publish a list of foreign producers, manufacturers, suppliers, sellers, exporters, or other foreign persons found to have violated 19 U.S.C. 1592 by using false, fraudulent or counterfeit documentation, labeling, or prohibited transshipment practices in connection with textiles and apparel products. Section 1592a also requires any importer of record who enters or otherwise attempts to introduce into United States commerce textile or apparel products that were directly or indirectly produced, manufactured, supplied, sold, exported, or transported by such named person(s) to show, to the Secretary's satisfaction, that the importer has exercised reasonable care to ensure that the importations are accompanied by accurate documentation, packaging, and labeling regarding the products' origin. Under section 1592a, reliance solely upon information from a person named on the list does not constitute the exercise of reasonable care. Textile and apparel importers who have a commercial relationship with any of the listed parties must exercise reasonable care in ensuring that the documentation covering the imported merchandise, its packaging, and its labeling, accurately identify the importation's country of origin. This demonstration of reasonable care must rely upon more information than that supplied by the named party.

In order to meet the reasonable care standard when importing textile or apparel products and when dealing with a party named on this list, an importer should consider the following questions to ensure that the documentation, packaging and labeling are accurate regarding country-of-origin considerations. This list is illustrative, not exhaustive:

1. Has the importer had a prior relationship with the named party?
2. Has the importer had any seizures or detentions of textile or apparel products that were directly or indirectly produced, supplied, or transported by the named party?
3. Has the importer visited the company's premises to ascertain that the company actually has the capacity to produce the merchandise?
4. Where a claim of an origin-conferring process is made in accordance with 19 CFR 102.21, has the importer ascertained that the named party actually performed that process?
5. Is the named party really operating from the country that he or she claims on the documentation, packaging, or labeling?

6. Have quotas for the imported merchandise closed, or are they near closing, from the main producer countries for this commodity?
7. Does the country have a dubious or questionable history regarding this commodity?
8. Have you questioned your supplier about the product's origin?
9. If the importation is accompanied by a visa, permit, or license, has the importer verified with the supplier or manufacturer that the document is of valid, legitimate origin? Has the importer examined that document for any irregularities that would call its authenticity into question?

10. Compliance Assessment/Compliance Measurement

Of primary interest to the trade community is the compliance assessment, which is the systematic evaluation of an importer's systems supporting his or her CBP-related operations. The assessment includes testing import and financial transactions, reviewing the adequacy of the importer's internal controls, and determining the importer's compliance levels in key areas. Compliance assessments are conducted in accordance with 19 U.S.C. 1509.

The assessment is conducted by an interdisciplinary team composed of a CBP auditor, import specialist, account manager, industry expert (highly knowledgeable of the electronics or auto parts or surgical equipment industries, for example), and possibly other CBP specialists (attorneys, inspectors, scientists). The compliance assessment utilizes professionally accepted statistical sampling and auditing techniques to review selected import transactions from the company's previous fiscal year.

Compliance assessments will evaluate the company's applicable customs operations such as:

■ Record keeping,
■ Merchandise classification/trade statistics,
■ Merchandise quantities,
■ Antidumping/countervailing duty operations,
■ Quota conformity,
■ Merchandise value,
■ Warehouse or foreign trade zone operations,
■ Merchandise transshipment,
■ Special trade programs (GSP, CBI, others).

Companies found in compliance with CBP laws and regulations will get a report stating that fact. Companies whose systems are determined to be noncompliant will also get a report and will be asked to formulate, in cooperation with CBP advisors, a compliance improvement plan specifying corrective actions the company will take to increase compliance levels. Serious violations of law or regulation may result in CBP referring the company for a formal investigation or other enforcement actions.

By law, CBP is required to provide the importer with advance notice of an intended assessment and an estimate of its duration. Importers are entitled to an entry conference, during which the assessment's purpose will be explained and its duration provided. Using information from CBP databases about the company or the importer's industry, the compliance assessment team may have prepared questionnaires seeking specific information about the importer's internal procedures. These questionnaires will be distributed at the entry conference.

Upon completion of the assessment, CBP will schedule a closing conference, at which its preliminary findings will be explained. A closing conference may not be scheduled for companies found to have serious enforcement issues. If no enforcement action is taken, CBP will provide the company with a written report of the assessment's results.

The Importer Audit/Compliance Assessment Team Kit (also called the CAT Kit), which provides extensive details of the assessment procedure, can be found at the CBP Web site, www.cbp.gov, or by calling the CBP Regulatory Audit Division office nearest you.

Compliance measurement is the primary tool that CBP uses to assess the accuracy of port-of-entry transactions and to determine the compliance rate for all commercial importations. By using statistical sampling methods, a valid compliance level for all commercial importations can be obtained. One of CBP's goals is to assure that at least 99 percent of the import revenues legally owed the United States government are collected. Cargo is sampled for compliance with international trade laws at the port of entry, at the time of entry into the United States. Importers should be aware that misclassification of merchandise, among other violations, will be detected through the compliance measurement process.

11. A Notice to Small-Business Importers

The Small Business Regulatory Enforcement Fairness Act was designed to create a more cooperative regulatory environment between federal agencies and small businesses.

Your comments are important. The Small Business and Regulatory Enforcement Ombudsman and 10 regional Fairness Boards were established to receive comments from small businesses about federal agency enforcement activities and to rate each agency's responsiveness to small business. If you wish to comment on the enforcement actions of U.S. Customs and Border Protection, call 1.888.REG.FAIR (1.888.734.3247).

Invoices

12. Commercial Invoice

A commercial invoice, signed by the seller or shipper, or his agent, is acceptable for CBP purposes if it is prepared in accordance with Section 141.86 through 141.89 of the CBP Regulations, and in the manner customary for a commercial transaction involving goods of the kind covered by the invoice. Importers and brokers participating in the Automated Broker Interface may elect to transmit invoice data via the Automated Invoice Interface or EDIFACT and eliminate the paper document. The invoice must provide the following information, as required by the Tariff Act:

- The port of entry to which the merchandise is destined,
- If merchandise is sold or agreed to be sold, the time, place, and names of buyer and seller; if consigned, the time and origin of shipment, and names of shipper and receiver,
- A detailed description of the merchandise, including the name by which each item is known, the grade or quality, and the marks, numbers, and symbols under which it is sold by the seller or manufacturer to the trade in the country of exportation, together with the marks and numbers of the packages in which the merchandise is packed,
- The quantities in weights and measures,
- If sold or agreed to be sold, the purchase price of each item in the currency of the sale,
- If the merchandise is shipped for consignment, the value of each item in the currency in which the transactions are usually made, or, in the absence of such value, the price in such currency that the manufacturer, seller, shipper, or owner would have received, or was willing to receive, for such merchandise if sold in the ordinary course of trade and in the usual wholesale quantities in the country of exportation,
- The kind of currency,
- All charges upon the merchandise, itemized by name and amount, including freight, insurance, commission, cases, containers, coverings, and cost of packing; and, if not included above, all charges, costs, and expenses incurred in bringing the merchandise from alongside the carrier at the port of exportation in the country of exportation and placing it alongside the carrier at the first U.S. port of entry. The cost of packing, cases, containers, and inland freight to the port of exportation need not be itemized by amount if included in the invoice price and so identified. Where the required information does not appear on the invoice as originally prepared, it shall be shown on an attachment to the invoice,
- All rebates, drawbacks, and bounties, separately itemized, allowed upon the exportation of the merchandise,
- The country of origin,
- All goods or services furnished for the production of the merchandise not included in the invoice price.

If the merchandise on the documents is sold while in transit, the original invoice reflecting this transaction and the resale invoice or a statement of sale showing the price paid for each item by the purchaser shall be filed as part of the entry, entry summary, or withdrawal documentation.

The invoice and all attachments must be in the English language, or shall be accompanied by an accurate English translation.

Each invoice shall state in adequate detail what merchandise is contained in each individual package.

If the invoice or entry does not disclose the weight, gauge, or measure of the merchandise necessary to ascertain duties, the importer of record shall pay expenses incurred to obtain this information prior to the release of the merchandise from CBP custody.

Each invoice shall set forth in detail, for each class or kind of merchandise, every discount from the list or other base price that has been or may be allowed in fixing each purchase price or value.

When more than one invoice is included in the same entry, each invoice with its attachments shall be numbered consecutively by the importer on the bottom of the face of each page, beginning with number 1. If an invoice is more than two pages, begin with number 1 for the first page of the first invoice and continue in a single series of numbers through all the invoices and attachments included in one entry. If an entry covers one invoice of one page and a second invoice of two pages, the numbering at the bottom of the page shall be as follows: Inv. 1, p.1; Inv. 2, p.2; Inv. 2, p.3, etc.

Any information required on an invoice may be set forth either on the invoice or on the attachment.

Specific Requirements

1. **Separate Invoice Required for Each Shipment.** Not more than one distinct shipment from one consignor to one consignee by one commercial carrier shall be included on the same invoice.
2. **Assembled Shipments.** Merchandise assembled for shipment to the same consignee by one commercial carrier may be included in one invoice. The original bills or invoices covering the merchandise, or extracts therefrom, showing the actual price paid or agreed to be paid, should be attached to the invoice.
3. **Installment Shipments.** Installments of a shipment covered by a single order or contract and shipped from one consignor to one consignee may be included in one invoice if the installments arrive at the port of entry by any means of transportation within a period not to exceed 10 consecutive days.

The invoice should be prepared in the same manner as invoices covering single shipments and should include any additional information that may be required for the particular class of goods concerned. If it is practical to do so, the invoice should show the quantities, values, and other invoice data with respect to each installment, and the identification of the importing conveyance in which each installment was shipped.

4. Production "Assist." The invoice should indicate whether the production of merchandise involved costs for "assists" (e.g., dies, molds, tooling, printing plates, artwork, engineering work, design and development, financial assistance, etc.) that are not included in the invoice price. If assists were involved, state their value, if known, and by whom supplied. Were they supplied without cost, or on a rental basis, or were they invoiced separately? If the latter, attach a copy of the invoice.

Whenever CBP requires information on the cost of production of goods for customs valuation, the importer will be notified by the port director. Thereafter, invoices covering shipments of such goods must contain a statement on the cost of production by the manufacturer or producer.

5. Additional Information Required. Special information may be required on certain goods or classes of goods in addition to the information normally required on the invoice. Although the United States importer usually advises the exporter of these special situations, section 141.89 of the CBP Regulations, which covers the requirements for these goods, has been reproduced in the addendum.

6. Rates of Exchange. In general, no rate(s) of exchange may be used to convert foreign currency for customs purposes other than the rate(s) proclaimed or certified in 31 U.S.C. 5151. For merchandise imported from a country having a currency for which two or more rates of exchange have been certified by the Federal Reserve Bank of New York, the invoice will show the exchange rate or rates used in converting the United States dollars received for the merchandise into the foreign currency and the percentage of each rate if two or more rates are used. If a rate or combination of rates used to pay costs, charges, or expenses is different from those used to pay for the merchandise, state that rate or combination of rates separately. When dollars have not been converted at the time the invoice is prepared, state that fact on the invoice, in which case the invoice shall also state the rate or combination of rates at which the dollars will be converted, or that it is not known what rate or rates will be used. Rates of exchange are not required for merchandise unconditionally free of duty or subject only to a specific rate of duty not depending on value.

13. Other Invoices

Pro Forma Invoice

If the required commercial invoice is not filed at the time the merchandise is entered, a statement in the form of an invoice (a *pro forma* invoice) must be filed by the importer at the time of entry. A bond is given for production of the required invoice not later than 120 days from the date of the entry summary, or entry if there is no entry summary. If the invoice is needed for statistical purposes, it must generally be produced within 50 days from the date on which the entry summary is required to be filed.

The exporter should bear in mind that unless he or she forwards the required invoice in time, the American importer will incur a liability under his bond for failure to file the invoice with the port director of CBP before the 120-day period expires.

Although a pro forma invoice is not prepared by the exporter, it is of interest to exporters as it gives a general idea of the kind of information needed for entry purposes. A pro forma invoice indicates what the importer may find necessary to furnish CBP officers at the time a formal entry is filed for a commercial shipment, if a properly prepared CBP or commercial invoice is not available at the time the goods are entered. An acceptable format for a pro forma invoice is reproduced in the addendum.

Some of the additional information specified for the commodities under section 141.89 of the CBP Regulations may not be required when entry is made on a pro forma invoice. However, the pro forma invoice must contain sufficient data for examination, classification, and appraisement purposes.

Special Invoices

Special invoices are required for some merchandise. See 19 CFR 141.89.

14. Frequent Errors in Invoicing

Foreign sellers or shippers must exercise care in preparing invoices and other documents used to enter goods into the commerce of the United States in order for their importers to avoid difficulties, delays, or possibly even penal sanctions. Each document must contain all information required by law or regulations, and every statement of fact contained in the documents must be true and accurate. Any inaccurate or misleading statement of fact in a document presented to a CBP officer in connection with an entry, or the omission from the document of required information, may result in delays in merchandise release, the detention of the goods, or a claim against the importer for domestic value. Even though the inaccuracy or omission was unintentional, the importer may be required to establish that he exercised due diligence and was not negligent, in order to avoid sanctions with consequent delay in obtaining possession of goods and closing the transaction. (See 19 U.S.C. 1592.)

It is particularly important that all statements relating to merchandise description, price or value, and amounts of discounts, charges, and commissions be truthfully and accurately set forth. It is also important that the invoices set forth the true name of the actual seller and purchaser of the goods, in the case of purchased goods, or the true name of the actual consignor and consignee when the goods are shipped otherwise than in pursuance of a purchase. It is important, too, that the invoice otherwise reflect the real nature of the transaction pursuant to which the goods were shipped to the United States.

The fundamental rule is that both the shipper and importer must furnish CBP officers with all pertinent information with respect to each import transaction to assist CBP officers in determining the tariff status of the goods. Examples of omissions and inaccuracies to be avoided are:

- The shipper assumes that a commission, royalty, or other charge against the goods is a so-called "nondutiable" item and omits it from the invoice.
- A foreign shipper who purchases goods and sells them to a United States importer at a delivered price shows on the invoice the cost of the goods to him instead of the delivered price.
- A foreign shipper manufactures goods partly with the use of materials supplied by the United States importer, but invoices the goods at the actual cost to the manufacturer without including the value of the materials supplied by the importer.
- The foreign manufacturer ships replacement goods to his customer in the United States and invoices the goods at the net price without showing the full price less the allowance for defective goods previously shipped and returned.
- A foreign shipper who sells goods at list price, less a discount, invoices them at the net price, and fails to show the discount.
- A foreign shipper sells goods at a delivered price but invoices them at a price f.o.b. the place of shipment and omits the subsequent charges.
- A foreign shipper indicates in the invoice that the importer is the purchaser, whereas he is in fact either an agent who is receiving a commission for selling the goods or a party who will receive part of the proceeds of the sale of the goods sold for the joint account of the shipper and consignee.
- Invoice descriptions are vague, listing only parts of numbers, truncated or coded descriptions, or lumping various articles together as one when several distinct items are included.

Assessment of Duty

15. Dutiable Status of Goods

Rates of Duty

All goods imported into the United States are subject to duty or duty-free entry in accordance with their classification under the applicable items in the Harmonized Tariff Schedule of the United States. An annotated loose-leaf edition of the tariff schedule may be purchased from the U.S. Government Printing Office, Washington, DC 20402. (See 19 U.S.C. 1202.)

When goods are dutiable, *ad valorem*, specific, or compound rates may be assessed. An ad valorem rate, which is the type of rate most often applied, is a percentage of the value of the merchandise, such as five percent ad valorem. A specific rate is a specified amount per unit of weight or other quantity, such as 5.9 cents per dozen. A compound rate is a combination of both an ad valorem rate and a specific rate, such as 0.7 cents per kilo plus 10 percent ad valorem.

Free of Duty or Dutiable

Rates of duty for imported merchandise may vary depending upon the country of origin. Most merchandise is dutiable under the most-favored-nation—now referred to as *normal trade relations*—rates in the General column under column 1 of the tariff schedule. Merchandise from countries to which these rates have *not* been extended is dutiable at the full or "statutory" rates in column 2 of the tariff schedule.

Free rates are provided for many subheadings in columns 1 and 2 of the tariff schedule. Duty-free status is also available under various conditional exemptions, which are reflected in the *Special* column under column 1 of the tariff schedule. It is the importer's burden to show eligibility for a conditional exemption from duty.

One of the more frequently applied exemptions from duty occurs under the Generalized System of Preferences (GSP). GSP-eligible merchandise qualifies for duty-free entry when it is from a beneficiary developing country. Exemptions are found under the subheadings in Chapter 98 of the tariff schedule. These subheadings include, among other provisions, certain personal exemptions, exemptions for articles for scientific or other institutional purposes, and exemptions for returned American goods.

Rulings on Imports

CBP makes its decision on the dutiable status of merchandise when the entry is liquidated after the entry documents have been filed. When advance information is needed, do not depend on a small "trial" or "test" shipment because there is no guarantee that the next shipment will receive the same tariff treatment. Small importations may slip by, particularly if they are processed under informal procedures that apply to small shipments or in circumstances warranting application of a flat rate. An exporter, importer, or other interested party may get advance information on any matter affecting the dutiable status of merchandise by writing to the port director where the merchandise will be entered or to:

Director, National Commodity Specialist Division
U.S. Customs and Border Protection
One Penn Plaza, 11th Floor
New York, New York 10119

or to:

U.S. Customs and Border Protection
Attention: Office of Regulations and Rulings
Washington, DC 20229

Detailed information on the procedures for the issuance of administrative rulings is given in 19 CFR Part 177.

Binding Decisions

While you will find that, for many purposes, CBP ports are your best sources of information, informal information obtained on tariff classifications is not binding. Under 19 CFR part 177, the importing public may obtain a binding ruling, which can be relied upon for placing or accepting orders or for making other business determinations, under Chapters 1 through 97 of the Harmonized Tariff Schedule or by writing to:

National Commodity Specialist Division
U.S. Customs and Border Protection
One Penn Plaza, 11th Floor
New York, New York 10119

The ruling will be binding at all ports of entry unless revoked by the CBP Office of Regulations and Rulings.

The following information is required in ruling requests:

■ The names, addresses and other identifying information of all interested parties (if known) and the manufacturer ID code (if known),
■ The name(s) of the port(s) at which the merchandise will be entered (if known),
■ A description of the transaction; for example, a prospective importation of (merchandise) from (country),
■ A statement that there are, to the importer's knowledge, no issues on the commodity pending before CBP or any court, and
■ A statement as to whether classification advice has previously been sought from a CBP officer, and if so, from whom, and what advice was rendered, if any.

A request for a tariff classification should include the following information:

■ A complete description of the goods. Send samples, if practical, sketches, diagrams, or other illustrative material that will be useful in supplementing the written description,
■ Cost breakdowns of component materials and their respective quantities shown in percentages, if possible,
■ A description of the principal use of the goods, as a class or kind of merchandise, in the United States,
■ Information as to commercial, scientific or common designations, as may be applicable, and
■ Any other information that may be pertinent or required for the purpose of tariff classification.

To avoid delays, your request should be as complete as possible. If you send a sample, do not rely on it to tell the whole story. Also, please note that samples may be subjected to laboratory analysis, which is done free of charge. If a sample is destroyed during laboratory analysis, however, it cannot be returned.

Information submitted and incorporated in response to a request for a CBP decision may be disclosed or withheld in accordance with the provisions of the Freedom of Information Act, as amended 5 U.S.C. 552, 19 CFR 177.8(a)(3).

Protests

The importer may disagree with the dutiable status after the entry has been liquidated. A decision at this stage of the entry transaction is requested by filing a protest and application for further review on CBP Form 19. The time limit is within 180 days after liquidation (see CFR part 174; see 19 USC 1514(c)(3) as amended by section 2103(2)(B), Pub. L.108-429. The same legislation also eliminated the 1 year to file protests for clerical errors and mistakes of fact for entries after 12/18/04). If CBP denies a protest, the adverse decision may be appealed to the U.S. Court of International Trade.

Liability for Duties

There is no provision under which U.S. duties or taxes may be prepaid in a foreign country before exportation to the United States. This is true even for gifts sent by mail.

In the usual case, liability for the payment of duty becomes fixed at the time an entry for consumption or for warehouse is filed with CBP. The obligation for payment is upon the person or firm in whose name the entry is filed. When goods have been entered for warehouse, liability for paying duties may be transferred to any person who purchases the goods and desires to withdraw them in his or her own name.

Paying a customs broker will not relieve the importer of his or her liability for customs charges (duties, taxes, and other debts owed CBP) should those charges not be paid by the broker. Therefore, if the importer pays the broker by check, he or she should give the broker a separate check, made payable to "U.S. Customs and Border Protection" for those customs charges, which the broker will then deliver to CBP.

If the entry is made in the name of a customs broker, the broker may obtain relief from statutory liability for the payment of increased or additional duties found due if (1) the actual owner of goods is named, and (2) the owner's declaration whereby the owner agrees to pay the additional duty and the owner's bond are both filed by the broker with the port director within 90 days of the date of entry.

16. Containers or Holders

CBP designates such items as lift vans, cargo vans, shipping tanks, pallets and certain articles used to ship goods internationally as *instruments of international traffic*. So long as this designation applies, these articles are not subject to entry or duty when they arrive, whether they are loaded or empty. Other classes of merchandise containers may also be designated as instruments of international traffic upon application to the Commissioner of CBP for such a designation. If any article so designated is diverted to domestic use, however, it must be entered and duty paid, if applicable.

Containers specially shaped or fitted to contain a specific article or set of articles, suitable for long term use and entered with the articles for which they are intended, are classifiable with the accompanying articles if they are of a kind normally sold therewith. Examples of such containers are: camera cases, musical instrument cases, gun cases, drawing instrument cases, and necklace cases. This rule does not apply to containers that give the importation as a whole its essential character.

Subject to the above rule, packing materials and packing containers entered with goods packed in them are classified with these goods if they are of a kind normally used for packing such goods. However, this does not apply to packing materials or containers that are clearly suitable for repetitive use.

17. Temporary Free Importations

Temporary Importation under Bond (TIB)

Goods of the types enumerated below, when not imported for sale or for sale on approval, may be admitted into the United States under bond, without the payment of duty, for exportation within one year from the date of importation. Generally, the amount of the bond is double the estimated duties. The one-year period for exportation may, upon application to the port director, be extended for one or more further periods which, when added to the initial one year, shall not exceed a total of three years. There is an exception in the case of articles covered in item 14: the period of the bond may not exceed six months and may not be extended.

Merchandise entered under TIB must be exported or destroyed before expiration of the bond period, or any extension, to avoid assessment of liquidated damages in the amount of the bond.

All goods entered under TIB are subject to quota compliance.

Classes of Goods

(1) Merchandise to be repaired, altered, or processed (including processes that result in an article being manufactured or produced in the United States), provided the following conditions are met:

The merchandise will not be processed into an article manufactured or produced in the United States if the article is:

■ Alcohol, distilled spirits, wine, beer, or any dilution or mixture of these,
■ Perfume or other commodity containing ethyl alcohol, whether denatured or not,

■ A product of wheat.

If merchandise is processed and results in an article being manufactured or produced in the United States other than those described above:

- A complete accounting will be made to CBP for all articles, wastes, and irrecoverable losses resulting from the processing, and
- All articles will be exported or destroyed under CBP supervision within the bonded period. Valuable waste must also be exported or so destroyed unless duty, if applicable, is paid.

(2) Models of women's wearing apparel imported by manufacturers for use solely as models in their own establishments; these articles require quota compliance.

(3) Articles imported by illustrators and photographers for use solely as models in their own establishments to illustrate catalogs, pamphlets, or advertising matter.

(4) Samples solely for use in taking orders for merchandise; these samples require quota compliance.

(5) Articles solely for examination with a view to reproduction or for examination and reproduction (except photoengraved printing plates for examination and reproduction); and motion-picture advertising films.

(6) Articles intended solely for testing, experimental, or review purposes, including plans, specifications, drawings, blueprints, photographs, and articles for use in connection with experiments or for study. If articles under this category are destroyed in connection with the experiment or study, proof of such destruction must be presented to satisfy the obligation under the bond to export the articles.

(7) Automobiles, motorcycles, bicycles, airplanes, airships, balloons, boats, racing shells, and similar vehicles and craft, and the usual equipment of the foregoing, if brought temporarily into the United States by nonresidents for the purpose of taking part in races or other specific contests. Port directors may defer the exaction of a bond for a period not to exceed 90 days after the date of importation for vehicles and craft to take part in races or other specific contests for other than money purposes. If the vehicle or craft is not exported or the bond is not given within the period of such deferment, the vehicle or craft shall be subject to forfeiture.

(8) Locomotives and other railroad equipment brought temporarily into the United States for use in clearing obstructions, fighting fires, or making emergency repairs on railroads within the United States or for use in transportation otherwise than in international traffic when the Secretary of the Treasury finds that the temporary use of foreign railroad equipment is necessary to meet an emergency. Importers can expedite approval of a request for temporary importation to meet an emergency by including evidence of the existence of the emergency, such as news reports.

(9) Containers for compressed gases, filled or empty, and containers or other articles used for covering or holding merchandise (including personal or household effects) during transportation and suitable for reuse for that purpose.

(10) Professional equipment, tools of trade, repair components for equipment or tools admitted under this item, and camping equipment imported by or for nonresidents for the nonresident's use while sojourning temporarily in the United States.

(11) Articles of special design for temporary use exclusively in connection with the manufacture or production of articles for export.

(12) Animals and poultry brought into the United States for the purpose of breeding, exhibition, or competition for prizes, and the usual equipment therefor.

(13) Works of free fine arts, drawings, engravings, photographic pictures, and philosophical and scientific apparatus brought into the United States by professional artists, lecturers, or scientists arriving from abroad for use by them for exhibition and in illustration, promotion, and encouragement of art, science, or industry in the United States.

(14) Automobiles, automobile chassis, automobile bodies, cutaway portions of any of the foregoing, and parts for any of the foregoing, finished, unfinished, or cutaway, when intended solely for show purposes. These articles may be admitted only on condition that the Secretary of the Treasury has found that the foreign country from which the articles were imported allows or will allow substantially reciprocal privileges with respect to similar exports to that country from the United States. If the Secretary finds that a foreign country has discontinued or will discontinue the allowance of such privileges, the privileges under this item shall not apply thereafter to imports from that country.

Relief from Liability

Relief from liability under bond may be obtained in any case in which the articles are destroyed under CBP supervision, in lieu of exportation, within the original bond period. However, in the case of articles entered under item 6, destruction need not be under CBP supervision where articles are destroyed during the course of experiments or tests during the bond period or any lawful extension, but satisfactory proof of destruction shall be furnished to the port director with whom the customs entry is filed.

ATA Carnet

ATA stands for the combined French and English words "Admission Temporaire—Temporary Admission." ATA carnet is an international customs document that may be used for the temporary duty-free importation of certain goods into a country in lieu of the usual customs documents required. The carnet serves as a guarantee against the payment of customs duties that may become due on goods temporarily imported and not reexported. Quota compliance is required on merchandise subject to quota; for example, textiles are subject to quota and visa requirements.

A carnet is valid for one year. The traveler or businessperson, however, may make as many trips as desired during the period the carnet is valid provided he or she has sufficient pages for each stop.

The United States currently allows ATA carnets to be used for the temporary admission of professional equipment, commercial samples, and advertising material. Most other countries allow the use of carnets for the temporary admission of these goods and, in some cases, other uses of the ATA carnet are permitted.

Local carnet associations, as members of the International Bureau of the Paris-based International Chamber of Commerce, issue carnets to their residents. These associations guarantee the payment of duties to local customs authorities should goods imported under cover of a foreign-issued carnet not be reexported. In the United States, CBP has designated the U.S. Council of the International Chamber of Commerce, located at 1212 Avenue of the Americas, New York, NY 10036, Tel. 212-354-4480, as the United States issuing and guaranteeing organization. The Council charges a fee for its service.

ATA carnets can be used in the following countries:

Algeria	Ivory Coast
Australia	Japan
Austria	Republic of South Korea
Belgium	Lebanon
Bulgaria	Luxembourg
Canada	Malaysia
Canary Islands	Malta
China	Mauritius
Croatia	Netherlands
Cyprus	New Zealand
Czech Republic	Norway
Denmark	Poland
Estonia	Portugal
Finland	Romania
France	Senegal
French Polynesia	Singapore
French West Indies	Slovakia
Germany	Slovenia
Gibraltar	South Africa
Greece	Spain
Hong Kong	Sri Lanka
Hungary	Sweden
Iceland	Switzerland
India	Thailand
Ireland	Turkey
Israel	United Kingdom
Italy	United States

Egypt and certain other countries have accepted the ATA convention, but have not implemented the use of carnets. As countries are being continuously added to the carnet system, please check with the U.S. Council if a country you wish to visit is not included in the above list.

18. The North American Free Trade Agreement (NAFTA)

The provisions of the North American Free Trade Agreement (NAFTA) were adopted by the United States with enactment of the North American Free Trade Agreement Implementation Act of 1993 (107 Stat. 2057, P.L. 103-182). Nineteen Code of Federal Regulation (19 CFR) Parts 10, 12, 123, 134, 162, 174, 177, and 178 were amended, and new parts 102 and 181 of the CBP Regulations were developed to implement NAFTA's duty provisions.

NAFTA phased out tariffs on almost all "originating" goods traded between Canada and the United States by January 1, 2003, and provides for an additional 5-year phase-out period on certain sensitive commodities traded between Mexico and the United States.

Article 401 of NAFTA eliminates both tariffs and the merchandise processing fees for goods that "originate." Transshipping goods through Mexico or Canada that were made in another country, or performing only minor processing or packaging operations on them in North America, will not invoke preferential NAFTA duty rates.

The term "originate" means those goods that meet the requirements of NAFTA Article 401. Article 401 defines "originate" in four ways:

1. Goods wholly obtained or produced entirely in the NAFTA region (these contain no foreign inputs);
2. Goods produced entirely in the NAFTA region exclusively from originating materials (these contain foreign materials that have been previously manufactured into originating materials);
3. Goods meeting an Annex 401 specific rule of origin such as a prescribed change in tariff classification, regional value content requirement; and in extremely limited instances,
4. Unassembled goods and goods classified with their parts, which do not meet the tariff-shift rule but contain 60 percent regional value content using the transaction-value method, or 50 percent using the net-cost method.

Annex 401 of NAFTA is codified in General Note 12(t) of the Harmonized Tariff Schedule of the United States and is available at www.cbp.gov/nafta/rulesorg.htm.

Entry Procedures

For NAFTA, as with other preferential trade programs, it is the importer's responsibility to claim the benefits. In the United States, a NAFTA claim is made as follows:

■ Non-Commercial (Personal) Importations
For a non-commercial importation of NAFTA goods, a NAFTA claim may be made in the United States without a certificate of origin or statement.

- Commercial Importations, Low-Value
  In order to claim preferential tariff treatment on a commercial shipment of NAFTA goods valued at US $2,500 or less, the entry packet must include the 19 CFR 181.22(d) statement certifying that the goods "originate" (www.cbp.gov/nafta/docs/us/181sec1-1.html#181.21).

- Commercial Importations, Other
  The importer must have a valid NAFTA certificate of origin, signed by the exporter or his agent, when claiming preferential tariff treatment on a commercial shipment of NAFTA goods valued at more than US $2,500.

- Post-Importation Claims
  Importers who may not have a valid NAFTA certificate of origin, or who are unsure whether their goods "originate," or who otherwise choose not to make a NAFTA claim at the time of entry summary have up to one year from the date of importation to make a post-importation claim.

Exporter's Certificate of Origin

NAFTA Article 502 requires that an importer's NAFTA claim be based on the exporter's certificate of origin. This may be CBP Form 434, the Canadian B-232, or the Mexican Certificado de Origen. When making a NAFTA claim in the United States, the importer must have one of these three certificates of origin or a CBP-approved, privately printed or alternate certificate of origin. For a single shipment, the certificate of origin shall be annotated with the invoice number or other distinguishing marks. For multiple shipments of identical goods, the certificate shall be annotated with a blanket period of up to 12 months.

NAFTA Certificates of Origin and NAFTA Claims Are Optional

The exporter or producer is never obligated to provide a certificate of origin to a customer. However, since the importer may not claim NAFTA preferential tariff treatment without one, it is in the exporter or producer's interest to provide it. By providing a certificate of origin, the producer is attesting that:

1. The goods originate,
2. He has the substantiating production and accounting documentation, and
3. He will make it available to the customs authorities upon request.

Country of Origin for Marking and Duty Purposes

For goods processed in Canada, Mexico or the United States, NAFTA codified the concept of "substantial transformation," the process by which a good's country of origin is determined for marking and duty purposes. Even though a good may be sufficiently processed in Canada, Mexico, or the United States to be marked with that country of origin, it may not be sufficiently manufactured to "originate" under the rules of origin for NAFTA tariff treatment purposes (Harmonized Tariff Schedule of the United States, General Note 12(t)). With certain limited exceptions, only originating goods benefit from NAFTA preferential treatment. For additional marking information, please see *NAFTA: A Guide to Customs Procedures*, available at www.cbp.gov/nafta/nafta_new.htm or 19 CFR 102 at www.gpoaccess.gov/cfr/index.html.

Special Provisions for Sensitive Sectors

The NAFTA Annex 401-origin criteria ensure that most textile- and apparel-related production occur in North America. The basic rule of origin for textiles and apparel is commonly referred to as "yarn forward." This means that the yarn used to form the fabric must be spun in the NAFTA territory, and all subsequent processing must take place in North America. Textiles and apparel of man-made filament fibers have an even more restrictive "fiber-forward" rule. Some apparel goods must additionally meet a "visible-lining rule," meaning that certain linings must be woven or knit in North America.

Transshipment

Goods that are entitled to NAFTA preferential duty rates by virtue of their originating status will lose that status if they leave customs control outside of North America or undergo any operation outside of North America other than unloading, reloading, or any other operation necessary to preserve them in good condition or to transport the goods to Canada, Mexico, or the United States.

Repair or Alteration

Goods may be exported from one NAFTA country to another for repair or alteration and returned free of duty regardless of the origin of the goods. This provision does not apply to alterations that are part of a manufacturing process.

Territory

With respect to the United States, the customs territory includes the 50 states, the District of Columbia, Puerto Rico, and the foreign trade zones located therein.

Additional NAFTA information can be obtained in *NAFTA: A Guide to Customs Procedures*, available on line at www.cbp.gov/nafta/nafta_new.htm or from the Code of Federal Regulations at www.cbp.gov/nafta/resource.htm.

19. Generalized System of Preferences (GSP)

The Generalized System of Preferences (GSP) is a preferential program that provides duty-free treatment to products of beneficiary designated countries and territories. The program was authorized by the Trade Act of 1974 (19 U.S.C. 2461 et seq.) as a means of promoting economic development in the developing countries and was instituted on January 1, 1976. The GSP periodically expires and must be renewed by Congress to remain in effect. CBP provides the trade community with notification of these expirations and renewals.

Eligible Items

The GSP eligibility list contains a wide range of products classifiable under 3,400 different subheadings in the Harmonized Tariff Schedule of the United States (Tariff Schedule). These items are identified by the symbols "A", "A*", or "A+" in the "Special" subcolumn under column 1 of the tariff schedule. Merchandise classifiable under a subheading designated in this manner may qualify for duty-free entry if imported into the United States directly from any of the designated countries and territories. Items identified by an "A*" may be excluded from the exemption if imported from certain designated countries.

The list of countries and exclusions, as well as the list of GSP-eligible articles, will change from time to time. For example, countries immediately lose GSP eligibility upon joining the European Union. Consult the *Federal Register* at www.ustr. gov for the most current information regarding country and/or commodity eligibility. Click on the link to "Trade and Development" and then the link for the "USTR Reference Programs." A GSP guidebook is available at http://www.ustr.gov/assets/ Trade_Development/Preference_Programs/GSP/asset_upload_file890_8359.pdf.

Importers and other interested parties may obtain an advance ruling to determine whether a particular product is eligible for GSP treatment.

Claims

For commercial shipments requiring a formal entry, a claim for duty-free status is made under the GSP by declaring on the entry summary that the country of origin is a designated beneficiary developing country and by placing the symbol "A" as a prefix to the subheading of the tariff schedule for each article for which such treatment is claimed. Eligible merchandise will be entitled to duty-free treatment provided the following conditions are met:

■ The merchandise must be the "product of" a beneficiary country. This requirement is satisfied when:
   (1) The goods are wholly the growth, product, or manufacture of a beneficiary country, or

(2) When an article is produced from materials imported into the beneficiary developing country and those imported materials are substantially transformed into a new or different article of commerce in a beneficiary country. A statement to that effect shall be included on the commercial invoice.

■ The merchandise must be imported *directly* from any beneficiary country into the customs territory of the United States.

■ The cost or value of materials produced in the beneficiary developing country and/or the direct cost of processing performed there must be at least 35 percent of the appraised value of the goods.

The cost or value of materials imported into the beneficiary developing country may be included in calculating the 35-percent value-content requirement of the GSP only if such materials undergo a "double substantial transformation" in the beneficiary developing country. That is, such materials must be substantially transformed in the beneficiary developing country into a new and different intermediate article of commerce, which is then transformed a second time in the production of the final good. The phrase "direct costs of processing" refers to costs directly incurred in, or which can be reasonably allotted to, the processing of the article. Such costs include, but are not limited to: all actual labor costs involved with production of the good; dies, molds, tooling, and depreciation on machinery and equipment; research and development; and costs of inspecting and testing the merchandise. Profit and general expenses are not considered direct costs of processing. General expenses are those that cannot be allocated to the good or costs that do not relate to production of the good, such as administrative salaries, insurance, advertising, and salaries for sales employees.

Sources of Additional Information

CBP rules and regulations on the GSP are incorporated in sections 10.171-10.178 of the CBP Regulations. Address any question you may have on the administrative or operational aspects of the GSP to:

CBP Trade Agreements Branch
U.S. Customs and Border Protection
1300 Pennsylvania Avenue, NW
Washington, DC 20229

Requests for information concerning additions to or deletions from the list of merchandise eligible under the GSP, or changes to the list of beneficiary developing countries, should be directed to:

Chairman, Trade Policy Staff Subcommittee
Office of U.S. Trade Representative

600 17th St., NW
Washington, DC 20506

GSP Independent Countries

Afghanistan
Albania
Algeria
Angola
Antigua and Barbuda
Argentina
Armenia
Bahrain
Bangladesh
Barbados
Belize
Benin
Bhutan
Bolivia
Bosnia and Herzegovina
Botswana
Brazil
Bulgaria
Burkina Faso
Burundi
Cambodia
Cameroon
Cape Verde
Central African Republic
Chad
Colombia
Comoros
Congo (Brazzaville)
Congo (Kinshasa)
Costa Rica
Côte d'Ivoire
Croatia
Djibouti
Dominica
Dominican Republic
Ecuador
Egypt
El Salvador

Equatorial Guinea
Eritrea
Ethiopia
Fiji
Gabon
Gambia, The
Georgia
Ghana
Grenada
Guatemala
Guinea
Guinea-Bissau
Guyana
Haiti
Honduras
India
Indonesia
Iraq
Jamaica
Jordan
Kazakhstan
Kenya
Kiribati
Kyrgyzstan
Lebanon
Lesotho
Macedonia, Former Yugoslav Republic of
Madagascar
Malawi
Mali
Mauritania
Mauritius
Moldova
Mongolia
Mozambique
Namibia
Nepal
Niger
Nigeria
Oman
Pakistan
Panama
Papua, New Guinea

Paraguay
Peru
Philippines
Romania
Russia
Rwanda
Saint Kitts and Nevis
Saint Lucia
Saint Vincent and the Grenadines
Samoa
Sao Tome and Principe
Senegal
Seychelles
Sierra Leone
Solomon Islands
Somalia
South Africa
Sri Lanka
Suriname
Swaziland
Tanzania
Thailand
Togo
Tonga
Trinidad and Tobago
Tunisia
Turkey
Tuvalu
Uganda
Uruguay
Uzbekistan
Vanuatu
Venezuela
Yemen, Republic of
Zambia
Zimbabwe

Non-Independent Countries and Territories

Anguilla
British Indian Ocean Territory
Christmas Island (Australia)
Cocos (Keeling) Island

Cook Islands
Falkland Islands (Islas Malvinas)
Gibraltar
Heard Island and McDonald Islands
Montserrat
Niue
Norfolk Island
Pitcairn Island
Saint Helena
Tokelau
Turks and Caicos Islands
Virgin Islands, British
Wallis and Funtuna
West Bank and Gaza Strip
Western Sahara

20. Caribbean Basin Initiative (CBI) and the Caribbean Basin Economic Recovery Act (CBERA)

The Caribbean Basin Initiative (CBI) is a program that allows duty-free entry of certain merchandise from designated beneficiary countries or territories. This program was enacted by the United States as the Caribbean Basin Economic Recovery Act (CBERA), which became effective January 1, 1984, and has no expiration date.

Beneficiary Countries

The following countries and territories have been designated as beneficiary countries for purposes of the CBI:

Antigua and Barbuda
Aruba
Bahamas
Barbados
Belize
Costa Rica
Dominica
Dominican Republic
El Salvador
Grenada
Guatemala
Guyana
Haiti

Honduras
Jamaica
Montserrat
Netherlands Antilles
Nicaragua
Panama
Saint Kitts and Nevis
Saint Lucia
Saint Vincent and the Grenadines
Trinidad and Tobago
Virgin Islands, British

Eligible Items

Most products from designated beneficiary countries may be eligible for CBI duty-free treatment. These items are identified by either an "E" or "E*" in the Special column under column 1 of the Harmonized Tariff Schedule. Merchandise classifiable under a subheading designated in this manner may qualify for duty-free entry if imported into the United States directly from any of the designated countries and territories.

Merchandise from one or more of these countries, however, may be excluded from time to time over the life of the program. Also, the list of beneficiary countries may change from time to time as well. Therefore, importers should consult the latest edition of the *Harmonized Tariff Schedule of the United States* for the most up-to-date information on eligible commodities. General Note 7(a) in the latest edition of the Harmonized Tariff Schedule contains updated information on the current list of beneficiary countries.

Claims

Merchandise will be eligible for CBI duty-free treatment only if the following conditions are met:

- The merchandise must have been produced in a beneficiary country. This requirement is satisfied when:
  1. The goods are wholly the growth, product, or manufacture of a beneficiary country, or
  2. The goods have been substantially transformed into a new or different article of commerce in a beneficiary country.
- The merchandise must be imported directly from any beneficiary country into the customs territory of the United States.
- For commercial shipments requiring a formal entry, a claim for preferential tariff treatment under CBI is made by showing that the country of origin is

a designated beneficiary country and by inserting the letter "E" as a prefix to the applicable tariff schedule number on CBP Form 7501.

■ At least 35 percent of the imported article's appraised value must consist of the cost or value of materials produced in one or more beneficiary countries and/ or the direct costs of processing operations performed in one or more beneficiary countries. The Commonwealth of Puerto Rico and the U.S. Virgin Islands are defined as beneficiary countries for purposes of this requirement; therefore, value attributable to Puerto Rico or to the Virgin Islands may also be counted. The cost or value of materials produced in the customs territory of the United States other than Puerto Rico may also be counted toward the 35 percent value-added requirement, but only to a maximum of 15 percent of the imported article's appraised value.

The cost or value of materials imported into a beneficiary country from a non-beneficiary country may be included in calculating the 35 percent value-added requirement for an eligible article if the materials are first substantially transformed into new or different articles of commerce that are subsequently used as constituent materials in the production of the eligible article. The phrase "direct costs of processing operations" includes costs directly incurred or reasonably allocated to the production of the article; for example, the cost of actual labor, dies, molds, tooling, depreciation of machinery, research and development, inspection, and testing. Business overhead, administrative expenses and profit, and general business expenses like casualty and liability insurance, advertising, and salespeople's salaries, are not considered direct costs of processing operations.

CBI II Sections 215 and 222

In addition to the origin rules enumerated above, the Customs and Trade Act of 1990 added new criteria for duty-free eligibility under the Caribbean Basin Initiative. First, articles that are the growth, product, or manufacture of Puerto Rico and that are subsequently processed in a CBI beneficiary country may also receive duty-free treatment if the three following conditions are met:

■ They are imported directly from a beneficiary country into the customs territory of the United States.
■ They are advanced in value or improved in condition by any means in a beneficiary country.
■ Any material added to the article in a beneficiary country must be a product of a beneficiary country or the United States.

In addition, articles that are assembled or processed in whole from U.S. components or ingredients (other than water) in a beneficiary country may be entered free of duty. Duty-free treatment will apply if the components or ingredients are exported directly to the beneficiary country, and the finished article is imported directly into the customs territory of the United States.

Importers and other interested parties may obtain an advance ruling to determine whether your commodity is eligible for CBI treatment.

Sources of Additional Information

CBP rules and regulations regarding CBI are incorporated in sections 10.191–10.198 of the CBP Regulations. Address any questions you may have about CBI's administrative or operational aspects to the port director where the merchandise will be entered, or to:

Director, Trade Enforcement and Facilitation Division
U.S. Customs and Border Protection
1300 Pennsylvania Avenue, NW
Washington, DC 20229

21. Andean Trade Preference Act (ATPA)/Andean Trade Promotion and Drug Eradication Act (ATPDEA)

The Andean Trade Preference Act (ATPA) provides for the duty-free entry of certain merchandise from designated beneficiary countries, Bolivia, Colombia, Ecuador, and Peru.

Eligible Items

When ATPA was renewed, portions of the Act were expanded into ATPDEA, which extends preferential treatment for merchandise previously excluded by ATPA. These include certain leather materials, watches and watch parts, petroleum and petroleum derivatives, tuna packaged in foil or other flexible packages, some footwear, and certain textile and apparel articles.

However, many products remain excluded from receiving preferential treatment, including certain textile and apparel items; rum and tafia; and above-quota imports of certain agricultural products like tuna in cans, syrups, sugars, and sugar products, which are subject to tariff-rate quotas.

Non-textile goods for which all ATPA countries are eligible for preferential treatment are identified by a "J" in the "Special" subcolumn under Column 1 of the Harmonized Tariff Schedule. Goods for which only some ATPA countries qualify for preferential treatment are identified by a "J*." Goods that qualify for preferential treatment in the expanded ATPDEA provision are identified by "J+."

Certain textile and apparel goods may enter the United States free of duty or restrictions on quantity if they meet certain requirements. The textile and apparel goods eligible for preferential treatment are listed in Chapter 98, subchapter XXI, of the Harmonized Tariff Schedule.

Rules of Origin

Commercial shipments from designated beneficiary countries that require formal entry may make a claim for preferential tariff treatment under ATPA/ATPDEA by entering the letter "J" on CBP Form 7501 (the entry summary) as a prefix to the appropriate tariff schedule number.

Non-textile merchandise will be eligible for ATPA/ATPDEA duty-free treatment only if the following conditions are met:

- The merchandise must have been produced in a beneficiary country. This requirement is satisfied when:
  1. The goods are wholly the growth, product, or manufacture of a beneficiary country, or
  2. The goods have been substantially transformed into a new or different article of commerce in a beneficiary country.
- The merchandise must be imported directly from any beneficiary country into the customs territory of the United States.
- At least 35 percent of the article's appraised value must consist of the cost or value of materials produced in one or more ATPA or CBI beneficiary countries and/or the direct costs of processing operations performed in one or more ATPA or CBI beneficiary countries. The Commonwealth of Puerto Rico and the U.S. Virgin Islands are defined as beneficiary countries for purposes of this requirement. In addition, the cost or value of materials produced in the customs territory of the United States (other than Puerto Rico) may be counted toward the 35 percent value-added requirement, but only to a maximum of 15 percent of the appraised value of the imported article.

Certain textile and apparel goods may enter the United States free of duty or restrictions on quantity if they meet certain requirements. The textile and apparel goods eligible for preferential treatment are listed in Chapter 98, subchapter XXI, of the Harmonized Tariff Schedule.

The cost or value of materials imported into ATPA or CBI beneficiary countries from non-beneficiary countries may be included when calculating the 35 percent value-added requirement for an eligible article if the materials are first substantially transformed into new or different articles of commerce and are then used as constituent materials in producing the eligible article. The phrase "direct costs of processing operations" means costs directly incurred or reasonably allocated to producing the article, including the cost of actual labor, dies, molds, tooling, depreciation of machinery, research and development, inspection, and testing. Business overhead, administrative expenses and profit, and other general business expenses like casualty and liability insurance, advertising, and salespeople's salaries, are not considered direct costs of processing operations.

Further information can be found at: cbp.gov/xp/cgov/import/international_agreements/atpa/

22. U.S.–Israel Free Trade Area Agreement (ILFTA)

The United States–Israel Free Trade Area agreement was originally enacted to provide for duty-free treatment for merchandise produced in Israel to stimulate trade between the two countries. This program was authorized by the United States in the Trade and Tariff Act of 1984, became effective September 1, 1985, and has no termination date. The Harmonized Tariff Schedule was amended to include General Note 8 implementing the U.S.–Israel Free Trade Area Implementation Act.

The ILFTA Implementation Act was amended on October 2, 1996, authorizing the president to implement certain changes affecting the duty status of goods from the West Bank, Gaza Strip, and qualifying industrial zones (QIZs). Presidential Proclamation 6955 of November 13, 1996, created General Note 3(v) to implement the new program for these goods. Pursuant to General Note 3(v), duty-free treatment is allowed for products of the West Bank, Gaza Strip, or a QIZ, imported directly from the West Bank, Gaza Strip, a QIZ or Israel, provided certain requirements are met. Presidential Proclamation 6955 also modified the eligibility requirements for duty-free treatment of articles that are the product of Israel.

General Note 3(a)(v)(G) of the Harmonized Tariff Schedule defines a QIZ as any area that:

1. Encompasses portions of the territory of Israel and Jordan or Israel and Egypt;
2. Has been designated by local authorities as an enclave where merchandise may enter without payment of duty or excise taxes; and
3. Has been designated as a QIZ by the United States Trade Representative in a notice published in the *Federal Register*.

Eligible Items

The ILFTA applies to a broad range of tariff items listed in the Harmonized Tariff Schedule and identified by "IL" in the "Special" column.

Products of Israel

An article imported into the customs territory of the United States is eligible for treatment as a "product of Israel" only if:

■ The merchandise has been produced in Israel. This requirement is satisfied when
  1. The goods are wholly the growth, product, or manufacture of Israel, or
  2. The goods have been substantially transformed into a new or different article of commerce in Israel;
■ That article is imported directly from Israel, the West Bank, Gaza Strip, or a QIZ into the customs territory of the United States;

■ The sum of:
1. The cost or value of the materials produced in Israel, the West Bank, Gaza Strip, or a QIZ, plus
2. The direct costs of processing operations performed in Israel, the West Bank, Gaza Strip, or a QIZ

is not less than 35 percent of the appraised value of such article at the time it is entered. If the cost or value of materials produced in the customs territory of the United States is included with respect to an eligible article, an amount not to exceed 15 percent of the appraised value of the article at the time it is entered may be applied toward determining the 35 percent.

Products of the West Bank, Gaza Strip, or a Qualifying Industrial Zone

An article imported into the customs territory of the United States is eligible for treatment as a product of the West Bank, Gaza Strip, or a QIZ only if:

■ The article is the growth, product, or manufacture of the West Bank, Gaza Strip, or a QIZ,
■ The article is imported directly from the West Bank, Gaza Strip, a QIZ, or Israel into the customs territory of the United States,
■ The sum of:
1. The cost or value of the materials produced in the West Bank, Gaza Strip, a QIZ, or Israel, plus
2. The direct costs of processing operations performed in the West Bank, Gaza Strip, a QIZ, or Israel

is not less than 35 percent of the appraised value of such article at the time it is entered. If the cost or value of materials produced in the customs territory of the United States is included with respect to an eligible article, an amount not to exceed 15 percent of the appraised value of the article at the time it is entered may be applied toward the 35 percent.

No article may be considered to meet these requirements by virtue of having undergone:

■ Simple combining or packaging operations, or
■ Mere diluting with water or another substance that does not materially alter the characteristics of the article.

The phrase "direct costs of processing operations" includes, but is not limited to:

- All actual labor costs involved in the growth, production, manufacture, or assembly of the specific merchandise, including fringe benefits, on-the-job training and the costs of engineering, supervisory, quality control, and similar personnel.
- Dies, molds, tooling, and depreciation on machinery and equipment that are allocable to the specific merchandise.

Direct costs of processing operations do not include costs that are not directly attributable to the merchandise concerned or are not costs of manufacturing the product, such as:

1. Profit,
2. General expenses of doing business that are either not allocable to the specific merchandise or are not related to the growth, production, manufacture, or assembly of the merchandise, such as administrative salaries, casualty and liability insurance, advertising and sales staff salaries, or commissions or expenses.

Certificate of Origin Form A

The United Nations Conference on Trade and Development Certificate of Origin Form A is used as documentary evidence to support duty-free and reduced-rate claims for Israeli articles covered by a formal entry. It does not have to be produced at the time of entry, however, unless CBP requests it at that time.

Form A may be presented on an entry-by-entry basis or may be used as a blanket declaration for a period of 12 months. Form A can be obtained from the Israeli authorizing issuing authority or from:

United Nations Conference on Trade and Development
Two U.N. Plaza
Room 1120
New York, NY 10017
Tel. 212-963-6895

Informal Entries

Form A is not required for commercial or non-commercial shipments covered by an informal entry. However, the port director may require other evidence of the country of origin as deemed necessary.

In order to avoid delays to passengers, the inspecting CBP officer will extend Israeli duty-free or reduced-rate treatment to all eligible articles accompanying the traveler if the available facts satisfy the officer that the merchandise concerned is a product of Israel. In such cases, Form A is not required.

Sources of Additional Information

Questions about the administrative or operational aspects of the ILFTA should be addressed to:

> Executive Director, Trade Compliance and Facilitation Division
> U.S. Customs and Border Protection
> Washington, DC 20229

> Requests for information about ILFTA policy issues should be directed to:

> Chairman, Trade Policy Staff Subcommittee
> Office of U.S. Trade Representative
> 600 17th St., NW
> Washington, DC 20506

23. U.S.–Jordan Free Trade Area Agreement (JFTA)

The United States–Jordan Free Trade Area agreement went into effect on December 17, 2001, and provides for the elimination of tariffs on almost all qualifying goods within 10 years.

Eligible Items

JFTA benefits apply to tariff items listed in the Harmonized Tariff Schedule and identified by "JO" in the Special column.

Eligibility Requirements, General

An article imported into the customs territory of the United States is eligible for JFTA preference if:

- It was wholly obtained or produced entirely in Jordan with no foreign inputs; or
- It is a "product of" Jordan, and the sum of (1) the cost of the materials produced in Jordan, plus (2) the direct costs of processing performed in Jordan is not less than 35 percent of the article's appraised value at the time it enters the commerce of the United States. Materials produced in the United States that do not to exceed 15 percent of the article's appraised value may be applied toward the 35 percent threshold; and
- The article is imported directly into the United States.

Eligibility Requirements, Textiles and Apparel

Textile and apparel articles, with exceptions, are subject to the same "substantial transformation plus 35 percent" value-content rule as non-textiles (see Harmonized Tariff Schedule, General Note 18(d)).

Qualified Industrial Zones

The JFTA does not affect merchandise entered from a Qualifying Industrial Zone (QIZ). Because duty reductions for some products will be staged, importers may choose to continue entering qualifying merchandise under the QIZ, rather than under the JFTA.

Certification

CBP does not require presentation of a certificate of origin. By making the preference claim, the importer is deemed to certify that the goods meet the requirements of the agreement.

Documentation

The importer shall be prepared to submit to CBP a declaration setting forth the pertinent information concerning the article's production or manufacture and all supporting documentation upon which the declaration is based. This information must be retained in the importer's files for five years. The importer's failure to provide the declaration and/or sufficient evidentiary documentation will result in the claim's denial.

Merchandise Processing Fees

The JFTA provides no exemption from payment of the merchandise processing fee.

Sources of Additional Information

Additional information is available on CBP's Web site at: www.cbp.gov/xp/cgov/import/international_agreements/free_trade/usjfta.xml or www.cbp.gov/xp/cgov/import/textiles_and_quotas/.

Information can also be found on the U.S. Trade Representative Web site, www.ustr.gov/Trade_Agreements/Bilateral/Jordan/Section_Index.html.

References

- Presidential Proclamation 7512, December 7, 2001,
- Public Law 107-43, September 28, 2001,
- Harmonized Tariff Schedule of the United States, General Note 18.

24. Compact of Free Association (FAS)

FAS is a program providing for the duty-free entry of certain merchandise from designated freely associated states. (U.S. Pub. Law 99-239, Compact of Free Assoc.

Act of 1985, 48 USC 1681 Note. 59 Stat. 1031 and amended Dec. 17, 2003 by House Jt. Res. 63; U.S. Pub. Law 180-188)

The Compact of Free Association between the Federated States of Micronesia and the United States was initialed by negotiators in 1980 and signed in 1982. The Compact was approved by the citizens of the FSM in a plebiscite held in 1983. Legislation on the Compact was adopted by the U.S. Congress in 1986, and signed into law on November 13, 1986.

Beneficiary Countries

The following freely associated states have been designated as beneficiary countries for purposes of the FAS:

Marshall Islands
Federated States of Micronesia
Republic of Palau

Eligible Items

The duty-free treatment is applied to most products from the designated beneficiaries. For commercial shipments requiring formal entry, a claim for duty-free status is made by placing the letter "Z" next to the eligible subheading. The following merchandise is excluded from the duty-free exemption:

- Textile and apparel articles that are subject to textile agreements.
- Footwear, handbags, luggage, flat goods, work gloves, and leather wearing apparel that were not eligible for GSP treatment, discussed in Chapter 17 of the Harmonized Tariff Schedule on, April 1, 1984.
- Watches, clocks, and timing apparatus of Chapter 91 of the Harmonized Tariff Schedule (except such articles incorporating an opto-electronic display and no other type of display).
- Buttons of subheading 9606.21.40 or 9606.29.20 of the Harmonized Tariff Schedule.
- Tuna and skipjack, prepared or preserved, not in oil, in airtight containers weighing with their contents not more than 7 kilograms each, "in excess" of the consumption quota quantity allowed duty-free entry.
- Any agricultural product of Chapters 2 through 52 inclusive, of the Harmonized Tariff Schedule that is subject to a tariff-rate quota, if entered in a quantity in excess of the in-quota quantity for such products.

Rules of Origin

Merchandise will be eligible for FAS duty-free treatment only if the following conditions are met:

■ The merchandise must have been produced in the freely associated state. This requirement is satisfied when (1) the goods are wholly the growth, product, or manufacture of the freely associated state, or (2) the goods have been substantially transformed into a new or different article of commerce in the freely associated state.

■ The merchandise must be imported directly from the freely associated state into the customs territory of the United States.

■ At least 35 percent of the appraised value of the article imported into the United States must consist of the cost or value of materials produced in the beneficiary country. In addition, the cost or value of materials produced in the customs territory of the United States may be counted toward the 35 percent value-added requirement, but only to a maximum of 15 percent of the appraised value of the imported article. The cost or value of the materials imported into the freely associated state from a non-beneficiary country may be included in calculating the 35 percent value-added requirement for an eligible article if the materials are first substantially transformed into new or different articles of commerce and are then used as constituent materials in the production of the eligible product.

Sources of Additional Information

Address any questions you may have about the administrative or operational aspects of the FAS to the port director where the merchandise will be entered or to:

Director
Commercial Compliance Division
U.S. Customs and Border Protection
Washington, DC 20229

25. African Growth and Opportunity Act (AGOA)

The African Growth and Opportunity Act provides duty-free treatment under the Generalized System of Preferences (GSP) for certain articles from sub-Saharan African countries that would normally be excluded from GSP provisions. AGOA also provides for the duty-free, quantity-free entry of specific textile and apparel articles provided that strict conditions are met. This preferential treatment for eligible textiles and apparel is subject to certain limitations.

Non-textile, non-apparel AGOA claims are designated by inserting the symbol "D" in the "Rates of Duty 1-Special" column of the Harmonized Tariff Schedule for subheadings covering such articles. Textile and apparel claims are made by entering the appropriate Chapter 98 tariff number, details of which may be found in subchapter XIX of Chapter 98 of the Harmonized Tariff Schedule.

Beneficiary Countries

There are three types of beneficiary-country designations under AGOA:

- Beneficiary sub-Saharan African countries;
- Lesser-developed beneficiary sub-Saharan African countries; and
- Beneficiary sub-Saharan African countries eligible for textile/apparel benefits.

The president will monitor and review annually the current or potential eligibility of sub-Saharan African countries to be designated as beneficiary countries. Thus, the list of such countries may change over the life of the program. Importers should consult General Note 16 of the latest edition of the Harmonized Tariff Schedule of the United States for the current information on designated countries.

Countries designated as *beneficiary* sub-Saharan African countries for AGOA purposes are listed in General Note 16 of the Harmonized Tariff Schedule. Sub-Saharan African countries designated as *lesser-developed beneficiary* countries for AGOA purposes are listed in Chapter 98, subchapter XIX, U.S. Note 2(d), of the Harmonized Tariff Schedule. Countries that have established visa systems and can import textiles and apparel merchandise for purposes of AGOA are listed in Chapter 98, subchapter XIX, U.S. Note 1, of the Harmonized Tariff Schedule.

Eligible Items

Expanded GSP Treatment

The Trade Act of 1974 authorizes the president to provide duty-free treatment under the GSP to certain articles that would otherwise be excluded from such treatment. A variety of products have been designated as eligible for duty-free treatment for beneficiary sub-Saharan African countries, including:

- Some watches and clocks,
- Certain electronics,
- Certain steel and metals,
- Certain textiles and wearing apparel, and
- Certain semi-manufactured and manufactured glass products.

A complete listing of products eligible for duty-free treatment under AGOA is available on the Web at www.agoa.gov. The president may extend duty-free treatment to imports of essentially all products except textiles and apparel, as long as the products:

- Are the "growth, product or manufacture" of a beneficiary sub-Saharan African country,
- Are imported directly from a beneficiary sub-Saharan African country into the customs territory of the U.S.,

- Meet a value-added requirement, and
- The president determines that the products are not import-sensitive in the context of imports from beneficiary sub-Saharan African countries. Sub-Saharan African beneficiary countries are also exempted from competitive-need limitations.

Sub-Saharan African beneficiary countries are also exempted from competitive-need limitations.

Preferential Treatment for Certain Textile and Apparel Articles

In order for textile or apparel articles to be eligible for preferential treatment, the beneficiary sub-Saharan African country must be designated as eligible for textile/apparel benefits. This designation requires that the United States determine whether the country has satisfied the requirements of AGOA regarding that country's procedures to protect against unlawful transshipments (including an effective visa system) and the implementation of procedures and requirements similar in all material respects to the relevant procedures and requirements under Chapter 5 of the NAFTA. The United States Trade Representative will publish a *Federal Register* notice when it designates a country as eligible for preferential treatment. This information will be available on the Web at www.ustr.gov and at www.agoa.gov.

AGOA provides duty-free and quota-free benefits to imports of certain textile and apparel articles produced in eligible sub-Saharan African countries. In most instances, these benefits are available regardless of the total volume of apparel exported from eligible countries to the United States. The six broad categories of textile and apparel articles that may receive preferential treatment are listed in Chapter 98, subchapter XIX, of the Harmonized Tariff Schedule.

Sources of additional information

The entire text of the AGOA agreement is available on the Web at www.agoa.gov.

CBP rules and regulations about AGOA are incorporated in sections 10.211–10.217 of the CBP Regulations. Additional regulations implementing the GSP provisions are incorporated in section 10.178 of the CBP Regulations. CBP regulations pertaining to AGOA are also available on the Web at www.agoa.gov.

For answers to specific questions or to request a ruling, send inquiries to:

Director
National Commodity Specialist Division
U.S. Customs and Border Protection
One Penn Plaza, 11th Floor
New York, NY 10119

Further information regarding importing procedures is also available on the CBP Web site, cbp.gov/xp/cgov/import/international_agreements/.

The Office of the United States Trade Representative has prepared an *African Growth and Opportunity Act Implementation Guide* available at the AGOA Web site, www.agoa.gov. Questions about AGOA not covered in the guidebook may be directed to:

Office of African Affairs
Office of the United States Trade Representative
600 17th Street, NW
Washington, DC 20508
Tel. 202-395-9514
Fax: 202-395-4505

Additional information on the GSP program is available at the United States Trade Representative Web site, www.ustr.gov, and from the GSP Information Center, Office of the U.S. Trade Representative, at the above address, tel. 202.395.6971.

Information on apparel cap, fabric and yarn not available in commercial quantities, and on hand-loomed, handmade, and folklore articles is available from the Department of Commerce, Office of Textile and Apparel, at otexa.ita. doc.gov.

26. United States–Caribbean Basin Trade Partnership Act (CBTPA)

The United States–Caribbean Basin Trade Partnership Act expands the trade benefits currently available to Caribbean and Central American countries under the Caribbean Basin Economic Recovery Act (CBERA; see Chapter 18.)

The CBTPA allows specific textile and apparel articles to enter the United States free of duty or restrictions on quantity, provided certain conditions are met. It also extends NAFTA standards of duty to non-textile articles that were previously excluded from duty-free treatment under the CBERA.

The U.S.-Caribbean Trade Partnership Act (CBTPA) trade benefits, which began on October 1, 2000, expands the list of duty-free products and offers more market access opportunities to CBTPA-eligible countries while meeting various criteria. Congress has reauthorized this program until September 20, 2020.

On August 6, 2002, the president signed into law the Trade Act of 2002, which made a number of changes to the textile and apparel provisions of paragraph (2)(A) of section 213(b) of the CBERA.

Beneficiary Countries

The list of beneficiary countries may change over the life of the program. A current listing of countries eligible for designation as beneficiary countries can be found in General Note 17 of the Harmonized Tariff Schedule.

CBTPA's enhanced trade benefits are available to countries designated as CBTPA beneficiary countries. To receive these benefits, CBTPA countries must have satisfied the trade pact's requirements that the eligible country has implemented procedures and requirements that are similar in all material respects to the relevant procedures and requirements under Chapter Five of NAFTA.

Eligible Items

Preferential Treatment for Certain Textile and Apparel Articles

Certain textile and apparel articles may enter the United States free of duty and restrictions on quantity. The textile and apparel articles eligible for preferential treatment are listed in Chapter 98 of the Harmonized Tariff Schedule.

The CBP regulations that implement the CBTPA include specific documentary, procedural, and other requirements that must be met in order to obtain CBTPA benefits. The CBP regulations and General Note 17 of the HTS should be consulted *before* importing merchandise in order to ensure that all requirements have been met.

NAFTA Parity

Except for textile and apparel articles, the CBTPA allows NAFTA tariff treatment for goods previously excluded from the CBI program. Thus, imported footwear, canned tuna, petroleum and petroleum products, watches and watch parts, handbags, luggage, flat goods, work gloves and leather wearing apparel, *when qualifying as CBTPA originating goods*, are eligible for a reduction in duty equal to the rate given to Mexican products under the staged duty-rate reductions set forth in NAFTA.

Claims

Articles that the president has designated as eligible for CBTPA treatment are those whose duty rate in the "Special" subcolumn is followed by the symbol "R" in Chapters 1 through 97 of the Harmonized Tariff Schedule. Whenever a rate of duty other than "free" appears in this subcolumn for any heading or subheading followed by the symbol "E" or "E*," and a lower rate of duty followed by the symbol "R" also appears in the subcolumn, an eligible article will receive the lower rate of duty.

Certain Beverages Made with Caribbean Rum

The CBTPA provides duty-free treatment to certain liqueurs and spirituous beverages produced in the territory of Canada from rum that is the growth, product, or manufacture of a CBTPA beneficiary country or of the U.S. Virgin Islands.

Sources of Additional Information

CBP rules and regulations on the CBTPA are incorporated in Sections 10.221–10.228 and 10.231–10.237 of the CBP regulations. Additional information can be found on the CBP Web site at www.cbp.gov/xp/cgov/import/international_agreements/ or at http://www.cbp.gov/xp/cgov/import/international_agreements/.

It is also necessary to consult General Note 17 of the Harmonized Tariff Schedule for specific requirements of CBTPA.

For answers to specific questions or to request a ruling, send inquiries to:

Director, National Commodity Specialist Division
U.S. Customs and Border Protection
One Penn Plaza, 10th Floor
New York, NY 10019

Information on CBTPA may also be obtained from:

Office of the United States Trade Representative
Office of the Western Hemisphere
600 17th Street, NW
Washington, DC 20508
Tel: 202-395-5190
Fax: 202-395-9675

Additional information on quantity limitations; fabric and yarn not available in commercial quantities; and hand-loomed, handmade, and folklore articles may be available at the Department of Commerce Office of Textile and Apparel Web site at otexa.ita.doc.gov. The Department of Commerce also provides detailed information on the CBTPA at www.mac.doc.gov/CBI/webmain/intro.htm.

27. The U.S.–Chile Free Trade Agreement (US–CFTA)

The U.S.–Chile Free Trade Agreement (US–CFTA) took effect January 1, 2004, with the enactment of the US-CFTA Implementation Act (P. L.108-77; 117 Stat. 909). (Presidential Proclamation 7746, the official announcement of US–CFTA, incorporates by reference Publication 3652 of the U.S. International Trade Commission. Publication 3652 amends the Harmonized Tariff Schedule by adding General Note 26, which implements the duty provisions of the US–CFTA. Title 19, Code of Federal Regulations is being amended to implement the US–CFTA.)

The US–CFTA eliminates duties on goods originating in Chile and the United States over a maximum transition period of 12 years. Under the schedule to eliminate duties, 85 percent of Chilean goods received immediate duty-free status. Duties on the remaining goods will phase out in four-, eight-, 10- and 12-year stages, although Chile and the United States may later choose to accelerate these phase-outs.

Eligible Items

According to the rules set forth in the Agreement and incorporated into our domestic legislation as General Note 26 of the Harmonized Tariff Schedule, merchandise that originates in Chile or the United States will receive a reduced or free rate of duty. Goods that originate elsewhere and are merely transshipped through Chile will not be entitled to these benefits.

Originating is a term used to describe goods that meet the requirements of Article 4.1 of the Agreement. Article 4.1 defines *originating* as goods that meet one of the following conditions:

- The good is wholly obtained or produced entirely in the territory of Chile or the United States,
- The good is produced in the territory of Chile or the United States and meets the rule specified in Annex 4.1, through either a tariff shift or tariff-shift-plus-regional-value content rules, or
- The good is produced entirely in the territory of Chile or the United States exclusively from originating materials.

Originating goods that subsequently undergo any operation outside of the territories of Chile or the United States other than unloading, reloading, or other processes necessary to preserve the condition of the good, will lose their originating status. Goods that have undergone simple combining or packaging operations or mere dilution with water or other substances will not be considered originating.

Entry Procedures

Importers may claim preferential duty treatment for commercial shipments requiring a formal entry by prefixing "CL" to the tariff classification number on the CF 7501 (Entry Summary).

Pursuant to Article 4.13(7) of the Agreement, the United States does not require a certificate of origin when the value of the originating goods is US $2,500 or less.

Certification of Origin

The US-CFTA requires the importer to substantiate the validity of a claim for preferential treatment. At CBP's request, an importer must submit a certification of origin or other supporting documentation to demonstrate that the imported goods "originate," as defined by the Act.

A US-CFTA certification of origin is not an official form, as it is in other trade agreements, and does not need to be in a prescribed format. The certification of origin may take many forms, such as a statement on company letterhead, a statement on a commercial invoice, or supporting documentation. Whatever form or format is used, however, must contain the following data elements to demonstrate that the goods are US-CFTA originating goods:

- Name and address of the importer,
- Name and address of the exporter,
- Name and address of the producer,
- Description of good,
- Harmonized tariff classification number,
- Preference criterion,
- Commercial invoice number on single shipments,
- Identify the blanket period in "mm/dd/yyyy to mm/dd/yyyy" format (12-month maximum) for multiple shipments of identical goods,
- Authorized signature, company, title, telephone, fax, e-mail and certification date,
- Certification that the information is correct.

The certification of origin may cover a single entry or multiple entries in a period not to exceed 12 months. The importer must retain the certificate of origin and supporting documentation in the United States and must provide it to CBP upon request.

Sources of Additional Information

CBP has drafted regulations that implement the provisions of the US-CFTA. These may be found in sections 10.401 through 10.490, CBP regulations. Also, information has been posted on the CBP Web site at: www.cbp.gov/xp/cgov/import/international_agreements/

28. The U.S.–Singapore Free Trade Agreement (US–SFTA)

The provisions of the U.S.–Singapore Free Trade Agreement Implementation Act (Public Law 108-78; 117 Stat. 948; 19 USC 3805 note) took effect on January

1, 2004. Upon implementation, the Harmonized Tariff Schedule was amended to include General Note 25, which contains specific information regarding the U.S.–Singapore Free Trade Agreement. The agreement provides for the immediate or staged elimination of duties and barriers to bilateral trade in goods and services originating in the United States and Singapore over a period of ten years. Customs regulations are being updated to implement the provisions of this agreement.

According to Section 202 of the US–SFTA Implementation Act, in general, non-textile goods shall qualify for preferential tariff treatment as a "product of Singapore" if:

- The good is wholly obtained or produced entirely in Singapore, the U.S., or both;
- Each non-originating material used in the production of the good imported from Singapore either:
  1. Undergoes an applicable change in tariff classification (tariff shift) specified in General Note 25(o) of the Harmonized Tariff Schedule as a result of production occurring entirely in Singapore, the United States, or both, or
  2. The good otherwise satisfies the applicable regional value content or other requirements specified in General Note 25(o).
- The good, as imported, is enumerated in General Note 25(m) as imported from Singapore, a provision known as the Integrated Sourcing Initiative.

A textile or apparel good must meet the terms of General Note 25 in order to receive the preferential tariff treatment under the US–SFTA.

Integrated Sourcing Initiative (ISI)

Per Article 3.2(1) of the US–SFTA, certain information technology and medical products listed in General Note 25(m) may be considered originating goods for purposes of the Agreement when shipped between the United States and Singapore, regardless of whether they satisfy the applicable rule of origin. Singapore must be the country of export in order for ISI-eligible goods to receive benefits under the US–SFTA; however, the country of origin of the good may be any country. An ISI product does not qualify as "originating" simply by being imported into Singapore or the United States—shipment from one US–SFTA country to another is required to obtain originating status.

The ISI provision eliminates the requirement that these products must meet specific rules of origin under "tariff shift" or "regional value content" requirements. The only way an ISI material, component, or product would affect a regional-value-content calculation is if an ISI product is shipped from a non-FTA party (Malaysia, for example) to Singapore and then to the United States (and is held there without undergoing any processing) and then shipped back to Singapore where the ISI product is used as input for the manufacture of a non-ISI good.

Upon request, documents must be provided to CBP verifying that goods claiming preferential treatment under this ISI provision were exported directly from the country of Singapore. For purposes of ISI, the territory of Singapore is defined as its land territory, internal waters, and territorial sea, plus certain maritime zones. The goods must still be marked with the true country of origin—despite receiving originating status under US–SFTA.

Entry Procedures

For commercial shipments requiring a formal entry, a claim for preferential tariff treatment may be filed at the time of entry summary by placing the symbol "SG" as a prefix to the Harmonized Tariff Schedule subheading for each good or line item for which treatment is being claimed. For non-originating apparel goods eligible for preferential treatment under a tariff-preference level (TPL), please refer to General Note 25 and Subchapter X of Chapter 99 of the Harmonized Tariff Schedule.

Customs Verification

If CBP requests, the importer must submit a statement or supporting documentation containing informational data elements to demonstrate that the imported goods qualify for preferential tariff treatment. There is no official CBP form or required format for certification, and the statement may be submitted electronically.

Importers are required to maintain all records relating to the importation of US–SFTA goods for five years after the date of importation. These include, but are not limited to, records concerning the purchase of, cost of, value of, and payment for the good, the purchase of, cost of, value of, and payment for all materials used in the production of the good, and the production of the good in its exported form.

Further information on the U.S.–Singapore Free Trade Agreement is available at: cbp.gov/xp/cgov/import/international_agreements/.

29. Antidumping and Countervailing Duties

Antidumping (AD) and countervailing (CVD) duties are additional duties that may be assessed on imported goods intended for sale in the United States at abnormally low prices. These low prices are the result of unfair foreign trade practices that give some imports an unearned advantage over competing U.S. goods.

Dumping is the practice of trying to sell products in the United States at lower prices than those same products would bring in the producer's home market. Dumping also includes trying to sell a product in the United States at a price lower than it cost to manufacture that item. Subsidizing is the practice by some governments of providing financial assistance to reduce manufacturers' costs in producing, manufacturing, or exporting particular commodities. Countervailing duties may be assessed to "level the playing field" between domestic and subsidized imported goods. However, to meet the criteria for assessing antidumping or countervailing duties, the imported merchandise must, in addition to being subsidized or sold at less than fair value, also injure a U.S. industry.*

The Department of Commerce, the International Trade Commission (ITC), and U.S. Customs and Border Protection each have a role in administering and enforcing antidumping and countervailing duty laws.

The Commerce Department is responsible for the general administration of these laws. Commerce determines whether the merchandise is being sold at less than fair value, whether it has been subsidized, and what percentage rate of duty will be assessed. The ITC determines whether the product poses an injury† to a particular U.S. industry. CBP assesses the actual duties—the amount—based upon the rate set by the Commerce Department once the ITC has determined that the import injures a particular industry.

In general, the following processes must be completed before AD or CVD duties are established.

Antidumping and countervailing duty investigations are usually initiated by the Commerce Department through the petition process. A domestic industry or another interested party such as a trade union or industry association petitions the department, although occasionally the Commerce Department may also initiate an investigation. If the party seeking the investigation also wants the ITC to test for injury, that party must simultaneously—on the same day—file the petition with both the Commerce Department and with the ITC.

If the petition contains the necessary elements, the Commerce Department and the ITC will initiate separate investigations that will yield preliminary and final determinations. If appropriate, the Department of Commerce will issue either an antidumping or countervailing duty order and will assess whatever AD or CVD duties the investigation determines are appropriate.

If a test is required for injury to a domestic industry, the ITC will make the first, preliminary determination concerning the likelihood of injury. If that determination is negative, there will be no further investigation or action by the ITC. If it is affirmative, however, the Commerce Department will issue its preliminary determination regarding sales (antidumping) or subsidy (countervailing duty) issues.

After additional review by the Commerce Department and analysis of public comments received in the case, Commerce will issue its final duty determinations. If either determination (AD or CVD) is affirmative, Commerce will direct CBP to suspend liquidation of entries for the merchandise subject to the investigation and to require cash deposits or bonds equal to the amount of the estimated dumping

---

* CVD cases apply only if the foreign country is a signatory to the World Trade Organization's Agreement on Subsidies and Countervailing Measures.
† Section 771(7)(a) of the Tariff Act of 1930 defines material injury to a U.S. industry as "harm [that] is not inconsequential, immaterial, or unimportant."

margin (the differential between the fair market value and the U.S. price) or the net subsidy.

After this step, the ITC follows with its final injury determination. If this determination is also affirmative, Commerce will issue an antidumping or countervailing duty order. At that time, Commerce will also direct CBP to collect, with a very limited exception for new shippers, cash deposits of estimated duties.

A negative final determination either by Commerce or the ITC would terminate the investigations, and that termination would remain final for this particular inquiry. Both agencies announce their determinations, including orders and the results of the administration reviews (described below), in the Federal Register.

Each year during the anniversary month of the AD or CVD order, interested parties may review the order with respect to the individual producers or resellers it covers. This review generally looks at the 12 months preceding the anniversary month, but the first review can also include any period for which the suspension of liquidations was directed prior to the normal 12-month period.

If no annual review is requested, Commerce will direct CBP to continue collecting deposits and assessing duties on the subject merchandise at the cash or bond rate in effect on the date of entry, and to continue requiring deposits at that rate for future entries of such merchandise. If a review is requested, Commerce will conduct a review similar to its original investigation, issue revised rates for duty assessment and deposits, and instruct CBP to collect duties and liquidate entries according to the results of its latest review.

30. Drawback—Refunds of Duties

Drawback is a refund of monies—customs duties, certain internal revenue taxes, and other fees—that were lawfully collected at the time of importation. The Continental Congress established drawback in 1789 to create jobs in the new United States and to encourage manufacturing and exporting.

For drawback to be paid, the imported merchandise must be exported or destroyed under CBP supervision after importation.

Types of Drawback

Although Section 1313, Title 19, of the United States Code provides for several types of drawback, there are three primary types of drawback of interest to most importers:

- Manufacturing drawback,
- Unused-merchandise drawback, or
- Rejected-merchandise drawback.

Manufacturing drawback is a refund of duties paid on imported merchandise specifically designated for use in manufacturing articles that are subsequently exported or destroyed. For example: two-inch speakers are imported and are incorporated into a certain model clock radio. The speakers themselves are not altered, just used in the production of a new and different article.

Manufacturing operations to produce the new and different article must take place within three years receipt by the manufacturer or producer of the merchandise. The drawback product must be exported or destroyed within five years from the date of importation. Drawback can be paid on merchandise used to manufacture or produce a different article if it was not the merchandise imported but is commercially interchangeable, i.e., of the same kind and quality, or if it falls under the same eight-digit Harmonized Tariff Schedule number as the merchandise to which it is compared, and the party claiming drawback has had possession of it for three years. This is called "substitution."

Unused-merchandise drawback is a refund of any duty, tax, or eligible fees paid on imported merchandise that is exported or destroyed without undergoing any manufacturing operations and that is never used in the United States. The imported merchandise must be exported within three years of the date it was imported.

Rejected-merchandise drawback is refund of duties on imported merchandise that is exported or destroyed because it:

■ Did not conform to sample or specifications,
■ Was shipped without the consignee's consent, or
■ Was defective at time of importation.

To qualify for rejected-merchandise drawback, the merchandise in question must be returned to CBP custody within three years of the date it was originally released from CBP custody.

Guidelines for completing drawback claims are provided in Title 19, Code of Federal Regulations, Part 191. Drawback claims can only be filed at one of the five CBP port offices that have drawback centers:

■ Chicago, IL,
■ Houston, TX,
■ Los Angles, CA,
■ New York/Newark, N.J., and
■ San Francisco, CA.

Rejected merchandise drawback was amended in 2004 to permit limited substitution of imported merchandise. The import merchandise on which drawback is claimed must be classified under the same 8-digit HTSUS subheading and have the same specific product indicator (such as a part number, product code, or sku) as the merchandise that is exported or destroyed and must have been imported within one year of the export or destruction.

Additional questions about drawback should be addressed to:

Chief, Entry and Drawback Management
Office of Field Operations
U.S. Customs and Border Protection
1300 Pennsylvania Avenue, NW
Washington, DC 20229

Classification and Value

31. Classification—Liquidation

Classification

Classification, and, when ad valorem rates of duty are applicable, appraisement, are the two most important factors affecting dutiable status. Classification and valuation, whether or not they are pertinent because an ad valorem rate of duty applies, must be provided by commercial importers when an entry is filed. In addition, classifications under the statistical suffixes of the tariff schedules must also be furnished, even though this information is not pertinent to dutiable status. Accordingly, classification is initially the responsibility of an importer, customs broker, or other person preparing the entry papers. Section 637 of the Customs Modernization Act imposes the requirement that importers exercise reasonable care when classifying and appraising merchandise.

Familiarity with the organization of the Harmonized Tariff Schedule of the United States facilitates the classification process. The tariff schedule is divided into various sections and chapters dealing separately with merchandise in broad product categories. These categories cover animal products, vegetable products, products of various basic materials such as wood, textiles, plastics, rubber, steel, and other metal products in various stages of manufacture, for example. Other sections encompass chemicals, machinery and electrical equipment, and other specified or non-enumerated products. The last section, Section XXII, covers certain exceptions from duty and special statutory provisions.

In Sections I through XXI, products are classifiable (1) under items or descriptions that name them, known as an *eo nomine* provision; (2) under provisions of general description; (3) under provisions that identify them by component material; or (4) under provisions that encompass merchandise in accordance with its actual or principal use. When two or more provisions seem to cover the same merchandise, the prevailing provision is determined in accordance with the legal notes and the General Rules of Interpretation for the tariff schedule. Also applicable are tariff classification principles contained in administrative precedents or in the case law of the U.S. Court of International Trade (formerly the U.S. Customs Court) or the U.S. Court of Appeals for the Federal Circuit (formerly the U.S. Court of Customs and Patent Appeals).

Liquidation

CBP officers at the port of entry or other officials acting on behalf of the port director review selected classifications and valuations, as well as other required import information, for correctness or as a proper basis for appraisement, as well as for agreement of the submitted data with the merchandise actually imported. The entry summary and documentation may be accepted as submitted without any changes. In this situation, the entry is liquidated as entered. Liquidation is the point at which CBP's ascertainment of the rate and amount of duty becomes final for most purposes. Liquidation is accomplished by posting a notice on a public bulletin board at the customhouse. However, an importer may receive an advance notice on CBP Form 4333A "Courtesy Notice" stating when and in what amount duty will be liquidated. This form is not the liquidation, and protest rights do not accrue until the notice is posted. Time limits for protesting do not start until the date of posting, and a protest cannot be filed before liquidation is posted.

CBP may determine that an entry cannot be liquidated as entered for one reason or another. For example, the tariff classification may not be correct or may not be acceptable because it is not consistent with established and uniform classification practice. If the change required by this determination results in a rate of duty more favorable to an importer, the entry is liquidated accordingly and a refund is authorized for the applicable amount of the deposited estimated duties. On the other hand, a change may be necessary that imposes a higher rate of duty. For example, a claim for an exemption from duty under a free-rate provision or under a conditional exemption may be found to be insufficient for lack of the required supporting documentation. In this situation, the importer will be given an advance notice of the proposed duty rate increase and an opportunity to validate the claim for a free rate or more favorable rate of duty.

If the importer does not respond to the notice, or if the response is found to be without merit, entry is liquidated in accordance with the entry as corrected, and the importer is billed for the additional duty. The port may find that the importer's response raises issues of such complexity that resolution is warranted by a CBP Headquarters decision through the internal advice procedure. Internal advice from CBP Headquarters may be requested by local CBP officers on their own initiative or in response to a request by the importer.

Protests

After liquidation, an importer may still pursue, on CBP Form 19 (19 CFR 174), any claims for an adjustment or refund filing a protest within 180 days after liquidation. In order to apply for a Headquarters ruling, a request for further review must be filed with the protest. The same Form 19 can be used for this purpose. If filed separately, application for further review must still be filed within 90 days of liquidation. However, if a ruling on the question has previously been issued in response to a request for a decision on a prospective transaction or a request for internal advice, further review will ordinarily be denied. If a protest is denied, an importer has the right to litigate the matter by filing a summons with the U.S. Court of International Trade within 180 days after denial of the protest. The rules of the court and other applicable statutes and precedents determine the course of customs litigation.

While CBP's ascertainment of dutiable status is final for most purposes at the time of liquidation, a liquidation is not final until any protest that has been filed against it has been decided. Similarly, the administrative decision issued on a protest is not final until any litigation filed against it has become final.

Entries must be liquidated within one year of the date of entry unless the liquidation needs to be extended for another one-year period not to exceed a total of four years from the date of entry. CBP will suspend liquidation of an entry when required by statute or court order. A suspension will remain in effect until the issue is resolved. Notifications of extensions and suspensions are given to importers, surety companies, and customs brokers who are parties to the transaction.

32. Conversion of Currency

The conversion of foreign currency for customs purposes must be made in accordance with the provisions of 31 U.S.C. 5151. This section states that CBP is to use rates of exchange determined and certified by the Federal Reserve Bank of New York. These certified rates are based on the New York market buying rates for the foreign currencies involved.

In the case of widely used currencies, rates of exchange are certified each day.

The rates certified on the first business day of each calendar quarter are used throughout the quarter except on days when fluctuations of five percent or more occur, in which case the actual certified rates for those days are used. For infrequently used currencies, the Federal Reserve Bank of New York certifies rates of exchanges upon request by CBP. The rates certified are only for the currencies and dates requested.

For CBP purposes, the date of exportation of the goods is the date used to determine the applicable certified rate of exchange. This remains true even though a different rate may have been used in payment of the goods. Information as to the applicable rate of exchange in converting currency for customs purposes in the case of a given shipment may be obtained from a CBP port director.

33. Transaction Value of Imported Merchandise

The entry filer is responsible for using reasonable care to value imported merchandise and provide any other information necessary to enable the CBP officer to properly assess the duty and determine whether any other applicable legal requirement is met. The CBP officer is then responsible for fixing the value of the imported merchandise. The valuation provisions of the Tariff Act of 1930 are found in section 402, as amended by the Trade Agreements Act of 1979.

Generally, the customs value of all merchandise exported to the United States will be the transaction value for the goods. If the transaction value cannot be used, then certain secondary bases are considered. The secondary bases of value, listed in order of precedence for use, are:

- Transaction value of identical merchandise,
- Transaction value of similar merchandise,
- Deductive value,
- Computed value.

The order of precedence of the last two values can be reversed if the importer so requests in writing at the time of filing the entry.

Inclusions

The transaction value of imported merchandise is the price actually paid or payable for the merchandise when sold for exportation to the United States, plus amounts for the following items if they are not included in the price:

- The packing costs incurred by the buyer,
- Any selling commission incurred by the buyer,
- The value of any assist,
- Any royalty or license fee that the buyer is required to pay as a condition of the sale,
- The proceeds, accruing to the seller, of any subsequent resale, disposal, or use of the imported merchandise.

The amounts for the above items are added only to the extent that each is not included in the price actually paid or payable and information is available to establish the accuracy of the amount. If sufficient information is not available, then the transaction value cannot be determined and the next basis of value, in order of precedence, must be considered for appraisement. A discussion of these added items follows.

Packing costs consist of the cost incurred by the buyer for all containers and coverings of whatever nature and for the labor and materials used in packing the imported merchandise so that it is ready for export.

Any selling commission incurred by the buyer with respect to the imported merchandise constitutes part of the transaction value. Buying commissions do not. A selling commission means any commission paid to the seller's agent, who is related to or controlled by, or works for or on behalf of, the manufacturer or the seller.

The apportioned value of any assist constitutes part of the transaction value of the imported merchandise. First the value of the assist is determined; then the value is prorated to the imported merchandise.

An assist is any of the items listed below that the buyer of imported merchandise provides directly or indirectly, free of charge or at a reduced cost, for use in the production or sale of merchandise for export to the United States.

- Materials, components, parts, and similar items incorporated in the imported merchandise,
- Tools, dies, molds, and similar items used in producing the imported merchandise,
- Merchandise consumed in producing the imported merchandise,
- Engineering, development, artwork, design work, and plans and sketches that are undertaken outside the United States.

"Engineering ...," will not be treated as an assist if the service or work is:

- Performed by a person domiciled within the United States,
- Performed while that person is acting as an employee or agent of the buyer of the imported merchandise, and
- Incidental to other engineering, development, artwork, design work, or plans or sketches undertaken within the United States.

In determining the value of an assist, the following rules apply:

- The value is either: (a) the cost of acquiring the assist, if acquired by the importer from an unrelated seller, or (b) the cost of the assist, if produced by the importer or a person related to the importer.
- The value includes the cost of transporting the assist to the place of production.
- The value of assists used in producing the imported merchandise is adjusted to reflect use, repairs, modifications, or other factors affecting the value of the assists. Assists of this type include such items as tools, dies, and molds.

For example, if the importer previously used the assist, regardless of whether he acquired or produced it, the original cost of acquisition or of production must be decreased to reflect the use. Alternatively, repairs and modifications may result in the value of the assist having to be adjusted upward.

- In case of engineering, development, artwork, design work, and plans and sketches undertaken elsewhere than in the United States, the value is:
  1. The cost of obtaining copies of the assist, if the assist is available in the public domain,

2. The cost of the purchase or lease, if the assist was bought or leased by the buyer from an unrelated person,
3. The value added outside the United States, if the assist was reproduced in the United States and one or more foreign countries.

So far as possible, the buyer's commercial record system will be used to determine the value of an assist, especially such assists as engineering, development, artwork, design work, and plans and sketches undertaken elsewhere than in the United States.

Having determined the value of an assist, the next step is to prorate that value to the imported merchandise. The apportionment is done in a reasonable manner appropriate to the circumstances and in accordance with generally accepted accounting principles. By the latter is meant any generally recognized consensus or substantial authoritative support regarding the recording and measuring of assets and liabilities and changes, the disclosing of information, and the preparing of financial statements.

Royalty or license fees that a buyer must pay directly or indirectly as a condition of the sale of the imported merchandise for exportation to the United States will be included in the transaction value. Ultimately, whether a royalty or license fee is dutiable will depend on whether the buyer had to pay it as a condition of the sale and to whom and under what circumstances it was paid. The dutiable status will have to be decided on a case-by-case basis.

Charges for the right to reproduce the imported goods in the United States are not dutiable. This right applies only to the following types of merchandise:

■ Originals or copies of artistic or scientific works,
■ Originals or copies of models and industrial drawings,
■ Model machines and prototypes,
■ Plant and animal species.

Any proceeds resulting from the subsequent resale, disposal, or use of the imported merchandise that accrue, directly or indirectly, to the seller are dutiable. These proceeds are added to the price actually paid or payable if not otherwise included.

The price actually paid or payable for the imported merchandise is the total payment, excluding international freight, insurance, and other c.i.f. charges, that the buyer makes to the seller. This payment may be direct or indirect. Some examples of an indirect payment are when the buyer settles all or part of a debt owed by the seller, or when the seller reduces the price on a current importation to settle a debt he owes the buyer. Such indirect payments are part of the transaction value.

However, if a buyer performs an activity on his own account, other than those that may be included in the transaction value, then the activity is not considered an indirect payment to the seller and is not part of the transaction value. This applies even though the buyer's activity might be regarded as benefiting the seller; for example, advertising.

Exclusions

The amounts to be excluded from transaction value are as follows:

- The cost, charges, or expenses incurred for transportation, insurance, and related services incident to the international shipment of the goods from the country of exportation to the place of importation in the United States.
- Any reasonable cost or charges incurred for:
  1. Constructing, erecting, assembling, maintaining, or providing technical assistance with respect to the goods after importation into the United States, or
  2. Transporting the goods after importation.
- The customs duties and other federal taxes, including any federal excise tax, for which sellers in the United States are ordinarily liable.

NOTE: Foreign inland freight and related charges in bullet 1 (see part 152, CBP Regulations), as well as bullets 2 and 3 above, must be identified separately.

Limitations

The transaction value of imported merchandise is the appraised value of that merchandise, provided certain limitations do not exist. If any of these limitations are present, then transaction value cannot be used as the appraised value, and the next basis of value will be considered. The limitations can be divided into four groups:

- Restrictions on the disposition or use of the merchandise,
- Conditions for which a value cannot be determined,
- Proceeds of any subsequent resale, disposal, or use of the merchandise accruing to the seller for which an appropriate adjustment to transaction value cannot be made,
- Related-party transactions where the transaction value is not acceptable.

The term "acceptable" means that the relationship between the buyer and seller did not influence the price actually paid or payable. Examining the circumstances of the sale will help make this determination.

Alternatively, "acceptable" can also mean that the transaction value of the imported merchandise closely approximates one of the following test values, provided these values relate to merchandise exported to the United States at or about the same time as the imported merchandise:

■ The transaction value of identical merchandise or of similar merchandise in sales to unrelated buyers in the United States,
■ The deductive value or computed value for identical merchandise or similar merchandise.

The test values are used for comparison only; they do not form a substitute basis of valuation. In determining whether the transaction value is close to one of the foregoing test values, an adjustment is made if the sales involved differ in:

■ Commercial levels,
■ Quantity levels,
■ The costs, commission, values, fees, and proceeds added to the transaction value (price paid) if not included in the price,
■ The costs incurred by the seller in sales in which he and the buyer are not related that are not incurred by the seller in sales in which he and the buyer are related.

As stated, the test values are alternatives to an examination of the circumstances of the sale. If one of the test values is met, it is not necessary to examine the circumstances of the sale to determine if the relationship influenced the price.

34. Transaction Value of Identical or Similar Merchandise

When the transaction value cannot be determined, then an attempt will be made to appraise the imported goods under the transaction value of identical merchandise method. If merchandise identical to the imported goods cannot be found or an acceptable transaction value for such merchandise does not exist, then the next appraisement method is the transaction value of similar merchandise. In either case the value used would be a previously accepted customs value.

The identical or similar merchandise must have been exported to the United States at or about the same time that the merchandise being appraised is exported to the United States.

The transaction value of identical or similar merchandise must be based on sales of identical or similar merchandise, as applicable, at the same commercial level and in substantially the same quantity as the sale of the merchandise being appraised. If no such sale exists, then sales at either a different commercial level or in different quantities, or both, can be used but must be adjusted to take account of any such difference. Any adjustment must be based on sufficient information, that is, information establishing the reasonableness and accuracy of the adjustment.

The term "identical merchandise" means merchandise that is:

■ Identical in all respects to the merchandise being appraised,
■ Produced in the same country as the merchandise being appraised,
■ Produced by the same person as the merchandise being appraised.

If merchandise meeting all three criteria cannot be found, then identical merchandise is merchandise satisfying the first two criteria but produced by a different person than the producer of merchandise being appraised.

NOTE: Merchandise can be identical to the merchandise being appraised and still show minor differences in appearance.

- *Exclusion*: Identical merchandise does not include merchandise that incorporates or reflects engineering, development, art work, design work, or plans and sketches provided free or at reduced cost by the buyer and undertaken in the United States. '

The term "similar merchandise" means merchandise that is:

- Produced in the same country and by the same person as the merchandise being appraised,
- Like the merchandise being appraised in characteristics and component materials,
- Commercially interchangeable with the merchandise being appraised.

If merchandise meeting the foregoing criteria cannot be found, then similar merchandise is merchandise having the same country of production, like characteristics and component materials, and commercial interchangeability but produced by a different person.

In determining whether goods are similar, some of the factors to be considered are the quality of the goods, their reputation, and existence of a trademark.

- *Exclusion*: Similar merchandise does not include merchandise that incorporates or reflects engineering, development, art work, design work, and plans and sketches provided free or at reduced cost to the buyer and undertaken in the United States.

It is possible that two or more transaction values for identical or similar merchandise, as applicable, will be determined. In such a case the lowest value will be used as the appraised value of the imported merchandise.

35. Other Bases: Deductive and Computed Value

Deductive Value

If the transaction value of imported merchandise, of identical merchandise, or of similar merchandise cannot be determined, then deductive value is the next basis of appraisement. This method is used unless the importer designates computed value as the preferred appraisement method. If computed value was chosen and subsequently determined not to exist for customs valuation purposes, then the basis of appraisement reverts to deductive value.

Basically, deductive value is the resale price in the United States after importation of the goods, with deductions for certain items. In discussing deductive value, the term "merchandise concerned" is used. The term means the merchandise being appraised, identical merchandise, or similar merchandise. Generally, the deductive value is calculated by starting with a unit price and making certain additions to and deductions from that price.

Unit Price. One of three prices constitutes the unit price in deductive value. The price used depends on when and in what condition the merchandise concerned is sold in the United States.

1. **Time and Condition:** The merchandise is *sold in the condition as imported at or about the date of importation of the merchandise being appraised.*
   Price: The price used is the unit price at which the greatest aggregate quantity of the merchandise concerned is sold at or about the date of importation.

2. **Time and Condition:** The merchandise concerned is *sold in the condition as imported but not sold at or about the date of importation* of the merchandise being appraised.
   Price: The price used is the unit price at which the greatest aggregate quantity of the merchandise concerned is sold after the date of importation of the merchandise being appraised but before the close of the 90th day after the date of importation.

3. **Time and Condition:** The merchandise concerned is *not sold in the condition as imported and not sold before the close of the 90th day* after the date of importation of the merchandise being appraised.
   Price: The price used is the unit price at which the greatest aggregate quantity of the merchandise being appraised, after further processing, is sold before the 180th day after the date of importation.

This third price is also known as the "further processing price" or "superdeductive."

The importer has the option to ask that deductive value be based on the further processing price.

Under the superdeductive method the merchandise concerned *is not sold in the condition as imported and not sold before the close of the 90th day* after the date of importation, but is sold before the 180th day after the date of importation.

Under this method, an amount equal to the value of the further processing must be deducted from the unit price in determining deductive value. The amount so deducted must be based on objective and quantifiable data concerning the cost of such work as well as any spoilage, waste, or scrap derived from that work. Items such as accepted industry formulas, methods of construction, and industry practices could be used as a basis for calculating the amount to be deducted.

Generally, the superdeductive method cannot be used if the further processing destroys the identity of the goods. Such situations will be decided on a case-by-case basis for the following reasons:

- Sometimes, even though the identity of the goods is lost, the value added by the processing can be determined accurately without unreasonable difficulty for importers or for CBP.
- In some cases, the imported goods still keep their identity after processing but form only a minor part of the goods sold in the United States. In such cases, using the superdeductive method to value the imported goods will not be justified.

The superdeductive method cannot be used if the merchandise concerned is sold in the condition as imported before the close of the 90th day after the date of importation of the merchandise being appraised.

Additions. Packing costs for the merchandise concerned are added to the price used for deductive value, provided these costs have not otherwise been included. These costs are added regardless of whether the importer or the buyer incurs the cost. "Packing costs" means the cost of:

- All containers and coverings of whatever nature, and
- Packing, whether for labor or materials, used in placing the merchandise in condition, packed ready for shipment to the United States.

Deductions. Certain items are not part of deductive value and must be deducted from the unit price. These items are as follows:

- Commissions or profit and general expenses. Any commission usually paid or agreed to be paid, or the addition usually made for profit and general expenses, applicable to sales in the United States of imported merchandise that is of the same class or kind as the merchandise concerned, regardless of the country of exportation.
- Transportation/insurance costs.
  (a) The actual and associated costs of transportation and insurance incurred with respect to international shipments concerned from the country of exportation to the United States, and
  (b) The usual and associated costs of transportation and insurance incurred with respect to shipments of such merchandise from the place of importation to the place of delivery in the United States, provided these costs are not included as a general expense under the preceding item 1.

- Customs duties/federal taxes. The customs duties and other federal taxes payable on the merchandise concerned because of its importation plus any federal excise tax on, or measured by the value of, such merchandise for which sellers in the United States are ordinarily liable.
- Value of further processing. The value added by processing the merchandise after importation, provided that sufficient information exists concerning the cost of processing. The price determined for deductive value is reduced by the value of further processing only if the third unit price (the superdeductive) is used as deductive value.

For purposes of determining the deductive value of imported merchandise, any sale to a person who supplies any assist for use in connection with the production or sale for export of the merchandise shall be disregarded.

Computed Value

The next basis of appraisement is computed value. If customs valuation cannot be based on any of the values previously discussed, then computed value is considered. This value is also the one the importer can select to precede deductive value as a basis of appraisement.

Computed value consists of the sum of the following items:

- The cost or value of the materials, fabrication, and other processing used in producing the imported merchandise,
- Profit and general expenses,
- Any assist, if not included in bullets 1 and 2,
- Packing costs.

Materials, Fabrication, and Other Processing. The cost or value of the materials, fabrication, and other processing of any kind used in producing the imported merchandise is based on (a) information provided by or on behalf of the producer, and (b) the commercial accounts of the producer if the accounts are consistent with generally accepted accounting principles applied in the country of production of the goods.
NOTE: If the country of exportation imposes an internal tax on the materials or their disposition and refunds the tax when merchandise produced from the materials is exported, then the amount of the internal tax is not included as part of the cost or value of the materials.

Profit and General Expenses

- The amount is determined by information supplied by the producer and is based on his or her commercial accounts, provided such accounts are consistent with generally accepted accounting principles in the country of production.

- The producer's profit and general expenses must be consistent with those usually reflected in sales of goods of the same class or kind as the imported merchandise that are made by producers in the country of exportation for export to the United States. If they are not consistent, then the amount for profit and general expenses is based on the usual profit and general expenses of such producers.
- The amount for profit and general expenses is taken as a whole.

Basically, a producer's profit could be low and his or her general expenses high, so that the total amount is consistent with that usually reflected in sales of goods of the same class or kind. In such a situation, a producer's actual profit figures, even if low, will be used provided he or she has valid commercial reasons to justify them and the pricing policy reflects usual pricing policies in the industry concerned.

Under computed value, "merchandise of the same class and kind" must be imported from the same country as the merchandise being appraised and must be within a group or range of goods produced by a particular industry or industry sector. Whether certain merchandise is of the same class or kind as other merchandise will be determined on a case-by-case basis.

In determining usual profit and general expenses, sales for export to the United States of the narrowest group or range of merchandise that includes the merchandise being appraised will be examined, providing the necessary information can be obtained.

If the value of an assist used in producing the merchandise is not included as part of the producer's materials, fabrication, other processing, or general expenses, then the prorated value of the assist will be included in computed value. It is important that the value of the assist not be included elsewhere because no component of computed value should be counted more than once in determining computed value.

NOTE: The value of any engineering, development, artwork, design work, and plans and sketches undertaken in the United States is included in computed value only to the extent that such value has been charged to the producer.

The cost of all containers and coverings of whatever nature, and of packing, whether for labor or material, used in placing merchandise in condition and packed ready for shipment to the United States is included in computed value.

Value If Other Values Cannot Be Determined

If none of the previous five values can be used to appraise the imported merchandise, then the customs value must be based on a value derived from one of the five previous methods, reasonably adjusted as necessary. The value so determined should be based, to the greatest extent possible, on previously determined values. Some examples of how the other methods can be reasonably adjusted are:

Identical Merchandise (or Similar Merchandise):

1. The requirement that the identical merchandise (or similar merchandise) should be exported at or about the same time as the merchandise being appraised could be flexibly interpreted.
2. Identical imported merchandise (or similar imported merchandise) produced in a country other than the country of exportation of the merchandise being appraised could be the basis for customs valuation.
3. Customs values of identical imported merchandise (or similar imported merchandise) already determined on the basis of deductive value and computed value could be used.

36. Rules of Origin

The *origin* of merchandise that is imported into the customs territory of the United States can affect the rate of duty, entitlement for special programs, admissibility, quota, anti-dumping or countervailing duties, procurement by government agencies and marking requirements. In order to determine a product's country of origin, the importer should consult the applicable rules of origin.

There are two basic types of rules of origin: *non-preferential* and *preferential*. Non-preferential rules generally apply in the absence of bilateral or multilateral trade agreements. Preferential rules are applied to merchandise to determine its eligibility for special treatment under various trade agreements or special legislation such as the Generalized System of Preferences (GSP), the North American Free Trade Agreement (NAFTA), or the African Growth and Opportunity Act (AGOA). There are also rules of origin for textile and apparel articles; these are provided for by statute.

A more detailed discussion of these rules may be found in the publications *What Every Member of the Trade Community Should Know About: Rules of Origin* and *What Every Member of the Trade Community Should Know About: Textile & Apparel Rules of Origin*, which are available on the CBP Electronic Bulletin Board and the CBP Web site, www.cbp.gov.

Marking

37. Country-Of-Origin Marking

U.S. customs laws require that each article produced abroad and imported into the United States be marked with the English name of the country of origin to indicate to the ultimate purchaser in the United States what country the article was manufactured or produced in. These laws also require that marking be located in a conspicuous place as legibly, indelibly, and permanently as the nature of the article permits. Articles that are otherwise specifically exempted from individual marking are also an exception to this rule. These exceptions are discussed below.

Marking Required

If the article—or its container, when the container and not the article must be marked—is not properly marked at the time of importation, a marking duty equal to 10 percent of the article's customs value will be assessed unless the article is exported, destroyed, or properly marked under CBP supervision before the entry is liquidated.

Although it may not be possible to identify the ultimate purchaser in every transaction, broadly stated, the "ultimate purchaser" may be defined as the last person in the United States who will receive the article in the form in which it was imported. Generally speaking, when an article is imported into and used in the United States to manufacture another article with a different name, character, or usage than the imported article, the manufacturer is the ultimate purchaser. If an article is to be sold at retail in its imported form, the retail customer is the ultimate purchaser. A person who subjects an imported article to a process that results in the article's substantial transformation is the ultimate purchaser, but if that process is only minor and leaves the identity of the imported article intact, the processor of the article will not be regarded as the ultimate purchaser.

When an article or its container is required to be marked with the country of origin, the marking is considered sufficiently permanent if it will remain on the article or container until it reaches the ultimate purchaser.

When an imported article is normally combined with another article after importation but before delivery to the ultimate purchaser, and the imported article's country of origin is located so that it is visible after combining, the marking must include, in addition to the country of origin, words or symbols clearly showing that the origin indicated is that of the imported article, and not of any other article with which it has been combined. For example, if marked bottles, drums, or other containers are imported empty to be filled in the United States, they shall be marked with such words as "Bottle (or drum or container) made in (name of country)." Labels and similar articles marked so that the name of the article's country of origin is visible after it is affixed to another article in this country shall be marked with additional descriptive words such as "label made (or printed) in (name of country)" or words of equivalent meaning.

In cases where the words "United States" or "American" or the letters "U.S.A." or any variation of such words or letters, or the name of any city or locality in the United States, or the name of any foreign country or locality in which the article was not manufactured or produced, appear on an imported article or container, and those words, letters, or names may mislead or deceive the ultimate purchaser about the article's actual country of origin, there shall also appear, legibly, permanently and in close proximity to such words, letters, or name, the name of the country of origin preceded by "made in," "product of," or other words of similar meaning.

If marked articles are to be repacked in the United States after release from CBP custody, importers must certify on entry that they will not obscure the marking on properly marked articles if the article is repacked, or that they will mark the repacked container. If an importer does not repack, but resells to a repacker, the importer must notify the repacker about marking requirements. Failure to comply with these certification requirements may subject importers to penalties and/or additional duties.

Marking Not Required

The following articles and classes or kinds of articles are not required to be marked to indicate country of origin, i.e., the country in which they were grown, manufactured, or produced. However, the outermost containers in which these articles ordinarily reach the ultimate purchaser in the United States must be marked to indicate the English name of the country of origin of the articles.

Art, works of,
Articles classified subheads 9810.00.15, 9810.00.25, 9810.00.40, and 9810.00.45, HTSUS,
Articles entered in good faith as antiques and rejected as unauthentic,
Bagging, waste,
Bags, jute,
Bands, steel,
Beads, unstrung,
Bearings, ball, 5/8-inch or less in diameter,
Blanks, metal, to be plated,
Bodies, harvest hat,
Bolts, nuts, and washers,
Briarwood, in blocks,
Briquettes, coal or coke,
Buckles, one inch or less in greatest dimension,
Burlap,
Buttons,
Cards, playing,
Cellophane and celluloid in sheets, bands, or strips,
Chemicals, drugs, medicinals, and similar substances, when imported in capsules, pills, tablets, lozenges, or troches,
Cigars and cigarettes,
Covers, straw bottle,
Dies, diamond wire, unmounted,
Dowels, wooden,
Effects, theatrical,

Eggs,

Feathers,

Firewood,

Flooring, not further manufactured than planed, tongued and grooved,

Flowers, artificial, except bunches,

Flowers, cut,

Glass, cut to shape and size for use in clocks, hand, pocket, and purse mirrors, and other glass of similar shapes and size, not including lenses or watch crystals,

Glides, furniture, except glides with prongs,

Hairnets,

Hides, raw,

Hooks, fish (except snelled fish hooks),

Hoops (wood), barrel,

Laths,

Livestock,

Lumber, except finished,

Lumber, sawed,

Metal bars except concrete reinforcement bars, billets, blocks, blooms, ingots, pigs, plates, sheets, except galvanized sheets, shafting, slabs, and metal in similar forms,

Mica not further manufactured than cut or stamped to dimension, shape, or form,

Monuments,

Nails, spikes, and staples,

Natural products, such as vegetables, fruit, nuts, berries, and live or dead animals, fish and birds; all the foregoing which are in their natural state or not advanced in any manner further than is necessary for their safe transportation,

Nets, bottle wire,

Paper, newsprint,

Paper, stencil,

Paper, stock,

Parchment and vellum,

Parts, for machines imported from same country as parts,

Pickets (wood),

Pins, tuning,

Plants, shrubs, and other nursery stock,

Plugs, tie,

Poles, bamboo,

Posts (wood), fence,

Pulpwood,

Rags (including wiping rags),

Rails, joint bars, and tie plates of steel,

Ribbon,

Rivets,

Rope, including wire rope, cordage, cords, twines, threads, and yarns,
Scrap and waste,
Screws,
Shims, track,
Shingles (wood), bundles of, except bundles of red-cedar shingles,
Skins, fur, dressed or dyed,
Skins, raw fur,
Sponges,
Springs, watch,
Stamps, postage and revenue, and government-stamped envelopes and postal
 cards bearing no printing other than the official imprint,
Staves (wood), barrel,
Steel, hoop,
Sugar, maple,
Ties (wood), railroad,
Tiles, not over one inch in greatest dimension,
Timbers, sawed,
Tips, penholder,
Trees, Christmas,
Weights, analytical and precision, in sets,
Wicking, candle,
Wire, except barbed.

Unless an article being shipped to the United States is specifically named in the foregoing list, it would be advisable for an exporter to obtain advice from CBP before concluding that it is exempted from marking. If articles on the foregoing list are repacked in the United States, the new packages must be labeled to indicate the country of origin of the articles they contain. Importers must certify on entry that if they repackage, they will properly mark the repackaged containers. If they do not package, but resell to repackagers, they must notify repackagers about these marking requirements. Failure to comply with these certification requirements may subject importers to penalties and marking duties.

Other Exceptions

The following classes of articles are also exempt from country-of-origin marking. (The usual container in which one of these articles is imported will also be exempt from marking.)

- An article imported for use by the importer and not intended for sale in its imported or any other form.
- An article to be processed in the United States by the importer or for his account other than for the purpose of concealing the origin of the article

and in such manner that any mark of origin would necessarily be obliterated, destroyed, or permanently concealed.

■ An article that the ultimate purchaser in the United States, by reason of the article's character or the circumstances of its importation, must necessarily know the country of origin even though the article is not marked to indicate it. The clearest application of this exemption is when the contract between the ultimate purchaser in the United States and the supplier abroad insures that the order will be filled only with articles grown, manufactured, or produced in a named country.

The following classes of articles are also exempt from marking to indicate country of origin:

■ Articles incapable of being marked,
■ Articles that cannot be marked prior to shipment to the United States without injury,
■ Articles that cannot be marked prior to shipment to the United States except at a cost economically prohibitive of their importation,
■ Articles for which marking of the containers will reasonably indicate their country of origin,
■ Crude substances,
■ Articles produced more than 20 years prior to their importation into the United States,
■ Articles entered or withdrawn from warehouse for immediate exportation or for transportation and exportation.

Although the articles themselves are exempted from marking to indicate country of origin, the outermost containers in which they ordinarily reach the ultimate purchaser in the United States must be marked to show the articles' country of origin.

When marking an article's container will reasonably indicate its country of origin, the article itself may be exempt from such marking. This exemption applies only when the article reaches the ultimate purchaser in an unopened container. For example, articles that reach the retail purchaser in sealed containers marked clearly to indicate the country of origin fall within this exception. Materials to be used in building or manufacture by the builder or manufacturer who will receive the materials in unopened cases also fall within the exemption. The following articles, as well as their containers, are exempt from country-of-origin marking:

■ Products of American fisheries that are free of duty,
■ Products of United States possessions,
■ Products of the United States that are exported and returned,
■ Articles valued at not more than $200 (or $100 for bona fide gifts) that are passed without entry.

Goods processed in NAFTA countries are subject to special country-of-origin marking rules that can be found in 19 CFR 102 at www.gpoaccess.gov/cfr/index.html. An overview of these rules can be found in *NAFTA: A Guide to Customs Procedures* available at http://www.cbp.gov/nafta/docs/us/guidproc.html

38. Special Marking Requirements

The country-of-origin marking requirements are separate and apart from any special marking or labeling required on specific products by other agencies. It is recommended that the specific agency be contacted for any special marking or labeling requirements.

Certain articles are subject to special country of origin marking requirements. Iron and steel pipe and pipe fittings; manhole rings, frames, or covers; and compressed gas cylinders must generally be marked by one of four methods: die-stamped, cast-in-mold lettering, etching (acid or electrolytic), or engraving. In addition, none of the exceptions from marking discussed above are applicable to iron and steel pipe and pipe fittings.

The following articles and parts thereof shall be marked legibly and conspicuously to indicate their origin by die-stamping, cast-in-the-mold lettering, etching (acid or electrolytic), engraving, or by means of metal plates that bear the prescribed marking and that are securely attached to the article in a conspicuous place by welding, screws, or rivets: knives, clippers, shears, safety razors, surgical instruments, scientific and laboratory instruments, pliers, pincers, and vacuum containers.

Watch movements are required to be marked on one or more of the bridges or top plates to show:

1. The name of the country of manufacture,
2. The name of the manufacturer or purchaser, and
3. In words, the number of jewels, if any, serving a mechanical purpose as frictional bearings.

Clock movements shall be marked on the most visible part of the front or back plate to show:

1. The name of the country of manufacture,
2. The name of the manufacturer or purchaser, and
3. The number of jewels, if any.

Watch cases shall be marked on the inside or outside of the back cover to show (1) the name of the country of manufacture, and (2) the name of the manufacturer or purchaser.

Clock cases and other cases provided for in Chapter 91, HTSUS, are required to be marked on the most visible part of the outside of the back to show the name of the country of manufacture.

The terms "watch movement" and "clock movement" refer to devices regulated by a balance wheel and hairspring, quartz crystal, or any other system capable of determining intervals of time, with a display or system to which a mechanical display can be incorporated. "Watch movements" include devices that do not exceed 12 mm in thickness and 50 mm in width, length, or diameter; "clock movements" include devices that do not meet the watch movement dimensional specifications. The term "cases" includes inner and outer cases, containers, and housings for movements, together with parts or pieces, such as, but not limited to, rings, feet, posts, bases, and outer frames, and any auxiliary or incidental features, which (with appropriate movements) serve to complete the watches, clocks, time switches, and other apparatus provided for in Chapter 91, HTSUS.

Articles required to be marked in accordance with the special marking requirements in Chapter 91, HTSUS, must be conspicuously and indelibly marked by cutting, die-sinking, engraving, stamping, or mold marking. Articles required to be so marked shall be denied entry unless marked in exact conformity with these requirements.

Movements with opto-electronic display only and cases designed for use therewith, whether entered as separate articles or as components of assembled watches or clocks, are not subject to the special marking requirements. These items need only be marked with the marking requirements of 19 U.S.C. 1304.

In addition to the special marking requirements set forth above, all watches of foreign origin must comply with the usual country of origin marking requirements. CBP considers the country of origin of watches to be the country of manufacture of the watch movement. The name of this country should appear either on the outside back cover or on the face of the dial.

Title IV of the Tariff Suspension and Trade Act of 2000 (P.L. 106-476), also known as the Imported Cigarette Compliance Act of 2000, imposes special requirements on the importation of cigarettes and other tobacco products. Importers of cigarettes or other tobacco products are urged to contact the United States port of entry at which their merchandise will arrive for information about the new requirements.

39. Marking—False Impression

Section 42 of the Trademark Act of 1946 (15 U.S.C. 1124) provides, among other things, that no imported article of foreign origin, which bears a name or mark calculated to induce the public to believe that it was manufactured in the United States or in any foreign country or locality other than the country or locality in which it was actually manufactured, shall be admitted to entry at any customhouse in the United States.

In many cases, the words "United States," the letters "U.S.A.," or the name of any city or locality in the United States appearing on an imported article of foreign origin, or on the containers thereof, are considered to be calculated to induce the public to believe that the article was manufactured in the United States unless the name of the country of origin appears in close proximity to the name which indicates a domestic origin.

Merchandise discovered after conditional release to have been missing a required country of origin marking may be ordered redelivered to CBP custody. If such delivery is not promptly made, liquidated damages may be assessed against the CBP bond. (See 19 CFR 141.113[a]; cf., 19 CFR Part 172 and CBP Form 4647.)

An imported article bearing a name or mark prohibited by Section 42 of the Trademark Act is subject to seizure and forfeiture. However, upon the filing of a petition by the importer prior to final disposition of the article, the CBP port director may release it upon the condition that the prohibited marking be removed or obliterated or that the article and containers be properly marked; or the port director may permit the article to be exported or destroyed under CBP supervision and without expense to the government.

Section 43 of the Trademark Act of 1946 (15 U.S.C. 1125) prohibits the entry of goods marked or labeled with a false designation of origin or with any false description or representation, including words or other symbols tending to falsely describe or represent the same. Deliberate removal, obliteration, covering, or altering of required country-of-origin markings after release from CBP custody is also a crime punishable by fines and imprisonment (19 U.S.C. 1304[l]).

40. User Fees

CBP user fees were established by the Consolidated Omnibus Budget Reconciliation Act of 1985. This legislation was expanded in 1986 to include a merchandise processing fee. Also in 1986, Congress enacted the Water Resources Development Act, which authorized the CBP Service to collect a harbor maintenance fee for the Army Corps of Engineers.

The merchandise processing fee (MPF) is 0.21 percent ad valorem on formally-entered imported merchandise (generally entries valued over $2,000), subject to a minimum fee of $25 per entry and a maximum fee of $485 per entry. On informal entries (those valued at less than $2,000), the MPFs are: $2 for automated entries, $6 for manual entries not prepared by CBP, and $9 for manual entries that are prepared by CBP.

Goods imported directly from Canada that qualify under NAFTA to be marked as goods originating in Canada are exempt from the MPF. This applies to all MPF fees: formal, informal, manually prepared, or automated. Goods that do not qualify under NAFTA are subject to all applicable MPFs.

Goods imported directly from Mexico are exempt from the MPF if the goods qualify under the NAFTA to be marked as goods originating in Mexico.

The harbor maintenance fee is an ad valorem fee assessed on port use associated with imports, admissions into foreign trades zones, domestic shipments, and passenger transportations. The fee is assessed only at ports that benefit from the expenditure of funds by the Army Corps of Engineers for maintaining and improving the port trade zones. The fee is 0.125 percent of the value of the cargo and is paid quarterly, except for imports, which are paid at the time of entry. CBP deposits the harbor maintenance fee collections into the Harbor Maintenance Trust Fund. The funds are made available, subject to appropriation, to the Army Corps of Engineers for the improvement and maintenance of United States ports and harbors.

Special Requirements

41. Prohibitions, Restrictions, Other Agency Requirements

The importation of certain classes of merchandise may be prohibited or restricted to protect the economy and security of the United States, to safeguard consumer health and well-being, and to preserve domestic plant and animal life. Some commodities are also subject to an import quota or a restraint under bilateral trade agreements and arrangements.

In addition to CBP requirements, many of these prohibitions and restrictions on importations are subject to the laws and regulations administered by other United States government agencies with which CBP cooperates in enforcement. These laws and regulations may, for example, prohibit entry; limit entry to certain ports; restrict routing, storage, or use; or require treatment, labeling, or processing as a condition of release. CBP clearance is given only if these various additional requirements are met. This applies to all types of importations, including those made by mail and those placed in foreign trade zones.

The foreign exporter should make certain that the United States importer has been provided with proper information so the importer can:

- Submit the necessary information concerning packing, labeling, etc., and
- Make necessary arrangements for entry of the merchandise into the United States.

Foreign exporters and U.S. importers should consult the agency mentioned for detailed information and guidance, as well as for any changes to the laws and regulations under which the commodities are controlled. Addresses, phone numbers, and Web sites for these agencies are listed in the Addendum.

Agricultural Commodities

1. Cheese, Milk, and Dairy Products. Cheese and cheese products are subject to requirements of the Food and Drug Administration and the Department of Agriculture (USDA). Most importations of cheese require an import license and are subject to quotas administered by the Department of Agriculture, Foreign Agricultural Service, Washington, DC 20250 (see Chapter 40).

The importation of milk and cream is subject to requirements of the Food, Drug and Cosmetic Act and the Import Milk Act. These products may be imported only by holders of permits from:

Department of Health and Human Services
Food and Drug Administration
Center for Food Safety and Applied Nutrition
Office of Food Labeling (HFS-156)
200 "C" Street, NW
Washington, DC 20204

and the Department of Agriculture.

2. Fruits, Vegetables, and Nuts. Certain agricultural commodities, including:

Fresh tomatoes
Avocados
Mangoes
Limes
Oranges
Grapefruit
Green peppers
Irish potatoes
Cucumbers
Eggplants
Dry onions
Processed dates
Prunes
Walnuts and filberts
Raisins, and
Olives in tin

must meet United States import requirements relating to grade, size, quality, and maturity (7 U.S.C. 608[e]). These commodities are inspected; an inspection certificate must be issued by USDA's Food Safety and Inspection Service to indicate import compliance. Inquiries on general requirements should be made to USDA's Agricultural Marketing Service, Washington, DC 20250. Additional restrictions may be imposed by the USDA's Animal and Plant Health Inspection Service, Washington, DC 20782, under the Plant Quarantine Act, and by the Food and Drug Administration, Division of Import Operations and Policy (HFC-170), 5600 Fishers Lane, Rockville, MD 20857, under the Federal Food, Drug, and Cosmetic Act.

3. **Insects.** Insects in a live state that is injurious to cultivated crops (including vegetables, field crops, bush fruit, and orchard, forest, or shade trees) and the eggs, pupae, or larvae of such insects are prohibited from importation, except for scientific purposes, under regulations prescribed by the Secretary of Agriculture.

All packages containing live insects or their eggs, pupae, or larvae that are not injurious to crops or trees are permitted entry into the United States only if:

- They have a permit issued by the Animal and Plant Health Inspection Service of the Department of Agriculture, and
- They are not prohibited by the U.S. Fish and Wildlife Service.

4. **Livestock and Animals.** Inspection and quarantine requirements of the Animal and Plant Health Inspection Service (APHIS) must be met for the importation of:

- All cloven-hoofed animals (ruminants), such as cattle, sheep, deer, antelope, camels, giraffes;
- Swine including the various varieties of wild hogs and the meat from such animals;
- Horses, asses, mules, and zebras;
- All avian species including poultry and pet birds;
- Animal by-products, such as untanned hides, wool, hair, bones, bone meal, blood meal, animal casings, glands, organs, extracts, or secretions of ruminants and swine (if animal by-products for food, drugs, or cosmetics, they are also regulated by the Food and Drug Administration);
- Animal germ-plasm, including embryos and semen; and
- Hay and straw.

A permit for importation must be obtained from APHIS before shipping from the country of origin.

In addition, a veterinary health certificate must accompany all animal imports. Entry procedures for livestock and animals from Mexico and Canada (except for birds from Mexico) are not as rigorous as those for animals from other countries. Entry of animals is restricted to specific ports that have been designated as quarantine stations. All nondomesticated animals must meet the requirements of the Fish and Wildlife Service.

5. Meat, Poultry and Egg Products.

NOTE: *The U.S. Department of Agriculture maintains a trade prohibition on the importation of poultry and unprocessed poultry products from countries where the H5N1 High Pathogen Avian Influenza strain has been detected. This list can be found on the Centers for Disease Control Web site at http://www.cdc.gov/flu/avian/outbreaks/embargo.htm.*

All imported live birds must be quarantined for 30 days at a USDA quarantine facility and tested for the avian influenza virus before entering the country. This requirement also applies to returning U.S.-origin pet birds from H5N1 HPAI affected countries.

Processed goods from H5N1 affected countries may enter the U.S. however; entry requires an Animal and Plant Health Inspection Service's (APHIS) Veterinary Services permit and certification that specified risk mitigation measures to eliminate the disease have been performed.

All commercial shipments of meat and meat food products (derived from cattle, sheep, swine, goats, and horses) offered for entry into the United States are subject to USDA regulations and must be inspected by the Food Safety and Inspection Service (FSIS) of that department and by CBP's Agriculture Program and Liaison Office.

Meat products from other sources (including, but not limited to wild game) are subject to APHIS regulations; to the provisions of the Federal Food, Drug, and Cosmetic Act, which is enforced by the Food and Drug Administration; and the U.S. Fish and Wildlife Service. Poultry, live, dressed, or canned; eggs, including eggs for hatching; and egg products are subject to the requirements and regulations of the Animal and Plant Heath Inspection Service and the Food Safety and Inspection Service of the Department of Agriculture.

The term "poultry" is defined as any live or slaughtered domesticated bird, for example:

- Chickens
- Doves
- Ducks
- Ducks, non-migratory
- Geese
- Guinea fowl
- Partridges
- Pea fowl
- Pigeons
- Swans
- Turkeys

Other birds, for example:

- Commercial, domestic, or pen-raised grouse
- Pheasants
- Quail
- Migratory birds, and
- Certain egg products

are also subject to USDA's trade prohibitions. When those prohibitions are lifted, the above birds are subject to APHIS regulations and to the provisions of the Federal Food, Drug, and Cosmetic Act, which is enforced by the Food and Drug Administration. Inquiry should also be made to the Fish and Wildlife Service, Washington, DC 20240, about their requirements, restrictions, and prohibitions.

Inspection certificates from the country of origin must accompany all imported meat, poultry, and egg products. These certificates must indicate the:

- Product name,
- Establishment number,
- Country of origin,
- Name and address of the manufacturer or distributor,
- Quantity and weight of contents,
- List of ingredients,
- Species of animals from which the product was derived,
- Identification marks.

The certificate must also bear the official seal of the government agency responsible for the inspection and the signature of an agency official. This certificate must be in both English and the language of the originating country.

An FSIS inspector will reinspect all meat and poultry upon arrival at a U.S. port of entry. Shipments that pass reinspection are then allowed to enter U.S. commerce and are treated as domestic product. Shipments from all countries except Canada are stamped with the official USDA mark of inspection. Canadian shipments carry the Canadian mark of inspection and an export stamp. Meat and poultry shipments remain under bond and subject to recall by CBP until the completion of a reinspection.

6. **Plants and Plant Products.** The importation of plants and plant products is subject to regulations of the Department of Agriculture and may be restricted or prohibited. Plants and plant products include:

- Fruits,
- Vegetables,

- Plants,
- Nursery stock,
- Bulbs,
- Roots,
- Seeds,
- Certain fibers including cotton and broomcorn,
- Cut flowers,
- Sugarcane,
- Certain cereals,
- Elm logs, and
- Elm lumber with bark attached.

Import permits are required. Further information should be obtained from APHIS. Also, certain endangered species of plants may be prohibited or require permits or certificates. The Food and Drug Administration also regulates plant and plant products, particularly fruits and vegetables.

7. **Seeds.** The provisions of the Federal Seed Act of 1939 and regulations of the Agricultural Marketing Service, Department of Agriculture, govern the importation into the United States of agricultural and vegetable seeds and screenings. Shipments are detained pending the drawing and testing of samples.

8. **Wood Packing Materials.** On September 16, 2005, CBP began enforcing the U.S. Department of Agriculture's and Animal and Plant Health Inspection Service's import regulation for wood packaging material. The rule requires wood packing material such as:

- Pallets,
- Crates,
- Boxes, and
- Dunnage used to support or brace cargo

to be treated and marked. In cases of noncompliance, the wood packing materials will be subject to immediate export along with the accompanying cargo.

The approved treatments for wood packaging material are:

- Heat treatment to a minimum wood core temperature of 56°C for a minimum of 30 minutes, or
- Fumigation with methyl bromide.

To certify treatment, the wood packing materials must be marked with the following International Plant Protection Convention (IPPC) logo. Paper certificates of treatment will not be accepted.

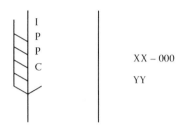

XX – 000

YY

XX represents the ISO country code.
000 represents the unique number assigned by the national plant protection organization.
YY represents either HT for heat treatment or MB for methyl bromide fumigation.

For further information, please see the APHIS Web site at www.aphis. usda.gov.

9. **Tobacco-Related Products** Importers of commercial quantities of tobacco products must obtain an import permit from the Alcohol and Tobacco Tax and Trade Bureau (TTB) of the Department of the Treasury. Chapter 52 of the Internal Revenue Code of 1986 (26 U.S.C.) defines tobacco products as:

   - Cigars,
   - Cigarettes,
   - Smokeless tobacco (snuff and chewing tobacco),
   - Pipe tobacco,
   - Roll-your-own tobacco.

   Tobacco products and cigarette papers and tubes imported into the United States are subject to the payment of federal excise taxes under the Internal Revenue Code unless they qualify for an exemption under the Harmonized Tariff Schedule. For example, tobacco products and cigarette papers and tubes are exempt from tax when brought in by returning residents within the quantity limitations set by the Harmonized Tariff Schedule. Under Section 5704 of the Internal Revenue Code, imported tobacco products and cigarette papers and tubes may be transferred in-bond to the bonded premises of a manufacturer of tobacco products or to an export warehouse proprietor.

   TTB regulations (27 CFR Part 41) require that tobacco products for sale or delivery to the consumer be put in packages that securely hold the product and that bear certain product description notices. These packages may also have to bear health-related notices required by laws administered by the Federal Trade Commission, Washington, DC 20580.

   Tobacco products manufactured in the U.S. and only labeled for export may only be imported into the U.S. in accord with 26 U.S.C. § 5754 and 26 U.S.C. § 5704.

Information regarding importation of tobacco products and cigarette papers and tubes is available on the TTB Web site, www.ttb.gov, or by telephone at 1-877-882-3277.

Arms, Ammunition, and Radioactive Materials

10. **Arms, Ammunition, Explosives, and Implements of War.** These items are prohibited importations except when a license is issued by the Bureau of Alcohol, Tobacco, Firearms and Explosives of the Department of Justice, Washington, DC 20226, Tel. 202-927-8320, or the importation is in compliance with the regulations of that department.

Imported firearms and ammunition are subject to the payment of an excise tax imposed under Chapter 32 of the Internal Revenue Code of 1986 (26 U.S.C. 4181). The Alcohol and Tobacco Tax and Trade Bureau of the Department of the Treasury administers this excise tax. Information regarding the tax is available on the TTB Web site, www.ttb.gov, or by telephone at 1-877-882-3277.

The temporary importation, in-transit movement, and exportation of arms and ammunition listed on the U.S. Munitions List in 22 CFR part 121, is prohibited unless the Directorate of Defense Trade Controls, Department of State, Washington, DC 20520, issues a license, or unless a license exemption is available as set forth in 22 CFR 123.4 and other sections of 22 CFR. Questions about exporting shotguns should be referred to:

U.S. Department of Commerce
Exporter Assistance Staff
Washington, DC 20230

11. **Radioactive Materials and Nuclear Reactors.** Many radioisotopes, all forms of uranium, thorium, and plutonium, and all nuclear reactors imported into the United States are subject to the regulations of the Nuclear Regulatory Commission in addition to import regulations imposed by any other agency of the United States government. Authority to import these commodities or articles containing these commodities requires a license from the Nuclear Regulatory Commission, Washington, DC 20555. (Refer to 10 CFR Part 110.)

Radioisotopes and radioactive sources intended for medical use are subject to the import restrictions set forth in 19 U.S.C. §1618a and the provisions of the Federal Food, Drug, and Cosmetic Act, enforced by the Food and Drug Administration.

In order to comply with the Nuclear Regulatory Commission requirements, the importer must be aware of the identity and amount of any NRC-controlled radioisotopes, or uranium, thorium, and plutonium, and of any nuclear reactor being imported into the United States. The importer must demonstrate to CBP which Nuclear Regulatory Commission authority the controlled commodity is being imported under. The authority cited may be the number of a specific or general license, or the specific section of the Nuclear Regulatory Commission regulations that establishes a general license or grants an exemption to the regulations. The foreign exporter may save time for the prospective importer by furnishing the importer with complete information concerning the presence of NRC-controlled commodities in U.S. importations.

Consumer Products — Energy Conservation

12. **Household appliances.** The Energy Policy and Conservation Act, as amended, calls for energy standards for certain major household appliances, and for these appliances to be labeled to indicate expected energy consumption or efficiency. The Department of Energy, Office of Codes and Standards, Washington, DC 20585, is responsible for test procedures and energy performance standards. The Federal Trade Commission, Division of Enforcement, Washington, DC 20580, regulates the labeling of these appliances.

The Act covers the following household appliances:
 – Refrigerators, refrigerator-freezers, and freezers;
 – Room air-conditioners;
 – Central air-conditioners and central air-conditioning heat pumps;
 – Water heaters;
 – Furnaces;
 – Dishwashers;
 – Clothes washers;
 – Clothes dryers;
 – Direct heating equipment;
 – Kitchen ranges and ovens;
 – Pool heaters; and
 – Fluorescent lamp ballasts.

13. **Commercial and industrial equipment.** The Energy Policy Act of 1992 (EPACT) calls for energy performance standards for certain commercial and industrial equipment. The Department of Energy, Office of Codes and Standards, Washington, DC 20585, is responsible for test procedures and energy performance standards. The EPACT covers the following equipment:

 – Small and large commercial-package air-conditioning and heating equipment;
 – Packaged terminal air-conditioners and heat pumps;
 – Warm-air furnaces;
 – Packaged boilers;

- Storage water heaters;
- Instantaneous water heaters;
- Unfired hot-water storage tanks;
- Large electric motors (one to 200 horsepower) whether shipped separately or as a part of a larger assembly;
- Four-foot medium bi-pin, two-foot U-shaped, eight-foot slimline, and eight-foot high-output fluorescent lamps; and
- Incandescent reflector lamps.

EPACT also calls for water conservation standards for the following plumbing products:

- Lavatory faucets,
- Lavatory replacement aerators,
- Kitchen faucets,
- Kitchen replacement faucets,
- Metering faucets,
- Gravity tank-type toilets,
- Flushometer tank toilets,
- Electromechanical hydraulic toilets,
- Blowout toilets, and
- Urinals.

Importation of these products must comply with the applicable Department of Energy and Federal Trade Commission requirements. Importers should contact these agencies for requirements in effect at the time of anticipated shipment. Be aware that not all appliances are covered by requirements of both agencies.

Consumer Products—Safety

Any consumer product offered for importation will be refused admission and/or seized if the product fails to comply with an applicable product safety standard or regulation, a specified labeling or certification requirement, or if it is determined to present a substantial product hazard. The U.S. Consumer Product Safety Commission (CPSC), Washington, DC 20207, administers these requirements.

14. **Toys and Children's Articles.** Toys and other children's articles cannot be imported into the United States unless they comply with applicable regulations issued under the Federal Hazardous Substances Act. CPSC's regulations also contain tests used to define hazardous sharp edges and points on toys and other children's articles.

      Toys or other articles intended for children under the age of three cannot have small parts that present choking hazards. The Child Safety Protection

Act (an amendment to the Federal Hazardous Substances Act) and its implementing regulations require warning labeling on toys and games designed for children between the ages of three and six, when these toys or games contain small parts that could present choking hazards. Similar regulations exist for balloons, small balls (small balls for children under age three are banned), and marbles. Electric toys, rattles, pacifiers, and cribs are subject to specific safety regulations. Lawn darts are banned.

15. Lead in Paint. Paint and other similar surface coating materials intended for consumer use are banned if they contain more than 0.06 percent lead by weight of the dried plant film. This ban also applies to furniture with paint that exceeds 0.06 percent lead and to toys or other articles intended for children if these toys/articles contain paint that exceeds 0.06 percent lead.

Such products cannot be admitted into the United States. Although this ban applies to "surface coatings," CPSC can take action, under the Federal Hazardous Substances Act, against other lead-containing products if the lead content results in a substantial risk of injury or illness.

16. Bicycles and Bicycle Helmets. Bicycles cannot be admitted unless they meet regulations issued under the Federal Hazardous Substances Act. The CPSC also has mandatory safety standards for bicycle helmets; such helmets will not be admitted unless they meet CPSC's Safety Standard for Bicycle Helmets and are accompanied by a Certificate of Compliance.

17. Fireworks. The fireworks regulations issued under the Federal Hazardous Substances Act set labeling requirements and technical specifications for consumer fireworks.

Large fireworks like cherry bombs and M-80s are banned for consumer use. Large reloadable mortar shell fireworks are also banned. Large multiple-tube mine and shell fireworks are subject to specific requirements to prevent tip-over. Fireworks not meeting these requirements cannot be imported into the United States.

18. Flammable Fabrics. Any article of wearing apparel, fabric, or interior furnishing cannot be imported into the United States if it fails to conform to an applicable flammability standard issued under the Flammable Fabrics Act. These flammability standards cover:

- General wearing apparel,
- Children's sleepwear,
- Mattresses,
- Mattress pads, including futons;
- Carpets and rugs.

Certain products can be imported into the United States, as provided in Section 11(c) of the Act, in order to finish or process them to render these products less highly flammable and thus less dangerous when worn by individuals. In such cases, the exporter must state on the invoice or other paper relating to the shipment that the shipment is being made for that purpose.

19. **Art Materials.** Art materials cannot be imported into the United States unless they meet the Labeling of Hazardous Art Materials Act (LHAMA) of 1988. LHAMA requires that a toxicologist review art materials for their potential to produce adverse heath effects. Art materials must bear appropriate chronic-hazard warnings in addition to any cautionary labeling required by the Federal Hazardous Substances Act.

The LHAMA mandated a voluntary standard, ASTM D-4236, with certain modifications, as a mandatory rule under Section 3(b) of the Federal Hazardous Substances Act. This standard also requires that an art material bear or be displayed with a label indicating that it has been reviewed in accordance with the standard, whether or not the product bears a chronic warning statement.

20. **Cigarette Lighters.** Disposable and novelty cigarette lighters cannot be admitted into the United States unless they meet the child-resistant safety standard; this standard is issued under the Consumer Product Safety Act. All nonrefillable lighters, and refillable lighters whose value is less than $2.25 (subject to change in 2008) and that use gas as a fuel, are considered to be "disposable lighters" and are covered by this standard.

Novelty lighters are lighters using any type of fuel that have entertaining audio or visual effects or that depict articles commonly recognized as intended for use by children less than five years of age. Manufacturers and importers must test lighters, keep records, and report the results to CPSC. A Certificate of Compliance must accompany each shipping unit of the product, or be furnished in another fashion to the distributor or retailer to whom the manufacturer, private labeler, or importer delivers the product.

21. **Multi-purpose lighters.** A multi-purpose lighter, also known as grill lighter, fireplace lighter, utility lighter, micro-torch, or gas match, is a flame-producing product that operates on fuel (less than 10 oz.), incorporates an ignition mechanism, and is used by consumers to ignite items such as candles, fuel for fireplaces, charcoal or gas-fired grills, camp fires, camp stoves, lanterns, fuel-PSC gas-fired appliances or devices, or pilot lights, or for uses such as soldering or brazing.

Multi-purpose lighters cannot be admitted into the United States unless they meet a child-resistant safety standard issued under the Consumer Product Safety Act. All manufacturers and importers must test lighters, keep records, and report the results to CPSC. A Certificate of Compliance must accompany each shipping unit of the product, or be furnished in another fashion to the distributor or retailer to whom the manufacturer, private labeler, or importer delivers the product.

22. **Other Regulations and Standards.** CPSC has issued a number of other safety standards, regulations, and bans. These have generally been of less interest to the importing community because fewer of these items are imported. These include:

- Architectural glazing,
- Matchbooks,
- CB and TV antennas,
- Walk-behind power lawn-mowers,
- Swimming-pool slides,
- Cellulose insulation,
- Garage-door operators,
- Unstable refuse bins,
- Flammable contact adhesives,
- Patching compounds with asbestos,
- Emberizing materials with asbestos,
- Household chemicals (hazardous household chemicals require labeling under the Federal Hazardous Substances Act),
- Refrigerator doors,
- Poison Prevention Packaging Act (certain cosmetics, drugs, and household chemicals—the PPPA regulates 32 substances—require special child-resistant packaging),
- Bunk beds.

Electronic Products

23. **Radiation- and Sonic Radiation-Producing Products.** The following products are subject to the Federal Food, Drug, and Cosmetic Act, Chapter V, Subchapter C—Electronic Product Radiation (formerly called the Radiation Control Health and Safety Act of 1968):

■ Television products that incorporate a cathode-ray tube,
■ Cold-cathode gas-discharge tubes,
■ Microwave ovens,
■ Cabinet and diagnostic x-ray equipment,
■ Laser products,
■ Ultrasound physical therapy equipment,

■ Sunlamps,
■ CD-ROMs,
■ Cellular and cordless telephones,
■ Other electronic products for which there are radiation-performance standards.

An electronic product: (a) for which there is a radiation performance standard, and (b) that is imported for sale or use in the United States may only be imported if a declaration (Form FDA 2877) is filed with each importer's entry. Form FDA 2877 is available from the Food and Drug Administration, Center for Devices and Radiological Health, Rockville, MD 20850.

The declaration must describe the product's compliance status. The importer must affirm that the product was:

– Not subject to a standard (e.g., manufactured prior to the effective date of the applicable federal standard); or
– Complies with the standard and has a label affixed by the manufacturer certifying compliance; or
– Does not comply with the standard but is being imported only for purposes of research, investigation, study, demonstration, or training; or
– Does not now comply with the standard, but will be brought into compliance.

The provisions of the Federal Food, Drug, and Cosmetic Act, Chapter V, Subchapter C—Electronic Product Radiation—apply to electronic products manufactured in the United States as well as to imported products.

24. Radio Frequency Devices. The following are subject to radio emission standards of the Federal Communications Commission, Washington, DC 20554, under the Communications Act of 1934, as amended:

– Radios,
– Televisions,
– Citizens-band radios or
– Combinations thereof
– Other radio frequency devices.

Importations of such products may be accompanied by an FCC declaration (FCC 740) certifying that the imported model or device is in conformity with, will be brought into conformity, or is exempt from, the Federal Communication Commission requirements.

Foods, Drugs, Cosmetics, and Medical Devices

The Public Health Security and Bio-Terrorism Preparedness and Response Act of 2002, or BTA, was implemented on December 12, 2003. All food imported or offered for import into the United States, both for human and animal consumption, is subject to the requirements of this Act.

The BTA's purpose is to ensure the security of food for human and animal consumption. "Food" is defined as:

■ Articles used for food or drink for man or other animals,
■ Chewing gum,
■ Articles used for components or any such article.

The BTA's key elements require that manufacturers and shippers register the facilities from which they export food and food products to the U.S. with the Food and Drug Administration. Manufacturers and shippers must also provide the FDA with *prior notification* (PN) for any food shipment covered by BTA regulations. Failure to provide the PN will result in refusal of the food importation, which could cause the shipment to be:

– Held at the port of arrival,
– Moved to secured storage pending compliance with PN requirements,
– Exported, or
– Destroyed.

For more information on the BTA and its requirements, please visit the FDA's Web site: www.fda.gov.

25. **Foods, Cosmetics, etc.** The importation into the United States of food, drugs, devices, and cosmetics is governed by provisions of the Federal Food, Drug, and Cosmetic Act. The Food and Drug Administration of the Department of Health and Human Services, Rockville, MD 20857, administers this Act.

   The Act prohibits the importation of articles that are adulterated or misbranded and products that are defective, unsafe, filthy, or produced under unsanitary conditions. The term *misbranded* includes statements, designs, or pictures in labeling that are false or misleading or that fail to provide the information required in labeling. The Act also prohibits the importation of pharmaceuticals that have not been approved by the FDA for admission into the United States.

   Imported products regulated by the FDA are subject to inspection at the time of entry. Shipments found not to comply with its laws and regulations are subject to refusal; these shipments must be brought into compliance, destroyed, or re-exported. At the FDA's discretion, an importer may be permitted to bring a nonconforming importation into compliance if it is possible to do so. Any sorting, reprocessing, or relabeling must be supervised by the FDA at the importer's expense.

Some imported foods regulated by the FDA, such as confectionery, dairy products, poultry, eggs and egg products, meats, fruits, nuts and vegetables, are also subject to other agencies' requirements. Certain aquatic species may also be subject to the requirements of the National Marine Fisheries Service of the National Oceanic and Atmosphere Administration of the Department of Commerce, 1335 East-West Highway, Silver Spring, MD 20910.

26. **Biological Drugs.** The manufacture and importation of biological products *for human consumption* are regulated under the Public Health Service Act. Domestic as well as foreign manufacturers of such products must obtain a U.S. license for both the manufacturing establishment and for the product intended to be produced or imported. Additional information may be obtained from the Food and Drug Administration, Department of Health and Human Services, Rockville, MD 20857, and from its Web site: www.fda.gov.

    Biological drugs *for animals* are regulated under the Virus Serum Toxin Act, which is administered by the Department of Agriculture. The importation of viruses, serums, toxins and analogous products, and organisms and vectors for use in the treatment of domestic animals, is prohibited unless the importer holds a permit from the Department of Agriculture covering the specific product. These importations are also subject to special labeling requirements.

27. **Biological Materials and Vectors.** The importation into the United States for sale, trade, or exchange of items such as the following, which are applicable to the prevention, treatment, or cure of human diseases or injuries, is prohibited unless they have been propagated or prepared at an establishment with an unsuspended, unrevoked U.S. license for such manufacturing issued by the Secretary of the Department of Health and Human Services:

    - Any virus,
    - Therapeutic serum,
    - Toxin, antitoxin, or analogous products,
    - Arsphenamine, its derivatives, or any other trivalent organic arsenic compound.

(This prohibition does not extend to materials to be used in research experiments; however, research materials are subject to other requirements.)

    Samples of the U.S.-licensed product must accompany each importation so that the CBP port director at the port of entry can forward them to:

Director
Center for Biologics Evaluation and Research
1401 Rockville Pike
Bethesda, MD 20852

A permit from the U.S. Public Health Service, Centers for Disease Control and Prevention, Atlanta, GA 30333, is required for shipments of any etiological agent; any insect, animal, or plant vector of human disease; or for any exotic living insect, animal, or plant capable of being a vector of human disease.

28. **Narcotic Drugs and Derivatives.** The importation of controlled substances including narcotics, marijuana, and other dangerous drugs, is prohibited except when imported in compliance with regulations of the Drug Enforcement Administration of the Department of Justice, Arlington, VA 22202. Examples of some prohibited controlled substances are:

   – Amphetamines,
   – Barbiturates,
   – Coca leaves and derivatives such as cocaine,
   – Hallucinogenic substances such as LSD, mescaline, peyote, and marijuana and other forms of cannabis,
   – Opiates, including methadone,
   – Opium, including opium derivatives such as morphine and heroin,
   – Synthetic substitutes for narcotic drugs, and
   – Anabolic steroids.

29. **Drug Paraphernalia.** Items of drug paraphernalia are prohibited from importation or exportation under Section 863, Title 21 of the United States Code.

   Under the Controlled Substances Act (Title II of Public Law 91-513), the term *drug paraphernalia* means any equipment, product, or material of any kind that is primarily intended or designed for use in manufacturing, compounding, converting, concealing, producing, processing, preparing, injecting, ingesting, inhaling, or otherwise introducing into the human body a controlled substance whose possession is unlawful under this Act.

   Items of drug paraphernalia include, but are not limited to, the following:

   – Metal, wooden, acrylic, glass, stone, plastic, or ceramic pipes, with or without screens, permanent screens, hashish heads, or punctured metal bowls;
   – Water pipes;
   – Carburetion tubes and devices;
   – Smoking and carburetion masks;
   – Roach clips, meaning objects used to hold burning material, such as a marijuana cigarette, that has become too small or too short to be held in the hand;

- Miniature spoons with level capacities of one-tenth cubic centimeter or less;
- Chamber pipes;
- Carburetor pipes;
- Electric pipes;
- Air-driven pipes;
- Chillums;
- Bongs;
- Ice pipes or chillers;
- Wired cigarette papers; or
- Cocaine freebase kits.

Conflict Diamonds

30. Conflict Diamonds. On April 25, 2003, President George W. Bush signed the Clean Diamond Trade Act, H.R. 1584 (Pub L. 108-19), into law. This Act enables the United States to implement procedures developed by more than 50 countries to exclude rough (uncut or unpolished) *conflict diamonds* from international trade while promoting legitimate trade in diamonds. Conflict diamonds are rough diamonds sold by rebel groups in Africa or their allies for the specific purpose of financing uprisings against legitimate, internationally recognized governments.

Rebel, military, and terrorist groups in parts of Africa have used conflict diamonds to finance unlawful insurrections against legitimate governments. Conflict diamonds are so called because of the atrocities committed on civilian populations during these insurrections. The United States played a key role in forging an international consensus to curb this trade and has therefore strongly supported the Kimberley Process.

The Kimberley Process Certification Scheme (KPCS) is an international initiative aimed at breaking the link between the legitimate diamond trade and trade in conflict diamonds by documenting and tracking all rough diamonds that enter participating KPCS countries and by shipping them in tamper-resistant containers.

The importation of rough diamonds into the United States requires a Kimberley Process Certificate and must be sealed in a tamper resistant container.

Gold, Silver, Currency, Stamps

31. Gold and Silver. The provisions of the National Stamping Act, as amended (15 U.S.C. 291-300), are enforced inpart by CBP and by the FBI. Articles made of gold or alloys thereof are prohibited importation into the United

States if the gold content is one-half carat divergence below the indicated fineness. In the case of articles made of gold or gold alloy, including the solder and alloy of inferior fineness, a one-carat divergence below the indicated fineness is permitted.

Articles marked "sterling" or "sterling silver" must assay at least 0.925 of pure silver with a 0.004 divergence allowed. Other articles of silver or silver alloys must assay not less than 0.004 part below their indicated fineness. Articles marked "coin" or "coin silver" must contain at least 0.900 part pure silver, with an allowable divergence of 0.004 part below.

A person placing articles of gold or silver bearing a fineness or quality mark such as 14K, sterling, etc., in the mail or in interstate commerce must place his name or registered trademark next to the fineness mark in letters the same size as the fineness mark. Because the trademark or name is not required at the time of importation, CBP has no direct responsibility for enforcing this aspect of the law. Anyone seeking further advice or interpretation of the law should consult the Department of Justice.

Articles bearing the words *United States Assay* are prohibited importations.

Articles made wholly or in part of inferior metal and plated or filled with gold, silver, or alloys thereof, and that are marked with the degree of fineness must also be marked to indicate the plated or filled content. In such cases, the use of the words *sterling* or *coin* is prohibited.

Restrictions on the purchase, holding, selling, or otherwise dealing in gold were removed as of December 31, 1974, and gold may be imported subject to the usual CBP entry requirements. Under the Hobby Protection Act, which is administered by the Bureau of Consumer Protection of the Federal Trade Commission, any imitation numismatic item must be plainly and permanently marked "copy"; items that do not comply with this marking requirement are subject to seizure and forfeiture.

Unofficial gold coin restrikes must be marked with the country of origin. It is advisable to obtain a copy of the legal proclamation under which the coins are issued, or, if the proclamation is unavailable, an affidavit of government sanction of coins should be secured from a responsible banking official.

32. **Counterfeit Articles.** Articles bearing facsimiles or replicas of coins or securities of the United States or of any foreign country cannot be imported. Counterfeits of coins in circulation in the United States; counterfeited, forged, or altered obligations or other securities of the United States or of any foreign government; plates, dies, or other apparatus which may be used in making any of the foregoing, are prohibited importations.

33. **Monetary Instruments.** Under the Currency and Foreign Transactions Reporting Act, 31 U.S.C. 5311 et seq., if a person knowingly transports,

is about to transport, or has transported, more than $10,000 in monetary instruments at one time to, through or from the United States, or if a person receives more than $10,000 at one time from or through a place outside the United States, a report of the transportation (form FINCEN 105) must be filed with CBP. Monetary instruments include:

- U.S. or foreign coin,
- Currency,
- Traveler's checks in any form,
- Personal and other checks, either in bearer-negotiable form or endorsed without restriction,
- Money orders, either in bearer-negotiable form or endorsed without restriction, and
- Securities or stocks in bearer form.

A bank check or money order made payable to a named person but not endorsed, or that bears a restrictive endorsement, is not considered to be a "monetary instrument." Department of the Treasury regulations governing the report of monetary instruments are set forth at 31 CFR part 103.

Pesticides, Toxic, and Hazardous Substances

34. **Pesticides.** The Federal Insecticide, Fungicide, and Rodenticide Act (FIFRA) as amended, 1988, provides the statutory authority governing the importation of pesticides and pesticide devices into the United States. Promulgated under Section 17(c) of this authority, CBP regulations at 19 CFR Parts 12.112-117 describe the procedures governing these importations. Among other requirements, these regulations require importers to submit to CBP an EPA Notice of Arrival (EPA form 3540-1) that the EPA has reviewed and approved before the importation arrives in the United States.

    Pesticides not registered in accordance with FIFRA Section 3 will be refused entry into the United States. Pesticide devices are not subject to product registration, but the labels of both pesticides and devices must bear the EPA registration number of the producing establishment.

    Pesticides and devices will be refused entry if they are identified as adulterated or misbranded, if they violate FIFRA provisions in any other way, or if they are otherwise injurious to health or the environment.

35. **Toxic Substances.** The Toxic Substances Control Act (TSCA), effective January 1, 1977, regulates the manufacturing, importation, processing, commercial distribution, use, or disposal of any chemical substances or mixtures broadly defined in Section 3 of TSCA. Section 3 specifies

that certain substances be excluded from the definition of "chemical substance" based upon their use. These substances include, but are not limited to:

- Foods,
- Drugs,
- Cosmetics,
- Active ingredients in pesticides.

Importations will not be released from CBP custody unless proper certification is presented CBP indicating that the import "complies with" or "is not subject to" TSCA requirements, or if it has already been identified as a food, drug, or active pesticide ingredient.

For further information from EPA, call the TSCA Assistance Information Service, Tel. 202-554-1404.

36. **Hazardous Substances.** The Hazardous Substance Act; the Caustic Poison Act; the Food, Drug, and Cosmetic Act; and the Consumer Product Safety Act all regulate the importation into the United States of dangerous, caustic, corrosive, and hazardous substances. Among the requirements is that such substances be shipped to the United States in packages suitable for household use. *

The Office of Hazardous Materials Transportation of the U.S. Department of Transportation, Washington, DC 20590, regulates the marking, labeling, packaging, and transportation of hazardous materials, substances, wastes, and their containers. Hazardous waste is a special sub-category of hazardous substances and is regulated by the Resource Recovery and Conservation Act. Such waste requires a special EPA manifest for both imports and exports.

CBP considers otherwise legitimate commodities that were produced with radiation-contaminated materials to be hazardous and therefore subject to seizure.

37. **Refrigerants.** The production, consumption, and importation of refrigerants and other ozone-depleting substances are regulated by the Title VI of the Clean Air Act as amended in 1990. Please consult the Addendum for lists of the more common trade names of Class I and Class II ozone-depleting substances.

Class I includes chlorofluorocarbons (CFCs), methyl chloroform, carbon tetrachloride, halons, and methyl bromide. Class II includes

---

* The FDA defines a container suitable for household use as any retail parcel, package, or container that can be readily adapted for fast or convenient handling in places where people dwell. Please consult 21 CFR, Subchapter L, Part 1230, or visit the FDA's Web site at www.fda.gov.

hydrofluorocarbons (HCFCs). Both Class I and Class II substances are commonly used as refrigerants, solvents, and fire-suppression agents. The EPA regulates the importation of all Class I and Class II ozone-depleting substances.

Textile, Wool, and Fur Products

38. Textile Products. All textile fiber products imported into the United States must be stamped, tagged, labeled, or otherwise marked with the following information, as required by the Textile Fiber Products Identification Act, unless exempted from marking under Section 12 of the Act:

- The generic names and percentages by weight of the constituent fibers present in the textile fiber product, exclusive of permissive ornamentation, in amounts greater than five percent.
- Constituent fibers must be listed in order of predominance by weight. Any fiber or fibers present in amounts of five percent or less must be designated as "other fiber" or "other fibers" and must appear last in this list.
- The name of the manufacturer, or the name or identification number issued by the Federal Trade Commission of the person(s) marketing or handling the textile fiber product. A word trademark, used as a house mark, that is registered with the United States Patent Office may be used on labels in lieu of the name otherwise required if the owner of such trademark furnishes a copy of the Patent Office registration to the Federal Trade Commission prior to use.
- The name of the country where the product was processed or manufactured.

A commercial invoice is required for each shipment of textile fiber products worth more than $500. Commercial invoices for textile fiber products that are subject to the Act's labeling requirements must contain the information noted previously in "Commercial Invoices", as well as the information normally required on invoices. Regulations and pamphlets containing the text of the Textile Fiber Products Identification Act may be obtained from the Federal Trade Commission, Washington, DC 20580.

Pursuant to Section 204 of the Agricultural Act of 1956, imported textiles and textile products may, in addition to labeling requirements, also be subject to quota, visa, export-license, or other entry requirements, including declarations that identify the fabricated components.

39. Wool. The Wool Products Labeling Act of 1939 requires that any imported product containing woolen fiber—with the exception of carpet, rugs, mats, upholsteries, and articles made more than 20 years prior to importation—be tagged, labeled, or otherwise clearly marked with the following information:

- The percentage of the wool product's total fiber weight, exclusive of ornamentation not exceeding five percent of the total fiber weight, of:
  1. Wool,
  2. Recycled wool,
  3. Every fiber other than wool if the percent by weight of such fiber is at least five percent, and
  4. The aggregate of all other fibers.
- The percent of the wool product's total weight composed of any nonfibrous loading, filling, or adulterating matter.
- The name of the manufacturer or importer. If the importer has a registered identification number issued by the Federal Trade Commission, that number may be used instead of the individual's name.

A commercial invoice is required for each shipment of wool products exceeding $500 in value. Commercial invoices for wool products subject to the Act's labeling requirements must contain the information noted previously in "Commercial Invoices".

The provisions of the Wool Products Labeling Act apply to products manufactured in the United States as well as to imported products. Pamphlets containing the text of the Wool Products Labeling Act and regulations may be obtained from the Federal Trade Commission, Washington, DC 20580.

40. **Fur.** The Fur Products Labeling Act requires that any imported article of wearing apparel made in whole or in part of fur or used fur, with the exception of articles made of new fur whose cost or manufacturer's selling price does not exceed $7, be tagged, labeled, or otherwise clearly marked to show the following information:

- The name of the manufacturer or importer. If the importer has a registered identification number, that number may be used instead of the individual's name.
- The name(s) of the animal or animals that produced the fur, as set forth in the Fur Products Name Guide and as determined under the FTC's rules and regulations.
- That the fur product contains used or damaged fur when such is the fact.
- That the fur product is bleached, dyed, or otherwise artificially colored when such is the fact.
- That the fur product is composed in whole or in substantial part of paws, tails, bellies, or waste fur when such is the fact.
- The country of origin of any imported furs incorporated in the fur product.

A commercial invoice is required for each shipment of furs or fur products exceeding $500 in value and must contain the information noted previously in "Commercial Invoices".

Dog or cat fur. The importation, exportation, transportation, distribution, or sale of any product that consists or is composed in whole or in part of any dog fur, cat fur, or both, is prohibited. Any such product that is imported, exported, transported, distributed, or sold will be seized and forfeited, and penalties may be imposed against any person who violates this law. Anyone found to have violated this prohibition may be barred from importing or exporting *any* fur product. This prohibition does not apply to the importation, exportation, or transportation, for noncommercial purposes, of personal pets that are deceased, including pets preserved through taxidermy.

The provisions of the Fur Products Labeling Act apply to fur and fur products in the United States as well as to imported furs and fur products. Regulations and pamphlets containing the text of the Fur Products Labeling Act may be obtained from the Federal Trade Commission, Washington, DC 20580.

Trademarks, Trade Names, and Copyrights

41. **Trademarks and Trade Names.** Articles bearing counterfeit trademarks are subject to seizure and forfeiture. A counterfeit trademark is defined as a spurious trademark that is identical with, or substantially indistinguishable from, a registered trademark. Articles with marks that copy or simulate a registered trademark that has been recorded with CBP are subject to detention and possible seizure and forfeiture. CBP may assess a civil penalty when merchandise is seized and forfeited under 19 U.S.C. § 1526(e). (See 19 U.S.C. § 1526(f))

    CBP may also determine that a registered and recorded trademark should be granted protection against the importation of *parallel*, or *gray-market*, goods. These are goods bearing a legitimate trademark but that were not intended for sale in the United States. Should CBP determine that a registered and recorded trademark receive protection against the importation of gray-market goods, any attempted importation of such goods will subject them to detention and possible seizure and forfeiture.

    A personal exemption for merchandise bearing an infringing mark is permitted for articles that accompany any person arriving in the United States *when such articles are for his or her personal use and not for sale.* Only one infringing item of each type bearing a registered trademark is permitted. An individual may take advantage of this exemption only once within a 30-day period (19 U.S.C. 1526 (d); 19 CFR 148.55).

42. **Copyrights.** Articles imported into the United States that are pirated (bootleg, counterfeit) copies of any registered copyright are subject to seizure and forfeiture.

Wildlife and Pets

43. **Wildlife and Pets.** The importation of live wildlife (i.e., game animals, birds, plants), any part or product made from them, and of birds' eggs, is subject to prohibitions, restrictions, permits and quarantine requirements administered by several government agencies.

Imports or exports of wildlife, their parts, or products must be declared at designated ports of the U.S. Fish and Wildlife Service (FWS) unless an exception is granted prior to the time of import or export. The Assistant Regional Director of Law Enforcement for the FWS region in which the import or export will take place should be contacted for additional information or to request an exception to designated-port-permit requirement.

Any commercial importer or exporter (there are some exceptions for exporters) planning to import or export wildlife must first obtain a license from the Fish and Wildlife Service. Applications and further information may be obtained from the Fish and Wildlife Service, Assistant Regional Director for Law Enforcement, for the region in which the importer or exporter is located.

Endangered species of wildlife and certain species of animals and birds are generally prohibited from entering the United States. Such species can only be imported or exported under a permit granted by the Fish and Wildlife Service. Specific information concerning permit requirements should be obtained from the Fish and Wildlife Service, Office of Management Authority, 4401 North Fairfax Drive, Arlington, VA 22203; or by calling 1-800-358-2104; or by visiting FWS's Web site, www.fws.gov.

Antique articles (articles that can be certified as being at least 100 years old) may be exempt from certain requirements of the U.S. Endangered Species Act. The Fish and Wildlife Service, Office of Management Authority, should be contacted for details.

Marine mammals. The taking and importation of marine mammals and their products are subject to the requirements of the Marine Mammal Protection Act (MMPA) of 1972, as amended in 1994. The National Marine Fisheries Service and FWS both have jurisdiction under the MMPA for certain species and import activities. Additional requirements of the U.S. Endangered Species Act and the Convention on International Trade in Endangered Species (CITES) may also apply. Prior to importing, both agencies should be contacted to learn their exact import requirements. Other import requirements administered by the National Marine Fisheries Service may also apply for certain species covered by the International Commission for the Conservation of Atlantic Tunas, e.g., Atlantic blue fin tuna. See the agency's Web site, www.nmfs.noaa.gov, for more information.

Certain plants, mammals, reptiles, amphibians, fish, snails, clams, insects, crustaceans, mollusks, and other invertebrates may be prohibited from entering the United States unless the importer has a permit from either from the exporting nation's (i.e., the foreign) wildlife authority or from the Fish and Wildlife Service, Office of Management Authority, before the importation takes place.

The importation into the United States of any wildlife, their parts, or products is prohibited if the wildlife was captured, taken, shipped, or possessed in any manner violating the laws of the foreign country in which it, or they, was/were taken.

The importation of the feathers or skins of any bird, other than for scientific or educational purposes, is prohibited except for the species noted in this paragraph. This prohibition does not apply to fully manufactured artificial flies used for fishing or to personally taken, noncommercial game birds. Feathers or skins of the following species are permitted entry under certain conditions:

- Chickens,
- Turkeys,
- Guinea fowl,
- Geese, ducks,
- Pigeons, ostriches,
- Rheas,
- English ring-necked pheasants,
- Pea fowl not taken from the wild.

On October 23, 1992, the Wild Bird Conservation Act became effective. This act focuses on the live species listed in the Appendices to the Convention on International Trade in Endangered Species (CITES). If you import live birds, you must meet the requirements of this law in addition to the requirements of CITES, the Endangered Species Act, the Migratory Bird Treaty Act, and any other applicable regulations. Import permits must be obtained in advance from the Fish and Wildlife Service, Office of Management Authority.

Live birds, their parts, and products that are protected under the Migratory Bird Treaty Act may be imported into the United States for scientific purposes or certain propagating purposes only under permits issued by the regional office of Fish and Wildlife Service, Office of Migratory Birds, in the region where the importation will occur or where the importer resides.

Imported birds (pets, migratory birds, falcons) are subject to the quarantine requirements of the USDA and Public Health Service. Quarantine space must be reserved *before* importing. Health certificates must be obtained from the birds' country of origin prior to exportation. Inquiries should be addressed to the appropriate agency.

On June 9, 1989, the U.S. Fish and Wildlife Service announced a ban on the importation of most African elephant ivory and any products made from it. The ban covers all commercial and noncommercial shipments, including personal baggage accompanying a tourist. There are limited exceptions for antiques, trophies, and personal household effects. For further information, contact the U.S. Fish and Wildlife Service, Office of Management Authority, 4401 N. Fairfax Drive, Arlington, VA 22203, Tel. 1-800-358-2104.

The importation of the following is subject to the requirements of the Quarantine Division of the U.S. Public Health Service, Centers for Disease Control, Atlanta, GA 30333; the Veterinary Services of the Animal and Plant Health Inspection Service, Department of Agriculture, Hyattsville, MD 20782; and of the U.S. Fish and Wildlife Service:

- Birds,
- Cats,
- Dogs,
- Monkeys,
- Turtles.

A current rabies certificate must accompany each live imported dog. Importers of dogs without a rabies certificate must complete a copy of CDC Form 75.37, "Notice to Owners & Importers of Dogs," prior to obtaining the dog's release from CBP custody. The importer must send copies of this completed form to the local quarantine station of the Public Health Service, a list of which can be found on the CDC's Web site, www.cdc.gov/ncidod/dq/quarantine_stations.htm. If the local quarantine station is unknown, importers may call 773-894-2960 (Chicago), 718-553-1685 (JFK-NY), or 310-215-2365 (LA) to learn the appropriate office for submitting this form.

The importation of live turtles, tortoises, and terrapins with a carapace length of less than four inches, and the viable eggs of turtles, tortoises and terrapins, is allowed by the U.S. Public Health Service only under strict requirements as to purpose and quantity. The U.S. Public Heath Service does not allow the importation of live, non-human primates, including monkeys, as pets.

Other Miscellaneous Prohibited or Restricted Merchandise

44. Matches, fireworks, knives. The following are all prohibited importations:

- White or yellow phosphorus matches,
- Fireworks banned under federal or state restrictions,
- Pepper shells,
- Switchblade knives,

45. Foreign Assets Control Restrictions. The Office of Foreign Assets Control (OFAC) of the U.S. Treasury Department administers regulations and executive orders that impose a variety of sanctions, including import or export bans, on countries, companies, and individuals. Restrictions imposed by the sanctions vary, and in some instances, including bans, certain products may be permissible even when most others are prohibited. Contact your local port of entry for complete information.

Full or partial trade embargoes are currently in place for:

- Cuba,
- Iran,
- North Korea,
- Sudan,
- Syria, and
- Burma.

Travelers should be aware that travel restrictions may also apply to these countries. Because of strict enforcement of these prohibitions, anyone anticipating travel to any of the countries listed above is advised to contact OFAC, 202-622-2500, well in advance of planned travel, or to write to the Office of Foreign Assets Control, Department of the Treasury, Washington, DC 20220.

OFAC also administers sanctions involving targeted persons in:

- The Western Balkans,
- Burma (Myanmar),
- Iraq,
- Liberia,
- Libya,
- Zimbabwe.

In addition, OFAC administers sanctions involving individuals or entities generally identified as having been involved in:

- Illegal diamond trading,
- Terrorist activities,
- Narcotics trafficking,
- Proliferation of weapons of mass destruction,
- Acts of violence,
- Threatening international stabilization efforts,
- Crimes against humanity.

Import and export transactions involving these persons or entities are ordinarily prohibited. Detailed information can be found at OFAC's Web site, www.treas.gov/offices/enforcement/ofac/sanctions or by contacting OFAC's Licensing Division at 202-622-2480.

46. Obscene, Immoral or Seditious Matter and Lottery Tickets. Section 305, Tariff Act of 1930, as amended, prohibits the importation of any book, writing, advertisement, circular, or picture containing:

- Any matter advocating or urging treason or insurrection against the United States,
- Any matter advocating or urging forcible resistance to any law of the United States,
- Any threat to take the life of or inflict bodily harm upon any person in the United States.

  It also prohibits the importation of:

- Any obscene book, writing, advertisement, circular, picture or other representation, figure, or image on or of paper or other material,
- Any instrument or other article that is obscene or immoral,
- Any drug or medicine for causing unlawful abortion that has not been approved by the FDA.
- Any lottery ticket, unless printed in Canada for use in a U.S.—or in some cases, other foreign—lottery.

47. Petroleum and Petroleum Products. Importations of petroleum and petroleum products are subject to the requirements of the Department of Energy. An import license is no longer required, but an import authorization may be needed. These importations may be subject to an oil-import license fee, which is collected and administered by the Department of Energy. Inquiries should be directed to the Department of Energy, Washington, DC 20585.

48. Products of Convict or Forced Labor. Merchandise produced, mined, or manufactured, wholly or in part by means of the use of convict labor, forced labor, or indentured labor under penal sanctions is prohibited from importation, provided that a finding has been published pursuant to section 12.42 of the CBP Regulations (19 CFR 12.42) that certain classes of merchandise from a particular country, produced by convict, forced, or indentured labor, either were being, or are likely to be, imported into the United States in violation of section 307 of the Tariff Act of 1930, as amended (19 U.S.C. 1307).

49. Unfair Competition. Section 337 of the Tariff Act, as amended, prohibits the importation of merchandise if the president finds that unfair methods of competition or unfair acts exist. This section is most commonly invoked in the case of patent violations, although a patent need not be at issue. The prohibition of entries of the merchandise in question is generally for the term of the patent, although a different term may be specified.

Following a Section 337 investigation, the International Trade Commission (ITC) may find that unfair methods of competition or unfair acts exist regarding the importation of particular merchandise. After the ITC has issued an order, the president is allowed 60 days to take action to communicate his approval or disapproval of the ITC's determination. Should the 60 days expire without presidential action, the order becomes final. During the 60-day period, or until the president acts, importation of the merchandise is allowed under a special bond. However, CBP must recall that merchandise if doing so becomes appropriate under the order's conditions once it becomes final. If the president determines that entry of the merchandise in question does not violate Section 337, the bond is canceled.

50. Artifacts/Cultural Property. A number of U.S. laws regulate the importation of cultural artifacts such as archaeological and ethnologic objects. For example, U.S. law prohibits the importation of pre-Columbian monumental and architectural sculpture and murals from countries in Central and South America without first obtaining export permits from the country of origin. CBP will not accept an export permit from a third country. Importers should also be aware that a treaty exists between the United States and Mexico regarding the recovery of cultural property.

Importations of certain archeological and ethnographic material from the following countries are specifically restricted from entering the United States unless an export certificate issued by the country of origin accompanies them:

- Bolivia,
- Cyprus,
- Cambodia,
- El Salvador,
- Guatemala,
- Honduras,
- Italy,
- Mali,
- Nicaragua,
- Peru.

Additionally, cultural property from Iraq is prohibited from entering the U.S. if it was illegally removed from Iraq after August 6, 1990.

All these restrictions are aimed at deterring the pillage of other countries' cultural heritage and at fostering opportunities for access to cultural objects for legitimate scientific, cultural, and educational purposes. CBP has published import restrictions on objects and artifacts of this nature in the *Federal Register*; these restrictions can also be found at the Web site of the Bureau of

Educational and Cultural Affairs, www.exchanges.state.gov/culprop/, of the U.S. Department of State.

Federal law also prohibits the importation of any article of cultural property stolen from museums or from religious or secular public monuments. Would-be buyers of such property should be aware that purchases of cultural objects, unlike purchases of customary tourist merchandise, do not confer ownership should the object be found to be stolen. The U.S. National Stolen Property Act may be applicable in such cases, particularly if the country of origin declares by law that it owns all cultural objects, known or unknown, within its present-day political boundaries.

Purveyors of merchandise described in this section have been known to offer fake export certificates. Prospective buyers should be aware that CBP officers are expert at spotting fraudulent export certificates that accompany cultural property. CBP officers will also examine import declaration forms to determine whether any false information has been entered because this also constitutes a violation.

For current information about countries for which the United States has issued specific import restrictions, contact the U.S. Department of State's Bureau of Educational and Cultural Affairs, Washington, DC 20547, or visit the agency's Web site: www.exchanges.state.gov/culprop/index.html. For information about how these restrictions are enforced, visit CBP's Web site, www.cbp.gov, and search on "cultural property."

51. **United States Trade Representative Actions.** As authorized by the Trade Act of 1974, the United States Trade Representative (USTR) administers Section 301 complaints against unfair foreign trade practices that harm U.S. exporters. USTR actions that may directly affect U.S. importers include the *suspension of concessions.* For example, the USTR may suspend the normal-trade-relations rate of duty and substitute a substantially higher duty rate on designated products from a foreign country found to be discriminating against U.S. products.

Importers and Internet shoppers should check the USTR Web site, www. ustr.gov, on a regular basis to determine whether their products may become subject to a substituted rate of duty. The USTR will normally propose a list of products and provide a comment period for businesses that may be affected by a higher duty rate.

The International Trade Administration at the Department of Commerce has set up a notification system that will advise importers of USTR actions that may affect imported products. Importers who wish to receive such notification should sign up at the following site: www.ita.doc.gov/td/industry/otea/301alert/form.html. Importers are advised that once the USTR has taken a Section 301 action, CBP is responsible for implementing that action as directed by USTR.

Information on USTR actions that CBP is currently implementing can be found at: www.cbp.gov/xp/cgov/import/commercial_enforcement/.

42. Alcoholic Beverages

Any person or firm wishing to engage in the business of importing into the United States distilled spirits, wines containing at least seven percent alcohol, or malt beverages must first obtain an importer's basic permit from the Alcohol and Tobacco Tax and Trade Bureau (TTB) of the U.S. Treasury Department. TTB is responsible for administering the Federal Alcohol Administration Act, 27 U.S.C. 201 et seq. and 27 CFR Subchapter A.

Under this act, TTB has the authority to:

- Prevent consumer deception,
- Require that labels on alcohol products provide consumers with "adequate information" regarding the identity and quality of the products, and
- Prohibit false or misleading statements.

Information on basic permits, labeling, and other importation issues is available on the TTB Web site, www.ttb.gov, or from TTB's National Revenue Center, 1-877-882-3277.

Distilled spirits imported in bulk containers whose capacity is more than one gallon can be only withdrawn from CBP custody by individuals to whom it is lawful to sell, or otherwise dispose of, distilled spirits in bulk. A copy of a bill of lading or other document such as an invoice, showing the name of the consignee, the nature of the contents, and the quantity the shipment contains must, at the time of importation, accompany each bulk or bottled shipment of imported spirits or distilled or intoxicating liquors (18 U.S.C. 1263).

CBP will not release to any state an alcoholic beverage(s) whose use would violate its laws. The importation of alcoholic beverages in the mails is prohibited.

The United States adopted the metric system of measurement with the enactment of the Metric Conversion Act of 1975. In general, imported wine had to conform to metric standards of fill if bottled or packed on or after January 1, 1979. Imported distilled spirits, with some exceptions, had to conform to metric standards of fill if bottled or packed on or after January 1, 1980. Distilled spirits or wines bottled or packed prior to the applicable date had to be accompanied by a statement confirming that fact and signed by an authorized official of the appropriate foreign country. This statement may be a separate document or may be shown on the invoice. Wine containing less than seven percent alcohol by volume and malt beverages, including beer, are not subject to metric standards of fill.

Under the Internal Revenue Code of 1986, 26 U.S.C. Chapter 51, all beverages containing at least 0.5 percent (one half of one percent) alcohol by volume are subject to an excise tax. This tax applies to all alcoholic products that are fit for beverage use even if they are imported for industrial use. The excise tax also applies to imported denatured alcohol, including fuel alcohol, unless it is transferred directly from CBP custody to the bonded premises of a registered distilled spirits plant (or, in the case of fuel alcohol, to a registered alcohol-fuel plant).

Distilled spirits (Section 5232 of the Internal Revenue Code), wine (Section 5364), and beer (Section 5418) imported in bulk may be transferred in-bond from CBP custody to the bonded premises of a distilled spirits plant, winery, or brewery without having to pay the excise tax (see 27 CFR Part 27).

Marking

Wines imported in bottles or other containers (except those containing less than seven percent alcohol by volume) must be packaged, marked, branded, and labeled in accordance with the regulations in 27 CFR Part 4. Wines with less than seven percent alcohol by volume are not subject to 27 CFR Part 4, but they must be marked in accordance with Food and Drug Administration rules. Imported malt beverages, including alcohol-free and nonalcoholic malt beverages, must be labeled in conformance with the regulations in 27 CFR Part 7. The labeling regulations governing imported distilled spirits can be found in 27 CFR Part 5.

Each bottle, cask or other immediate container of imported distilled spirits, wines, or malt beverages must be marked for CBP purposes to indicate the country of origin of its contents unless the shipment comes within one of the exceptions outlined in Chapter 32 ("Rules of Origin") of this book.

Health Warning Statement

TTB regulations in 27 CFR Part 16 require the following health warning to appear on the labels of containers of alcoholic beverages bottled on or after Nov. 18, 1989:

Certificate of Label Approval

Labels affixed to bottles of imported distilled spirits, wine and malt beverages must be covered by certificates of label approval issued by TTB to the importer. Certificates of label approval or photostatic copies of these certificates must be filed with CBP before the goods can be released for sale in the United States. These requirements do not apply to wines containing less than seven percent alcohol, but they do apply to fermented malt beverages if the state in which the malt beverage is withdrawn for consumption imposes labeling requirements similar to federal requirements.

Foreign Documentation

Importers of wines and distilled spirits should consult TTB about certificates of origin, identity, age, and proper cellar treatment. Certain wines or distilled spirits require original certificates of origin as a condition of entry. Also, an importer of natural wine must possess, at the time of importation, certification regarding proper cellar treatment, as provided in 27 CFR 27.140.

Requirements of Other Agencies

The importation of alcoholic beverages is also subject to the specific requirements of the Food and Drug Administration. Certain plant materials, when used in bottle jackets for wine or other liquids, are subject to special restrictions under plant quarantine regulations of the Animal and Plant Health Inspection Service. All bottle jackets made of dried or unmanufactured plant materials are subject to inspection upon arrival and are referred to the Department of Agriculture.

43. Motor Vehicles and Boats

Automobiles, Vehicles, and Vehicle Equipment

Safety, Bumper, and Emission Requirements. As a general rule, all imported motor vehicles less than 25 years old and items of motor vehicle equipment must comply with all applicable Federal Motor Vehicle Safety Standards (FMVSS) in effect when these vehicles or items were manufactured. A CBP inspection at the time of entry will determine such compliance, which is verified by the original manufacturer's certification permanently affixed to the vehicle or merchandise. An entry declaration form, HS-7, must be filed when motor vehicles or items of motor vehicle equipment are entered. The HS-7 can be obtained from customs brokers or ports of entry.

Certain temporary importations may be exempt from the requirements for conformance if written approval is obtained in advance from both the U.S. Department of Transportation and the Environmental Protection Agency. This includes vehicles brought in for research, demonstrations, investigation, studies, testing, or competitive events. Also, EPA form 3520-1 and DOT form HS-7 must be submitted to CBP at the time entry for such vehicles is made.

Vehicles imported for temporary use by certain nonresidents or by members of foreign governments or foreign armed forces may not be required to comply with safety, bumper, emission, or theft-prevention standards. Nonconforming vehicles imported by nonresidents for personal use must be exported at the end of one year. Vehicles described in this paragraph may also require EPA and DOT declarations (forms 3520-1 and HS-7, respectively).

A DOT bond in the amount of 150 percent of the vehicle's dutiable value must be posted at the port of entry when a noncertified or nonconforming vehicle is imported for permanent use. The importer must also sign a contract with a DOT-registered importer, who will modify the vehicle to conform with all applicable safety and bumper standards and who can certify the modification(s). A copy of this contract must be furnished to CBP with the HS-7 at the port of entry. Furthermore, the vehicle model and model year must be determined to be eligible for importation.

For additional information or details on these requirements, contact:

U.S. Department of Transportation
National Highway Traffic Safety Administration
Director of the Office of Vehicle Safety Compliance (NEF-32)
400 Seventh Street, SW
Washington, DC 20590
Tel. 1-800-424-9393

The Clean Air Act, as amended, prohibits the importation of any motor vehicle or motor vehicle engine not in conformity with emission requirements prescribed by the U.S. Environmental Protection Agency. This restriction applies whether the motor vehicle or motor-vehicle engine is new or used, and whether it was originally produced for sale and use in a foreign country or originally produced (or later modified) to conform to EPA requirements for sale or use in the United States. In addition to passenger cars, all trucks, multipurpose vehicles (e.g., all-terrain vehicles, campers), motorcycles, etc., that are capable of being registered by a state for use on public roads or that the EPA has deemed capable of being safely driven on public roads, are subject to these requirements. The term "vehicle" is used below to include all EPA-regulated vehicles and engines.

Nonroad Engine Imports

In accordance with the Clean Air Act and implementing regulations, 40 CFR Parts 89, 90 and 91, the Environmental Protection Agency began regulating certain nonroad diesel and gasoline engines, requiring that they meet federal emission standards beginning January 1, 1996.

Nonroad, also referred to as *off-road* or *off-highway* is a term that covers a diverse group of engines and equipment. The nonroad category includes lawn and garden equipment, outdoor power equipment, recreational equipment, farm equipment, construction equipment, marine engines, and locomotives.

Prior to importation into the United States, regulated nonroad engines must be covered by an EPA-issued Certificate of Conformity. EPA issues the certificate to the engine manufacturer; the certificate declares that the engine family named on the certificate conforms with all applicable emissions standards and other requirements. It also permits the manufacturer to sell, offer for sale, introduce into commerce, or import into the United States the named engine family. Certificates are issued for only one model year at a time. A label confirming that the engine meets emission standards must be affixed to the engine and readily visible.

Upon request, an importer must provide an EPA Form 3520-21 to CBP at the time of entry into the United States. This form must contain the following information about the engine:

- Model,
- Model number,
- Serial number,
- Horsepower,
- Build date, and
- Manufacturer.

It must also include a description of the equipment or vehicle containing the engine, including:

- The equipment manufacturer,
- Equipment serial number,
- Location of the EPA emissions label, and
- Engine serial number.

For additional information and specific guidelines regarding the importation of nonroad engines subject to EPA emissions standards, please refer to the EPA's Web page, "Importing Vehicles and Engines," at www.epa.gov/otaq/imports/. To obtain the EPA Form 3520-21, please refer to EPA's Web site, www.epa.gov/otaq/imports/forms/3520-21.pdf.

For technical assistance, please contact EPA's Office of Civil Enforcement, Air Enforcement Division, at 202-564-8673.

U.S.-Version Vehicles: Any person may import U.S.-version vehicles. *All such 1971 and later models are required to have a label in a readily visible position in the engine compartment stating that the vehicle conforms to U.S. requirements.* This label will read "Vehicle Emission Control Information" and will have a statement by the manufacturer that the vehicle meets EPA emission requirements at the time of manufacture. If this label is not present, the importer should obtain a letter of conformity from the manufacturer's United States representative—not from a dealership—prior to importation.

Non-U.S.-Version Vehicles: Individuals are not permitted to import non-U.S.-version vehicles (unless otherwise excluded or exempted; see next sections). These vehicles must be imported (entered) by an Independent Commercial Importer (ICI) having a currently valid qualifying certificate of conformity for each vehicle being imported. The ICI will be responsible for performing all necessary modifications, testing, and labeling, as well as providing an emissions warranty identical to the emissions warranty required of new vehicles sold in the U.S.

A list of approved ICIs is available from the EPA. Vehicles at least 21 years old are exempt from these provisions and may be imported without modification.

Words of Caution:

- Not all nonconforming vehicles are eligible for importation, and ICIs are not required to accept vehicles for which they have qualifying certificates of conformity.
- EPA certification of ICIs does not guarantee the actions or work of the ICIs, nor does it regulate contractual agreements and working relationships with vehicle owners.
- EPA strongly recommends that prospective importers buy only U.S.-version (labeled) vehicles, because of the expense and potential difficulties involved with importing a non-U.S.-version vehicle.
- EPA strongly recommends that current owners of non-U.S.-version vehicles sell or otherwise dispose of them overseas rather than ship and import them into the U.S., because of the expense and potential difficulties involved with importing a non-U.S.-version vehicle.
- Before shipping a nonconforming vehicle for importation, EPA strongly recommends that the importer either make final arrangements with an ICI for modifications and testing or obtain EPA approval in writing for importation. Storage fees at the ports are costly, and the vehicle may not be eligible for importation.
- The EPA policy that permitted importers a one-time exemption for vehicles at least five years old has been eliminated.
- EPA considers a U.S.-version vehicle that has had modifications to its drive train or emission control system to be a non-U.S.-version vehicle, even though it may be labeled a U.S.-version vehicle.

For Further Information:

Environmental Protection Agency
2000 Traverwood Drive
Ann Arbor, Michigan 48105
Attn: Imports Division
Tel. 734-214-4100

Final Word of Caution. *Modifications necessary to bring a nonconforming vehicle into conformity with safety, bumper, or emission standards may require extensive engineering, be impractical or impossible, or the labor and materials may be unduly* *expensive. It is highly recommended that these modifications be investigated before a vehicle is purchased for importation.*

Boat Safety Standards

Imported boats and associated equipment are subject to U.S. Coast Guard safety regulations or standards under the Federal Boat Safety Act of 1971. Products subject to standards must have a compliance certification label affixed to them. Certain hulls also require a hull identification number to be affixed. A U.S. Coast Guard import declaration is required to be filed with entries of nonconforming boats. Further information may be obtained from the Commandant, U.S. Coast Guard, Washington, DC 20593.

Dutiability

Vessels brought into the United States for use in trade or commerce are not dutiable. Yachts or pleasure boats brought into the United States by nonresidents for their own use in pleasure cruising are also not dutiable.

Yachts or pleasure boats owned by a resident or brought into the United States for sale or charter to a resident are dutiable. Further information may be found in CBP's pamphlet *Pleasure Boats*.

Restrictions on Use

Vessels that are foreign-built or of foreign registry may be used in the United States for pleasure purposes and in the foreign trade of the United States. However, federal law prohibits the use of such vessels in the coastwise trade, i.e., the transportation of passengers or merchandise between points in the United States, including carrying fishing parties for hire. Questions concerning the use of foreign-built or foreign-flag vessels should be addressed to:

Chief, Cargo Security
Carriers and Immigration Branch
Office of Regulations and Rulings
U.S. Customs and Border Protection
1300 Pennsylvania Avenue, NW, Mint Annex
Washington, DC 20229

44. Import Quotas

An import quota is a quantity control on imported merchandise for a certain period of time. Quotas are established by legislation, by directives, and by proclamations issued under the authority contained in specific legislation. The majority of import quotas are administered by CBP. The Commissioner of CBP controls the importation of quota merchandise but has no authority to change or modify any quota.

United States import quotas may be divided into two types: absolute and tariff-rate. Under the North American Free Trade Agreement (NAFTA), there are tariff-preference levels, which are administered like tariff-rate quotas.

Tariff-rate quotas provide for the entry of a specified quantity of the quota product at a reduced rate of duty during a given period. There is no limitation on the amount of the product that may be entered during the quota period, but quantities entered in excess of the quota for the period are subject to higher duty rates. In most cases, products of Communist-controlled areas are not entitled to the benefits of tariff-rate quotas.

Absolute quotas are quantitative, that is, no more than the amount specified may be permitted entry during a quota period. Some absolute quotas are global, while others are allocated to specified foreign countries. Imports in excess of a specified quota may be held for the opening of the next quota period by placing it in a foreign trade zone or by entering it for warehouse, or it may be exported or destroyed under CBP supervision.

The usual CBP procedures generally applicable to other imports apply with respect to commodities subject to quota limitations.

The quota status of a commodity subject to a tariff-rate quota cannot be determined in advance of its entry. The quota rates of duty are ordinarily assessed on such commodities entered from the beginning of the quota period until such time in the period as it is determined that imports are nearing the quota level. CBP port directors are then instructed to require the deposit of estimated duties at the over-quota duty rate and to report the time of official presentation of each entry. A final determination is then made of the date and time when a quota is filled, and all port directors are advised accordingly.

Some of the absolute quotas are invariably filled at or shortly after the opening of the quota period. Each of these quotas is therefore officially opened at noon Eastern Standard Time, or the equivalent in other time zones, on the designated effective date. When the total quantity for these entries filed at the opening of the quota period exceeds the quota, the merchandise is released on a pro rata basis, the pro rata being the ratio between the quota quantity and the total quantity offered for entry. This assures an equitable distribution of the quota.

Merchandise is not regarded as presented for purposes of determining quota priority until an entry summary or withdrawal from warehouse for consumption has been submitted in proper form and the merchandise is located within the port limits.

Commodities Subject to Quotas Administered by CBP

As provided in the Harmonized Tariff Schedule of the United States, the commodities listed below are subject to quota limitations currently in effect. Local CBP officers can be consulted about any changes.

Information may also be obtained by contacting:

Quota Staff
U.S. Customs and Border Protection
1300 Pennsylvania Avenue, NW
Washington, DC 20229
Tel. 202-863-6560

Tariff-Rate Quotas

- Anchovies,
- Brooms,
- Broom corn brooms,
- Ethyl alcohol,
- Lamb,
- Line pipe,
- Milk and cream,
- Olives,
- Satsumas (mandarins),
- Tuna,
- Upland cotton, and
- Wire rod.

NAFTA

Presidential Proclamation 6641 implemented the North American Free Trade Agreement and established tariff-preference levels on the following qualifying imported goods:

Imported from Mexico:

- Chapter 99, Subchapter VI, U.S. Note 4 (99 USN 4)—Milk and cream,
- 99 USN 5—Dried milk and dried cream,
- 99 USN 6—Dried milk and dried cream,
- 99 USN 7—Milk and cream (condensed and evaporated),
- 99 USN 8—Cheese,
- 99 USN 9—Tomatoes,
- 99 USN 10—Tomatoes,
- 99 USN 11—Onions and shallots,
- 99 USN 12—Eggplants,
- 99 USN 13—Chili peppers,
- 99 USN 14—Squash,

- 99 USN 15—Watermelons,
- 99 USN 16—Peanuts,
- 99 USN 18—Sugars derived from sugar cane or sugar beets,
- 99 USN 19—Blended syrups,
- 99 USN 20—Sugars derived from sugar cane or sugar beets,
- 99 USN 21—Orange juice,
- 99 USN 22—Orange juice,
- 99 USN 25—Cotton,
- 9906.96.01—Brooms,
- Section XI Additional U.S. Notes—cotton or man-made fiber apparel, wool apparel, cotton or man-made fiber fabrics and made-ups, and cotton or man-made fiber yarns.

Imported from Canada:

- Section XI Additional U.S. Notes—cotton or man-made fiber apparel, wool apparel, cotton or man-made fiber fabrics and made-ups, and cotton or man-made fiber yarns.

Tariff-Rate Quotas—GATT:

Presidential Proclamation 6763 implemented the GATT Uruguay Round Agreements for the following tariff-rate commodities:

- Chapter 2, Additional U.S. Note 3 (2 AUSN 3)—Beef,
- 4 AUSN 5—Milk and cream,
- 4 AUSN 9—Dried milk and dried cream,
- 4 AUSN 10—Dairy products,
- 4 AUSN 11—Milk and cream (condensed or evaporated),
- 4 AUSN 12—Dried milk, dried cream, and dried whey (in excess of 224,981 kilograms),
- 4 AUSN 18—Canadian cheddar cheese,
- 12 AUSN 2—Peanuts,
- 17 AUSN 5—Sugar (including sugar cane),
- 17 AUSN 7—Articles containing more than 65 percent by dry weight of sugar described in 17 AUSN 2,
- 17 AUSN 8—Articles containing more than 10 percent by dry weight of sugar described in 17 AUSN 3,
- 17 AUSN 9—Blended syrups,
- 18 AUSN 1—Cocoa powder,
- 18 AUSN 2—Chocolate,
- 18 AUSN 3—Chocolate and low-fat chocolate crumb,

- 19 AUSN 2—Infant formula,
- 19 AUSN 3—Mixes and doughs,
- 20 AUSN 5—Peanut butter and paste,
- 21 AUSN 4—Mixed condiments and mixed seasonings,
- 21 AUSN 5—Ice cream,
- 23 AUSN 2—Animal feed,
- 24 ASUN 5—Tobacco,
- 52 AUSN 5—Cotton,
- 52 AUSN 6—Harsh or rough cotton,
- 52 AUSN 7—Cotton,
- 52 AUSN 8—Cotton,
- 52 AUSN 9—Card strips made from cotton,
- 52 AUSN 10—Fibers of cotton.

Tariff-Rate Quotas: U.S.–Israel Agreement on Trade in Agricultural Products

Presidential Proclamation 6962 implemented the U.S.–Israel agreement for the following agricultural products:

- Chapter 99, Subchapter VIII, U.S. Note 3—Butter, fresh or sour cream,
- Chapter 99, Subchapter VIII, U.S. Note 4—Dried milk,
- Chapter 99, Subchapter VIII, U.S. Note 5—Cheese and substitutes for cheese,
- Chapter 99, Subchapter VIII, U.S. Note 6—Peanuts,
- Chapter 99, Subchapter VIII, U.S. Note 7—Ice cream.

Textile Articles

CBP administers import controls on certain cotton, wool, man-made fiber, silk blend, and other vegetable-fiber articles manufactured or produced in designated countries. CBP administers the Special Access Program and the Andean Trade Preference Act on certain products that are made of U.S.-formed-and-cut fabric. These controls are imposed on the basis of directives issued to the Commissioner of CBP by the Chairman of the Committee for the Implementation of Textile Agreements.

Information concerning specific import controls may be obtained from the Commissioner of CBP. Other information concerning the textile program may be obtained from:

Chairman
Committee for the Implementation of Textile Agreements
U.S. Department of Commerce
Washington, DC 20230

Textile Visa and Export License Requirements

A textile visa is an endorsement in the form of a stamp on an invoice or export control license that is executed by a foreign government. It is used to control the exportation of textiles and textile products to the United States and to prohibit the unauthorized entry of the merchandise into this country. A visa may cover either quota or nonquota merchandise. Conversely, quota merchandise may or may not require a visa depending upon the country of origin. A visa does not guarantee entry of the merchandise into the United States. If the quota closes between the time the visa is issued in the foreign country and the shipment's arrival in the United States, the shipment will not be released to the importer until the quota opens again.

Electronic Visa Information System (ELVIS)

ELVIS is the electronic transmission of visa information for textile merchandise from a specific country to the U.S. CBP.

Quotas or Licenses Administered by Other Government Agencies

Watches and Watch Movements. There are no licensing requirements or quotas on watches and watch movements entering the United States unless the watches and watch movements are produced in the insular possessions (U.S. Virgin Islands, American Samoa, Guam). The Departments of Commerce and the Interior administer a program that establishes an annual allocation for watches and watch movements assembled in the insular possessions to enter the United States free of duty under statistical notes (91/5) to Chapter 91 of the Harmonized Tariff Schedule. Licenses are issued only to established insular producers. Further information on the insular watch program may be obtained from:

Statutory Import Programs Staff
Import Administration
U.S. Department of Commerce
Washington, DC 20230

Dairy Products. Certain dairy products are subject to annual import quotas administered by the Department of Agriculture and may be imported at the in-quota rate only under import licenses issued by that department. Detailed information on the licensing of these products, or the conditions under which limited quantities of the products may be imported without licenses, may be obtained from:

Dairy Import Group
Foreign Agricultural Service

U.S. Department of Agriculture
Washington, DC 20250
Tel. 202-720-0638

- Chapter 4, Additional U.S. Note 6 (4 AUSN 6)—Butter and fresh or sour cream,
- 4 AUSN 7—Dried milk,
- 4 AUSN 8—Dried milk or dried cream,
- 4 AUSN 12—Dried milk, dried cream, or dried whey (up to 224,981 kilograms),
- 4 AUSN 14—Butter substitutes,
- 4 AUSN 16—Cheeses and substitutes for cheese,
- 4 AUSN 17—Blue-molded cheese,
- 4 AUSN 18—Cheddar cheese (except Canadian cheddar),
- 4 AUSN 19—American-type cheese,
- 4 AUSN 20—Edam and Gouda cheese,
- 4 AUSN 21—Italian-type cheese,
- 4 AUSN 22—Swiss or Emmentaler cheese,
- 4 AUSN 23—Cheese and substitutes for cheese,
- 4 AUSN 25—Swiss or Emmentaler cheese.

The above products may be imported at the over-quota rate without an import license.

45. Fraud

Civil and Criminal Enforcement Provisions

Section 592 of the Tariff Act of 1930, as amended (19 U.S.C. 1592), generally provides that persons shall be subject to a monetary penalty if they enter, introduce, or attempt to enter or introduce merchandise into the commerce of the United States by fraud, gross negligence, or negligence; by using material and false electronically transmitted data; written or oral statement; or by document, act, or material omission. In limited circumstances, the merchandise of such individuals may be seized to insure payment of the penalty and forfeited if the penalty is not paid.

CBP has applied the civil fraud statute in cases where individuals and companies in the United States and abroad have negligently, gross negligently, or intentionally provided false information concerning importations into the United States. Individuals presenting false information to CBP officers may also be liable for sanctions under a criminal fraud statute. Title 18, United States Code, Section 542, provides a maximum of two years' imprisonment, a fine, or both, for each violation involving a fraudulent importation or attempted importation. Although Congress initially enacted the civil and criminal fraud statutes to discourage individuals from evading payment of lawful duties owed to the United

States, these laws apply today regardless of whether the United States is deprived of lawful duties.

Under Section 596 of the Tariff Act of 1930, as amended (19 U.S.C. 1595a(c)), CBP is required to seize and forfeit all merchandise that is stolen, smuggled, or clandestinely imported or introduced. CBP is also required to seize and forfeit controlled substances, certain contraband articles, and plastic explosives that do not contain a detection agent.

Merchandise may also be seized and forfeited if:

- Its importation is restricted or prohibited because of a law relating to health, safety, or conservation;
- The merchandise is lacking a federal license required for the importation;
- The merchandise or packaging is in violation of copyright, trademark, trade name, or trade dress protections;
- The merchandise is intentionally or repetitively marked in violation of country of origin marking requirements; or
- The imported merchandise is subject to quantitative restrictions requiring a visa or similar document from a foreign government, and the document presented with the entry is counterfeit.

Federal laws relating to criminal activities commonly known as money laundering (e.g., 18 U.S.C. 1956) created criminal and civil provisions that, along with fines and imprisonment, enable the government to prosecute persons for, and seize and forfeit property involved in or traceable to, such violations. Criminal penalties include fines of not more than $500,000 or twice the value of the property, funds, or monetary instruments involved in the violation, whichever is greater, or imprisonment for not more than twenty years, or both. There is also a civil penalty of not more than $10,000 or the value of the property, funds, or monetary instruments involved in the violation, whichever is greater.

Special agents from U.S. Immigration and Customs Enforcement, who operate throughout the United States and in the world's major trading centers, enforce the criminal fraud, civil fraud, and money laundering statutes. Suspected or known violations of any laws that involve importing merchandise into the United States can be reported toll-free and anonymously by calling 1-800-BE ALERT (1-800-232-5378). Rewards are applicable in many instances of reporting fraud.

46. Foreign-Trade Zones

Foreign-Trade Zones

Foreign-trade zones are secure areas legally outside the customs territory of the United States. Their purpose is to attract and promote international trade and commerce. Subzones are special-purpose facilities for companies that cannot operate effectively at public zone sites.

Foreign-trade zones are usually located in or near CBP ports of entry, industrial parks, or terminal warehouse facilities. These zones must be within 60 miles or 90 minutes' driving time from the port of entry limits, while subzones have no limit and are located in the zone user's private facility.

The Foreign-Trade Zones Board, which is under the Department of Commerce, authorizes operations within these zones based upon demonstrating that the intended operations are legal and not detrimental to the public interest. Created by the Foreign-Trade Zones Act of 1934, the Board reviews and approves applications to establish, operate, and maintain foreign-trade zones.

CBP is responsible for activating foreign-trade zones, securing them, controlling dutiable merchandise moving in and out of them, protecting and collecting the revenue, assuring that there is no evasion or violation of U.S. laws and regulations governing imported and exported merchandise, and assuring that the zones program is free from terrorist activity. It is important to note that although foreign-trade zones are treated as being outside the customs territory of the United States for tariff and entry purposes, all other federal laws—the Federal Food, Drug, and Cosmetic Act, for example—are applicable to products and establishments within these zones.

Foreign exporters planning to open or expand new American outlets may forward their goods to a foreign-trade zone in the United States to be held for an unlimited period while awaiting a favorable market in the United States or nearby countries. During this time, their goods will not be subject to CBP entry requirements, payment of duty, tax, or bond.

Treatment of Goods

Merchandise lawfully brought into these zones may be stored, sold, exhibited, broken up, repacked, assembled, distributed, sorted, tested, repaired, sampled, salvaged, relabeled, destroyed, processed, graded, cleaned, mixed with foreign or domestic merchandise, or otherwise manipulated or manufactured. Merchandise imported for use in the zone, such as construction materials or production equipment, may be admitted into the zone and assembled prior to entry for consumption. Payment of duty would be deferred until such equipment goes into use as production equipment in a Board-authorized activity.

The Foreign-Trade Zones Board may at any time order any goods, process, or treatment to be excluded from the zone if, in its judgment, they would be detrimental to the public interest, health, or safety. Any resulting merchandise would thereafter have to be exported.

When foreign goods are admitted to a zone in privileged foreign status, the importer may choose to have the merchandise treated, for tariff purposes, in the same condition as it was at the time of admission to the zone. By choosing this status, the importer "freezes" the goods' rate of duty and tariff classification in their condition at the time of filing the application for privileged foreign status. The rate of duty in force when privileged foreign status was chosen will apply regardless of when the merchandise is entered into United States customs territory, even though its condition or form may have been changed by processing in the zone. By selecting nonprivileged foreign status, the importer chooses to have the merchandise treated, for tariff purposes, in its condition and quantity as it is constructively transferred from the zone into United States customs territory and entered for consumption.

In most instances the importer may choose the status of the merchandise when it is admitted to the zone. The Foreign-Trade Zones Board may require that certain commodities be placed in privileged foreign status because of certain trade requirements such as antidumping and countervailing-duty considerations. Merchandise may be considered exported, for customs or other purposes, upon its admission to a zone in zone-restricted status; however, the merchandise taken into a zone under zone-restricted status must be for the sole purpose of exportation, destruction (except destruction of distilled spirits, wines, and fermented malt liquors) or storage.

An important feature of foreign-trade zones for foreign merchants entering the American market is that the goods may be brought to the threshold of the market, making immediate delivery certain and avoiding possible cancellation of orders due to shipping delays.

Producing articles in zones through the combined use of domestic and foreign materials makes it unnecessary to send domestic materials abroad for manufacture or to pay duty or obtain a bond for foreign materials that have been imported for this purpose. Duty on foreign goods involved in such processing or manufacture are calculated only on the actual quantity of the foreign goods incorporated into the merchandise and transferred from a zone for entry into the commerce of the United States. Allowances are made for unrecoverable waste resulting from such manufacture or manipulation, thereby eliminating payment of duty except on the articles that are actually entered. Recoverable waste will be placed in privileged foreign status and will be dutiable according to the condition it was in when it was admitted to the zone and according to the quantity entered into the commerce of the United States.

The Foreign-Trade Zones Act also allows exhibiting merchandise within a zone. Zone facilities may be utilized for the full exhibition of foreign merchandise for an unlimited length of time with no requirement for exportation or payment of duty. Merchandise exhibited in a zone would be held under the operator's bond. Thus, the owner of goods in a zone may display the goods where they are stored, establish his or her own showrooms, or join with other importers to display merchandise in a permanent exhibition. The importer may also sell from stock in a zone wholesale quantities. Retail trade is prohibited in zones.

Domestic merchandise may be taken into a zone and, providing its identity is maintained in accordance with regulations, may be returned to customs territory free of quotas, duty, or tax, even though while in the zone it may have been combined with or made part of other articles. However, domestic distilled spirits, wine, and beer, and a limited number of other kinds of merchandise generally may not be processed while in the zone.

Advantages

Manipulation and manufacture in a zone may produce cost savings. For example, many products shipped to a zone in bulk can be dried, sorted, graded, cleaned, bagged, or packed, resulting in savings of duties and taxes on moisture taken from content or dirt removed and culls thrown out. Damaged packages or broken bottles can be removed from shipments of packaged or bottled goods. If evaporation results during shipment or while goods are stored in the zone, contents of barrels or other containers can be regauged and savings obtained, as duty is not payable on the portions lost or removed. In other words, the contents of barrels or other containers can be measured at the time of transfer to customs territory to insure that duty is not charged on any portion lost to evaporation, leakage, breakage, or otherwise. These operations may also be conducted in bonded warehouses.

Savings in shipping charges, duty, and taxes may also result from such operations as shipping unassembled or disassembled furniture, machinery, etc., to the zone and assembling or reassembling it there.

Merchandise otherwise up to standard may be re-marked or relabeled in the zone (or bonded warehouse) to conform to requirements for entry into the commerce of the United States. Re-marking or relabeling that is misleading is not permitted in the zone. Substandard foods and drugs may, in certain cases, be reconditioned to meet the requirements of the Food, Drug, and Cosmetic Act.

There is no time limit on how long foreign merchandise may be stored in a zone or when it must be entered into United States customs territory, re-exported, or destroyed.

Transfer of Goods in Bonded Warehouses

Foreign merchandise in CBP bonded warehouses may be transferred to foreign-trade zones at any time before their retention date in the bonded warehouse expires, but such a transfer may only be made for the purpose of eventual exportation, destruction, or permanent storage.

When foreign merchandise is transferred to a zone from a CBP bonded warehouse, the bond is cancelled and all obligations regarding duty payment or when merchandise must be re-exported are terminated. Similarly, the owner of domestic merchandise stored in Internal Revenue bonded warehouses may transfer his or her goods to a zone and obtain cancellation of bonds. In addition, domestic goods moved into a zone under zone-restricted status are, upon entering the zone, considered exported for purposes of excise and internal revenue tax rebates. A manufacturer operating in U.S. customs territory using dutiable imported materials in his or her product may, upon transferring the product to the zone for export and complying with appropriate regulations, also obtain drawback of duties paid or cancellation of bond.

General information about United States foreign-trade zones and their locations may be obtained from:

Foreign-Trade Zones Board
Department of Commerce
Washington, DC 20330

Questions about the legal aspects of CBP responsibilities in regard to foreign-trade zones should be addressed to:

Chief, Cargo Control
U.S. Customs and Border Protection
Washington, DC 20229

Questions about the operational aspects of such responsibilities should be addressed to the appropriate CBP port director. The Foreign-Trade Zones Manual may be purchased from the Superintendent of Documents, U.S. Government Printing Office, Washington, DC 20402. When ordering, refer to CBP Publication No.0000-0559.

The Foreign-Trade Zones Manual may also be viewed at or downloaded from CBP's Web site, www.cbp.gov.

Appendix C

Addendum to Importing Into the United States

Addendum

Invoices; Additional Information; Customs Valuation; Other Forms; Other Agencies

Contents

6. Other Agencies

Addresses, Phone Numbers, and Web sites

1. Invoices

§ 141.83 Type of invoice required.

(a)–(b) [Reserved]

(c) *Commercial invoice.* (1) A commercial invoice shall be filed for each shipment of merchandise not exempted by paragraph (d) of this section. The commercial invoice shall be prepared in the manner customary in the trade, contain the information required by Secs. 141.86 through 141.89, and substantiate the statistical information required by Sec. 141.61(e) to be given on the entry, entry summary, or withdrawal documentation.

(2) The port director may accept a copy of a required commercial invoice in place of the original. A copy, other than a photostatic or photographic copy, shall contain a declaration by the foreign seller, the shipper, or the importer that it is a true copy.

(d) *Commercial invoice not required.* A commercial invoice shall not be required in connection with the filing of the entry, entry summary, or withdrawal documentation for merchandise listed in this paragraph. The importer, however, shall present any invoice, memorandum invoice, or bill pertaining to the merchandise which may be in his possession or available to him. If no invoice or bill is available, a pro forma (or substitute) invoice, as provided for in Sec. 141.85, shall be filed, and shall contain information adequate for the examination of merchandise and the determination of duties, and information and documentation which verify the information required for statistical purposes by Sec. 141.61(e). The merchandise subject to the foregoing requirements is as follows:

(1) [Reserved]

(2) Merchandise not intended for sale or any commercial use in its imported condition or any other form, and not brought in on commission for any person other than the importer.

(3)–(4) [Reserved]

(5) Merchandise returned to the United States after having been exported for repairs or alteration under subheadings 9802.00.40 and 9802.00.60, Harmonized Tariff Schedule of the United States (19 U.S.C. 1202).

(6) Merchandise shipped abroad, not delivered to the consignee, and returned to the United States.

(7) Merchandise exported from continuous CBP custody within 6 months after the date of entry.

(8) Merchandise consigned to, or entered in the name of, any agency of the U.S. Government.

(9) Merchandise for which an appraisement entry is accepted.

(10) Merchandise entered temporarily into the customs territory of the United States under bond or for permanent exhibition under bond.

(11) Merchandise provided for in section 466, Tariff Act of 1930 (19 U.S.C. 1466), which pertain to certain equipment, repair parts, and supplies for vessels.

(12) Merchandise imported as supplies, stores, and equipment of the importing carrier and subsequently made subject to entry pursuant to section 446, Tariff Act of 1930, as amended (19 U.S.C. 1446).

(13) Ballast (not including cargo used for ballast) landed from a vessel and delivered for consumption.

(14) Merchandise, whether privileged or nonprivileged, resulting from manipulation or manufacture in a foreign trade zone.

(15) Screenings contained in bulk importations of grain or seeds.

[T.D. 73-175, 38 FR 17447, July 2, 1973, as amended by T.D. 78-53, 43 FR 6069, Feb. 13, 1978; T.D. 79-221, 44 FR 46820, Aug. 9, 1979; T.D. 82- 224, 47 FR 53728, Nov. 29, 1982; T.D. 84-213, 49 FR 41184, Oct. 19, 1984; T.D. 85-39, 50 FR 9612, Mar. 11, 1985; T.D. 89-1, 53 FR 51256, Dec. 21, 1988; T.D. 93-66, 58 FR 44130, Aug. 19, 1993; T.D. 94-24, 59 FR 13200, Mar. 21, 1994; T.D. 97-82, 62 FR 51771, Oct. 3, 1997]

NOTE: *The Customs Service waived the requirement for a special invoice on March 1, 1982. However, it may still be used. If a commercial invoice is used, it must be signed by the seller and shipper or their agents.*

(PRO FORMA INVOICE HERE)

2. Additional Information

§ 141.89 Additional Information for certain classes of merchandise.

(a) Invoices for the following classes of merchandise, classifiable under the Harmonized Tariff Schedule of the United States (HTSUS), shall set forth the additional information specified: [T.D. 75-42, 75-239, 78-53, 83-251, 84-149.]

Aluminum and alloys of aluminum classifiable under subheadings 7601.10.60, 7601.20.60, 7601.20.90, or 7602.00.00, HTSUS (T.D. 53092, 55977, 56143)—Statement of the percentages by weight of any metallic element contained in the article.

Articles manufactured of textile materials, Coated or laminated with plastics or rubber, classifiable in Chapter(s) 39, 40, and 42, HTSUS—Include a description indicating whether the fabric is coated or laminated on both sides, on the exterior surface or on the interior surface.

Bags manufactured of plastic sheeting and not of a reinforced or laminated construction, classified in Chapter 39 or in heading 4202, HTSUS—Indicate the gauge of the plastic sheeting.

Ball or roller bearings classifiable under subheading 8482.10.50 through 8482.80.00, HTSUS (T.D. 68-306)—(1) Type of bearing (i.e. whether a ball or roller bearing); (2) If a roller bearing, whether a spherical, tapered, cylindrical, needled, or other type; (3) Whether a combination bearing (i.e., a bearing containing both ball and roller bearings, etc.); and (4) If a ball bearing (not including ball bearing with integral shafts or parts of ball bearings), whether or not radial, the following: (a) outside diameter of each bearing; and (b) whether or not a radial bearing (the definition of radial bearing is, for customs purposes, an antifriction bearing primarily designed to support a load perpendicular to shaft axis).

Beads (T.D. 50088, 55977)—(1) The length of the string, if strung; (2) The size of the beads expressed in millimeters; (3) The material of which the beads are composed, i.e. ivory, glass, imitation pearl, etc.

Bed Linen and Bedspreads—Statement as to whether or not the article contains any embroidery, lace, braid, edging, trimming, piping, or applique work.

Chemicals—Furnish the use and Chemical Abstracts Service number of chemical compounds classified in Chapters 27, 28 and 29, HTSUS.

Colors, dyes, stains and related products provided for under heading 3204, HTSUS—The following information is required: (1) Invoice name of product; (2) Trade name of product; (3) Identity and percent by weight of each component; (4) Color Index number (if none, so state); (5) Color Index generic name (if none so state); (6) Chemical Abstracts Service number of the active ingredient; (7) Class of merchandise (state whether acid type dye, basic dye, disperse dye, fluorescent brightener, soluble dye, vat dye, toner, or other (describe); (8) Material to which applied (name the material for which the color, dye, or toner is primarily designed).

Copper (T.D. 45878, 50158, 55977) articles classifiable under the provisions of Chapter 74, HTSUS—A statement of the weight of articles of copper, and a statement of percentage of copper content and all other elements—by weight—of articles classifiable according to copper content.

Copper ores and concentrates (T.D. 45878, 50158, 55977) classifiable in heading 2603, and subheadings 2620.19.60, 2620.20.00, 2620.30.00, and heading 7401—Statement of the percentage by weight of the copper content and any other metallic elements.

Cotton fabrics classifiable under the following HTSUS headings: 5208, 5209, 5210, 5211, and 5212—(1) Marks on shipping packages; (2) Numbers on shipping packages; (3) Customer's call number, if any; (4) Exact width of the merchandise; (5) Detailed description of the merchandise; trade name, if any; whether bleached, unbleached, printed, composed of yarns of different color, or dyed; if composed of cotton and other materials, state the percentage of each component material by weight; (6) Number of single threads per square centimeter (All ply yarns must be counted in accordance with the number of single threads contained in the yarn; to illustrate: a cloth containing 100 two-ply yarns in one square centimeter must be reported as 200 single thread); (7) Exact weight per square meter in grams; (8) Average yarn number use this formula:

$$\frac{100 \times (\text{total single yarns per square centimeter})}{(\text{number of grams per square meter})}$$

(9) Yarn size or sizes in the warp; (10) Yarn size or sizes in the filling; (11) Specify whether the yarns are combed or carded; (12) Number of colors or kinds (different yarn sizes or materials) in the filling; (13) Specify whether the fabric is napped or not napped; and (14) Specify the type of weave, for example, plan, twill, sateen, oxford, etc., and (15) Specify the type of machine on which woven: if with Jacquard (Jacq), if with Swivel (Swiv), if with Lappet (Lpt.), if with Dobby (Dobby).

Cotton waste (T.D. 50044)—(1) The name by which the cotton waste is known, such as "cotton card strips"; "cotton comber waste"; "cotton fly waste"; etc.; (2) Whether the length of the cotton staple forming any cotton card strips covered by the invoice is less than 3.016 centimeters (1 3/16 inches) or is 3.016 centimeters (1 3/16 inches) or more.

Earthenware or crockeryware composed of a nonvitrified absorbent body (including white granite and semiporcelain earthenware and cream-colored ware, stoneware, and terra cotta, but not including common brown, gray, red, or yellow earthenware), embossed or plain; common salt-glazed stoneware; stoneware or earthenware crucibles; Rockingham earthenware; china, porcelain, or other vitrified wares, composed of a vitrified nonabsorbent body which, when broken, shows a vitrified, vitreous, semi-vitrified, or semivitreous fracture; and bisque or Parian ware (T.D. 53236)—(1) If in sets, the kinds of articles in each set in the shipment and the quantity of each kind of article in each set in the shipment; (2) The exact maximum diameter, expressed in centimeters, of each size of all plates in the shipment; (3) The unit value for each style and size of plate, cup, saucer, or other separate piece in the shipment.

Fish or fish livers (T.D. 50724, 49640, 55977) imported in airtight containers classifiable under Chapter 3, HTSUS—(1) Statement whether the articles contain an oil, fat, or grease, (2) The name and quantity of any such oil, fat, or grease.

Footwear, classifiable in headings 6401 through 6405 of the HTSUS—
1. Manufacturer's style number.
2. Importer's style and/or stock number.
3. Percent by area of external surface area of upper (excluding reinforcements and accessories) that is:

Leather	a. _____%	
Composition leather	b. _____%	
Rubber and/or plastics	c. _____%	
Textile materials	d. _____%	
Other		
(give separate	e. _____%	
percent for each	f. _____%	
type of material)		

4. Percent by area of external surface area of outersole (excluding reinforcements and accessories) that is:

Leather	a. _____%	
Composition leather	b. _____%	
Rubber and/or plastics	c. _____%	
Textile materials	d. _____%	
Other		
(give separate	e. _____%	
percent for each	f. _____%	
type of material)		

You may skip this section if you choose to answer all questions A through Z below:

I. If 3(a) is larger than any other percent in 3 and if 4(a) is larger than any other percent in 4, answer questions F, G, L, M, O, R, S, and X.
II. If 3(a) is larger than any other percent in 3 and if 4(c) is larger than any other percent in 4, answer questions F, G, L, M, O, R, S, and X.
III. If 3(a) plus 3(b) is larger than any single percent in 3 and 4(d), 4(e) or 4(f) is larger than any other percent in 4, stop.
IV. If 3(c) is larger than any other percent in 3 and if 4(a) or 4(b) is larger than any other percent in 4, stop.

V. If 3(c) is larger than any other percent in 3 and if 4(c) is larger than any other percent in 4, answer questions B, E, F, G, H, J, K, L, M, N, O, P, T, and W.

VI. If 3(d) is larger than any other percent in 3 and if 4(a) plus 4(b) is greater than any single percent in 4, answer questions C and D.

VII. If 3(d) is larger than any other percent in 3 and if 4(c) is larger than any single percent in 4, answer questions A, C, J, K, M, N, P, and T.

VIII. If 3(d) is larger than any other percent in 3 and if 4(d) is larger than any other percent in 4, answer questions U, Y and Z.

IX. If the article is made of paper, answer questions V and Z.

If the article does not meet any of the conditions I through IX above, answer all questions A through Z, below:

A. Percent of external surface area of upper (including leather reinforcements and accessories).

    Which is leather   _____%

B. Percent by area of external surface area of upper (including all reinforcements and accessories).

    Which is rubber   _____%

    and/or plastics   _____%

C. Percent by weight of rubber and/or plastics is

    _____%

D. Percent by weight of textile materials plus rubber and/or plastics is

    _____%

E. Is it waterproof?

F. Does it have a protective metal toe cap?

G. Will it cover the wearer's ankle bone?

H. Will it cover the wearer's knee cap?

I. [Reserved.]

J. Is it designed to be a protection against water, oil, grease, or chemicals or cold or inclement weather?

K. Is it a slip-on?

L. Is it a downhill or cross-country ski boot?

M. Is it serious sports footwear other than ski boots? (Chapter 64, HTSUS, subheading note defines sports footwear.)

N. Is it a tennis, basketball, gym, or training shoe or the like?

O. Is it made on a base or platform of wood?

P. Does it have open toes or open heels?

Q. Is it made by the (lipped insole) welt construction?

R. Is it made by the turned construction?

S. Is it worn exclusively by men, boys, or youths?

T. Is it made by an exclusively adhesive construction?

U. Are the fibers of the upper, by weight, predominately vegetable fibers?

V. Is it disposable, i.e., intended for one-time use?

W. Is it a "Zori"?

X. Is the leather in the upper pigskin?

Y. Are the sole and upper made of wool felt?

Z. Is there a line of demarcation between the outer sole and upper?

The information requested above may be furnished on CBPF 5523 or other appropriate format by the exporter, manufacturer, or shipper.

Also, the following information must be furnished by the importer or his authorized agent if classification is claimed under one of the subheadings below, as follows:

If subheading 6401.99.80, 6402.19.10, 6402.30.30, 6402.91.40, 6402.99.15, 6402.99.30, 6404.11.40, 6404.11.60, 6404.19.35, 6404.19.40, or 6404.19.60 is claimed:

Does the shoe have a foxing or foxing-like band? If so, state its material(s).

Does the sole overlap the upper other than just at the front of the toe and/or at the back of the heel?

Definitions for some of the terms used in questions A to Z above: For the purpose of this section, the following terms have the approximate definitions below. If either a more complete definition or a decision as to its application to a particular article is needed, the marker or importer of record (or the agent of either) should contact CBP prior to entry of the article.

a. In an exclusively adhesive construction, all of the pieces of the bottom would separate from the upper or from each other if all adhesives, cements, and glues were dissolved. It includes shoes in which the pieces of the upper are stitched to each other, but not to any part of the bottom. Examples include:
   1. Vulcanized construction footwear;
   2. Simultaneous molded construction footwear;
   3. Molded footwear in which the upper and the bottom is one piece of molded rubber or plastic, and
   4. Footwear in which staples, rivets, stitching, or any of the methods above are either primary or even just extra or auxiliary, even though adhesive is a major part of the reason the bottom will not separate from the upper.

b. Composition leather is made by binding together leather fibers or small pieces of natural leather. It does not include imitation leathers not based on natural leather.

c. Leather is the tanned skin of any animal from which the fur or hair has been removed. Tanned skins coated or laminated with rubber and/or plastics are "leather" only if leather gives the material its essential character.

d. A line of demarcation exists if one can indicate where the sole ends and the upper begins. For example, knit booties do not normally have a line of demarcation.

e. Men's, boy's, and youth's sizes cover footwear of American youths size 11 and larger for males, and does not include footwear commonly worn by both sexes. If more than 4% of the shoes sold in a given size will be worn by females, that size is "commonly worn by both sexes."

f. Footwear is designed to protect against water, oil, or cold or inclement weather only if it is substantially more of a protection against those items than the usual shoes of that type. For example, leather oxfords will clearly keep your feet warmer and drier than going barefoot, but they are not a protection in this sense. On the other hand, the snow-jogger is the protective version of the nonprotective jogging shoe.

g. Rubber and/or plastics includes any textile material visibly coated (or covered) externally with one or both of those materials.

h. Slip-on includes:
   1. A boot that must be pulled on.
   2. Footwear with elastic cores that must be stretched to get it on, but not a separate piece of elasticized fabric that forms a full circle around the foot or ankle.

i. Sports footwear includes only:
   1. Footwear that is designed for a sporting activity and has, or has provision for, the attachment of spikes, sprigs, cleats, stops, clips, bars, or the like;
   2. Skating boots (without skates attached), ski boots and cross-country ski footwear, wrestling boots, boxing boots, and cycling shoes.

j. Tennis shoes, basketball shoes, gym shoes, training shoes, and the like cover athletic footwear other than sports footwear, whether or not principally used for such athletic games or purposes.

k. Textile materials are made from cotton, other vegetable fibers, wool, hair, silk, or man-made fibers. Note: Cork, wood, cardboard, and leather are not textile materials.

l. In turned construction, the upper is stitched to the leather sole wrong side out and the shoe is then turned right side out.

m. Vegetable fibers include cotton, flax, and ramie, but does not include either rayon or plaiting materials such as rattan or wood strips.

n. Waterproof footwear includes footwear designed to protect against penetration by water or other liquids, whether or not such footwear is primarily designed for such purposes.

o. Welt footwear means footwear construction with a welt, which extends around the edge of the outer sole, and in which the welt and shoe upper are sewed to a lip on the surface of the insole, and the outer sole of which is sewed or cemented to the welt.

p. A zori has an upper consisting only of straps or thongs of molded rubber or plastic. This upper is assembled to a formed rubber or plastic sole by means of plugs.

Fur products and furs (T.D. 53064)—(1) Name or names (as set forth in the Fur Products Name Guide (16 CFR 301.0) of the animal or animals that produced the fur, and such qualifying statements as may be required pursuant to § 7(c) of the Fur Products Labeling Act (15 U.S.C. 69e(c)); (2) A statement that the fur product contains or is composed of used fur, when such is the fact; (3) A statement that the fur product contains or is composed of bleached, dyed, or otherwise artificially colored fur, when such is the fact; (4) A statement that the fur product is composed in whole or in substantial part of paws, tails, bellies, or waste fur, when such is the fact; (5) Name and address of the manufacturer of the fur product; (6) Name of the country of origin of the furs or those contained in the fur product.

Glassware and other glass products (T.D. 53079, 55977)—Classifiable under Chapter 70, HTSUS—Statement of the separate value of each component article in the set.

Gloves—classifiable in subheadings 6116.10.20 and 6216.00.20—Statement as to whether or not the article has been covered with plastics on both sides. Grain or grain and screenings (T.D. 51284)—Statement on CBP invoices for cultivated grain or grain and screenings that no screenings are included with the grain, or, if there are screenings included, the percentage of the shipment that consists of screenings commingled with the principal grain.

Handkerchiefs—(1) State the exact dimensions (length and width) of the merchandise; (2) If of cotton indicate whether the handkerchief is hemmed and whether it contains lace or embroidery.

Hats or headgear—(1) If classifiable under subheading 6502.00.40 or 6502.00.60, HTSUS—Statement as to whether or not the article has been bleached or colored; (2) If classifiable under subheading 6502.00.20 through 6502.00.60 or 6504.00.30 through 6504.00.90, HTSUS—Statement as to whether or not the article is sewed or not sewed, exclusive of any ornamentation or trimming.

Hosiery—(1) Indicate whether a single yarn measures less than 67 decitex. (2) Indicate whether the hosiery is full length, knee length, or less than knee length. (3) Indicate whether it contains lace or net.

Iron or Steel classifiable in Chapter 72 or headings 7301 to 7307, HTSUS (T.D. 53092, 55977)—Statement of the percentages by weight of carbon and any metallic elements contained in the articles, in the form of a mill analysis or mill test certificate.

Iron oxide (T.D. 49989, 50107)—For iron oxide to which a reduced rate of duty is applicable, a statement of the method of preparation of the oxide, together with the patent number, if any.

Machines, equipment and apparatus—Chapters 84 and 85, HTSUS—A statement as to the use or method of operation of each type of machine.

Machine parts (T.D. 51616)—Statement specifying the kind of machine for which the parts are intended, or if this is not known to the shipper, the kinds of machines for which the parts are suitable.

Machine tools: (1) Heading 8456 through 8462—machine tools covered by these headings equipped with a CNC (Computer Numerical Control) or the facings (electrical interface) for a CNC must state so; (2) heading 8458 through 8463—machine tools covered by these headings if used or rebuilt must state so; (3) subheading 8456.30.10—EDM: (Electrical Discharge Machines) if a Traveling Wire (Wire Cut) type must state so. Wire EDM's use a copper or brass wire for the electrode; (4) subheading 457.10.0010 through 8457.10.0050—Machining Centers. Must state whether or not they have an ATC (Automatic Tool Changer). Vertical spindle machine centers with an ATC must also indicate the Y-travel; (5) subheadings 8458.11.0030 through 8458.11.00.90—horizontal lathes: numerically controlled. Must indicate the rated HP (or KW rating) of the main spindle motor. Use the continuous rather than 30-minute rating.

Madeira embroideries (T.D. 49988)—(1) With respect to the materials used, furnish: (a) country of production; (b) width of the material in the piece; (c) name of the manufacturer; (d) kind of material, indicating manufacturer's quality number; (e) landed cost of the material used in each item; (f) date of the order; (g) date of the invoice; (h) invoice unit value in the currency of the purchase; (i) discount from purchase price allowed, if any, (2) with respect to the finished embroidered articles, furnish: (a) manufacturer's name, design number, and quality number; (b) importer's design number, if any; (c) finished size; (d) number of embroidery points per unit of quantity; (e) total for overhead and profit added in arriving at the price of value of the merchandise covered by the invoice.

Motion-picture films—(1) Statement of footage, title, and subject matter of each film; (2) declaration of shipper, cameraman, or other person with knowledge of the acts identifying the films with the invoice and stating that the basic films were to the best of his knowledge and belief exposed abroad and returned for use as newsreel; (3) declaration of importer that he believes the films entered by him are the ones covered by the preceding declaration and that the films are intended for use as newsreel.

Paper classifiable in Chapter 48—Invoices covering paper shall contain the following information, or will be accompanied by specification sheets containing such information: (1) weight of paper in grams per square meter; (2) thickness, in micrometers (microns); (3) if imported in rectangular sheets, length and width sheets, in cm; (4) if imported in strips, or rolls, the width, in cm. In the case of rolls, the diameter of rolls in cm; (5) whether the paper is coated or impregnated, and with what materials; (6) weight of coating, in grams per square meter; (7) percentage by weight of the total fiber content consisting of wood fibers contained by a mechanical process, chemical sulfate or soda process, chemical sulfite process, or semi-chemical process, as appropriate; (8) commercial designation, as "writing," "cover," "drawing," "Bristol," "newsprint," etc.; (9) ash content; (10) color; (11) glaze, or finish; (12) Mullen bursting strength, and Mullen index; (13) stretch factor, in machine direction and in cross direction; (14) tear and tensile readings; in machine direction, in cross direction, and in machine direction plus cross direction; (15) identification of fibers as "hardwood" where appropriate; (16) crush resistance; (17) brightness; (18) smoothness; (19) if bleached, whether bleached uniformly through-out the mass; (20) whether embossed, perforated, creped, or crinkled.

Plastic plates, sheets, film, foil, and strip of headings 3920 and 3921—(1) Statement as to whether the plastic is cellular or noncellular; (2) specification of the type of plastic; (3) indication of whether or not flexible and whether combined with textile or other material.

Printed matter classifiable in Chapter 49—Printed matter entered in the following headings shall have, on or with the invoices covering such matter, the following information: (1) Heading 4901—(a) whether the books are: dictionaries, encyclo-pedias, textbooks, bound newspapers or journals or periodicals, directories, bibles or other prayer books, technical, scientific or professional books, art or pictorial books, or "other" books; (b) if "other" books, whether hardbound or paperbound; (c) if "other" books, paperbound, other than "rack size": number of pages (exclud-ing covers). (2) Heading 4902—(a) whether the journal or periodical appears at least four times a week. If the journal or periodical appears other than at least four times a week, whether it is a newspaper supplement printed by a gravure process, is a newspaper, business or professional journal or periodical, or other than these; (3) Heading 4904—whether the printed or manuscript music is sheet music, not bound (except by stapling or folding); (4) Heading 4905—(a) whether globes, or not; (b) if not globes, whether in book form, or not; (c) in any case, whether or not in relief; (5) cards, greeting cards, or other; (7) Heading 4910—(a) whether or not printed on paper by a lithographic process; (b) if printed on paper by a lithographic process, the thickness of the paper, in mum (modularization unitization and metrication); (8) Subheading not printed over 20 years at time of importation, whether suitable for use in the production of articles of heading 4902; (c) if not printed over 20 years at time of importation, and not suitable for use in the production of articles of heading 4901, whether the merchandise is lithographs on paper or paperboard; (d) if lithographs on paper or paperboard, under the terms of the immediately preced-ing description, thickness of the paper or paperboard, and whether or not posters; (e) in any case, whether or not posters; (f) in any case, whether or not photographic negatives or positives on transparent bases; (b) Subheading 4911.99—If not car-nets, or parts thereof, in English or French, whether or not printed on paper in whole or in part by a lithographic process.

Pulp classifiable in Chapter 47—(1) Invoices covering chemical woodpulp, dis-solving trades, in Heading 4702 shall state the insoluble fraction (as percentage) after one hour in a caustic soda solution containing 18 percent sodium hydroxide

(NaOH) at 20° C; (2) Subheading 4702.00.0020—Pulp entered under this subheading shall in addition contain on or with the invoice the ash content as a percentage by weight.

Refrigeration equipment (1) Refrigerator-freezers classifiable under subheading 8418.10.00 and (2) refrigerators classifiable under 8418.21.00—(a) statement as to whether they are compression or absorption type; (b) statement of other refrigerated volume in liters; (3) freezers classifiable under subheading 8418.30.00 and 8418.40.00—statement as to whether they are chest or upright type; (4) liquid chilling refrigerating unless classifiable under subheading 8418.69.0045 through 8418.69.0060—statement as to whether they are centrifugal open-type, centrifugal hermetic-type, absorption-type or reciprocating type.

Rolling mills—Subheading 8455.30.0005 through 8455.30.0085. Rolls for rolling mills: Indicate the composition of the roll—gray iron, cast steel or other—and the weight of each roll.

Rubber products of Chapter 40 of the HTSUS—(1) Statement as to whether combined with textile or other material; (2) statement whether the rubber is cellular or noncellular, unvulcanized or vulcanized, and if vulcanized, whether hard rubber or other than hard rubber.

Screenings or scalpings of grains or seeds (T.D. 51096)—(1) Whether the commodity is the product of a screening process; (2) if so, whether any cultivated grains have been added to such commodity; (3) If any such grains have been added, the kind and percentage of each.

Textile fiber products (T.D. 55095—(1) The constituent fiber or combination of fibers in the textile fiber product, designating with equal prominence each natural or manufactured fiber in the textile fiber product by its generic name in the order of predominance by the weight thereof if the weight of such fiber is 5 percent or more of the total fiber weight of the product; (2) percentage of each fiber present, by weight, in the total fiber content of the textile fiber product; (3) the name, or other identification issued and registered by the Federal Trade Commission, of the manufacturer of the product or one or more persons subject to § 3 of the Textile Fiber Products Identification Act (15 U.S.C. 70a) with respect to such product; (4) the name of the country where processed or manufactured. See also "Wearing Apparel" below.

Tires and tubes for tires, of rubber or plastics—(1) Specify the kind of vehicle for which the tire is intended, i.e. airplane, bicycle, passenger car, on-the-highway light or heavy truck or bus, motorcycle; (2) if designed for tractors provided for in subheading 8701.90.10, or for agricultural or horticultural machinery or implements provided for in Chapter 84 of the HTSUS or in subheading 8716.80.10, designate whether the tire is new, recapped, or used; pneumatic or solid; (3) indicate whether the tube is designed for tires provided for in subheading 4011.91.10, 4011.99.10, 4012.10.20, or 4012.20.20.

Tobacco (including tobacco in its natural state) (T.D. 44854, 45871)—(1) Specify in detail the character of the tobacco in each bale by giving (a) country and province of origin, (b) year of production, (c) grade or grades in each bale, (d) number of carrots or pounds of each grade if more than one grade is packed in a bale, (e) the time when, place where, and person from whom purchased, (f) price paid or to be paid for each bale or package, or price for the vega or lot is purchased in bulk, or if obtained otherwise than by purchase, state the actual market value per bale; (2) if an invoice covers or includes bales of tobacco that are part of a vega or lot purchased in bulk, the invoice must contain or be accompanied by a full description of the vega or lot purchased; or if such description has been furnished with a previous importation, the date and identity of such shipment; (3) packages or bales containing only filler leaf shall be invoiced as filler; when containing filler and wrapper but not more than 35 percent of wrapper, they shall be invoiced as mixed; and when containing more than 35 percent of wrapper, they shall be invoiced as wrapper.

Watches and watch movements classifiable under Chapter 91 of the HTSUS—For all commercial shipments of such articles, there shall be required to be shown on the invoice, or on a separate sheet attached to and constituting a part of the invoice, such information as will reflect with respect to each group, type, or model, the following:

(A) For watches, a thorough description of the composition of the watch cases, the bracelets, bands, or straps, the commercial description (ebauche caliber number, ligne size, and number of jewels) of the movements contained in the watches, and the type of battery (manufacturer's name and reference number), if the watch is battery operated.

(B) For watch movements, the commercial description (ebauche caliber number, ligne size, and number of jewels). If battery-operated, the type of battery (manufacturer's name and reference number).

(C) The name of the manufacturer of the exported watch movements and the name of the country in which the movements were manufactured.

Wearing apparel—(a) All invoices for textile wearing apparel should indicate a component material breakdown in percentages by weight for all component fibers present in the entire garment, as well as separate breakdowns of the fibers in the (outer) shell (exclusive of linings, cuffs, waistbands, collars, and other trimmings) and in the lining; (2) for garments that are constructed of more than one component or material (combination of knits and not knit fabric or combinations of knit and/or not knit fabric with leather, fur, plastic including vinyl, etc.), the invoice must show a fiber breakdown in percentages by weight for each separate textile material in the garment and a breakdown in percentages by weight for each nontextile material for the entire garment; (3) for woven garments, indicate whether the fabric is yarn dyed and whether there are "two or more colors in the warp and/or filling"; (4) for all-white T-shirts and singlets, indicate whether or not the garment contains pockets, trim, or embroidery; (5) for mufflers, state the exact dimensions (length and width) of the merchandise.

Wood products—(1) Wood sawed or chipped lengthwise, sliced or peeled, whether or not planed, sanded, or finger-jointed, of a thickness exceeding 6 mm (lumber), classifiable under Chapter 44 heading 4407, HTSUS, and wood continuously shaped along any of its edges or faces, whether or not planed, sanded or finger-jointed; coniferous: Subheading 4409.10.90 and nonconiferous: Subheading 4409.20.90, HTSUS, and dutiable on the basis of cubic meters—Quantity in cubic meter (m) before dressing; (2) fiberboard of wood or other ligneous materials whether or not bonded with resins or other organic substances, under Chapter 44, Heading 4411, HTSUS, and classifiable according to its density–density in grams per cubic centimeter (cm); (3) plywood consisting solely of sheets of wood, classifiable under Chapter 44, Subheading 4412.11,4412.12, and 4412.19, HTSUS, and classifiable according to the thickness of the wood sheets–thickness of each ply in millimeters (mm);

Wool and hair—See 151.62 of Chapter 44, HTSUS, for additional information required on invoices.

Wool products, except carpets, rugs, mats, and upholsteries, and wool products made more than 20 years before importation (T.D. 50388, 51019) (1) The percentage of the total fiber weight of the wool product, exclusive of ornamentation not exceeding 5 per cent of said total fiber weight, of (a) wool; (b) reprocessed wool; (c) reused wool; (d) each fiber other than wool if said percentage by weight of such fiber is 5 per cent or more; and (e) the aggregate of all fibers; (2) the maximum percentage of the total weight of the wool product, of any nonfibrous loading, filling, or adulterating matter; and (3) the name of the manufacturer of the wool product, except when such product consists of mixed wastes, residues, and similar merchandise obtained from several suppliers or unknown sources.

Woven fabric of man-made fibers in headings 5407, 5408, 5512, 5513, 5514, 5515, 5516—

(1) State the exact width of the fabric.
(2) Provide a detailed description of the merchandise, (trade name, if any).
(3) Indicate whether bleached, unbleached, dyed, or yarns of different colors and/or printed.
(4) If composed of more than one material, list percentage by weight in each.
(5) Identify the man-made fibers as artificial or synthetic, filament or staple, and state whether the yarns are high tenacity. Specify the number of turns per meter in each yarn.
(6) Specify yarn sizes in warp and filling.
(7) Specify how the fabric is woven (plain weave, twill, sateen, dobby, jacquard, swivel, lappet, etc.)
(8) Indicate the number of single threads per square centimeter in both warp and filling.
(9) Supply the weight per square meter in grams.

(10) Provide the average yarn number using this formula:

$$\frac{100 \times (\text{number of single threads per square centimeter})}{(\text{number of grams per square meter})}$$

(11) For spun yarns, specify whether textured or not textured.

(12) For filament yarns, specify whether textured or not textured.

Yarns—(1) All yarn invoices should show: (a) fiber content by weight; (b) whether single or plied; (c) whether or not put up for retail sale (See Section XI, Note 4, HTSUS); (d) whether or not intended for use as sewing thread.

    (2) If chief weight of silk, show whether spun or filament.

    (3) If chief weight of cotton, show:

        (a) whether combed or uncombed

        (b) metric number (mn)

        (c) whether bleached and/or mercerized.

    (4) If chief weight of man-made fiber, show:

        (a) whether filament, or spun, or a combination of filament and spun

        (b) If a combination of filament and spun, give percent age of filament and spun by weight.

    (5) If chief weight of filament man-made fiber, show:

        (a) whether high tenacity (See Section XI, note 6, HTSUS)

        (b) whether monofilament, multifilament, or strip

        (c) whether texturized

        (d) yarn number in decitex

        (e) number of turns per meter

        (f) for monofilaments-show cross-sectional dimension in millimeters

        (g) for strips, show the width of the strip in millimeters (measure in folded or twisted condition if so imported)

Items or classes of goods may be added to or removed from the list from time to time.

3. Customs Valuation

93 STAT. 194 PUBLIC LAW 96-39—JULY 26, 1979

Tariff Act of 1930

"SEC. 402, VALUE. [19 U.S.C. 1401a]

"(a) IN GENERAL—(1) Except as otherwise specifically provided for in this Act, imported merchandise shall be appraised, for the purposes of this Act, on the basis of the following:

    "(A) The transaction value provided for under subsection (b).

    "(B) The transaction value of identical merchandise provided for under subsection (c), if the value referred to in subparagraph (A) cannot be determined, or can be determined but cannot be used by reason of subsection (b)(2).

"(C)   The transaction value of similar merchandise provided or under subsection (c), if the value referred to in subparagraph (B) cannot be determined.

"(D)   The deductive value provided for under subsection (d), if the value referred to in subparagraph (C) cannot be determined and if the importer does not request alternative valuation under Paragraph (2).

"(E)   The computed value provided for under subsection (e), if the value referred to in subparagraph (D) cannot be determined.

"(F)   The value provided for under subsection (f), if the value referred to in subparagraph (E) cannot be determined.

"(2)   If the value referred to in paragraph (1)(C) cannot be determined with respect to imported merchandise, the merchandise shall be appraised on the basis of the computed value provided for under paragraph (1)(E), rather than the deductive value provided for under paragraph (1)(D), if the importer makes a request to that effect to the CBP officer concerned within such time as the Secretary shall prescribe. If the computed value of the merchandise cannot subsequently be determined, the merchandise may not be appraised on the basis of the value referred to in paragraph (1) (F) unless the deductive value of the merchandise cannot be determined under paragraph (1)(D).

"(3)   Upon written request therefor by the importer of merchandise, and subject to provisions of law regarding the disclosure of information, the CBP officer concerned shall provide the importer with a written explanation of how the value of that merchandise was determined under this section.

"(b)   TRANSACTION VALUE OF IMPORTED MERCHANDISE.—(1) The transaction value of imported merchandise is the price actually paid or payable for the merchandise when sold for exportation to the United States, plus amounts equal to—

"(A)   The packing costs incurred by the buyer with respect to the imported merchandise;

"(B)   Any selling commission incurred by the buyer with respect to the imported merchandise;

"(C)   The value, apportioned as appropriate, of any assist;

"(D)   Any royalty or license fee related to the imported merchandise that the buyer is required to pay directly or indirectly, as a condition of the sale of the imported merchandise for exportation to the United States; and

"(E)   The proceeds of any subsequent resale, disposal, or use of the imported merchandise that accrue, directly or indirectly, to the seller.

The price actually paid or payable for imported merchandise shall be increased by the amounts attributable to the items (and no others) described in subparagraphs (A) through (E) only to the extent that each such amount (i) is not otherwise included within the price actually paid or payable; and (ii) is based on sufficient information. If sufficient information is not available, for any reason, with respect to any amount referred to in the preceding sentence, the transaction value of the imported merchandise concerned shall be treated, for purposes of this section, as one that cannot be determined.

"(2)(A) The transaction value of imported merchandise determined under paragraph (1) shall be the appraised value of that merchandise for the purposes of this Act only if—

"(i) there are no restrictions on the disposition or use of the imported merchandise by the buyer other than restrictions that—

"(I) are imposed or required by law,

"(II) limit the geographical area in which the merchandise may be resold, or

"(III) do not substantially affect the value of the merchandise;

"(ii) the sale of, or the price actually paid or payable for, the imported merchandise is not subject to any condition or consideration for which a value cannot be determined with respect to the imported merchandise;

"(iii) no part of the proceeds of any subsequent resale, disposal, or use of the imported merchandise by the buyer will accrue directly or indirectly to the seller, unless an appropriate adjustment therefor can be made under paragraph (1)(E); and

"(iv) the buyer and seller are not related, or the buyer and seller are related but the transaction value is acceptable, for purposes of this subsection, under subparagraph (B).

(B) The transaction value between a related buyer and seller is acceptable for the purposes of this subsection if an examination of the circumstances of the sale of the imported merchandise indicates that the relationship between such buyer and seller did not influence the price actually paid or payable; or if the transaction value of the imported merchandise closely approximates—Amended by P.L. 96—490, effective 1/1/81:

"(i) the transaction value of identical merchandise, or of similar merchandise in sales to unrelated buyers in the United States; or

"(ii) the deductive value or computed value for identical merchandise or similar merchandise; but, only if each value referred to in clause (i) or (ii) that is used for comparison relates to merchandise that was exported to the United States at or about the same time as the imported merchandise

"(C) In applying the values used for comparison purposes under subparagraph (B), there shall be taken into account differences with respect to the sales involved (if such differences are based on sufficient information whether supplied by the buyer or otherwise available to the CBP officer concerned) in—

"(i)   commercial levels;

"(ii)   quantity levels;

"(iii)   the costs commissions, values, fees, and proceeds described in paragraph (1); and

"(iv)   the costs incurred by the seller in sales in which he and the buyer are not related that are not incurred by the seller in sales in which he and the buyer are related.

"(3)   The transaction value of imported merchandise does not include any of the following, if identified separately from the price actually paid or payable and from any cost or other item referred to in paragraph (1):

"(A)   Any reasonable cost or charge that is incurred for—

"(i)   the construction, erection, assembly, or maintenance of, or the technical assistance provided with respect to, the merchandise after its importation into the United States; or

"(ii)   the transportation of the merchandise after such importation.

"(B)   The customs duties and other Federal taxes currently payable on the imported merchandise by reason of its importation, and any Federal excise tax on, or measured by the value of, such merchandise for which vendors in the United States are ordinarily liable.

"(4)   For purposes of this subsection—

Price Actually Paid or Payable:

"(A)   The term 'price actually paid or payable' means the total payment (whether direct or indirect, and exclusive of any costs, charges, or expenses incurred for transportation, insurance, and related services incident to the international shipment of the merchandise from the country of exportation to the place of importation in the United States) made, or to be made, for imported merchandise by the buyer to, or for the benefit of, the seller.

"(B)   Any rebate of, or other decrease in, the price actually paid or payable that is made or otherwise effected between the buyer and seller after the date of the importation of the merchandise into the United States shall be disregarded in determining the transaction value under paragraph (1).

"(C)   transaction value of identical merchandise and similar merchandise—(1) The transaction value of identical merchandise, or of similar merchandise, is the transaction value (acceptable as the appraised value for purposes of this Act under subsection (b) but adjusted under paragraph (2) of this subsection) of imported merchandise that is—

"(A)   with respect to the merchandise being appraised, either identical merchandise or similar merchandise, as the case may be; and

"(B)   exported to the United States at or about the time that the merchandise being appraised is exported to the United States.

"(2) Transaction values determined under this subsection shall be based on sales of identical merchandise or similar merchandise, as the case may be, at the same commercial level and in substantially the same quantity as the sales of the merchandise being appraised. If no such sale is found, sales of identical merchandise or similar merchandise at either a different commercial level or in different quantities, or both, shall be used, but adjusted to take account of any such difference. Any adjustment made under this paragraph shall be based on sufficient information. If in applying this paragraph with respect to any imported merchandise, two or more transaction values for identical merchandise, or for similar merchandise, are determined, such imported merchandise shall be appraised on the basis of the lower or lowest of such values.

Merchandise concerned:

"(d) DEDUCTIVE VALUE—(1) For purposes of this subsection, the term 'merchandise concerned' means the merchandise being appraised, identical merchandise, or similar merchandise.

"(2)(A) The deductive value of the merchandise being appraised is whichever of the following prices (as adjusted under paragraph (3)) is appropriate depending upon when and in what condition the merchandise concerned is sold in the United States:

"(i) if the merchandise concerned is sold in the condition as imported at or about the date of importation of the merchandise being appraised, the price is the unit price at which the merchandise concerned is sold in the greatest aggregate quantity at or about such date.

"(ii) If the merchandise concerned is sold in the condition as imported but not sold at or about the date of importation of the merchandise being appraised, the price is the unit price at which the merchandise concerned is sold in the greatest aggregate quantity after the date of importation of the merchandise being appraised but before the close of the 90th day after the date of such importation.

"(iii) If the merchandise concerned was not sold in the condition as imported and not sold before the close of the 90th day after the date of importation of the merchandise being appraised, the price is the unit price at which the merchandise being appraised, after further processing, is sold in the greatest aggregate quantity before the 180th day after the date of such importation. This clause shall apply to appraisement of merchandise only if the importer so elects and notifies the CBP officer concerned of that election within such time as shall be prescribed by the Secretary.

Unit Price:

"(B) For purposes of subparagraph (A), the unit price at which merchandise is sold in the greatest aggregate quantity is the unit price at which such merchandise is sold to unrelated persons, at the first commercial level after importation (in cases to which subparagraph (A)(iii) applies) at which such sales take place, in a total volume that is (i) greater than the total volume sold at any other unit price, and (ii) sufficient to establish the unit price.

"(3)(A) The price determined under paragraph (2) shall be reduced by an amount equal to—

"(i) any commission usually paid or agreed to be paid, or the addition usually made for profit and general expenses, in connection with sales in the United States of imported merchandise that is of the same class or kind, regardless of the country of exportation as the merchandise concerned;

"(ii) the actual costs and associated costs of transportation and insurance incurred with respect to international shipments of the merchandise concerned from the country of exportation to the United States;

"(iii) the usual costs and associated costs of transportation and insurance incurred with respect to shipments of such merchandise from the place of importation to the place of delivery in the United States, if such costs are not included as a general expense under clause (i);

"(iv) the customs duties and other Federal taxes currently payable on the merchandise concerned by reason of its importation, and any Federal excise tax on, or measured by the value of, such merchandise for which vendors in the United States are ordinarily liable: and

"(v) (but only in the case of a price determined under paragraph (2) (A)(iii)) the value added by the processing of the merchandise after importation to the extent that the value is based on sufficient information relating to cost of such processing.

"(B) For purposes of applying paragraph (A)—

"(i) the deduction made for profits and general expenses shall be based upon the importer's profits and general expenses, unless such profits and general expenses are inconsistent with those reflected in sales in the United States of imported merchandise of the same class or kind, in which case the deduction shall be based on the usual profit and general expenses reflected in such sales, as determined from sufficient information; and

"(ii) any State or local tax imposed on the importer with respect to the sale of imported merchandise shall be treated as a general expense.

"(C) The price determined under paragraph (2) shall be increased (but only to the extent that such costs are not otherwise included) by an amount equal to the packing costs incurred by the importer or the buyer, as the case may be, with respect to the merchandise concerned.

"(D) For purposes of determining the deductive value of imported merchandise, any sale to a person who supplies any assist for use in connection with the production or sale for export of the merchandise concerned shall be disregarded.

"(e) computed value.—(1) The computed value of imported merchandise is the sum of—

"(A)   the cost or value of the materials and the fabrication and other processing of any kind employed in the production of the imported merchandise

"(B)   an amount for profit and general expenses equal to that usually reflected in sales of merchandise of the same class or kind as the imported merchandise that are made by the producers in the country of exportation for export to the United States;

"(C)   any assist, if its value is not included under subparagraph (A) or (B); and

"(D)   the packing costs.

"(2)   For purposes of paragraph (1)—

"(A)   the cost or value of materials under paragraph (1)(A) shall not include the amount of any internal tax imposed by the country of exportation that is directly applicable to the materials or their disposition if the tax is remitted or refunded upon the exportation of the merchandise in the production of which the materials were used; and

"(B)   the amount for profit and general expenses under paragraph (1)(B) shall be used upon the producer's profits and expenses, unless the producer's profits and expenses are inconsistent with those usually reflected in sales of merchandise of the same class or kind as the imported merchandise that are made by producers in the country of exportation for export to the United States, in which case the amount under paragraph (1)(B) shall be used on the usual profit and general expenses of such producers in such sales, as determined from sufficient information.

"(f) value if other values cannot be determined or used.—(1) If the value of imported merchandise cannot be determined, or otherwise used for the purposes of this Act, under subsections (b) through (e), the merchandise shall be appraised for the purposes of this Act on the basis of a value that is derived from the methods set forth in such subsections, with such methods being reasonably adjusted to the extent necessary to arrive at a value.

Imported Merchandise Appraisal:

"(2)   Imported merchandise may not be appraised, for the purposes of this Act, on the basis of—

"(A)   the selling price in the United States of merchandise produced in the United States;

"(B)   a system that provides for the appraisement of imported merchandise at the higher of two alternative values

"(C)   the price of merchandise in the domestic market of the country of exportation

"(D) a cost of production, other than a value determined under subsection (c) for merchandise that is identical merchandise or similar merchandise to the merchandise being appraised;

"(E) the price of merchandise for export to a country other than the United States;

"(F) minimum values for appraisement; or

"(G) arbitrary or fictitious values.

This paragraph shall not apply with respect to the ascertainment, determination, or estimation of foreign market value or United States price under title VII.

Ante, p. 150:

"(g) special rules—(1) for purposes of this section, the persons specified in any of the following subparagraphs shall be treated as persons who are related:

"(A) Members of the same family, including brothers and sisters (whether by whole or half blood), spouse, ancestors, and lineal descendants.

"(B) Any officer or director of an organization and such organization.

"(C) Any officer or director of an organization and an officer or director of another organization, if each such individual is also an officer or director in the other organization.

"(D) Partners.

"(E) Employer and employee.

"(F) Any person directly or indirectly owning, controlling, or holding with power to vote, 5 percent or more of the outstanding voting stock or shares of any organization and such organization.

"(G) Two or more persons directly or indirectly controlling, controlled by, or under common control with, any person.

"(2) For purposes of this section, merchandise (including, but not limited to, identical merchandise and similar merchandise) shall be treated as being of the same class or kind as other merchandise if it is within a group or range of merchandise produced by a particular industry or industry sector.

Generally Accepted Accounting Principles:

"(3) For purposes of this section, information that is submitted by an importer, buyer, or producer in regard to the appraisement of merchandise may not be rejected by the CBP officer concerned on the basis of the accounting method by which that information was prepared, if the preparation was in accordance with generally accepted accounting principles. The term generally accepted accounting principles' refers to any generally recognized consensus or substantial authoritative support regarding—

"(A) which economic resources and obligations should be recorded as assets and liabilities;

"(B)   which changes in assets and liabilities should be recorded;

"(C)   how the assets and liabilities and changes in them should be measured;

"(D)   what information should be disclosed and how it should be disclosed; and

"(E)   which financial statements should be prepared.

The applicability of a particular set of generally accepted accounting principles will depend upon the basis on which the value of the merchandise is sought to be established.

"(h) definitions.—As used in this section—

"(1)(A)   The term 'assist' means any of the following if supplied directly or indirectly, and free of charge or at reduced cost, by the buyer of imported merchandise for use in connection with the production or the sale for export to the United States of the merchandise:

"(i)   Materials, components, parts, and similar items incorporated in the imported merchandise.

"(ii)   Tools, dies, molds, and similar items used in the production of the imported merchandise.

"(iii)   Merchandise consumed in the production of the imported merchandise.

"(iv)   Engineering, development, artwork, design work, and plans and sketches that are undertaken elsewhere than in the United States and are necessary for the production of the imported merchandise.

"(B)   No service or work to which subparagraph (A)(iv) applies shall be treated as an assist for purposes of this section if such service or work—

"(i)   is performed by an individual who is domiciled within the United States;

"(ii)   is performed by that individual while he is acting as an employee or agent of the buyer of the imported merchandise; and

"(iii)   is incidental to other engineering, development, artwork, design work, or plans or sketches that are undertaken within the United States.

"(C)   For purposes of this section, the following apply in determining the value of assists described in subparagraph (A)(iv):

"(i)   The value of an assist that is available in the public domain is the cost of obtaining copies of the assist,

"(ii)   If the production of an assist occurred in the United States and one or more foreign countries, the value of the assist is the value thereof that is added outside the United States.

"(2) The term 'identical merchandise' means—

"(A)   merchandise that is identical in all respects to, and was produced in the same country and by the same person as, the merchandise being appraised; or

"(B) if merchandise meeting the requirements under subparagraph (A) cannot be found (or for purposes of applying subsection (b)(2)(B)(i), regardless of whether merchandise meeting such requirements can be found), merchandise that is identical in all respects to, and was produced in the same country as, but not produced by the same person as, the merchandise being appraised.

Such term does not include merchandise that incorporates or reflect any engineering, development, artwork, design work, or plan or sketch that—

"(I)   was supplied free or at reduced cost by the buyer or the merchandise for use in connection with the production or the sale for export to the United States of the merchandise; and

"(II)   is not an assist because undertaken within the United States.

"(3)   The term 'packing costs' means the cost of all containers and coverings of whether nature and of packing, whether for labor or materials, used in placing merchandise in condition, packed ready for shipment to the United States.

"(4)   The term 'similar merchandise' means—

"(A)   merchandise that—

"(i)   was produced in the same country and by the same person as the merchandise being appraised,

"(ii)   is like the merchandise being appraised in characteristics and component material, and

"(iii)   is commercially interchangeable with the merchandise being appraised; or

"(B)   if merchandise meeting the requirements under subparagraph (A) cannot be found (or for purposes of applying subsection (b)(2)(B)(i), regardless of whether merchandise meeting such requirements can be found), merchandise that—

"(i)   was produced in the same country as, but not produced by the same person as, the merchandise being appraised, and

"(ii)   meets the requirement set forth in subparagraph (A)(ii) and (iii).

Such term does not include merchandise that incorporates or reflects any engineering, development, artwork, design work, or plan or sketch that—

"(I)   was supplied free or at reduced cost by the buyer of the merchandise for use in connection with the production or the sale for export to the United States of the merchandise; and

"(II)   is not an assist because undertaken within the United States.

"(5)   The term 'sufficient information', when required under this section for determining—

"(A)   any amount—

"(i)   added under subsection (b)(1) to the price actually paid or payable, "(ii)   deducted under subsection (d)(3) as profit or general expense or value from further processing, or

"(iii)   added under subsection (e)(2) as profit or general expense;

"(B)   any difference taken into account for purposes of subsection (b)(2)(C); or

"(C)   any adjustment made under subsection (c)(2); means information that establishes the accuracy of such amount, difference, or adjustment."

5. EPA-Regulated Refrigerants

Class I

Chemical Name	Trade Names	CAS Number
CFC-113 (C2F3Cl3) Trichlorotrifluoroethane	Algofrene 11 - Ausimont SPA	75-69-4
	Arcton 11 - INEOS Fluor	
	Asahifron R-11 - Asahi Glass Co. Ltd.	
	CFC-11 - Firefreeze International	
	CFC-11 - Chemicals and Plastics India Ltd.	
	CFC-11 - Gujarat Fluorochemicals Ltd.	
	CFC-11 - Hankook Shin Hwa	
	CFC-11 - Navin Fluorine Industries	
	CFC-11 - Roche Chemicals Inc.	
	CFC-11 - Spolek	
	CFC-11 - Changshu 3F Refrigerant Plant	
	CFC-11 - Jiangsu Meilan Electric Chemical Plant	
	CFC-11 - Suzhou Xinye Chemical Co. Ltd.	
	CFC-11 - Zhejiang Linhai Limin Chemical Plant	
	CFC-11 - Zhejiang Juhua Fluorochemical Co. Ltd.	
	CFC-11 - Chemical Industries of Northern Greece SA	
	Daiflon 11 - Daikin Industries Ltd.	
	Dional 11 - Solvay Fluor GMBH	
	Electro-CF 11 - Unknown	
	Eskimon 11 - Unknown	
	FCC-11 - Akzo Chemicals International B.V.	
	Flon Showa 11 - Showa Denko K.K.	
	Floron 11 - SRF Limited	
	Forane 11 - ARKEMA SA	
	Freon-11 - DuPont Fluoroproducts	
	Frigen 11 - Solvay Fluor GMBH	

Class I (Continued)

Chemical Name	Trade Names	CAS Number
	Genetron 11 - Honeywell (formerly Allied-Signal Inc.)	
	Genetron 11 - Quimobasicos s.a. de c.v.	
	ISCEON 11 - Rhodia	
	Isotron 11 - Unknown	
	Khaladon 11 - Unknown	
	Korfron 11 - Ulsan Chemical Co., Ltd.	
	Ledon 11 - Unknown	
	Mafron 11 - Navin Fluorine Industries	
	R11 - Protocol Resource Management Inc.	
CFC-12 (CCl_2F_2) Dichlorodifluoromethane	Algofrene 12 - Ausimont SPA	75-71-8
	Algofrene 12 - Montefluos S.P.A.	
	Arcton 12 - INEOS Fluor	
	Asahifron R-12 - Asahi Glass Co. Ltd.	
	Asahifron R-500 - Asahi Glass Co. Ltd.	
	CFC-12 - Zhejiang Juhua Fluorochemical Co. Ltd.	
	CFC-12 - Chemicals and Plastics India Ltd.	
	CFC-12 - Firefreeze International	
	CFC-12 - Gujarat Fluorochemicals Ltd.	
	CFC-12 - Hankook Shin Hwa	
	CFC-12 - Navin Fluorine Industries	
	CFC-12 - Roche Chemicals Inc.	
	CFC-12 - SRF Limited	
	CFC-12 - Changshu 3F Refrigerant Plant	
	CFC-12 - Zhejiang Dongyang Chemical Plant	
	CFC-12 - Jiangsu Meilan Electric Chemical Plant	
	CFC-12 - Fujian Shaowu Fluorochemical Plant	
	CFC-12 - Guangdong Zengcheng Xiangsheng Chemical Co. Ltd.	
	CFC-12 - Spolek	
	Daiflon 12 - Daikin Industries Ltd.	
	Daiflon 500 - Daikin Industries Ltd.	
	Electro-CF 12 - Unknown	

(Continued)

Class I (Continued)

Chemical Name	Trade Names	CAS Number
	Eskimon 12 - Unknown	
	FCC-12 - Akzo Chemicals International B.V.	
	Flon Showa 12 - Showa Denko K.K.	
	Flon Showa 500 - Showa Denko K.K.	
	Floron 12 - SRF Limited	
	Forane 12 - ARKEMA SA	
	Forane 500 - ARKEMA SA	
	Freon-12 - DuPont Fluoroproducts	
	Frigen 12 - Solvay Fluor GMBH	
	Frigen 500 - Solvay Fluor GMBH	
	Friogas 12 - Galco	
	G12 - AlliedSignal Fluorochemicals Europe BV	
	Genetron 12 - Quimobasicos s.a. de c.v.	
	Genetron 500 - Quimobasicos s.a. de c.v.	
	Genetron 500 - Honeywell (formerly AlliedSignal Inc.)	
	ISCEON 12 - Rhodia	
	ISCEON 500 - Rhodia	
	Isotron 12 - Unknown	
	Korfron 12 - Ulsan Chemical Co., Ltd.	
	Ledon 12 - Unknown	
	Mafron 12 - Navin Fluorine Industries	
	Oxyfume 12 - Honeywell (formerly AlliedSignal Inc.)	
	R12 - Protocol Resource Management Inc.	
	R-500	
	R-501	
	R-505	
	Taisoton 12 - Formosa Plastics	
	AF-113 - Asahi Glass Co. Ltd.	
	Algofrene 113 - Ausimont SPA	
	Arklone AM - INEOS Fluor	
	Arklone AMD - INEOS Fluor	
	Arklone AS - INEOS Fluor	
	Arklone EXT - INEOS Fluor	
	Arklone K - INEOS Fluor	
	Arklone L - INEOS Fluor	
	Arklone P - INEOS Fluor	

Class I (Continued)

Chemical Name	Trade Names	CAS Number
CFC-113 (C2F3Cl3) 1,1,2-Trichlorotrifluoroethane	Arklone PSM - INEOS Fluor Arklone W - INEOS Fluor Asahifron R-113 - Asahi Glass Co. Ltd. CFC-113 - Jiangsu Changshu Yudong Chemical Plant CFC-113 - Changshu 3F Refrigerant Plant CG Triflon - Central Glass Co. Ltd. CG Triflon A - Central Glass Co. Ltd. CG Triflon C1 - Central Glass Co. Ltd. CG Triflon CP - Central Glass Co. Ltd. CG Triflon D3 - Central Glass Co. Ltd. CG Triflon DI - Central Glass Co. Ltd. CG Triflon E - Central Glass Co. Ltd. CG Triflon EC - Central Glass Co. Ltd. CG Triflon EE - Central Glass Co. Ltd. CG Triflon ES - Central Glass Co. Ltd. CG Triflon FD - Central Glass Co. Ltd. CG Triflon M - Central Glass Co. Ltd. CG Triflon MES - Central Glass Co. Ltd. CG Triflon P - Central Glass Co. Ltd. CG Triflon WI - Central Glass Co. Ltd. Daiflon S3 - Daikin Industries Ltd. Daiflon S3-A - Daikin Industries Ltd. Daiflon S3-E - Daikin Industries Ltd. Daiflon S3-EN - Daikin Industries Ltd. Daiflon S3-ES - Daikin Industries Ltd. Daiflon S3-HN - Daikin Industries Ltd. Daiflon S3-MC - Daikin Industries Ltd. Daiflon S3-P35 - Daikin Industries Ltd. Daiflon S3-W6 - Daikin Industries Ltd. Delifrene 113 - Ausimont SPA Diflon S-3 - Unknown Dional 113 - Solvay Fluor GMBH F-113 - Tosoh Flon Showa FS-3 - Showa Denko K.K. Flon Showa FS-3A - Showa Denko K.K. Flon Showa FS-3D - Showa Denko K.K. Flon Showa FS-3E - Showa Denko K.K. Flon Showa FS-3ES - Showa Denko K.K.	76-13-1

(Continued)

Class I (Continued)

Chemical Name	Trade Names	CAS Number
	Flon Showa FS-3M - Showa Denko K.K.	
	Flon Showa FS-3MS - Showa Denko K.K.	
	Flon Showa FS-3P - Showa Denko K.K.	
	Flon Showa FS-3W - Showa Denko K.K.	
	Fluorisol - Rhodia	
	Fluorisol - ISC Chemicals	
	Forane 113 - ARKEMA SA	
	Freon MCA - DuPont Fluoroproducts	
	Freon MCA - DuPont-Mitsui Fluorochemicals Co. Ltd.	
	Freon PCA - DuPont Fluoroproducts	
	Freon SMT - DuPont-Mitsui Fluorochemicals Co. Ltd.	
	Freon SMT - DuPont Fluoroproducts	
	Freon TA - DuPont Fluoroproducts	
	Freon TA - DuPont-Mitsui Fluorochemicals Co. Ltd.	
	Freon T-B1 - DuPont-Mitsui Fluorochemicals Co. Ltd.	
	Freon T-DA35 - DuPont-Mitsui Fluorochemicals Co. Ltd.	
	Freon T-DA35X - DuPont-Mitsui Fluorochemicals Co. Ltd.	
	Freon T-DEC - DuPont-Mitsui Fluorochemicals Co. Ltd.	
	Freon T-DECR - DuPont-Mitsui Fluorochemicals Co. Ltd.	
	Freon TDF - DuPont Fluoroproducts	
	Freon T-DFC - DuPont-Mitsui Fluorochemicals Co. Ltd.	
	Freon T-DFCX - DuPont-Mitsui Fluorochemicals Co. Ltd.	
	Freon TE - DuPont-Mitsui Fluorochemicals Co. Ltd.	
	Freon T-E35 - DuPont-Mitsui Fluorochemicals Co. Ltd.	
	Freon T-E6 - DuPont-Mitsui Fluorochemicals Co. Ltd.	
	Freon TES - DuPont-Mitsui Fluorochemicals Co. Ltd.	
	Freon TES - DuPont Fluoroproducts	

Class I (Continued)

Chemical Name	Trade Names	CAS Number
	Freon TF - DuPont-Mitsui Fluorochemicals Co. Ltd.	
	Freon TF - DuPont Fluoroproducts	
	Freon TMC - DuPont-Mitsui Fluorochemicals Co. Ltd.	
	Freon TMC - DuPont Fluoroproducts	
	Freon TMS - DuPont-Mitsui Fluorochemicals Co. Ltd.	
	Freon TMS solvents - DuPont Fluoroproducts	
	Freon TP35 - DuPont Fluoroproducts	
	Freon T-P35 - DuPont-Mitsui Fluorochemicals Co. Ltd.	
	Freon TWD 602 - DuPont Fluoroproducts	
	Freon T-WD602 - DuPont-Mitsui Fluorochemicals Co. Ltd.	
	Freon-113 - DuPont Fluoroproducts	
	Frigen 113 - Solvay Fluor GMBH	
	Frigen TR 113 - Solvay Fluor GMBH	
	Fronsolve - Asahi Glass Co. Ltd.	
	Fronsolve AD-17 - Asahi Glass Co. Ltd.	
	Fronsolve AD-7 - Asahi Glass Co. Ltd.	
	Fronsolve AD-9 - Asahi Glass Co. Ltd.	
	Fronsolve AD-I9 - Asahi Glass Co. Ltd.	
	Fronsolve AE - Asahi Glass Co. Ltd.	
	Fronsolve AES - Asahi Glass Co. Ltd.	
	Fronsolve AM - Asahi Glass Co. Ltd.	
	Fronsolve AMS - Asahi Glass Co. Ltd.	
	Fronsolve AP - Asahi Glass Co. Ltd.	
	Fronsolve R 113 - Nagase & Co.	
	G Triflon E35 - Central Glass Co. Ltd.	
	Genesolv D - Honeywell (formerly Allied-Signal Inc.)	
	Genetron 113 - Honeywell (formerly AlliedSignal Inc.)	
	ISCEON 113 - Rhodia	
	Kaltron - Kali-Chemie AG	
	Magicdry MD 201 - Daikin Industries Ltd.	
	Magicdry MD 202 - Daikin Industries Ltd.	

(Continued)

Class I (Continued)

Chemical Name	Trade Names	CAS Number
	Magicdry MD 203 - Daikin Industries Ltd.	
	Magicdry MD-E35 - Daikin Industries Ltd.	
	Magicdry MD-E6 - Daikin Industries Ltd.	
	SonicSolve - London Chemical Co. (Lonco)	
	TCTFE - Solvay Fluor GMBH	
CFC-114 (C2F4Cl2) Dichlorotetrafluoroethane	Algofrene 114 - Ausimont SPA	76-15-1
	Arcton 114 - INEOS Fluor	
	Asahifron R-114 - Asahi Glass Co. Ltd.	
	Daiflon 114 - Daikin Industries Ltd.	
	Flon Showa 114 - Showa Denko K.K.	
	Forane 114 - ARKEMA SA	
	Freon-114 - DuPont Fluoroproducts	
	Frigen 114 - Solvay Fluor GMBH	
	Genetron 114 - Quimobasicos s.a. de c.v.	
	Genetron 114 - Honeywell (formerly AlliedSignal Inc.)	
	ISCEON 114 - Rhodia	
	R114 - Protocol Resource Management Inc.	
	R-506	
CFC-115 (C2F5Cl) Monochloropentafluoroethane	Algofrene 115 - Ausimont SPA	76-15-3
	Algofrene 502 - Ausimont SPA	
	Arcton 115 - INEOS Fluor	
	Arcton 502 - INEOS Fluor	
	Asahifron R-115 - Asahi Glass Co. Ltd.	
	Asahifron R-502 - Asahi Glass Co. Ltd.	
	CFC-115 - Zhejiang Chemical Research Institute	
	CFC-115 - Changshu 3F Refrigerant Plant	
	Daiflon 115 - Daikin Industries Ltd.	
	Daiflon 502 - Daikin Industries Ltd.	
	Flon Showa 502 - Showa Denko K.K.	
	Forane 115 - ARKEMA SA	
	Forane 502 - ARKEMA SA	
	Freon-115 - DuPont Fluoroproducts	
	Freon-502 - DuPont Fluoroproducts	
	Frigen 115 - Solvay Fluor GMBH	
	Genetron 115 - Honeywell (formerly AlliedSignal Inc.)	
	Genetron 502 - Quimobasicos s.a. de c.v.	

Class I (Continued)

Chemical Name	Trade Names	CAS Number
	Genetron 502 - Honeywell (formerly AlliedSignal Inc.)	
	ISCEON 115 - Rhodia	
	ISCEON 502 - Rhodia	
	R502 - Protocol Resource Management Inc.	
	R-504	
Halon 1211 (CF2ClBr) Bromochlorodifluoromethane	Halon 1211 - Hanju Chemical Co. Ltd.	353-59-3
	Halon-1211 - Jiangsu Wuxian Chemical Plant	
	Halon-1211 - Zhejiang Chemical Research Institute	
	Halon-1211 - Foshan Electrical-Chemical General Plant	
	Halon-1211 - Shandong Shouguang Plant	
	Halon-1211 - Zhejiang Dongyang Chemical Plant	
	Halon-1211 - Navin Fluorine Industries	
	Halon-1211 - Dalian Fire Extinguishing Agent Plant	
Halon 1301 (CF3Br) Bromotrifluoromethane	Freon FE 1301 - Ansul Fire Protection	75-63-8
	Freon FE 1301 - DuPont Fluoroproducts	
	Halon 1301 - Hanju Chemical Co. Ltd.	
	Halon-1301 - Zhejiang Chemical Industry Research Institute	
Halon 2402 (C2F4Br2) Dibromotetrafluoroethane		124-73-2
CFC-13 (CF3Cl) Chlorotrifluoromethane	Arcton 13 - INEOS Fluor	75-72-9
	Asahifron R-13 - Asahi Glass Co. Ltd.	
	Daiflon 13 - Daikin Industries Ltd.	
	FCC-13 - Akzo Chemicals International B.V.	
	Flon Showa 13 - Showa Denko K.K.	
	Forane 13 - ARKEMA SA	
	Freon-13 - DuPont Fluoroproducts	
	Frigen 13 - Solvay Fluor GMBH	
	Genetron 13 - Quimobasicos s.a. de c.v.	
	Genetron 13 - Honeywell (formerly AlliedSignal Inc.)	
	Genetron 503 - Quimobasicos s.a. de c.v.	

(Continued)

Class I (Continued)

Chemical Name	Trade Names	CAS Number
	Genetron 503 - Honeywell (formerly AlliedSignal Inc.)	
	ISCEON 13 – Rhodia	
	R-503	
CFC-111 (C2FCl5) Pentachlorofluoroethane	R-111	354-56-3
CFC-112 (C2F2Cl4) Tetrachlorodifluoroethane	R-112	76-12-0
CFC-211 (C3FCl7) Heptachlorofluoropropane		422-78-6
CFC-212 (C3F2Cl6) Hexachlorodifluoropropane		3182-26-1
CFC-213 (C3F3Cl5) Pentachlorotrifluoropropane		2354-06-5
CFC-214 (C3F4Cl4) Tetrachlorotetrafluoropropane		29255-31-0
CFC-215 (C3F5Cl3) Trichloropentafluoropropane		4259-43-2
CFC-216 (C3F6Cl2) Dichlorohexafluoropropane		661-97-2
CFC-217 (C3F7Cl) Chloroheptafluoropropane		422-86-6
CCl4 Carbon tetrachloride	Carbon tetrachloride - Riedelde Haen AG. Carbon tetrachloride - Mitsui Toatsu Chemicals Inc. Carbon tetrachloride - Kureha Chemical Industry Co., Ltd. Dowfume 75 - Dow AgroSciences LLC Freon 10 - DuPont Fluoroproducts Necatorina - Unknown Necatorine - Unknown Sienkatanso - Kanto Denka Kogyo Co. Sienkatanso - Kanto Denka Kogyo Co. Tetrafinol - Unknown Tetraform - Unknown Tetrasol - Unknown Univerm - Unknown Vermoestricid - Unknown Volcan Formula 72 – Unknown	56-23-5
Methyl Chloroform (C2H3Cl3) 1,1,1-trichloroethane	1,1,1-tri - Vulcan Chemicals 111 Tri - Vulcan Chemicals	71-55-6

Class I (Continued)

Chemical Name	Trade Names	CAS Number
	A D Delco Fabric - Chem-Tek America	
	Aerolex - National Chemsearch	
	Aerothene (R) TA Solvent - Dow Chemical Co.	
	Aerothene (R) TT Solvent (Aerosol Grade) - Dow Chemical Co.	
	Alpha 1220 - Alpha Metals	
	Aquadry 50 - Asahi Chemical Industry Co. Ltd.	
	Ardrox - Chemetall Asia Pte. Ltd. (formerly Brent Asia)	
	Ardrox D495A Developer - Chemetall Asia Pte. Ltd. (formerly Brent Asia)	
	Ardrox K410C Remover - Chemetall Asia Pte. Ltd. (formerly Brent Asia)	
	Arrow C190 LEC - Arrow Chemicals	
	Asahitriethane ALS - Asahi Glass Co. Ltd.	
	Asahitriethane BS - Asahi Glass Co. Ltd.	
	Asahitriethane EC Grade - Asahi Glass Co. Ltd.	
	Asahitriethane LS - Asahi Glass Co. Ltd.	
	Asahitriethane UT - Asahi Glass Co. Ltd.	
	Asahitriethane V5 - Asahi Glass Co. Ltd.	
	Baltane - ARKEMA SA	
	B-Lube - National Chemsearch	
	C-60 - Sprayway, Inc.	
	CG Triethane F - Central Glass Co. Ltd.	
	CG Triethane N - Central Glass Co. Ltd.	
	CG Triethane NN - Central Glass Co. Ltd.	
	CG Triethane NNA - Central Glass Co. Ltd.	
	Chemlok 252 - Lord Corp.	
	Chem-Slich - National Chemsearch	
	Chem-Slick - National Chemsearch	
	Chlorothene (R) - Dow Chemical Co.	
	Chlorothene (R) NU - Dow Chemical Co.	
	Chlorothene (R) SL - Dow Chemical Co.	
	Chlorothene (R) SM - Dow Chemical Co.	
	Chlorothene (R) VG - Dow Chemical Co.	
	Chlorothene (R) XL - Dow Chemical Co.	
	CRC226 - CRC Industries Australia Pty Ltd.	

(Continued)

Class I (Continued)

Chemical Name	Trade Names	CAS Number
	Dowclene (R) EC - Dow Chemical Co.	
	Dowclene (R) EC-CS - Dow Chemical Co.	
	Dowclene (R) LS - Dow Chemical Co.	
	Electrosolv - Unitor Ships Service	
	Ethana AL - Asahi Chemical Industry Co. Ltd.	
	Ethana FXN - Asahi Chemical Industry Co. Ltd.	
	Ethana HT - Asahi Chemical Industry Co. Ltd.	
	Ethana IRN - Asahi Chemical Industry Co. Ltd.	
	Ethana NU - Asahi Chemical Industry Co. Ltd.	
	Ethana RD - Asahi Chemical Industry Co. Ltd.	
	Ethana RS - Asahi Chemical Industry Co. Ltd.	
	Ethana SL - Asahi Chemical Industry Co. Ltd.	
	Ethana TS - Asahi Chemical Industry Co. Ltd.	
	Ethana VG - Asahi Chemical Industry Co. Ltd.	
	Film Cleaning Grade methyl chloroform - Dow Chemical Co.	
	Genklene A - INEOS Fluor	
	Genklene LV - INEOS Fluor	
	Genklene LVJ - INEOS Fluor	
	Genklene LVS - INEOS Fluor	
	Genklene LVX - INEOS Fluor	
	Genklene N - INEOS Fluor	
	Genklene P - INEOS Fluor	
	Genklene PT - INEOS Fluor	
	Gex - National Chemsearch	
	GEX - National Chemsearch	
	JS-536B - Chiland Enterprise Co. Ltd.	
	Kanden Triethane E - Kanto Denka Kogyo Co.	
	Kanden Triethane EL - Kanto Denka Kogyo Co.	

Class I (Continued)

Chemical Name	Trade Names	CAS Number
	Kanden Triethane ELV - Kanto Denka Kogyo Co.	
	Kanden Triethane EP - Kanto Denka Kogyo Co.	
	Kanden Triethane H - Kanto Denka Kogyo Co.	
	Kanden Triethane HA - Kanto Denka Kogyo Co.	
	Kanden Triethane HAK - Kanto Denka Kogyo Co.	
	Kanden Triethane HB - Kanto Denka Kogyo Co.	
	Kanden Triethane HC - Kanto Denka Kogyo Co.	
	Kanden Triethane HF - Kanto Denka Kogyo Co.	
	Kanden Triethane HG - Kanto Denka Kogyo Co.	
	Kanden Triethane HS - Kanto Denka Kogyo Co.	
	Kanden Triethane HT - Kanto Denka Kogyo Co.	
	Kanden Triethane N - Kanto Denka Kogyo Co.	
	Kanden Triethane ND - Kanto Denka Kogyo Co.	
	Kanden Triethane R - Kanto Denka Kogyo Co.	
	Kanden Triethane SR - Kanto Denka Kogyo Co.	
	Kanden Triethane SRA - Kanto Denka Kogyo Co.	
	Krylon Dulling Spray - Sherwin Williams Co.	
	Lectra Clean - CRC Industries Australia Pty Ltd.	
	Methyl Chloroform Low Stabilized - Dow Chemical Co.	
	Methyl Chloroform Low Stabilized - PW - Dow Chemical Co.	

(Continued)

Class I (Continued)

Chemical Name	Trade Names	CAS Number
	Methyl Chloroform Technical - Dow Chemical Co.	
	Molybkombin UMFT4 - Klueber Lubrification	
	Molybkombin UMFT4 Spray - Klueber Lubrification	
	MS-136N - Miller Stephenson Chemical Company Inc.	
	MS-136N/CO2 - Miller Stephenson Chemical Company Inc.	
	MV3 - Rocol Ltd.	
	NC-123 - National Chemsearch	
	New Dine T - Yokohama Polymer Co., Ltd.	
	Nicrobraz Cement 500RTS - Wall Colmonoy	
	Nicrobraz Cement xxx - Wall Colmonoy	
	Nilos Solution TLT70 - Nilos Hans Ziller-KG	
	Norchem ACC 572 - Goldcrest International	
	PC81x - Multicore Solders Inc.	
	Prelete® - Dow Chemical Co.	
	Proact® - Dow Chemical Co.	
	Propaklone - INEOS Fluor	
	Rust Inhibitor B007 - Crown Industrial Products	
	S.E.M.I. Grade - Dow Chemical Co.	
	Safety Solvent 8060 - Crown Industrial Products	
	Shine Pearl - Toagosei Co.	
	Solvent Cleaner/Degreas. C60 - Sprayway, Inc.	
	Solvethane - Solvay Fluor GMBH	
	SonicSolve xxx - London Chemical Co. (Lonco)	
	SS-25 - National Chemsearch	
	Sunlovely - National Chemsearch	
	Sunlovely - Asahi Glass Co. Ltd.	
	Super solution - Pang Rubber Co.	
	Swish - National Chemsearch	

Class I (Continued)

Chemical Name	Trade Names	CAS Number
	Tafclen - Asahi Chemical Industry Co. Ltd.	
	Tempilaq - Tempil, Inc.	
	Three Bond 1802 - Three Bond Tec(s) Pte. Ltd.	
	Three Bond xxx - Three Bond Tec(s) Pte. Ltd.	
	Three one - Toagosei Co.	
	Three One-A - Toagosei Co.	
	Three One-AH - Toagosei Co.	
	Three One-EX - Toagosei Co.	
	Three One-F - Toagosei Co.	
	Three One-HS - Toagosei Co.	
	Three One-R - Toagosei Co.	
	Three One-S - Toagosei Co.	
	Three One-S(M) - Toagosei Co.	
	Three One-T - Toagosei Co.	
	Three One-TH - Toagosei Co.	
	Tipp-Ex - Toagosei Co.	
	Toyoclean - Tosoh	
	Toyoclean AL - Tosoh	
	Toyoclean ALS - Tosoh	
	Toyoclean EE - Tosoh	
	Toyoclean EM - Tosoh	
	Toyoclean HS - Tosoh	
	Toyoclean IC - Tosoh	
	Toyoclean NH - Tosoh	
	Toyoclean O - Tosoh	
	Toyoclean SE - Tosoh	
	Toyoclean T - Tosoh	
	Triethane PPG - Tosoh	
Methyl Bromide (CH3Br)	50-50 Preplant Soil Fumigant - AmeriBrom, Inc. (subsidiary of Dead Sea Bromine Group)	74-83-9
	57-43 Preplant Soil Fumigant - AmeriBrom, Inc. (subsidiary of Dead Sea Bromine Group)	
	67-33 - Great Lakes Chemical Corporation	
	67-33 Preplant Soil Fumigation - AmeriBrom, Inc. (subsidiary of Dead Sea Bromine Group)	

(Continued)

Class I (Continued)

Chemical Name	Trade Names	CAS Number
	70-30 Preplant Soil Fumigation - AmeriBrom, Inc. (subsidiary of Dead Sea Bromine Group)	
	75-25 Preplant Soil Fumigation - AmeriBrom, Inc. (subsidiary of Dead Sea Bromine Group)	
	80-20 Preplant Soil Fumigation - AmeriBrom, Inc. (subsidiary of Dead Sea Bromine Group)	
	98-2 - Great Lakes Chemical Corporation	
	98-2 - AmeriBrom, Inc. (subsidiary of Dead Sea Bromine Group)	
	Agrobromo 50 - Agroquímicos de Levante S.A.	
	Agrobromo 98 - Agroquímicos de Levante S.A.	
	Agro-O-Gas 50 - Cerexagri SA	
	Ameribrom Methyl Bromide - Grain Fumigant - AmeriBrom, Inc. (subsidiary of Dead Sea Bromine Group)	
	Bercema - Unknown	
	BROM 70/30 - Soil Chemicals Corporation	
	Brom O Gas - Cerexagri SA	
	BROM-76 - Soil Chemicals Corporation	
	BRO-MEAN C-2R - Reddick Fumigants Inc.	
	BRO-MEAN C-33 - Reddick Fumigants Inc.	
	BRO-MEAN C-O - Reddick Fumigants Inc.	
	Bromocoop (with methyl bromide) - Vinexport S.A.	
	Bromofifty - Bromine Compounds Ltd. (a subsidiary of Dead Sea Bromine Group Ltd.	
	Brom-O-Gas - Great Lakes Chemical Corporation	
	Brom-O-Gas 0.25% - Great Lakes Chemical Corporation	
	Brom-O-Gas 0.5% - Great Lakes Chemical Corporation	
	Brom-O-Gas 2% - Great Lakes Chemical Corporation	

Class I (Continued)

Chemical Name	Trade Names	CAS Number
	Brom-O-Gas R - Great Lakes Chemical Corporation	
	Bromopic - Bromine Compounds Ltd. (a subsidiary of Dead Sea Bromine Group, Ltd.)	
	Brom-O-Sol - Great Lakes Chemical Corporation	
	Brom-O-Sol 90 - Great Lakes Chemical Corporation	
	Brozone Preplant Soil Fumigant - Dow AgroSciences LLC	
	Celfume - Unknown	
	Curafume - Unknown	
	Dowfume MC-2 soil fumigant - Unknown	
	Dowfume MC-33 soil fumigant - Albemarle Corporation	
	EDCO - Unknown	
	Embafume - Unknown	
	Halon 1001 - Unknown	
	Haltox - Unknown	
	Iscabrome - Unknown	
	Iscobrome - Unknown	
	Kayafume - Unknown	
	MB 98-2 Penetrating Fumigant - Asgrow Florida Co.	
	MBC Soil Fumigant - Hendrix and Dail, Inc.	
	MBC Soil Fumigant Concentrate - Hendrix and Dail, Inc.	
	MBC-33 Soil Fumigant - Hendrix and Dail, Inc.	
	M-B-R 2 Penetrating Fumigating - Albemarle Corporation	
	M-B-R 75 - Albemarle Corporation	
	Mebrom 100 - Mebrom N.V.	
	Mebrom 50/50 - Mebrom N.V.	
	Mebrom 67/33 - Mebrom N.V.	
	Mebrom 75/25 - Mebrom N.V.	
	Mebrom 98 - Mebrom N.V.	
	Mebrom AA - Mebrom N.V.	

(Continued)

Class I (Continued)

Chemical Name	Trade Names	CAS Number
	Metabrom - Bromine Compounds Ltd. (a subsidiary of Dead Sea Bromine Company, Ltd.)	
	Metabrom 100 - AmeriBrom, Inc. (subsidiary of Dead Sea Bromine Group)	
	Metabrom 98 - AmeriBrom, Inc. (subsidiary of Dead Sea Bromine Group)	
	Metabrom 99 - AmeriBrom, Inc. (subsidiary of Dead Sea Bromine Group)	
	Metabrom Q - AmeriBrom, Inc. (subsidiary of Dead Sea Bromine Group)	
	Metafume - Unknown	
	Meth-O-Gas 100 - Great Lakes Chemical Corporation	
	Meth-O-Gas Q - Great Lakes Chemical Corporation	
	Methyl bromide - ARKEMA SA	
	Methyl bromide - Ethyl Corporation	
	Methyl bromide - Nippoh Chemical Co., Ltd.	
	Methyl bromide - Sanko Chemical Industry Co. Ltd.	
	Methyl bromide - Dohkai Chemical Industry Co., Ltd.	
	Methyl bromide - SC Sinteza SA	
	Methyl bromide - Ichikawa Gohsei Chemical Co., Ltd.	
	Methyl bromide - Chemicrea Co. Ltd.	
	Methyl bromide - Lianyungang Seawater Chemical First Plant (Linanyung Dead Sea Bromine)	
	Methyl bromide - Zhejiang Linhai Limin Chemical Plant	
	Methyl bromide - M/S Tata Chemicals Ltd.	
	Methyl bromide - Saki Chemical Plant	
	Methyl Bromide - Great Lakes Chemical Corporation	

Class I (Continued)

Chemical Name	Trade Names	CAS Number
	Methyl bromide - Teijin Chemicals Ltd.	
	Methyl bromide - Asahi Glass Co. Ltd.	
	Methyl Bromide 100 - AmeriBrom, Inc. (subsidiary of Dead Sea Bromine Group)	
	Methyl Bromide 100 - Soil Chemicals Corporation	
	Methyl Bromide 100% - Dead Sea Bromine Group, Ltd.	
	Methyl Bromide 50% - Dead Sea Bromine Co., Ltd.	
	Methyl Bromide 50kg cylinder - Taizhou Xingye Chemical Factory	
	Methyl Bromide 67% - Dead Sea Bromine Co., Ltd.	
	Methyl Bromide 681g/Tin, 24Tin/box - Taizhou Xingye Chemical Factory	
	Methyl Bromide 89.5% - Trical	
	Methyl Bromide 98 (M-B-R 98) - Albemarle Corporation	
	Methyl Bromide 98% - Dead Sea Bromine Group, Ltd.	
	Methyl Bromide 98% - Soil Chemicals Corporation	
	Methyl Bromide 99.5 - Great Lakes Chemical Corporation	
	Methyl Bromide 99.5% - Shadow Mountain Products Corporation	
	Methyl Bromide 99.5% - Soil Chemicals Corporation	
	Methyl Bromide 99.75% - Soil Chemicals Corporation	
	Methyl Bromide Quarantine Fumigant - Soil Chemicals Corporation	
	Methyl Bromide Technical (M-B-R 98 Technical) - Albemarle Corporation	
	Methyl Bromide, 100% - Penglai Chemical, Inc.	
	Methyl Bromide, 98%+2% Chloropicrin - Penglai Chemical, Inc.	

(Continued)

Class I (Continued)

Chemical Name	Trade Names	CAS Number
	Pestmaster - Michigan Chemical Corp.	
	PIC BROM 25 - Soil Chemicals Corporation	
	PIC BROM 33 - Soil Chemicals Corporation	
	PIC BROM 43 - Soil Chemicals Corporation	
	PIC BROM 50 - Soil Chemicals Corporation	
	PIC BROM 55 - Soil Chemicals Corporation	
	PIC BROM 67 - Soil Chemicals Corporation	
	Rootect Oil (with DCIP) - Unknown	
	Rotox - Unknown	
	Sanibrom S Biocide Technical - Great Lakes Chemical Corporation	
	SCL Methyl Bromide 98 - Soil Chemicals Corporation	
	Terabol - Unknown	
	Terr-O-Cide II - Great Lakes Chemical Corporation	
	Terr-O-Gas - Cerexagri SA	
	Terr-O-Gas 33 preplant soil fumigant - Great Lakes Chemical Corporation	
	Terr-O-Gas 33 preplant soil fumigant - Great Lakes Chemical Corporation	
	Terr-O-Gas 45 preplant soil fumigant - Great Lakes Chemical Corporation	
	Terr-O-Gas 50 preplant soil fumigant - Great Lakes Chemical Corporation	
	Terr-O-Gas 57 preplant soil fumigant - Great Lakes Chemical Corporation	
	Terr-O-Gas 67 preplant soil fumigant - Great Lakes Chemical Corporation	
	Terr-O-Gas 70 preplant soil fumigant - Great Lakes Chemical Corporation	
	Terr-O-Gas 75 preplant soil fumigant - Great Lakes Chemical Corporation	
	Terr-O-Gas 80 preplant soil fumigant - Great Lakes Chemical Corporation	

Class I (Continued)

Chemical Name	Trade Names	CAS Number
	Terr-O-Gas 98 preplant soil fumigant - Great Lakes Chemical Corporation	
	Terrogel 67 - Great Lakes Chemical Corporation	
	TRI-BROM - TriCal	
	TRI-CON 45/55 - TriCal	
	TRI-CON 50/50 Preplant Soil Fumigant - TriCal	
	TRI-CON 57/43 Preplant Soil Fumigant - TriCal	74-83-9
	TRI-CON 67/33 Preplant Soil Fumigant - TriCal	
	TRI-CON 75/25 Preplant Soil Fumigant - TriCal	
	TRI-CON 76/24 Preplant Soil Fumigant - TriCal	
	TRI-CON 80/20 Preplant Soil Fumigant - TriCal	
	Zytox - Unknown	
CHFBr2 Dibromofluoromethane		1868-53-7
HBFC-12B1 (CHF2Br) Bromodifluoromethane		1511-62-4
CH2FBr Bromofluoromethane		373-52-4
C2HFBr4		
C2HF2Br3		
C2HF3Br 2 1,2-Dibromo-1,1,2-trifluoroethane	FC-123B2	354-04-1
C2HF4Br 1,1,1,2-Tetrafluoro-2-bromoethane 1-Bromo-1,1,2,2-tetrafluoroethane		124-72-1 354-07-4
C2H2FBr3		
C2H2F2Br2 1,1-Dibromo-2,2-difluoroethane 1,2-Dibromo-1,1-difluoroethane		359-19-3 75-82-1
C2H2F3Br		
C2H3FBr2 1,2-Dibromo-1-fluoroethane; 1,2-Dibromofluoroethane		358-97-4

(*Continued*)

Class I (Continued)

Chemical Name	Trade Names	CAS Number
C2H3F2Br 2-Bromo-1,1-difluoroethane 1-Bromo-1,1-difluoroethane		359-07-9 420-47-3
C2H4FBr 1-Bromo-2-fluoroethane; 2-Fluoroethyl bromide	FC-151B1	762-49-2
C3HFBr6		
C3HF2Br5		
C3HF3Br4		
C3HF4Br3		
C3HF5Br2		
C3HF6Br 1-Bromo-1,1,2,3,3,3- hexafluoropropane		2252-78-0
C3H2FBr5		
C3H2F2Br4		
C3H2F3Br3 1,2,2-Tribromo-3,3,3- trifluoropropane		
C3H2F4Br2 1,3-Dibromo-1,1,3,3- tetrafluoropropane		
C3H2F5Br		
C3H3FBr4		
C3H3F2Br3 1,2,3-Tribromo-3,3- difluoropropane		
C3H3F3Br2 1,2-Dibromo-3,3,3- trifluoropropane; 2,3- Dibromo-1,1,1- trifluoropropane		431-21-0
C3H3F4Br		
C3H4FBr3		
C3H4F2Br2 1,3-Dibromo-1,1- difluoropropane		460-25-3
C3H4F3Br 3-Bromo-1,1,1- trifluoropropane		460-32-2
C3H5FBr2		
C3H5F2Br		

Class I (Continued)

Chemical Name	Trade Names	CAS Number
C3H6FBr Propane, 1-bromo-2-fluoro- 1-Bromo-3-fluoropropane		1871-72-3 352-91-0
CH2BrCl Chlorobromomethane		74-97-5
Restricted blends	Free Zone Freeze 12 FRIGC FR-12 FX-10 FX-56 GHG-HP GHG-X4 GHG-X5 G2018C Hotshot HP-80 HP-81 Isceon 69-L MP-39 MP-52 MP-66 NARM-502 R-176 R-401A R-401B R-401C R-402A R-402B R-403B R-406A R-408A R-409A R-411A R-411B R-414A R-414B	

Class II

Chemical Name	Trade Names	CAS Number
HCFC-21 (CHFCl2) Dichlorofluoromethane	Khladon Fluorocarbon R21 Fluorodichloromethane - JSC "Halogen" Russia	75-43-4
HCFC-22 (CHF2Cl) Monochlorodifluoromethane	Algofrene 22 - Montefluos S.P.A. Algofrene 22 - Ausimont SPA Algofrene 502 - Ausimont SPA Arcton 22 - INEOS Fluor Arcton 402A - INEOS Fluor Arcton 402B - INEOS Fluor Arcton 408A - INEOS Fluor Arcton 409A - INEOS Fluor Arcton 412A - INEOS Fluor Arcton 502 - INEOS Fluor Arcton 509 - INEOS Fluor Arcton TP5R - INEOS Fluor Arcton TP5R2 - INEOS Fluor Asahifron R-22 - Asahi Glass Co. Ltd. Asahifron R-502 - Asahi Glass Co. Ltd. Daiflon 22 - Daikin Industries Ltd. Daiflon 502 - Daikin Industries Ltd. Di 36 - Ausimont SPA Di 44 - Ausimont SPA Dymel 22 - DuPont-Mitsui Fluorochemicals Co. Ltd. Flon Showa 22 - Showa Denko K.K. Flon Showa 502 - Showa Denko K.K. Floron 22 - SRF Limited Flugene 22 - Continental Industries Flugene 22 - Sicno Chemical Industries of Northern Greece Forane 22 - ARKEMA SA Forane 502 - ARKEMA SA Forane FX 10 - ARKEMA SA Forane FX 20 - ARKEMA SA Forane FX 55 - ARKEMA SA Forane FX 56 - ARKEMA SA Forane FX 57 - ARKEMA SA Formacel S - DuPont-Mitsui Fluorochemicals Co. Ltd. Freon 22 - DuPont Fluoroproducts	75-45-6

Class II (Continued)

Chemical Name	Trade Names	CAS Number
	Freon-22 - DuPont Fluoroproducts	
	Freon-502 - DuPont Fluoroproducts	
	Frigen 22 - Solvay Fluor GMBH	
	FX-56 - ARKEMA SA	
	G2015 - Greencool	
	G2018A - Greencool	
	G2018B - Greencool	
	G2018C - Greencool	
	Genetron 22 - Quimobasicos s.a. de c.v.	
	Genetron 22 - Honeywell (formerly AlliedSignal Inc.)	
	Genetron 408A - Honeywell (formerly AlliedSignal Inc.)	
	Genetron 409A - Honeywell (formerly AlliedSignal Inc.)	
	Genetron 502 - Honeywell (formerly AlliedSignal Inc.)	
	Genetron 502 - Quimobasicos s.a. de c.v.	
	Genetron HP80 - Honeywell (formerly AlliedSignal Inc.)	
	Genetron HP81 - Honeywell (formerly AlliedSignal Inc.)	
	Genetron MP39 - Honeywell (formerly AlliedSignal Inc.)	
	Genetron MP66 - Honeywell (formerly AlliedSignal Inc.)	
	GHG - Monroe Air Tech	
	GHG12 - ICOR International (formerly Indianapolis Refrigeration Co. Inc.)	
	GHG-HP - People's Welding Supply	
	GHG-X4 - People's Welding Supply	
	GHG-X5 - People's Welding Supply	
	HCFC-22 - Chemical Industries of Northern Greece SA	
	HCFC-22 - Chemicals and Plastics India Ltd.	
	HCFC-22 - Firefreeze International	
	HCFC-22 - Gujarat Fluorochemicals Ltd.	
	HCFC-22 - Hankook Shin Hwa	
	HCFC-22 - SRF Limited	

(Continued)

Class II (Continued)

Chemical Name	Trade Names	CAS Number
	HCFC-22 - Daikin Industries Ltd.	
	Hot Shot - ICOR International (formerly Indianapolis Refrigeration Co. Inc.)	
	ISCEON 22 – Rhodia	
	ISCEON 502 - Rhodia	
	ISCEON 69-L - Rhodia	
	ISCEON 69S - Rhodia	
	Khladon Fluorocarbon R22	
	Difluorochloromethane - JSC "Halogen" Russia	
	Korfron 22 - Ulsan Chemical Co., Ltd.	
	McCool R-12 - McMullen Oil Products Inc.	
	NAF P-III - North American Fire Guardian	
	NAF S III - Safety Hi-Tech srl	
	NAF S-III - North American Fire Guardian	
	NARM-502 - Moncton Refrigerants	
	Oxyfume 2002 - Honeywell (formerly AlliedSignal Inc.)	
	R22 - Protocol Resource Management Inc.	
	R502 - Protocol Resource Management Inc.	
	Solkane 22 - Solvay Fluor GMBH	
	Solkane 22/142b blends - Solvay Fluor GMBH	
	Solkane 406A - Solvay Fluor GMBH	
	Solkane 409A - Solvay Fluor GMBH	
	Suva HP80 - DuPont Fluoroproducts	
	Suva HP81 - DuPont Fluoroproducts	
	Suva MP39 - DuPont Fluoroproducts	
	Suva MP52 - DuPont Fluoroproducts	
	Suva MP66 - DuPont Fluoroproducts	
	Taisoton 22 - Formosa Plastics	
HCFC-31 (CH2FCl) Monochlorofluoromethane		593-70-4
HCFC-121 (C2HFCl4) Tetrachlorofluoroethane		354-14-3

Class II (Continued)

Chemical Name	Trade Names	CAS Number
HCFC-122 (C2HF2Cl3) Trichlorodifluoroethane		354-21-2
HCFC-123 (C2HF3Cl2) Dichlorotrifluoroethane	Asahiklin AK-123 - Asahi Glass Co. Ltd. Blitz III - North American Fire Guardian FE-232 - DuPont Fluoroproducts Forane 123 - ARKEMA SA Genesolv 2123 - Honeywell (formerly AlliedSignal Inc.) Genesolv 2127 - Honeywell (formerly AlliedSignal Inc.) Genetron 123 - Honeywell (formerly AlliedSignal Inc.) Halotron 1 - North American Fire Guardian Halotron I - American Pacific Corporation/Halotron, Inc. HCFC-123 - Especial Gas Inc. HCFC-123 Generic - Kanto Denka Kogyo Co. Meforex 123 - Ausimont SPA NAF P III - Safety Hi-Tech srl NAF P IV - Safety Hi-Tech srl NAF P-III - North American Fire Guardian NAF S III - Safety Hi-Tech srl NAF S-III - North American Fire Guardian R123 - Protocol Resource Management Inc. R-123 - Foosung Tech Corporation Solkane 123 - Solvay Fluor GMBH Suva 123 - DuPont Fluoroproducts Vertrel 423 - DuPont-Mitsui Fluorochemicals Co. Ltd.	306-83-2
HCFC-124 (C2HF4Cl) Monochlorotetrafluoroethane	Arcton 409A - INEOS Fluor Asahiklin AK-124 - Asahi Glass Co. Ltd. Di 24 - Ausimont SPA Di 36 - Ausimont SPA FE-241 - DuPont Fluoroproducts Forane FX 56 - ARKEMA SA Forane FX 57 - ARKEMA SA FRIGC - IGC Intermagnetics General RIGC FR-12 - Intermagnetics General FRIGC FR-12 - CFC Refimax, LLC	

(Continued)

Class II (Continued)

Chemical Name	Trade Names	CAS Number
	FX-56 - ARKEMA SA	
	Genetron 124 - Honeywell (formerly AlliedSignal Inc.)	
	Genetron 409A - Honeywell (formerly AlliedSignal Inc.)	
	Genetron MP39 - Honeywell (formerly AlliedSignal Inc.)	
	Genetron MP66 - Honeywell (formerly AlliedSignal Inc.)	
	GHG-X4 - People's Welding Supply	
	HCFC-124 - InterCool Energy Corporation	
	Hot Shot - ICOR International (formerly Indianapolis Refrigeration Co. Inc.)	
	Meforex 124 - Ausimont SPA	2837-89-0
	NAF P III - Safety Hi-Tech srl	
	NAF P-III - North American Fire Guardian	
	NAF S III - Safety Hi-Tech srl	
	NAF S-III - North American Fire Guardian	
	NARM-505 - Moncton Refrigerants	
	Oxyfume 2002 - Honeywell (formerly AlliedSignal Inc.)	
	Solkane 409A - Solvay Fluor GMBH	
	Suva 124 - DuPont Fluoroproducts	
	Suva MP39 - DuPont Fluoroproducts	
	Suva MP52 - DuPont Fluoroproducts	
	Suva MP66 - DuPont Fluoroproducts	
HCFC-131 ($C_2H_2FCl_3$) Trichlorofluoroethane		359-28-4
HCFC-132b ($C_2H_2F_2Cl_2$) Dichlorodifluoroethane		1649-08-7
HCFC-133a ($C_2H_2F_3Cl$) Monochlorotrifluoroethane		75-88-7
HCFC-141b ($C_2H_3FCl_2$) Dichlorofluoroethane	Asahiklin AK-141b - Asahi Glass Co. Ltd. Forane 141b - ARKEMA SA Friogas 141 - Galco Genesolv 2000 - Honeywell (formerly AlliedSignal Inc.)	1717-00-6

Class II (Continued)

Chemical Name	Trade Names	CAS Number
	Genesolv 2004 - Honeywell (formerly AlliedSignal Inc.) Genetron 141b - Honeywell (formerly AlliedSignal Inc.) HCFC-141b - Roche Chemicals Inc. HCFC-141b - Central Glass Co. Ltd. HCFC-141b - Daikin Industries Ltd. HCFC-141b MS - Daikin Industries Ltd. HyperClean Circuit Cleaner - Micro Care Corp. Korfron 141b - Ulsan Chemical Co., Ltd. Meforex 141b - Ausimont SPA Polioi Poliuretano ICI - INEOS Fluor Solkane 141b - Solvay Fluor GMBH Solkane 141b CN - Solvay Fluor GMBH Solkane 141b DH - Solvay Fluor GMBH Solkane 141b MA - Solvay Fluor GMBH Solkane 141b WE - Solvay Fluor GMBH	
HCFC-142b (C2H3F2Cl) Monochlorodifluoroethane	Arcton 409A - INEOS Fluor Arcton 412A - INEOS Fluor Arcton TP5R - INEOS Fluor Asahiklin AK-142b - Asahi Glass Co. Ltd. Daiflon 142b - Daikin Industries Ltd. Dymel 142b - DuPont-Mitsui Fluorochemicals Co. Ltd. Forane 142b - ARKEMA SA Forane FX 55 - ARKEMA SA Forane FX 56 - ARKEMA SA Forane FX 57 - ARKEMA SA Free Zone RB-276 - Refrigerant Gases Freeze 12 - Technical Chemical Co. Freezone - Freezone Inc. (formerly Patriot Consumer Products Inc.) FX-56 - ARKEMA SA G2015 - Greencool Genetron 142b - Honeywell (formerly AlliedSignal Inc.) Genetron 409A - Honeywell (formerly AlliedSignal Inc.) GHG - Monroe Air Tech	75-68-3

(Continued)

Class II (Continued)

Chemical Name	Trade Names	CAS Number
	GHG12 - ICOR International (formerly Indianapolis Refrigeration Co. Inc.)	
	GHG-HP - People's Welding Supply	
	GHG-X4 - People's Welding Supply	
	GHG-X5 - People's Welding Supply	
	HCFC-142b - Daikin Industries Ltd.	
	HCFC-142b - Central Glass Co. Ltd.	
	HCFC-142b - Roche Chemicals Inc.	
	Hot Shot - ICOR International (formerly Indianapolis Refrigeration Co. Inc.)	
	Korfron 142b - Ulsan Chemical Co., Ltd.	
	McCool R-12 - McMullen Oil Products Inc.	
	Meforex 142b - Ausimont SPA	
	Solkane 142b - Solvay Fluor GMBH	
	Solkane 22/142b blends - Solvay Fluor GMBH	
	Solkane 406A - Solvay Fluor GMBH	
	Solkane 409A - Solvay Fluor GMBH	
HCFC-221 (C3HFCl6) Hexachlorofluoropropane		422-26-4
HCFC-222 (C3HF2Cl5) Pentachlorodifluoropropane		422-49-1
HCFC-223 (C3HF3Cl4) Tetrachlorotrifluoropropane		422-52-6
HCFC-224 (C3HF4Cl3) Trichlorotetrafluoropropane		422-54-8
HCFC-225ca (C3HF5Cl2) Dichloropentafluoropropane		422-56-0
HCFC-225cb (C3HF5Cl2) Dichloropentafluoropropane		507-55-1
HCFC-226 (C3HF6Cl) Monochlorohexafluoropropane		431-87-8
HCFC-231 (C3H2FCl5) Pentachlorofluoropropane		421-94-3
HCFC-232 (C3H2F2Cl4) Tetrachlorodifluoropropane		460-89-9
HCFC-233 (C3H2F3Cl3) Trichlorotrifluoropropane		7125-84-0
HCFC-234 (C3H2F4Cl2) Dichlorotetrafluoropropane		425-94-5

Class II (Continued)

Chemical Name	Trade Names	CAS Number
HCFC-235 (C3H2F5Cl) Monochloropentafluoropropane		460-92-4
HCFC-241 (C3H3FCl4) Tetrachlorofluoropropane		666-27-3
HCFC-242 (C3H3F2Cl3) Trichlorodifluoropropane		460-63-9
HCFC-243 (C3H3F3Cl2) Dichlorotrifluoropropane		460-69-5
HCFC-244 (C3H3F4Cl) Monochlorotetrafluoropropane		679-85-6
HCFC-251 (C3H4FCl3) Trichlorofluoropropane		421-41-0
HCFC-252 (C3H4F2Cl2) Dichlorodifluoropropane		819-00-1
HCFC-253 (C3H4F3Cl) Monochlorotrifluoropropane		460-35-5
HCFC-261 (C3H5FCl2) Dichlorofluoropropane		420-97-3
HCFC-262 (C3H5F2Cl) Monochlorodifluoropropane		421-02-03
HCFC-271 (C3H6FCl) Monochlorofluoropropane		430-55-7

6. Government Contacts (Chapters 36, 37, 38 of HTSUS)
U.S. Department of Agriculture

Agricultural Marketing Service
Washington, DC 20250
Tel. 202-720-8998
www.ams.usda.gov

Animal and Plant Health Inspection Service (APHIS)

Animals:
USDA-APHIS-VS
Riverdale, MD 20737–1231
Tel. 301-734-7885

Plants:
USDA-APHIS-PPQ
Riverdale, MD 20737–1231
Tel. 301-734-8896
www.aphis.usda.gov

Food Safety and Inspection Service
Import Inspection Division
Landmark Center
1299 Farnam, Suite 300
Omaha, NE 68102
Tel. 402-221-7400

Foreign Agricultural Service
Room 5531-S
Washington, D.C. 20250-1000
Tel. 202-720-2916
Fax 202-720-8076
www.usda.gov

U.S. Department of Commerce

Exporter Counseling Division
14th Street & Pennsylvania Ave., N.W.
Washington, DC 20230
Tel. 202-482-4811
www.bxa.doc.gov

National Marine Fisheries Service Headquarters
National Oceanic and Atmospheric Administration
1315 East-West Highway
Silver Spring, MD 20910
Tel. 301-713-2289
NMFS Southwest Region

Protected Species Management Division
501 West Ocean Blvd.
Long Beach, CA 90802-4213
Tel. 562-980-4019
www.kingfish.ssp.nms.gov

Federal Communications Commission

Laboratory Division
7435 Oakland Mills Road
Columbia, MD 21046
Tel. 301-362-3000
www.fcc.gov

U.S. Consumer Product Safety Commission

Office of Compliance
4330 East West Highway
Bethesda, MD 20814

Tel. 301-504-0608
Fax 301-504-0359
www.cpsc.gov

Environmental Protection Agency

Hazardous Materials Hotline
1-800-424-9346

TSCA Assistance Information Service
Tel. 202-554-1404

Motor Vehicles Investigation/Imports Section
2000 Traverwood Drive
Ann Arbor, MI 48105
Attn: Imports Division
Tel. 734-214-4100

U.S. Department of Health and Human Services

Food and Drug Administration
Center for Biologics Evaluation and Research
1401 Rockville Pike
Suite 200 North
Rockville, MD 20852
Tel. 301-827-6201
www.fda.gov/cber

Center for Drug Evaluation and Research
7520 Standish Place
Rockville, MD 20855
Tel. 301-594-3150
www.fda.gov/cber

Center for Devices and Radiological Health
Rockville, MD 20850
Tel. 301-594-4692
www.fda.gov/cber

Division of Import Operations and Policy (HFC–170)
5600 Fishers Lane
Rockville, MD 20857
Tel. 301-443-6553
Fax 301-594-0413
www.fda.gov/ora/import

Center for Food Safety and Applied Nutrition
Office of Food Labeling (HFS–156)
200 "C" St., NW

Washington, DC 20204
Tel. 202-205-4606
http//vm.cfsan.fda.gov

Office of Seafood
Washington, DC 20005
Tel. 202-418-3150

Centers for Disease Control and Prevention
Office of Health and Safety
1600 Clifton Road
Atlanta, Georgia 30333
Tel. 404-639-3235
www.cdc.gov

U.S. Department of Energy

Office of Codes and Standards
Washington, DC 20585
Tel. 202-586-9127
www.eren.doe.gov

Office of Boating Safety
U.S. Coast Guard
2100 Second Street, SW
Washington, DC 20593-0001
Tel. 202-267-1077

National Vessel Documentation Center
U.S. Coast Guard
792 T.J. Jackson Drive
Falling Waters, W.Va. 25419-9502
Tel. 304-271-2400
Fax 304-271-2405

Office of Regulations and Rulings
1300 Pennsylvania Avenue NW
Washington, DC 20229
Tel. 202-572-8700

National Commodity Specialist Division
One Penn Plaza
11th Floor
New York, NY 10119
Tel. 201-443-0367
Fax 201-443-0595

Office of Field Operations
Trade Programs Division
1300 Pennsylvania Ave. NW
Washington, DC 20229
Tel. 202-344-0300

U.S. Department of the Interior

Fish and Wildlife Service
Office of Management Authority
4401 N. Fairfax Drive
Arlington, VA 22203
Tel. 703-358-2093
www.fws.gov

U.S. Department of Justice

Bureau of Alcohol, Tobacco, Firearms and Explosives
650 Massachusetts Avenue NW
Washington, DC 20226
Tel. 1-866-662-2750 (arms, ammunition, and explosives import licenses)

Drug Enforcement Administration
700 Army-Navy Drive
Arlington VA 22202
Tel. 202-307-7977
www.usdoj.gov/dea

Nuclear Regulatory Commission

Office of International Programs
One White Flint North
11555 Rockville Pike
Rockville, MD 20852
Tel. 301-415-7000

Federal Trade Commission

Bureau of Consumer Protection
Washington, DC 20580
Tel. 202-326-2996

Division of Enforcement
Washington, DC 20580
Tel. 202-326-2996
www.ftc.gov

International Trade Commission

500 "E" Street, SW

Washington, DC 20436
Tel. 202-205-2000
www.usitc.gov

U.S. Department of State

Office of Defense Trade Controls
Bureau of Political/Military Affairs
2401 "E" Street, NW
Washington, DC 20037
Tel. 202-663-2700
www.pmdtc.org

U.S. Department of Transportation

National Highway Traffic Safety Administration
Office of Vehicle Safety Compliance (NEF-32)
400 7th Street SW
Washington, DC 20590
Tel. 1-800-424-9393
Fax 202-366-1024
www.nhtsa.dot.gov

Office of Hazardous Materials
400 7th Street SW
Washington, DC 20590-0001
Tel. 202.366.4488

U.S. Department of the Treasury

Alcohol and Tobacco Tax and Trade Bureau
Washington, DC 20220
Tel. 1.877.882.3277
E-mail: ttbimport@ttb.gov (alcohol importer's basic permit, alcohol excise
    taxes)
    alfd@ttb.gov (alcohol labeling, advertising, and formulation)
    ttbtobacco@ttb.gov (tobacco products)
    ttbfaet@ttb.gov (firearms and ammunition excise tax)
Main Web site: www.ttb.gov

Office of Foreign Assets Control

1500 Pennsylvania Avenue NW
Washington, DC 20220
Tel. 202-622-2500
Fax 202-622-1657
www.treas.gov/offices/enforcement/ofac/index.shtml
U.S. Customs and Border Protection
Washington, D.C. 20229

Appendix D

Additional Export Agencies

C-TPAT

C-TPAT is a voluntary government-business initiative to build cooperative relationships that strengthen and improve overall international supply chain and U.S. border security. C-TPAT recognizes that U.S. Customs and Border Protection (CBP) can provide the highest level of cargo security only through close cooperation with the ultimate owners of the international supply chain such as importers, carriers, consolidators, licensed customs brokers, and manufacturers. Through this initiative, CBP is asking businesses to ensure the integrity of their security practices and communicate and verify the security guidelines of their business partners within the supply chain.

C-TPAT offers trade-related businesses an opportunity to play an active role in the war against terrorism. By participating in this first worldwide supply chain security initiative, companies will ensure a more secure and expeditious supply chain for their employees, suppliers, and customers. Beyond these essential security benefits, CBP will offer benefits to certain certified C-TPAT member categories, including:

- A reduced number of CBP inspections (reduced border delay times)
- Priority processing for CBP inspections. (Front of the Line processing for inspections when possible.)
- Assignment of a C-TPAT Supply Chain Security Specialist (SCSS) who will work with the company to validate and enhance security throughout the company's international supply chain.
- Potential eligibility for CBP Importer Self-Assessment program (ISA) with an emphasis on self-policing, not CBP audits.
- Eligibility to attend C-TPAT supply chain security training seminars.

CBP recognizes that a safe and secure supply chain is the most critical part of our work in keeping our country safe. For this reason, CBP is seeking a strong anti-terrorism partnership with the trade community through C-TPAT. Trade partners will have a commitment to both trade security and trade compliance rooted in their business practices. CBP wants to work closely with companies whose good business practices ensure supply chain security and compliance with trade laws.

CBP encourages all companies to take an active role in promoting supply chain and border security. C-TPAT is not just a big-company program. Medium and small companies may want to evaluate the requirements and benefits of C-TPAT carefully in deciding whether to apply for the program. Moreover, even without official participation in C-TPAT, companies should still consider employing C-TPAT guidelines in their security practices.

For More Information

Contact Industry Partnership Programs at (202) 344-1180 or fax (202) 344-2626 or e-mail us, at industry.partnership@dhs.gov

Export Enforcement

Mission

The mission of the Bureau of Industry and Security (BIS) Export Enforcement is to protect U.S. national security, homeland security, foreign policy, and economic interests through a law enforcement program focused on: sensitive exports to hostile entities or those that engage in onward proliferation; prohibited foreign boycotts; and related public safety laws. BIS's Export Enforcement (EE) is an elite law enforcement organization recognized for its expertise, professionalism, integrity, and accomplishments. EE accomplishes its mission through preventative and investigative enforcement activities and then, pursuing appropriate criminal and administrative sanctions against export violators.

In the post-9/11 world, the export control challenge is to enable legitimate global trade in U.S. goods and technology, while keeping these items out of the hands of weapons proliferators and terrorists. BIS addresses this challenge through assisting legitimate export traders to comply with export control and antiboycott requirements, preventing violations before they occur, and bringing willful export control violators to justice.

EE works with the Department of Justice to impose criminal sanctions for violations, including incarceration and fines, and with the Office of Chief Counsel for Industry and Security to impose civil fines and denials of export privileges. EE also works closely with other Federal law enforcement agencies, including the FBI and the Department of Homeland Security, when conducting investigations or preventative actions.

EE consists of the Office of Export Enforcement (OEE), the Office of Enforcement Analysis (OEA), and the Office of Antiboycott Compliance (OAC). Together with BIS's licensing officers and policy staff, EE employees apply their law enforcement and export control expertise to prevent and deter exports of the most sensitive items to illicit end-users and uses, to embargoed destinations, and to ensure that parties involved in U.S. commercial transactions do not engage in prohibited boycott activities.

Office of Export Enforcement (OEE)

OEE works to keep the most sensitive goods out the most dangerous hands. OEE conducts its enforcement operations from Headquarters and nine field locations in Boston, Chicago, Dallas, Houston, Los Angeles, Miami, New York, San Jose, and Washington, DC. OEE works cooperatively with the exporting community to prevent violations, and conducts investigations to gather evidence to support criminal and administrative sanctions.

Investigations:

OEE Special Agents are sworn Federal law enforcement officers with authority to make arrests, execute search and arrest warrants, serve subpoenas, and detain and seize goods about to be illegally exported. OEE investigations are initiated on information and intelligence obtained from a variety of sources, and are conducted to objectively and thoroughly gather testimony and evidence of alleged or suspected violations of dual-use export control laws. OEE works closely with attorneys in the Department of Justice and the Office of Chief Counsel for Industry and Security to prosecute criminal and administrative cases.

Sentinel Program:

Many end-use checks are conducted through BIS's Sentinel Program. Trained OEE Special Agents are deployed from the United States to countries to visit the end-users of sensitive controlled commodities and determine whether these items are being used in accordance with license conditions. Sentinel teams assess the suitability of foreign end-users to receive U.S.-origin licensed goods and technology, assess prospective end-users on pending license applications for diversion risk, and conduct educational outreach to foreign trade groups. In this way, Sentinel trips help to create the confidence needed to foster trade while strengthening U.S. national security.

Compliance:

Informed, voluntary compliance with U.S. export controls by the export trade community is an important contribution to U.S. National Security and a key component of BIS's export administration and enforcement programs. All parties to U.S. export transactions must ensure that their exports fully comply with all statutory and regulatory requirements. Compliance not only involves controlled goods and technologies, but also restrictions on shipping to certain countries, companies, organizations, and/or individuals. BIS works closely with the export trade community to raise awareness of compliance best practices and "red flags" of potential illicit export activities, and to identify and act on export violations.

These tools include:

- Know Your Customer Guidance
- Red Flag Indicators
- Iran Web Guidance
- How Do I Avoid Dealing with Unauthorized Parties?
- Lists To Check
- Freight Forwarder Guidance
- Fastener Quality Act Compliance
- How to Recognize and Report Possible Violations
- Reporting Possible Violations (Enforcement Hotline 1-800-424-2980)
- E-Commerce

An Export Management and Compliance Program (EMCP) can assist you in developing a system to capture analysis, decisions, and accountability, and implementing procedures to stay in compliance with the Export Administration Regulations (EAR). See EMCP section for more information.

Temporary Denial Orders:

Temporary Denial Orders are issued by the Assistant Secretary for Export Enforcement, denying any or (typically) all of the export privileges of a company or individual to prevent an imminent or on-going export control violation. These orders are issued ex parte for a renewable 180-day period and cut off not only the right to export from the United States, but also the right to receive or participate in exports from the United States.

Section 11(h) Denials:

Section 11(h) of the Export Administration Act provides that, at the discretion of the Secretary of Commerce, no person convicted of a violation of the EAA, IEEPA, or Section 38 of the Arms Export Control Act (or any regulation, license, or order issued under any of these laws), or one of several espionage-related statutes will be eligible to apply for or use any export license issued under the EAA for up to ten years from the date of the conviction. In addition, Section 11(h) provides that the Secretary of Commerce may revoke any export license which the party had at the time of the conviction.

Voluntary Self-Disclosures:

BIS encourages the submission of Voluntary Self Disclosures (VSDs) by parties who believe they may have violated the EAR. VSDs are an excellent indicator of a party's intent to comply with U.S. export control requirements and may provide

BIS important information on other ongoing violations. BIS carefully reviews VSDs received from disclosing parties to determine if violations of the EAR have occurred and to determine the appropriate corrective action when violations have taken place. Most VSDs are resolved by means other than the issuance of an administrative penalty. Of the VSDs received and resolved in Fiscal Year 2005, 97% were resolved with either a finding that no violation of the EAR had occurred (55%) or with the issuance of a warning letter (42%). Of VSDs received and resolved in Fiscal Year 2006, 100% were resolved with either a finding that no violation of the EAR had occurred (52%) or with the issuance of a warning letter (48%). In instances in which BIS determines that the issuance of an administrative penalty is appropriate for the resolution of a VSD, BIS affords the submission of a VSD "great weight" in assessing and mitigating the penalty. In appropriate cases, fines and other administrative penalties may be significantly reduced. Guidance regarding administrative penalties is provided in Supplement No. 1 of Section 766 of the EAR. Additional information is also available at Voluntary Self-Disclosures.

Pursuant to Part 764.5 of the EAR, the information constituting a VSD or any other correspondence pertaining to a VSD may be submitted to:

Director, Office of Export Enforcement
1401 Constitution Ave.
Room H4514
Washington, DC 20230
Tel: (202) 482-1208
Facsimile: (202) 482-5889

Office of Enforcement Analysis (OEA)

OEA's efforts focus on ensuring that export transactions are in compliance with the Export Administration Act, thus facilitating trade and promoting commerce abroad while protecting our nations' security from unauthorized use of our nation's sensitive goods and technology.

Pre-License Screening and End-Use Checks:

OEA screens all export license applications to ensure that export control enforcement information is considered before any final license decision is made. An interagency committee reviews license applications to assess diversion risks, to identify potential violations, and to determine the reliability of those receiving controlled U.S-origin commodities or technical data. In some instances, a pre-license check is conducted to determine the bona fides of the transaction and the end-user as well as confirming that nothing has changed with a known end-user. EE factors the result of this check into the licensing recommendation that EE makes to BIS's licensing offices. Post-shipment verifications also help the U.S. Government ensure that an item that was exported is being used in accordance with U.S. export control regulations and the terms of the export license.

Overseas Export Control Officer Program:

As part of BIS's international efforts to achieve its enforcement mission, BIS sends experienced Department of Commerce Special Agents overseas as Export Control Officers (ECOs) at key U.S. embassies in Beijing and Hong Kong, China; Abu Dhabi, UAE; New Delhi, India; and Moscow, Russia. The principal mission of the ECOs is to ensure that U.S. dual-use goods entering their region are used in accordance with U.S. export control laws and regulations. Compliance verification is accomplished through targeted end-use checks and by working with the host governments and local businesses to ensure that they understand and comply with U.S. export control laws and regulations. ECOs also work with host governments and local businesses to provide information and appropriate training to facilitate better understanding of U.S. dual-use export control requirements, and to help develop indigenous export control capabilities.

Unverified List:

When BIS cannot conduct a pre-license check or a post-shipment verification for reasons outside of the U.S. Government's control, the names and countries of foreign persons who were parties to the transaction are placed on the Unverified List. That list includes persons involved in export transactions where BIS has not been able to verify the existence or authenticity of the end user, intermediate consignee, ultimate consignee, or other party to the export transaction. Any transaction to which a listed person is a party will be deemed by BIS to raise a "Red Flag" with respect to such transaction within the meaning of the guidance set forth in Supplement No. 3 to 15 C.F.R. Part 732.

SED Review Program:

OEA conducts reviews of selected Shipper's Export Declarations of past shipments and identifies those that may have violated the Export Administration Regulations and refers them to the Office of Export Enforcement (OEE) for further investigation. Hundreds of investigations of suspected export control violations occur annually, based on the routine review of SEDs.

Visa Application Review Program:

The Visa Application Review Program is conducted to prevent unauthorized access to controlled U.S. technology or technical data by foreign nationals visiting the United States. EE reviews information on visa applications to detect and prevent possible violations of the EAR. Under this program, EE makes recommendations to the U.S. Department of State against issuing visas for technology control reasons, and identifies U.S. parties visited by foreign nationals for outreach contacts by OEE Special Agents.

Office of Antiboycott Compliance (OAC)

Through OAC, EE ensures compliance with the antiboycott provisions of the EAA. EE investigates violations (such as furnishing boycott-related information, refusing to deal with blacklisted businesses, and religious discrimination), and pursues the appropriate administrative or criminal sanctions, including civil penalties, imposition of periods of export denial, and referral to the Department of Justice for criminal prosecution. Cases warranting administrative action are settled by OAC, when authorized by the Administrative Case Review Board to do so, or referred to the Office of Chief Counsel for Industry and Security for the initiation of administrative proceedings. EE also compiles and publishes statistics about unsanctioned foreign boycotts and carries out extensive public education and counseling in antiboycott matters, via its telephone and e-mail advice line, to encourage compliance with the law.

OAC provides extensive guidance to the exporting community concerning the application of the regulations and trends in boycott activity through its telephone and e-mail advice line and speaking engagements to trade associations and banking groups. When preventative measures fail, OAC pursues criminal and administrative sanctions in matters that include furnishing boycott-related information, refusal to deal with blacklisted businesses, and discrimination for a boycott purpose based on religion or national origin. Please visit the antiboycott section of the BIS Web site for detailed information and if you have a question about any boycott-related matter, please contact the OAC advice line at (202) 482-2381 or via the e-mail link.

- Antiboycott Compliance
- U.S. Antiboycott Laws
- Examples of Boycott Requests
- Boycott Request Reporting Forms

Voluntary Self-Disclosures of Antiboycott Violations:

Voluntary Self Disclosure (VSD) of violations of the antiboycott provisions of EAR is provided for in Part 764.8 of the Regulations. If you believe you may have violated the antiboycott provisions, BIS urges you to disclose to the Office of Antiboycott Compliance (OAC) via the procedures described in Part 764.8. These procedures include: timing of the disclosure, requisites for initial notification, nature of the narrative account of the violation, documentation, and certification.

After receipt of the appropriate narrative and supporting documentation, OAC will give the disclosing party written notification of receipt of the disclosure. Following thorough review and any necessary investigation by OAC, BIS will inform the party making the disclosure of any action it intends to take. The criteria BIS uses in determining whether to pursue an enforcement action and what sanctions it will recommend are described in Supplement 2 of part 766. As indicated in Supplement 2, BIS encourages VSDs by giving the disclosing party "great weight" in the assessment of penalties. This may provide significant reduction in administrative penalties.

Voluntary self-disclosures of antiboycott violations shall be submitted to:

Office of Antiboycott Compliance
1401 Constitution Avenue, NW
Room 6098
Washington, DC 20230
Tel: (202) 482-2381
Fax: (202)482-0913

Export Management and Compliance Program (EMCP)

The requirements described in the Export Administration Regulations (EAR) may seem overwhelming without a system to capture analysis, decisions, accountability and implementing procedures. An EMCP takes individual decisions and pieces of information and builds them into an organized, integrated system. It is a program that can be established to manage export-related decisions and transactions to ensure compliance with the EAR and license conditions.

An EMCP can:

- Reinforce senior management commitment to comply with U.S. export laws and regulations to all parties within the company.
- Provide management structure and organization for the processing of export transactions.
- Enhance accountability for export control tasks by identifying who is responsible for performing each part of the process and who is responsible for overall effectiveness of the EMCP.
- Provide compliance safeguards throughout a company's supply chain to ensure that order processing due diligence checks produce consistent export decisions.
- Provide written instructions for employees to blend into their daily responsibilities to "screen" export transactions against general prohibitions of exports, re-exports, and selected transfers to certain end-uses and end-users.
- Serve as a vehicle to communicate red flag indicators that raise questions about the legitimacy of a customer or transaction.
- Provide personnel with tools to help them ensure they are performing their export control functions accurately and consistently.

- Identify transactions that could normally be exported without a license, but because of the end-use or end-user, require a license.
- Streamline the process and reduce time spent on compliance activities when employees have written instructions, tools and on-going training.
- Protect employees through training and awareness programs from inadvertently violating the EAR.

Compliance Contacts:

For EMCP or compliance related inquiries, please contact any of the following compliance specialists in the Export Management and Compliance Division or send an e-mail inquiry through the BIS Web site system to "EMS inquiry."

Tom Andrukonis, phone 202-482-6393; e-mail tandruko@bis.doc.gov
Renee Osborne, phone 202-482-5619; e-mail rosborne@bis.doc.gov
Rejineta Carroll, phone 202-482-3541; e-mail rcarroll@bis.doc.gov
Orestes Theocharides, phone 202-482-6751; e-mail otheocha@bis.doc.gov

Commerce Department Export Controls

Overview

The Bureau of Industry and Security (BIS) is responsible for implementing and enforcing the Export Administration Regulations (EAR), which regulate the export and reexport of most commercial items. We often refer to the items that BIS regulates as "dual-use"—items that have both commercial and military or proliferation applications—but purely commercial items without an obvious military use are also subject to the EAR.

The EAR do not control all goods, services, and technologies. Other U.S. government agencies regulate more specialized exports. For example, the U.S. Department of State has authority over defense articles and defense services. A list of other agencies involved in export controls can be found on this Web site or in Supplement No. 3 to Part 730 of the EAR, which is available on the Government Printing Office Web site.

This is designed to give people who are new to exporting, and, in particular, new to export controls, a general understanding of the regulations and how to use them. However, nothing provided here can substitute for consulting the EAR. The EAR include answers to frequently asked questions, detailed step-by-step instructions for determining if a transaction is subject to the regulations, how to request a commodity classification or advisory opinion, and how to apply for a license. In using the EAR, you may want to first look at Part 732 for the steps you follow to determine your obligations.

If you would like to review a specific part of the EAR referenced in this document, go to the on-line EAR database on the EAR Web site maintained by the Government Printing Office.

NOTE: The EAR contain provisions relating to matters not discussed in this short overview. Two examples of important concepts not discussed here are controls on the activities of U.S. persons in support of proliferation programs (see EAR §744.6) and the antiboycott provisions contained in EAR §760.

What Is an Export?

Any item that is sent from the United States to a foreign destination is an export. "Items" include commodities, software, or technology, such as clothing, building materials, circuit boards, automotive parts, blue prints, design plans, retail software packages, and technical information.

How an item is transported outside of the United States does not matter in determining export license requirements. For example, an item can be sent by regular mail or hand-carried on an airplane. A set of schematics can be sent via facsimile to a foreign destination, software can be uploaded to or downloaded from an Internet site, or technology can be transmitted via e-mail or during a telephone conversation. Regardless of the method used for the transfer, the transaction is considered an export for export control purposes. An item is also considered an export even if it is leaving the United States temporarily, if it is leaving the United State but is not for sale, (e.g. a gift), or if it is going to a wholly-owned U.S. subsidiary in a foreign country. Even a foreign-origin item exported from the United States, transmitted or transhipped through the United States, or being returned from the United States to its foreign country of origin is considered an export. Finally, release of technology or source code subject to the EAR to a foreign national in the United States is "deemed" to be an export to the home country of the foreign national under the EAR.

How to Determine If You Need a Commerce Export License

A relatively small percentage of total U.S. exports and reexports require a license from BIS. License requirements are dependent upon an item's technical characteristics, the destination, the end-user, and the end-use. You, as the exporter, must determine whether your export requires a license. When making that determination consider:

- What are you exporting?
- Where are you exporting?
- Who will receive your item?
- What will your item be used for?

What Are You Exporting?

The Export Control Classification Number and the Commerce Control List

COMMERCE CONTROL LIST CATEGORIES

A key in determining whether an export license is needed from the Department of Commerce is knowing whether the item you are intending to export has a specific Export Control Classification Number (ECCN). The ECCN is an alpha-numeric code, e.g., 3A001, that describes a particular item or type of item, and shows the controls placed on that item. All ECCNs are listed in the Commerce Control List (CCL) (Supplement No. 1 to Part 774 of the EAR), which is available on the Government Printing Office Web site. The CCL is divided into ten broad categories, and each category is further subdivided into five product groups. The CCL is available on the EAR Web site.

> 0 = Nuclear Materials, Facilities, and Equipment (and Miscellaneous Items)
> 1 = Materials, Chemicals, Microorganisms, and Toxins
> 2 = Materials Processing
> 3 = Electronics
> 4 = Computers
> 5 = Telecommunications and Information Security
> 6 = Sensors and Lasers
> 7 = Navigation and Avionics
> 8 = Marine
> 9 = Propulsion Systems, Space Vehicles, and Related Equipment

Five Product Groups
A. Systems, Equipment and Components
B. Test, Inspection, and Production Equipment
C. Material
D. Software
E. Technology

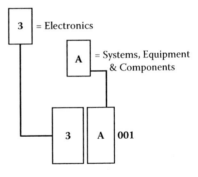

3 = Electronics
A = Systems, Equipment & Components
3 A 001

EXAMPLE

Assume that you have polygraph equipment that is used to help law enforcement agencies. What would be your ECCN? Start by looking in the Commerce Control List under the category of electronics (Category 3) and product group that covers equipment (Product Group A). Then read through the list to find whether your item is included in the list. In this example the item is 3A981 as shown below.

Classifying Your Item

The proper classification of your item is essential to determining any licensing requirements under the Export Administration Regulations (EAR). You may classify the item on your own, check with the manufacturer, or submit a classification request to have BIS determine the ECCN for you.

When reviewing the CCL to determine if your item is specified by an ECCN, you will first need to determine in which of the ten broad categories of the Commerce Control List your item is included and then consider the applicable product group.

3A981 Polygraphs (except biomedical recorders designed for use in medical facilities for monitoring biological and neurophysical responses); fingerprint analyzers, cameras and equipment, n.e.s.; automated fingerprint and identification retrieval systems, n.e.s.; psychological stress analysis equipment; electronic monitoring restraint devices; and specially designed parts and accessories, n.e.s.

License Requirements

Reason for Control: CC

Control(s)	Country Chart
CC applies to entire entry	CC Column 1

License Exceptions

LVS: N/A

GBS: N/A

CIV: N/A

List of Items Controlled

Unit: Equipment in number

Related Controls: N/A

Related Definitions: N/A

The list of items controlled is contained in the ECCN heading.

If Your Item Is Not on the Commerce Control List - EAR99

If your item falls under U.S. Department of Commerce jurisdiction and is not listed on the CCL, it is designated as EAR99. EAR99 items generally consist of low-technology consumer goods and do not require a license in many situations. However, if your proposed export of an EAR99 item is to an embargoed country, to an end-user of concern, or in support of a prohibited end-use, you may be required to obtain a license.

EAR99 Items subject to the EAR that are not elsewhere controlled by this CCL Category or in any other category in the CCL are designated by the number EAR99.

Where Are You Exporting?

Restrictions vary from country to country. The most restricted destinations are the embargoed countries and those countries designated as supporting terrorist activities, including Cuba, Iran, North Korea, Sudan, and Syria. There are restrictions on some products, however, that are worldwide.

How to Cross-Reference the ECCN with the Commerce Country Chart

Once you have classified the item, the next step is to determine whether you need an export license based on the "reasons for control" of the item and the country of ultimate destination.

You begin this process by comparing the ECCN with the Commerce Country Chart (Supplement No. 1 to Part 738). The ECCNs and the Commerce Country Chart, taken together, define the items subject to export controls based solely on the technical parameters of the item and the country of ultimate destination.

Below the main heading for each ECCN entry, you will find "Reason for Control" (e.g., NS for National Security, AT for Anti-Terrorism, CC for Crime Control, etc.). Below this, you will find the "Country Chart" designator that shows the specific export control code(s) applied to your item (e.g., NS Column 2, AT Column 1, CC Column 1, etc.). These specific control codes for your ECCN need to be cross-referenced against the Commerce Country Chart.

Commerce Conutry Chart
Reason for Control

Countries	Chemical & Biological Weapons			Nuclear Nonproliferation		National Security		Missile Tech	Regional Stability		Fine-arms Convention	Crime Control			Ant Terror
	CB 1	CB 2	CB 3	NP 1	NP 2	NS 1	NS 2	MT 1	RS 1	RS 2	FC 1	CC 1	CC 2	CC 3	AT 1
Guyana	X	X		X		X	X	X	X	X	X	X		X	
Haiti	X	X		X		X	X	X	X	X	X	X		X	
Honduras	X	X		X		X	X	X	X	X	X	X		X	
Hong Kong	X	X		X		X		X	X	X		X		X	
Hungary	X					X		X	X						
Iceland	X			X		X		X	X						
India	X	X	X	X	X	X	X	X	X	X		X		X	
Indonesia	X	X		X		X	X	X	X	X		X		X	

If there is an "X" in the box based on the reason(s) for control of your item and the country of destination, a license is required, unless a License Exception is available. Part 742 of the EAR sets forth the license requirements and licensing policy for most reasons for control.

EXAMPLE

Question: You have polygraph equipment classified as 3A981 for export to Honduras. Would you be required to obtain an export license from the Department of Commerce before selling and shipping it to your purchaser?

Answer: Yes. 3A981 is controlled for Crime Control (CC) reasons under CC Column 1 and the Country Chart shows that such items require a license for Honduras.

If there is no "X" in the control code column(s) specified under your ECCN and country of destination, you will not need an export license unless you are exporting to an end-user or end-use of concern.

EXAMPLE

Question: You have polygraph equipment classified as 3A981 for export to Iceland. Would you be required to obtain an export license from the Department of Commerce before selling and shipping it to your purchaser?

Answer: No. As you can see from the Commerce Country Chart (above) 3A981 is controlled for Crime Control (CC) reasons under CC Column 1 and the Country Chart shows that such items do not require a license for Iceland unless you are exporting to an end-user or end-use of concern.

Although a relatively small percentage of all U.S. exports and reexports require a BIS license, virtually all exports and many reexports to embargoed destinations and countries designated as supporting terrorist activities require a license. These countries are Cuba, Iran, North Korea, Sudan, and Syria. Part 746 of the EAR describes embargoed destinations and refers to certain additional controls imposed by the Office of Foreign Assets Control of the Treasury Department.

Who Will Receive Your Item?

Certain individuals and organizations are prohibited from receiving U.S. exports and others may only receive goods if they have been licensed, even items that do not normally require a license based on the ECCN and Commerce Country Chart or based on an EAR99 designation. You must be aware of the following lists:

Entity List—EAR Part 744, Supplement 4—A list of organizations identified by BIS as engaging in activities related to the proliferation of weapons of mass destruction. Depending on your item, you may be required to obtain a license to export to an organization on the Entity List even if one is not otherwise required.

Treasury Department Specially Designated Nationals and Blocked Persons List —EAR Part 764, Supplement 3—A list maintained by the Department of Treasury's Office of Foreign Assets Control comprising individuals and organizations deemed to represent restricted countries or known to be involved in terrorism and narcotics trafficking.

The Unverified List is composed of firms for which BIS was unable to complete an end-use check. Firms on the unverified list present a "red flag" that exporters have a duty to inquire about before making an export to them.

Denied Persons—You may not participate in an export or reexport transaction subject to the EAR with a person whose export privileges have been denied by the BIS. A list of those firms and individuals whose export privileges have been denied is available on this Web site. Note that some denied persons are located within the United States. If you believe a person whose export privileges have been denied wants to buy your product in order to export it, you must not make the sale and should report the situation to BIS's Office of Export Enforcement. If you have questions about Denied Persons, you may contact BIS's Office of Enforcement Analysis at (202) 482-4255.

What Will Your Item Be Used For?

Some end-uses are prohibited while others may require a license. For example, you may not export to certain entities involved in the proliferation of weapons of mass destruction (e.g., nuclear, biological, chemical) and the missiles to deliver them, without specific authorization, no matter what your item is. For more information on prohibited end-uses, please refer to Part 744 of the EAR.

Ways to Export

Authorization to export is determined by the transaction: what the item is, where it is going, who will receive it, and what it will be used for. The majority of U.S. commercial exports do not require a license.

NLR – ("No License Required")

Most exports from the United States do not require a license, and are therefore exported under the designation "NLR." Except in those relatively few transactions when a license requirement applies because the destination is subject to embargo or because of a proliferation end-use or end-user, no license is required when:

1. The item to be shipped is not on the CCL (i.e. it's EAR99); or
2. The item is on the CCL but there is no "X" in the box on the Country Chart under the appropriate reason for control column on the row for the country of destination. (See the Country Chart example above.)

In each of these situations, you would enter "NLR" on your export documents.

License Exception

If a license is required for your transaction, a license exception may be available. License Exceptions, and the conditions on their use, are set forth in Part 740 of the EAR. If your export is eligible for a license exception, you would use the designation of that license exception (e.g. LVS, GBS, TMP) on your export documents.

License

If your item requires a license to be exported, you must apply to BIS for an export license. If your application is approved, you will receive a license number and expiration date to use on your export documents. A BIS-issued license is usually valid for two years.

Where to Get Assistance

A good starting point for information on export licensing requirements and the regulations is to attend an export control seminars.

For counseling assistance, you may call one of our export counselors at 202-482-4811 (Washington, DC) or 408-998-8806 (Northern California) or email us in Washington or California. You may also register to receive email notifications of upcoming seminars.

Summary of Steps to Take to Process Your Export

■ Ensure that your export is under U.S. Department of Commerce jurisdiction.
■ Classify your item by reviewing the Commerce Control List.
■ If your item is classified by an Export Control Classification Number (ECCN), identify the Reasons for Control on the Commerce Control List.
■ Cross-reference the ECCN Controls against the Commerce Country Chart to see if a license is required. If yes, determine if a License Exception is available before applying for a license.

- Ensure that no proscribed end-users or end-uses are involved with your export transaction. If proscribed end-users or end-uses are involved, determine if you can proceed with the transaction or must apply for a license.
- Export your item using the correct ECCN and the appropriate symbol (e.g., NLR, license exception, or license number and expiration date) on your export documentation (e.g., Shipper's Export Declaration).

Prosecution of Cases When Improperly Exporting

Exporter Charged With Sale of Sensitive Technology to China

Former Cupertino Man Allegedly Sold Restricted Microwave Amplifier Technology to the People's Republic of China without a License

SAN JOSE, CALIF. - A federal grand jury in San Jose, Calif. indicted Fu-Tain Lu, formerly of Cupertino, Calif., as well as two companies Lu founded, on charges that they conspired to violate United States export regulations, United States Attorney Joseph P. Russoniello announced. The indictment also charges Lu with lying to federal agents who were investigating his conduct.

According to the indictment, Lu, 61, along with two companies he founded—Fushine Technology, Inc. ("Fushine") of Cupertino, Calif, and Everjet Science and Technology Corporation ("Everjet"), based in the People's Republic of China ("the PRC")—conspired to export sensitive microwave amplifier technology to the PRC without obtaining the required licenses or other approvals from the United States Department of Commerce. The indictment alleges that the items Fushine shipped and attempted to ship were restricted for export to China for reasons of national security.

The indictment further alleges that the defendants knew about the licensing restrictions and specifically sought to circumvent them. The indictment quotes from an internal company e-mail in which an Everjet employee told a Fushine employee, "Since these products are a little bit sensitive, in case the maker asks you where the location of the end user is, please do not mention it is in China." The indictment also quotes from another e-mail in which Lu advises a subordinate to pretend that the intended end-user for an item is in Singapore rather than China.

"Exporters may consider the requirement that they obtain a license before shipping controlled technology to restricted countries to be burdensome, yet those regulations are necessary to protect the security of the United States," Russoniello said. "My office will vigorously prosecute willful violations of export regulations to the fullest extent of the law."

Russoniello also expressed his appreciation to the agencies who conducted and assisted with the investigation, including the Department of Commerce Office of

Export Enforcement, the Federal Bureau of Investigation, U.S. Immigration and Customs Enforcement, and Customs and Border Protection.

The indictment was returned on April 1 but had been filed under seal until the defendant's arrest and appearance in federal court.

Lu was arrested at the San Francisco International Airport after disembarking from a flight on the evening of April 7. He made his initial appearance in federal court in San Jose today before United States Magistrate Judge Patricia V. Trumbull. Judge Trumbull ordered the defendant to be held without bail until his detention hearing, which is scheduled to be held before her on April 13 at 1:15 p.m.

For Lu (as opposed to the corporate defendants, for whom the penalties differ), the maximum statutory penalties for Count One—conspiracy to violate export regulations (18 U.S.C. § 371)—and for each of Counts Three and Four—false statements to a government agency (18 U.S.C. § 1001(a)(2))—are five years imprisonment and a $250,000 fine, or twice the gross financial gain from the offense. The maximum statutory penalty for Count Two—violation of export regulations (50 U.S.C. § 1705(b) and 15 C.F.R. 764.2(a))—is 10 years imprisonment, a $50,000 fine, or twice the gross gain from the offense. Any sentence following conviction, however, would be imposed by the court after consideration of the U.S. Sentencing Guidelines and the federal statute governing the imposition of a sentence, 18 U.S.C. § 3553.

David R. Callaway is the Assistant U.S. Attorney who is prosecuting the case with the assistance of Tracey Andersen. The prosecution is the result of a long-term, joint investigation by the Department of Commerce Office of Export Enforcement, the Federal Bureau of Investigation, and Immigration and Customs Enforcement.

Please note, an indictment contains only allegations and, as with all defendants, Mr. Lu and the two charged companies should be presumed innocent unless and until proven guilty.

Iowa-Based Company Settles Export Allegations on Crime Control Items

WASHINGTON, D.C. –The Commerce Department's Bureau of Industry and Security (BIS) announced today that Syrvet, Inc., a veterinary supply wholesaler based in Waukee, Iowa, has agreed to pay a $250,000 civil penalty to settle allegations involving sixteen unlicensed exports of electric cattle prods, from the United States to Mexico, Chile, South Africa, Dominican Republic, Columbia, and El Salvador in violation of the Export Administration Regulations. These items are listed on the Commerce Control List for crime control reasons. Syrvet and the BIS have agreed to suspend $150,000 of the fine provided that no additional violations occur and payment of the remaining $100,000 is made in accordance with the agreed upon payment schedule. Supplement 1 to Part 766 of the EAR allows BIS to suspend part of a penalty under certain circumstances.

"Preventing the illegal export of items that can be used to commit human rights abuses is an enforcement priority," said Mario Mancuso, the Undersecretary of Commerce for Industry and Security.

Undersecretary Mancuso praised the BIS Chicago Field Office for its outstanding work on this case

BIS controls exports and re-exports of dual-use commodities, technology, and software for reasons of national security, missile technology, nuclear non-proliferation, chemical and biological weapons non-proliferation, crime control, regional stability, and foreign policy. Criminal penalties and administrative sanctions can be imposed for violations of the Export Administration Regulations. For more information, please visit www.bis.doc.gov.

Illinois-Based Manufacturer of Scientific Equipment Settles Charges of Export Violations

WASHINGTON, D.C. –The Commerce Department's Bureau of Industry and Security (BIS) announced today that Buehler Limited of Lake Bluff, Illinois has agreed to pay a $200,000 civil penalty to settle allegations that it made 81 unlicensed exports of a lubricant containing Triethanolamine (TEA) in violation of the Export Administration Regulations. Buehler Limited is a global manufacturer of scientific equipment and supplies for use in materials research and analysis.

"Targeted and effective controls on materials that could be used in biological and chemical weapons are critical to preserving U.S. national security," said Mario Mancuso, the Undersecretary of Commerce for Industry and Security. "Companies should be mindful of the chemical make-up of their exports."

BIS alleged that between November 2001 and July 2006, Buehler Limited made 80 exports of a product called "Coolmet," a mixture containing TEA that is used as a lubricant with cutting tools, to various destinations including China, Hong Kong, Thailand, India, Brazil, and Israel without the required BIS licenses. Additionally, on one occasion in August 2005, the company's German affiliate re-exported Coolmet from Germany to Iran without the required U.S. Government authorization. TEA is a Schedule 3 chemical precursor and is controlled for Chemical/Biological, Anti-Terrorism, and Chemical Weapons reasons.

Buehler Limited voluntarily disclosed the violations and cooperated fully in the investigation.

Undersecretary Mancuso praised the BIS Chicago Field Office for its outstanding work on this case.

BIS controls exports and re-exports of dual-use commodities, technology, and software for reasons of national security, missile technology, nuclear non-proliferation, chemical and biological weapons non-proliferation, crime control, regional stability, and foreign policy. Criminal penalties and administrative sanctions may be imposed for violations of the Export Administration Regulations. For more information, please visit www.bis.doc.gov.

Nebraska Outdoor Equipment Outfitter, Cabela's Incorporated, Settles Export Allegations

WASHINGTON, D.C. – The Commerce Department's Bureau of Industry and Security (BIS) announced today that Cabela's Incorporated, an outdoor equipment outfitter based in Sidney, Nebraska, has agreed to pay a civil penalty of $680,000 to settle allegations that it committed 152 violations of the Export Administration Regulations (EAR) involving the export of controlled optical sighting devices to various countries worldwide.

"Compliance programs must be routinely reviewed and updated so that they keep pace with ever-changing business practices," said Darryl W. Jackson, the Assistant Secretary of Commerce for Export Enforcement. "Failing to do so can result in numerous violations occurring over time, which undermines our foreign policy objectives."

The allegations involved 76 exports of optical sighting devices for firearms in 2004 and 2005 to Argentina, Brazil, Canada, Chile, Finland, Ireland, Malaysia, Malta, Mexico, Pakistan, the Philippines, South Africa, Sweden, and Taiwan. These devices are controlled on the Commerce Control List for crime control and firearms convention reasons and require a license to export to the various destinations at issue. BIS also alleged that Cabela's failed to file the required Shipper's Export Declaration for each of the 76 exports in question.

In 2005, Cabela's settled similar allegations made by BIS that, on 685 occasions between April 1999 and September 2000, Cabela's made unlicensed exports of optical sighting devices to a number of countries, including Argentina, Brazil, Canada, Chile, and Mexico.

Assistant Secretary Jackson praised the BIS Office of Export Enforcement's Chicago Field Office for its outstanding work on this case.

Background — BIS controls exports and re-exports of dual-use commodities, technology, and software for reasons of national security, missile technology, nuclear non-proliferation, chemical and biological weapons non-proliferation, crime control, regional stability, firearms conventions, and anti-terrorism. Criminal penalties and administrative sanctions can be imposed for violations of the Export Administration Regulations. For more information, please visit http://www.bis.doc.gov.

Florida Co. Agrees to $180,000 Civil Penalty for Violations of the Export Administration Regulations

WASHINGTON, D.C. – The U.S. Department of Commerce's Bureau of Industry and Security (BIS) announced today that Marysol Technologies Inc., of Clearwater, Fla., agreed to pay a $180,000 civil penalty to settle allegations that it committed nine violations of the Export Administration Regulations (EAR) when it exported laser equipment to the People's Republic of China (PRC), India, Belarus, and Russia without the required export licenses.

"Companies must be careful when self-classifying products and should consult with a BIS licensing officer who may advise that a formal commodity classification for their products or technology is warranted," said Darryl W. Jackson, Assistant Secretary of Commerce for Export Enforcement. "Doing so is especially important when dealing with items controlled for national security reasons."

BIS alleged that between December 2003 and April 2006, Marysol Technologies committed nine violations of the EAR equipment resonator modules, module cavities, or components or parts for resonator modules and module cavities. These items are classified on the Commerce Control List under Export Control Classification Number 6A005, and are controlled for National Security reasons to the PRC, India, Belarus, and Russia.

Assistant Secretary Jackson commended the Office of Export Enforcement's Miami Office for its outstanding work in this case.

Background — BIS controls exports and reexports of dual-use commodities, technology, and software for reasons of national security, foreign policy, nuclear nonproliferation, chemical and biological weapons, regional stability, and short supply. Criminal penalties and administrative sanctions can be imposed for violations of the EAR.

Houston Company Settles Charges of Antiboycott Violations

WASHINGTON, D.C. –The U.S. Department of Commerce's Bureau of Industry and Security (BIS) announced today that American Rice, Inc. of Houston, TX, has agreed to pay a $30,000 civil penalty to settle allegations that it violated the antiboycott provisions of the Export Administration Regulations (EAR).

"The Department of Commerce is committed to vigorous enforcement of the antiboycott regulations," Darryl W. Jackson, Assistant Secretary of Commerce for Export Enforcement, reminded U.S. companies. "To avoid enforcement actions, companies should establish effective compliance programs that include such core elements as management commitment, employee training, and internal controls for reporting and responding to boycott issues."

BIS's Office of Antiboycott Compliance alleged that during the years 2002 through 2006, in connection with fifteen transactions involving the sale of U.S. origin goods to the U.A.E., American Rice, Inc. failed to report in a timely manner its receipt of a request to engage in a restrictive trade practice or boycott.

Background — The antiboycott provisions of the EAR prohibit U.S. persons from complying with certain requirements of unsanctioned foreign boycotts, including furnishing information about business relationships with or in a boycotted country.

In addition, the EAR requires that persons report their receipt of certain boycott requests to the Department of Commerce.

Florida Electronics Wholesaler Settles Export Allegations

WASHINGTON, D.C. – The Commerce Department's Bureau of Industry and Security (BIS) announced today that America II Electronics, Inc., an electronics wholesaler based in St. Petersburg, Florida, has agreed to pay a $170,000 civil penalty to settle allegations that it exported certain electronic components from the United States to Russia in violation of the Export Administration Regulations.

"It is very important to comply with licensing requirements, especially with goods controlled for national security reasons," said Darryl W. Jackson, Assistant Secretary of Commerce for Export Enforcement. "Proper commodity classification is essential. Exporters need to thoroughly review the description of the Export Control Classification Number or ECCN and pay particular attention to the conditions proscribed in the subparagraphs of certain ECCNs of the Commerce Control list."

The allegations involved four exports of analog-to-digital converters to Russia in 2003 and 2004. These electronic components are controlled on the Commerce Control List for National Security reasons and require a BIS license prior to export to Russia.

Assistant Secretary Jackson praised the BIS Office of Export Enforcement's Miami Field Office for its outstanding work on this case.

BIS controls exports and re-exports of dual-use commodities, technology, and software for reasons of national security, missile technology, nuclear non-proliferation, chemical and biological weapons non-proliferation, crime control, regional stability, and foreign policy. Criminal penalties and administrative sanctions can be imposed for violations of the Export Administration Regulations. For more information, please visit www.bis.doc.gov.

Taiwan Firm Settles Charges of Illegal Exports to the PRC

WASHINGTON – The U.S. Department of Commerce's Bureau of Industry and Security (BIS) announced today that Johnson Trading & Engineering Company, Ltd. of Taiwan has agreed to a $90,000 civil penalty to settle charges that it knowingly caused the unlicensed export of computer chips to the People's Republic of China (PRC) in violation of the Export Administration Regulations (EAR). BIS also charged that Johnson Trading took action to evade the EAR.

"BIS is taking a hard-line with license exceptions being used to evade licensing requirements," said Kevin Delli-Colli, Deputy Assistant Secretary for Export Enforcement at BIS. "The conditions and restrictions on all EAR license exceptions should be strictly adhered to by both exporters and consignees."

BIS charged that, between February 2003 and December 2003, Johnson Trading took action to evade the EAR and knowingly caused the unlicensed exports of computer chips from the United States, via Taiwan and Hong Kong, to the PRC. On seven occasions, Johnson Trading ordered the computer chips from a U.S. exporter and falsely represented to that exporter that the country of ultimate destination was Taiwan. Following the shipment of the computer chips to Taiwan, Johnson Trading arranged and facilitated for the items' subsequent shipment to the PRC via Hong Kong. The computer chips in question were subject to the EAR and controlled for national security and anti-terrorism reasons.

Johnson Trading also agreed to a suspended five-year denial of export privileges and to an audit of the company's export compliance program. If the company complies with other terms of the agreement, $30,000 of the $90,000 penalty will be suspended.

Deputy Assistant Secretary for Export Enforcement Delli-Colli commended the Washington Field Office for its work on the investigation.

Background — BIS controls exports and re-exports of dual-use items, technology, and software for reasons of national security, foreign policy, nuclear nonproliferation, chemical and biological weapons, nuclear non-proliferation, regional stability, and short supply. Criminal penalties and administrative sanctions can be imposed for violations of the EAR.

French Corporation Pleads Guilty to Conspiracy, Illegal Export, and Attempted Illegal Export of Cryogenic Submersible Pumps to Iran

Washington, D.C. – Cryostar SAS, formerly known as Cryostar France ("CRYOSTAR"), a French corporation, headquartered in Hesingue, France, has pleaded guilty to conspiracy, illegal export, and attempted illegal export of cryogenic submersible pumps to Iran, U.S. Attorney Jeffrey A. Taylor and Assistant Secretary of Commerce for Export Enforcement Darryl W. Jackson announced today.

CRYOSTAR pled guilty earlier today before the Honorable Colleen Kollar-Kotelly of the U.S. District Court for the District of Columbia to one count of Conspiracy, one count of Export without an Export License, and one count of Attempted Export without an Export License. Pursuant to a written plea agreement, CRYOSTAR must be sentenced to a criminal fine of $500,000 and corporate probation of two years when the company is sentenced by Judge Kollar-Kotelly on July 17, 2008.

"Foreign parties that choose to export U.S.-origin goods to embargoed destinations, such as Iran, violate our export control laws," said Assistant Secretary Jackson. "As this case demonstrates, we will vigorously pursue such violations."

"Export restrictions should not be viewed as avoidable obstacles, but rather as fundamental safeguards for the protection of our national interests," stated U.S. Attorney Taylor. "This prosecution should serve as a reminder that failure to comply with U.S. export control laws can have severe consequences."

The evidence in this case established that CRYOSTAR, with business locations around the world including in the United States, specialized in the design and manufacturing of cryogenic equipment, such as pumps, turbines, compressors, and automatic filling stations that were used to transport and process natural gases at extremely cold temperatures. Ebara International Corp., Inc. ("Ebara") was a Delaware corporation with its principal place of business in Nevada. Ebara engaged in the business of designing and manufacturing cryogenic pumps for various uses, including for pumping fluid hydrocarbons that have been cooled to cryogenic temperatures (280 degrees below zero). Ebara specialized in the design and manufacturing of cryogenic equipment, such as pumps, turbines, compressors, and automatic filling stations that were used to transport and process natural gases at extremely cold temperatures. "TN" was a French company with a U.S. subsidiary.

In 2001, TN arranged to purchase cryogenic submersible pumps from Ebara for delivery to an Iranian company for installation at the 9th and 10th Olefin Petrochemical Complexes in Iran. CRYOSTAR agreed to facilitate this transaction by serving as the middleman for TN and Ebara, by purchasing the pumps from Ebara, by reselling them to TN (which forwarded the pumps to Iran), and by falsely indicating that the final purchaser was a French company that would install the pumps in France, when all parties to the transaction knew that the ultimate and intended destination of the pumps was Iran.

The conspirators developed a plan to conceal the export of cryogenic pumps to Iran, under which Ebara would sell and export the pumps to CRYOSTAR in France, which would then resell the pumps to TN, with the ultimate and intended destination being Iran. The conspirators set forth the plan on a "matrix," which they used as a roadmap, including various procedures to be followed by each company to protect their conduct from detection by United States law enforcement, which included the following:

1. Requiring that all paperwork be passed through the London office of Ebara, which would eliminate references to Iran and TN on paperwork going to Ebara in the United States and which would replace Ebara references with the letterhead and template of CRYOSTAR on engineering drawings, letters, and reports on paperwork going to TN and Iran;
2. Creating false purchase orders
    i. from CRYOSTAR to Ebara stating that CRYOSTAR, not TN, was the purchaser, and France, not Iran, was the ultimate and intended destination and
    ii. from TN to CRYOSTAR stating that CRYOSTAR, not Ebara, was the supplier, and that France, not the United States, was the country of origin for the pumps;
3. Permitting only limited witness testing of the pumps in the United States by TN and not at all by the Iranian customer;
4. Transferring responsibility for all installation, commissioning, maintenance, testing, and training in Iran from Ebara to CRYOSTAR and allowing

participation by Ebara personnel from Ebara's London office only in "extreme situations" and no participation by Ebara personnel from the United States "under any circumstances";

5. Omitting all Ebara labels and stamps on the pumps' component parts before export to conceal the true country of their origin;

6. Replacing Ebara labeling and stamping of the pumps' component parts and accompanying shipping documents with CRYOSTAR identifiers after export to France so the country of their origin appeared to be France rather than the United States;

7. Purchasing as many component parts as possible from non-U.S. suppliers and importing them into the United States for assembly by Ebara to avoid using parts with U.S. certificates of origin and addressing questions from U.S. suppliers regarding end-users; and

8. Shipping the pumps from the United States through Canada, and then to France for re-labeling, before shipment to Iran for installation at the 9th Olefin Petrochemical Complex.

Following the procedures set forth in the "matrix," the conspirators manufactured four pumps, and shipped them, in January 2003, for installation at the 9th Olefin Petrochemical Complex in Iran, ("First CRYOSTAR Order"). The total value of the First CRYOSTAR Order was approximately $746,756.

The conspirators prepared three additional pumps to be shipped to Iran in the fall of 2003, for installation at the 10th Olefin Petrochemical Complex in Iran ("Second CRYOSTAR Order"). The total value of the Second CRYOSTAR Order was approximately $1,125,055. The conspirators halted shipment of the Second CRYOSTAR Order because of this investigation.

The conspirators attempted to cover up their illegal conduct by creating false correspondence confirming that none of the pumps were sent, or were intended to be sent, to Iran.

None of the conspirators sought and obtained export licenses for either the First CRYOSTAR Order or the Second CRYOSTAR Order.

Ebara and its former president pled guilty and were sentenced at an earlier stage in this investigation.

CRYOSTAR's guilty plea is the result of an investigation by the U.S. Department of Commerce, Bureau of Industry and Security.

In announcing today's guilty plea, U.S. Attorney Taylor and Assistant Secretary Jackson commended the efforts of Commerce Special Agent Norma Curtis. They also praised Assistant U.S. Attorney Jonathan M. Malis, who is prosecuting the case.

Index

About the Author

Thomas A. Cook is a seasoned veteran of global supply chain management, with over thirty-five years of experience specifically directed to the elements of transportation, importing, exporting, logistics, freight, and overall business management.

Tom is a veteran author of over nine books, such as *Post 9/11 Security and Compliance, Mastering Import and Export Trade,* and *Global Sourcing.*

Tom began his career as a NYS Maritime Academy graduate with numerous years serving our country in the Navy and Dutch and U.S. Merchant Marine.

Tom has been directly involved in manufacturing, insurance, banking, trading, logistics vendor services, freight forwarding, customs brokerage, 3PL, and many other related services to global supply chains.

Tom is considered a leader in education, training, and consulting to many of the Fortune 1,000 Companies on an array of topics hosted by various government agencies, the World Trade Institute, the American Management Association, the World Academy, CCSMP, the Department of State, ISM, and NAPM, to name a few.

He has been the recipient of numerous awards and accolades—more recently the International Partnership Award bestowed by former President Bill Clinton at the State University of New York in Westbury.

Tom is currently on the New York District Export Council and is managing director of American River International (www.americanriverintl.com).